D1125114

In Quest of the Sacred Baboon

HANS
KUMMER

In Quest
of the Sacred
Baboon

A Scientist's Journey

Translated by
M. Ann Biederman-Thorson

Princeton University Press

Originally published as *Weisse Affen am roten Meer: Das soziale Leben der Wüstenpaviane*, by R. Piper GmbH & Co. KG, Munich (1992)

Library of Congress Cataloging-in-Publication Data

Kummer, Hans, 1930–
[Weisse Affen am roten Meer. English]
In quest of the sacred baboon : a scientist's journey / Hans Kummer :
translated by M. Ann Biederman-Thorson.
p.   cm.
Includes bibliographical references and index.
ISBN 0-691-03701-9
ISBN 0-691-04838-X (pbk.)
1. Hamadryas baboon—Behavior.   2. Social behavior in animals.   I. Title.
QL737.P93K8213   1995
599.8'2—dc20   95-10732

This book has been composed in Sabon and Futura

Princeton University Press books are printed on acid-free paper
and meet the guidelines for permanence and durability
of the Committee on Production Guidelines for Book
Longevity of the Council on Library Resources

Second printing, and first paperback printing, 1997

Printed in the United States of America

3   5   7   9   10   8   6   4   2

For Verena

CONTENTS

ILLUSTRATION CREDITS

Drawings are by Roland Hausheer.

Map: The study area near Erer in Ethiopia. Modified from Abegglen 1984.

Unless otherwise credited, photos are by the author.

Figures 14, 18, 22, 23, 37, 38 are from the book *Social Organization of Hamadryas Baboons* (1968) by Hans Kummer, reprinted with the kind permission of S. Karger AG, Basel.

Figures 1, 12, and 44 are from the article, "Social Units of a Free-Living Population of Hamadryas Baboons," by Hans Kummer and Fred Kurt (*Folia Primatologica* 1(1963):4–19), reprinted with the kind permission of S. Karger AG, Basel.

Figures 9 and 10 are from the book *Soziales Verhalten einer Mantelpavian-Gruppe* (1957) by Hans Kummer, reprinted with the kind permission of Hans Huber, Bern.

Figures 3, 4, and 24 are from the book *Primate Societies* (1971) by Hans Kummer, reprinted with the kind permission of Harlan Davidson, Arlington Heights, Illinois.

The study area near Erer in Ethiopia,
showing the baboons' sleeping cliffs (●),
the railway (++++), and the road from
Djibouti to Addis Ababa (———).

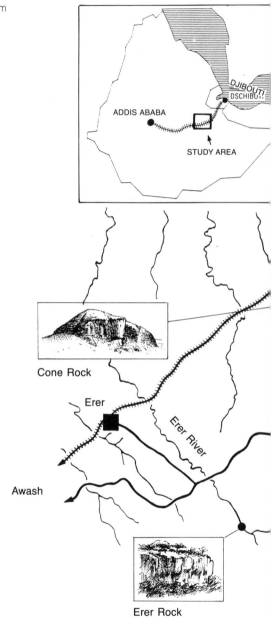

ADDIS ABABA

DJIBOUTI
DSCHIBUTI

STUDY AREA

Cone Rock

Erer

Erer River

Awash

Erer Rock

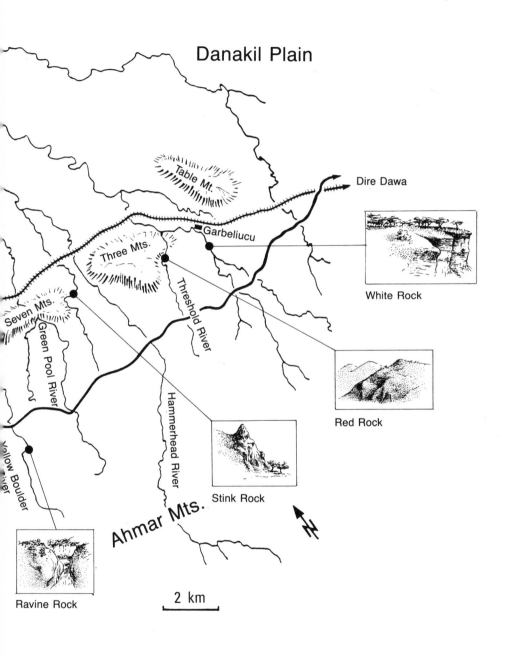

Danakil Plain

Table Mt.

Dire Dawa

Garbeliucu

Three Mts.

White Rock

Threshold River

Seven Mts.

Red Rock

Green Pool River

Hammerhead River

Stink Rock

Yellow Boulder River

Ahmar Mts.

N

Ravine Rock

2 km

Return to Red Rock

The moon must have come out early that night. In any case, I could see well enough to begin running as soon as I was out of view of the film people. The crooked thorns of the acacia bushes scratched across my freshly ironed khaki shirt, and I clumsily caught my foot on a stone at the edge of the small cattle track. I hadn't been here for three years—here where Fred Kurt and I had first observed wild hamadryas baboons. Now I had come back with a camera crew to film them. Before we set off, I had had my doubts: were the baboons still there? Maybe they had wandered off into the Danakil Desert, or up into the Ahmar Mountains? And what if they had been killed off by an epidemic? This was nomad land, not a national park, and no one could have protected the baboons from a disaster or informed us about it. As I ran, I realized that I wasn't merely worried about keeping my promise to lead the film people to the baboons. I was returning to the source of experiences that had become deeply lodged, far below the layer of my research and thinking—experiences as powerful and colorful as some of those we retain from early childhood. I had to see "them" again. That was why I had left the puzzled filmmakers and their baggage behind, at an isolated hut used by railway workers on the Addis Ababa–Djibouti line. With only a few words of explanation, I had plunged ahead into my baboon world.

I still knew the plains and hills of Garbellucu as well as my own hands. Traveling southwest, I trotted along winding trails over the acacia-covered plateau and, after one mile, reached the edge of the Red Rock wadi. The hard, grainy soil on the furrowed laterite slopes crunched under my soles as I ran down to the dry riverbed. There the sand slowed my steps. The wadi snaked up toward the Ahmar Mountains to the south, between steep, rocky cliffs. A dark mass lay ahead, where the bank jutted out in the shadow of a large fig tree, and as I advanced around it, the three walls of Red Rock rose before me. I seized my binoculars and pressed them against my eyes, the skin surrounding them slippery with sweat. The horizon of the left rock looked as though a line of bristles ran along it. Scattered among these were sturdier shapes, silhouetted against the night sky in delicate silver under the light of the moon: male hamadryas baboons! They were still there.

I settled down against a large rock in the wadi and watched them through the field glasses. Even in the darkness the lighter mantles of the old males stood out, identifying the leaders of the harems. Between them sat the darker, smaller forms of the females and young. A high, whining shriek pierced the silence—probably a young animal trying to work its way to a better place in its mother's arms. A male murmured soothingly in deep bass tones, putting an end to the little disturbance. From the distance came the laughing call of a spotted hyena. The sounds I remembered were still here too.

How can an animal species captivate someone so thoroughly? For me the hamadryas baboons are like a tribe of people whose customs no one since the ancient Egyptians has perhaps understood as well as my collaborators and I. To the Egyptians they were the incarnation of a divinity; to me they embody an idea of survival, being so molded by shape and society that they can exist in these semideserts. Every species of animal masters a particular ecological niche; that is its calling in life. To understand the desert baboons has, for twenty years, been part of my own calling.

This book, itself, is a return. Not to my youth, though—the young man who inhabits the first half of the book, and whom I can no longer quite recognize as myself, should be regarded with a smile. What I mean is a return from the tables and graphs of professional science to full-color, hands-on research: to a life of adventures, encounters, of observing and marveling, thinking and doubting, which are the roots from which science has sprung. As reported in the professional journals, the results of such work are often without appeal, an insipid broth abstracted from the bare bones of some investigation. In this book I will attempt to keep the full flavor, recounting the story not in scientific jargon but in my own words.

There are many roads to understanding nature. An Ice Age hunter may have had one kind of feeling for his reindeer, and the first horse tamer may have sensed the moods of his stallion through yet other ways, each as best suited his purpose; and so do scientists today. We biologists try to give a rational interpretation to what we observe in nature, and we must rely on critical, abstract thinking. Sometimes a new idea carries us away with excitement; yet the results of analysis are often richer and more beautiful than even our first impression. To some the conclusions may seem coldly abstract, and to others their truth is frightening. We love these icy peaks, sculpted by past research and given another supplementary touch—we hope—by our own publications. But we also love the lower slopes, the colorful paths leading upward and the conditions and people we meet there that have no place in the scientific journals. In this book, I want to do something that behavioral scientists don't ordinarily do, and may even be discouraged from doing: to describe the ascent along these paths and the joy of looking up toward the peaks. I will keep the less pleasant aspects of the journey in the background, both for the sake of the reader and because I no longer remember them so well.

While including our firsthand experiences, I shall also keep strictly to scientific truth. Professionals can thus use the book as a summary of our hamadryas research. For their convenience, the description of a research result is often followed by a number or name and date in parentheses; these refer to the literature (by the Zurich group and by others, respectively) cited at the back of the book, where references to the original works can be found. I am not writing only for professionals, however, but for the people who paid for our research and experiences without being able to be there with us. I particularly remember one of them. He was a businessman who had come to Addis Ababa as a tourist; the Swiss chargé d'affaires had recommended that he visit us in our camp at the Awash Falls. For days he drove with me through dust and thorns, helping to trap baboons and listening to my descriptions and theories. Once while we were waiting for our troop in the piercing afternoon sun, he suddenly declared, "At least you are doing something meaningful here." I was startled, and it took me a while to understand what he meant. My guest wasn't looking for material benefits, as others in his line of work might have been. Since then his remark has often encouraged me in moments of doubt.

In this book I relate the history of the "Project Hamadryas." It begins with the family life of baboons in the zoo and ends with the decision processes of large groups in the wild, the anatomy of social relationships, and the presumed evolution of hamadryas society. The sequence of individual projects was, however, not dictated by a larger plan but simply grew like a tree, wherever a new, imagined, or suspected horizon beckoned us onward.

The theories of ethologists and sociobiologists are discussed in abbreviated form as necessary so that the reader can develop a feeling for them. Here and there I interpret an observation in several ways and try to show how researchers analyze such problems.

I try to avoid scientific jargon as much as possible and write in everyday language. But one thing should be made clear: ordinary language has words for social behaviors such as fleeing and attack, for motivations, and for group structures, but these words were coined for *human* behavior, motivations, and group structures. Since there are no alternatives that everyone can understand, I must use this human-related ordinary language for the animals. Therefore please understand that I am not "humanizing" the animals by my choice of words. When I call the upper portion of the baboon a "head," no reasonable person will deny that it looks quite different from the head of a person. Thinking readers will apply the necessary qualifications on their own and recognize the common features along with the differences. It is surely fair to expect the same thoughtful flexibility when I am dealing with behavior. When I write "marriage," I mean the relationship of a permanently bonded pair that raises children and travels, forages, and rests as a unit. I do not mean a human marriage, not a cultural institution with legal status, relating to a "correct" norm about which the partners and others may dispute. When I say "the juvenile wants to flee to its mother," the word "wants" does not imply conscious intention but merely that every movement the juvenile makes would bring it to the mother if nothing were in its way.

Occasionally the reader will be tempted to interpret behavior that appears especially clever as implying humanlike motives and considerations—for example, to suspect that one baboon is consciously trying to mislead another. This is called an "anthropomorphic" explanation. In such cases I shall propose a simpler explanation that is equally plausible. Anthropomorphic thinking about higher animals does raise fascinating questions, but it must be critically examined. Simply to assume that animals think the way we do is both unrealistic and uninteresting; the interesting things are those foreign to our experience. Usually, however, I shall leave the workings of the inner life of the baboons to the reader's own intuition, because even professionals in the field still rarely know what animals are thinking in particular situations.

Sometimes the reader will be asked to stop and consider a view off the main track, but here again I shall not impose an interpretation in every last detail, especially not the often compelling comparisons with us humans, although I may hint at some of them. I would like my readers to think about what they read, and beyond. "By leaving something out, one gives the reader a creative pleasure" (Reiners 1967). The focus should be on what the animals are doing, and readers should be able to think their own thoughts about that just as I do, even though more work has gone into mine.

Now I must add one more warning. Although the ancient Egyptians saw the hamadryas baboon as a sacred figure, it is no saint. Its social life is not the idyll we fondly hope to find among animals. It lives in a patriarchal community, in which the male has evolved both of the fundamental aspects of fighting: a sharp canine tooth and a network of alliances. This finding was a surprise to us. In most related primate species the network of alliances is the specialty of females. When I started my research I wasn't looking for a patriarchal society, nor was I aware that this was one, and this book should by no means be taken as subliminal propaganda for male superiority. What animals do is no argument for what humans ought to do. My colleagues and I tried hard to decipher the female influences and roles, which are not at all obvious. Experiments had to be designed to bring them to light. If the war against Somalia in the Ogaden had not prevented us from continuing our project, we would probably have been able to uncover still more.

The fascinating thing about the patriarchal hamadryas males is their double role as husbands and as members of a male clan. In most animal species a permanent marriage prevents close, cooperative relations among males, so that families live apart from one another. The male hamadryas baboons have managed to integrate permanent marriage into a cooperative male society, despite sharp competition for the females: surrounded by their harem, they live side by side with their rivals. This social structure is found in only two other primate species: the gelada baboon of the high mountains in Ethiopia, and the human.

ACKNOWLEDGMENTS

The scientific content of these memoirs derives not only from my own efforts but, to an even greater extent, from those of my coworkers and former students: Fred Kurt, my assistant and colleague on the first expedition to Erer-Gota, Ethiopia, 1960 to 1961, which revealed the three main levels of the social structure; Walter Götz and Walter Angst, my coworkers in the second, experimental Ethiopia project from 1967 to 1969, which was concerned with two pillars of social structure: the herding behavior of the males and their respect for one another's possession of females; Ueli Nagel and Hansueli Müller, who in 1968 and 1971–72 investigated the pair behavior of the hybrids at the Awash Falls, the boundary between the two subspecies *anubis* and *hamadryas*; Jean-Jacques and Helga Abegglen and Ruedi Wey, who between 1971 and 1977 discovered the fourth level, that of the clans, and investigated the life cycle and the presexual pair bonds formed by the followers; Alex and Vreni Stolba, who from 1973 to 1975 found out how the bands decide in the morning where they are going to reassemble at noon; and Hans and Leonie Sigg, who in the same years discovered how various roles are distributed among the females in a harem.

During the following years, Eduard Stammbach, Christian Bachmann, and Marietta Fritz observed our hamadryas colony in Zurich and in the Munich Zoo in preparation for their Master's degrees and shed light on the internal programs by which the hamadryas baboons structure their one-male units.

I am grateful to all of them for hours of mutual intellectual stimulation and argument.

In addition, Dali Götz and Christine Müller each worked with us for a year under harsh field conditions, helping with hands and minds. From 1973 on, Jeanine Stocker competently and reliably organized the rear guard at the University of Zurich, typed many manuscripts, and gave encouragement to those who found it hard to become reoriented to Zurich after their year in Africa. Verena Baumann, Lore Valentin, and, with particular thoroughness, my daughter Kathrin Kummer and my colleague Dr. Gustl Anzenberger devoted their critical skills to various versions of this text. I thank Ann Biederman-Thorson for her outstanding cooperation in preparing the English translation, and Alice Calaprice for the sound advice contained in her editing of the manuscript. Jane

Goodall, Bernhard Hassenstein, and Robert Seyfarth improved the contents of the book with their valuable suggestions. My greatest thanks, however, are owed to my wife Verena. She let me go out into my world at great sacrifice to herself, and later shared my life in the bush with our small children. Without her support and criticism this book would not have come into being.

Finally, I am thankful to all the people who appear on these pages, and to the many who are not mentioned. Whether governor, beggar, police chief, or nomad chieftain, barmaid, diplomat, Greek garage mechanic or French railway official—all made the "Project Hamadryas" a feast of my life.

For my growth as a scientist, apart from the formative influences of my teachers Ernst Hadorn and Heini Hediger, the most fruitful experiences have been conversations with my colleagues William A. Mason and Emil W. Menzel.

Special thanks are due to the Swiss ambassadors and deputies in Addis Ababa and Jeddah, especially Mr. and Mrs. Jean de Stoutz in Addis Ababa in 1960 and 1961, who treated us as friends. I thank the following institutions for financing the hamadryas projects: the Swiss National Science Foundation, the U.S. National Science Foundation, the Swiss Natural Science Society, the Georges and Antoine Claraz Donation, the Wenner-Gren Foundation for Anthropological Research in New York, the Delta Regional Primate Research Center in Covington, Louisiana, the King Abdulaziz University in Jeddah, the Hescheler Foundation, and the University of Zurich. Some of their representatives became personally involved beyond the call of duty. As homage to all of them I shall add here a short story about a Bedouin, Osayis al Nomassy (plate 1, top), who was my driver in Saudi Arabia in 1980.

We had been at the Wadi Ranyah for three days, searching in vain for my first hamadryas baboons in Arabia. Early on the fourth morning we seated ourselves again in the blue Toyota, and Osayis asked with his eyes, "Where now?" I pointed toward the ford across the river. But Osayis, despite his incredible sense of direction, no longer seemed to know the way; instead, he drove westward past the Djebel Ablah. Suddenly he stopped so abruptly that he killed the engine. Pointing to the left, he looked at me, his usually serious face laughing. There were the baboons, sitting between a pair of umbrella acacias on a gravel rise. Osayis gestured toward the silent engine, then up toward heaven, and said happily, "Allah!" Later, from the Egyptian assistant Saleh, who knows some English, I learned some background to this story. On the previous evening the two Bedouin drivers had left "to visit our friends." In reality they had driven to the tent of an experienced Bedouin on the other side of the wadi and had gone out with him until midnight, climbing to three different sleeping rocks used by the baboons in the surrounding mountains. All of them were empty. Their adviser told them that there was one other place left, where we might see the hamadryas in the morning. It was to get to this place that Osayis now pretended to have lost his way. On other occasions he had no trouble communicating with me by signs, but he had wanted to keep his off-hour nocturnal labors to himself.

In Quest of the Sacred Baboon

The Hamadryas Baboon: A Desert Saint and Lecher

The last authentic experts on the hamadryas baboon were the ancient Egyptians. In the lower Nile Valley itself, the hamadryas was apparently nonexistent, as it is today. Yet at the time of Akhenaten's dynasty, about 1350 B.C., this baboon was considered an incarnation of Thoth, the god of scribes and scholars, the inventor of the sciences and of writing. The Egyptians had seen the living originals in the fabulous southern country called Punt, whose location is still unknown today. They brought the hamadryas baboons from there to the Nile. It was reported in Greek sources that Egyptian priests placed writing implements in front of the newly arrived hamadryas males. If the animals picked these up and began to scribble—behavior that seems entirely possible to me—the baboons were consecrated to Thoth (Macdonald 1965). According to the Egyptians, in the divine assembly Thoth stood with his tablet next to the king of the gods, and his duty among humans was to weigh the souls of the dead. In Egyptian illustrations of this event, the hamadryas baboon is often seated on the tip of the scale. Ramses III in 1168 B.C. let it be noted in a list of his donations to the god Ra: "I made for thee a scale of bright gold. Nothing of the kind has been produced since the time of Ra. Thoth sits on it as comrade (guardian) of the scale, as a powerful honorable baboon of embossed gold, so that thou weighest on it before thy countenance, O my father Ra" (Roeder 1959).

Earthly scribes prayed to Thoth that they might rise to a better position in life through the noble art of writing. One Egyptian statuette represents Thoth as a hamadryas with raised hands, gigantic and protective behind a seated man, probably a scribe. In his tomb statue the official and writer Ramses-nach reads a papyrus while a hamadryas baboon sits behind his head and inspires him with wisdom. The hamadryas—always a male—also appears in tomb paintings as a mediator between the praying human and the eye of a god. On a papyrus from the twenty-first dynasty, originating in about 1000 B.C., the music priestess Hent-Tawi prays, with the mediation of a hamadryas, to the sun rising above red desert mountains. The sun bears the eye of the god Horus (plate 1, bottom). Thoth and his baboons were associated with the moon. Perhaps the Egyptians derived this association from the round genital swelling of the female, which grows and shrinks in a monthly rhythm. They also believed that the hamadryas baboons greeted the rising sun with raised hands. We never saw this gesture among the wild hamadryas, but figure 1 shows a posture that the Egyptians may have interpreted in this way.

Among the symbols in Egyptian hieroglyphic writing are some elegant, true-to-life miniature drawings of animals. Depicted are the elephant, the quail, the ibis, and the hippopotamus, as well as a pacing male baboon with the unmistakable mantle of the hamadryas. The picture has various meanings. After some symbols it stands for "sacred baboon," but after others it means "to be angry" (Gardiner 1973). Whoever captured the hamadryas in Punt, brought them to the Nile by boat, and cared for them in the temples must have experienced the threatening and violent temperament, the swiftness and the power of a baboon. Nevertheless, Egyptian paintings show the hamadryas baboons to be a part of everyday human life. Males help to pick figs, allow themselves be led on a leash like dogs, or sit solemnly and apparently unchained on ships on the high seas. Either there were outstanding animal trainers at that time, or the Egyptians for their own greater glory depicted the hamadryas as more docile than it is, just as they painted foreign envoys as miniature figures in subservient poses before the pharaoh.

The reverence in which the hamadryas baboon was held by the inhabitants of the Nile Valley may have been inspired by its massive head and mantle and by its majestic, almost always symmetrical posture while seated, or perhaps by its deep, resonant call.

Though in Egypt the hamadryas was considered sacred, in Europe during the Middle Ages it was merely a lecher. There monkeys were viewed as incarnations of greed, conceit, and shamelessness. Even at the beginning of modern times, the influential Zurich naturalist Conrad Gessner (whose works dating from 1551 to 1587 were freely translated into English in 1607 by Edward Topsell) adopted the judgments of classical authors, saying of the "dog-head" or baboon, for example: "They are as lustfull and venereous as goats, attempting to defile all sorts of women." Even the lion, so he claimed, was not spared this animal's ardor. However, from his own observations Gessner reported more accurately that the monkey is "such an altogether adventurous, crafty, inquisitive animal that by nature he can imitate all kinds of tricks." Because the mothers carry their nursing infants around with them day and night, he concludes, "For its young the monkey has a special love, more than other animals do." But the moral judgments of the Middle Ages do not die so easily; as late as 1913 the biologist Elliot wrote that the hamadryas was "the lowest of the catarrhine monkeys, and as they are generally of large size they are dangerous animals when adult, possessing savage and ugly dispositions."

Fig. 1. A young male hamadryas lifts his arm so that his flank hairs can be groomed. Did the Egyptians see this gesture as a greeting to the rising sun (cf. plate 1, bottom)?

Monkeys were and are an annoyance to Europeans even in this century because they are uninhibited—but as we shall see, not in every respect—and yet similar to humans. That baboons would actually rape human women was something we also heard in Ethiopia. As far as I know there is no verified case of such an occurrence, yet no monkey would be more likely to fuel such a rumor than the male hamadryas. His mantle reaches barely to his hips, leaving his bottom bare and, to our sensibilities, embarrassingly unprotected; it's as though his clothes are worn the wrong way around. Furthermore, the large penis is driven exuberantly erect even by friendly interest, and the red hindquarters are resplendent at any time.

The naked red patch extends forward at his sides, where it is further emphasized by the contrasting border of white hairs. While humans conceal their lower body, the hamadryas flaunts it. In comparison, a tomcat appears very decent, with everything compact and nicely clothed in soft fur. But here we are deluding ourselves. A tomcat flaunts his sex just as much, but he does it through smell, by spraying strongly scented urine. The world of mammals apart from the higher primates is full of actively produced odors, which are even more effective in exciting conspecifics than the "sexy" costume of the baboon. It is just that our noses are usually unable to detect those scents. The hamadryas baboon has the bad luck to be a visual animal, like the human. His sexual stimuli are designed for the eye, so they affect us too. My copy of a cave drawing near Ursu in eastern Ethiopia, of unknown age, in all its simplicity shows what in the male hamadryas most impressed the shepherd who drew it (see fig. 2).

The present-day highland Ethiopians call the hamadryas baboon "nedj djindjero," the "white monkey" in Amharic, from the light color of the males' mantle. For them it is primarily an agricultural pest. They catch it in snares or shoot it because it steals grain from their fields. They give the name "tokur djindjero," or "black monkey," to the gelada baboons (*Theropithecus gelada*) of the high mountains in Ethiopia; this species is also mantled but dark brown. The old authors judged the appearance of these baboons by human criteria, too, but here the geladas were more fortunate than the hamadryas. They also have a naked, red area of skin bordered by white hairs, but theirs is on the chest rather than the buttocks. Because of their high, richly modulated voice, their round face, and their bare breast, they were regarded as mythical women. Conrad Gessner described them as "maiden monkeys" and gave them the early scientific name *Sphinx*: "As Ausonius and Varinus say, the face and hand of a mayde, the body of a Dogge, the winges of a byrd, the voice of a man, the clawes of a Lyon, and the tayle of a Dragon." The tail of the real gelada has a tuft at the end that makes it more like a lion's than a dragon's, but when an adult male is galloping his dark mantle rises and falls and it does indeed resemble a pair of wings. Perhaps the sphinx of the Egyptians, which lived on in the Greek saga of Oedipus, was a distorted image of the gelada in the inaccessibly distant high mountains beyond which lay the source of the blue Nile, long to remain unknown. As far as I know, the gelada was never imported to Egypt, and the Egyptian sculptors probably knew it only from hearsay, perhaps something like, "A mane on the head and a face like a human, voice and breast like a human woman, wings like an eagle, body and legs and tail like a lion." Topsell's *Historie* adds a fairly accurate description of the naked, reddish patch on the chest of the gelada: "In that part of their body which is bare without haire, there is a

Fig. 2. Cave drawing at Ursu, province of Hararghe, original size, black, age unknown. The artist apparently wanted to represent a male hamadryas. The mantle and sex organs in particular seem to have impressed him.

certaine red thing rising in a round circle like Millet seed, which giueth great grace and comelinesse to their coulour." These skin pearls do in fact surround the entire chest area of the female gelada, and they swell and subside during the menstrual cycle.

The Desert Baboon, *Papio cynocephalus hamadryas:* A Modern Summary

From the Egyptians to Gessner, the old truth is confirmed that every person sees the world and its creatures in a different way. As members of the human species we are of course alike in perceiving things primarily with our eyes, in developing concepts and naming them, in being able to sympathize with others and in making moral judgments. But it is almost inevitable that each person will also perceive and judge through the lenses of his or her own culture, which has endowed individuals with *particular* ideas and moral attitudes. Even modern scientists are predisposed to seeing things in certain ways. They cannot rid themselves of preconceptions completely, but they must do all they can to recognize the distortion preconceived ideas may produce. Present-day biological research on animal behavior, a field called ethology or psychobiology, emphasizes three important aspects that set it apart from animal studies of earlier times: (1) to observe with one's own eyes, for years on end; (2) to evaluate animal behavior according to its function for the animal itself, not according to its value for humans or to human moral criteria; (3) to understand not only the direct internal and external causes of behavior and how they change during a lifetime, but also the evolution of behavior. With an eye to these three concerns, I shall now introduce the hamadryas baboons.

First, like all natural scientists, ethologists want to see for themselves. For millennia, those who wrote books knew baboons, and other animals, mainly from hearsay. Those who knew them firsthand, the shepherds of the mountains and deserts, didn't write books. Long-term observation and writing were first combined by the behavioral researchers of the twentieth century. However, they made it a condition of their work that they would use only the observations perceptible with their own senses. What an animal might signify in an invisible, spiritual world is not to be found in our books. In this respect, the Egyptians were more daring.

Carolus Linnaeus chose the modern scientific name for the desert baboon, *Papio hamadryas*, now called *Papio cynocephalus hamadryas*. *Papio* is Latin for "baboon," *cynocephalus* means "dog-head," and *hamadryas* is a wood nymph in ancient Greek. Why Linnaeus associated this rugged creature with a nymph I cannot imagine. As viewed by modern zoologists, the hamadryas baboon is a medium-sized monkey that lives mainly on the ground. It inhabits both coasts of the Red Sea. On the African side it is thought to be distributed from a northern limit approximately at Suakin, near Port Sudan, southward to the mouth of the Webi Shebelle River in Somalia; the precise boundaries of its range in Africa are unknown. Going inland from the coast, it occupies those areas of the Danakil Desert where it can find drinking water, and in the west it sometimes ascends into the Ethiopian highlands. In Arabia it can live only in the coastal mountains, where rain sometimes falls, from Al Akhal, 200 kilometers north of Tajif, to Yemen in the south. It has been seen at altitudes from 0 to 8,450 feet and in areas where the annual rainfall is only four inches (Biquand et al. 1992). It has never been seen in the central Arabian desert and in the mountains of Oman.

The hamadryas baboon has a marked sexual dimorphism, which

means that males look very different from females. The female has short, brown hair and weighs about twenty-two pounds. The fully grown males weigh forty to forty-five pounds and are about twenty-four inches tall when seated. Their upper canine teeth are as much as one and a half inches long (plate 4, top left) and their back edge is sharp as a knife, because during threat behavior the male whets them against the teeth of the lower jaw. His powerful appearance is further exaggerated by the airy mantle of long hairs. Its hair coloration is a finely grained pattern of alternating dark and white rings, which gives the total impression of light gray, shading toward brown or almost white in some individuals. With this mantle, which reaches only to the hips, the male looks large shouldered like a bison bull. The faces of the hamadryas baboons are hairless, dark to reddish, with a long, squared-off muzzle; the hands are sturdy but not very dextrous tools for climbing and digging. The buttocks are naked in both sexes. The hamadryas weighs somewhat less than the more powerfully built savanna baboons, as if the desert requires a more economical construction of the body. Similarly, the oryx of the Arabian deserts is of lighter weight than those of the African savannas.

Pregnancy in a female hamadryas baboon lasts about six months. The infant is weaned at about fourteen months. A female gives birth about every twenty-two months; however, if the previous offspring dies as an infant, she can conceive sooner. The young females have their first monthly cycle when they are four to five years old. Males become sexually mature somewhat later. Then they begin to grow a short cape over their shoulders, which does not grow into a real mantle until age ten, when they have reached full adulthood.

A hamadryas can live for up to thirty years, as has been demonstrated in the Augsburg Zoo in Germany. My former student Jean-Jacques Abegglen has estimated that in our Ethiopian study area monkeys can live for a little over twenty years.

This description of physical characteristics is just the starting point for our biological investigation: that is what the animals known as "desert baboons" look like. But what is their actual relation to the desert, their ecological niche? What can they do there? Why do they do it in groups?

This brings us to the second concern of ethology, which is not, as it was among the ancients, whether the animal is dangerous or an amusing trickster *to us* or whether it is an incarnation that could lead *us* to the gods. Rather, we want to know what it is to *itself*, how it gets along in its world. How have the millennia through which it has survived in this kind of terrain shaped its body, its inclinations, its abilities, and its knowledge? How does it communicate—not with humans but with its group companions? The glowing red bottom of the male hamadryas, for instance, is not offensive to other hamadryas. It is a flag of peace. The members of the troop present it to one another in moments of tension, and it is probably in this way that friendship is preserved.

In trying to be objective we by no means close our eyes to the things the ancients thought they saw in our animals: the greeting to the rising sun, the tendency to fly into a rage, the boundless sexual drive. Our thinking is not so sterile that we would not enjoy such observations ourselves. But it has to be said, unfortunately, that forty years of field research on free-living primates have not confirmed most of the old stories. A social scientist could still find traces today of how such fables were first concocted. Eyewitnesses in Ethiopia told us, for example, that they had observed hamadryas performing what they interpreted as a funeral rite or evidence that our baboons are superstitious. We shall return to their tales later. Now, however, consider what hamadryas baboons do in their own world.

Hamadryas baboons, like the other species of the African genus *Papio*, are predominantly vegetarian (6). In Ethiopia they eat mainly grass seeds and acacia flowers in the rainy season, and in the dry season primarily acacia pods and a few leaves; they also dig in the stony ground for small, carrotlike roots. Sometimes they catch and eat a hare or a young dik-dik antelope. When locust swarms descend, they exploit this rare source of protein and eagerly pluck the insects from the bushes. Of all the baboons, the hamadryas are the only ones to have specialized in life in the rocky dwarf-shrub semidesert and the open savanna where thorn trees grow (plate 3). During the dry season, in many areas water can be found only below ground. The hamadryas baboons know where to look in the usually dry, sandy beds of the wadis, and they dig up these places with their hands. In contrast to almost all other monkeys, they do not spend the night in tall trees, which are too rare in semideserts, but rather on rock walls that are almost inaccessible to leopards.

Perhaps the most important means by which the hamadryas cope with desert life, however, is their social structure. On any one day, they can be found in gatherings of hundreds and, at other times and places, in groups as small as two to five. The larger groups divide along predetermined lines, as though a zipper were being opened, and they later reassemble (17). I have called this the "fusion-fission system." The size of the group is even more significant for the ecology of hamadryas baboons than for other animals. For protection against predators in the almost treeless semidesert, the group should be as large as possible. But when feeding sites are very far apart and can be as small as one bush bearing pods, so that only a few animals can feed there at once, a group of, say, fifty baboons would have to travel very far to find enough to eat, and at each site most of them would have to wait rather than eat. The fusion-fission system provides a flexible solution. It allows groups to form of a size suitable for various resource concentrations: for large sleeping rocks, a *troop* of over a hundred individuals; for permanent water holes, a *band* of about fifty; for fairly small feeding sites, a *clan* of about fifteen; and for single bushes or small trees, a *family* with a male at its head, the so-called one-male group of about five baboons. This four-layered organization is unique among animals, as far as we know. Even the closest relatives of the hamadryas, the savanna baboons, have only one type of group, of about the same size as a band.

To make more certain whether a special feature such as the fusion-fission system of the hamadryas has really evolved especially for the animals' life in the desert, it is necessary to find out how this system differs from the groupings of its relatives who have other modes of life. We shall take the fundamental question of how large a group should be to suit a specific ecological situation as an example of such a comparison. Among the baboons and their more distant kin, which include the mangabeys, the guenons, and the macaques, there is a simple relationship between group size and environment. The species that inhabit the crowns of the jungle trees live in groups of ten to twenty individuals, most including only one adult male. The further a set of species has departed from life in the tree crowns, the larger are the groups that it forms. The forest baboons, which live largely on the ground but still within the primary forest—that is, the drills (*Mandrillus leucophaeus*) and mandrills (*Mandrillus sphinx*)—and the forest macaques with similar habits have groups of twenty to thirty members. Those of the savanna baboons, which no longer have tree refuges available at intervals of only a few paces, number forty to seventy and contain more males. The boldest step into the open was taken by the geladas (*Theropithecus*), which invaded entirely treeless grasslands. When the Ice Age began in Europe, *Theropithecus oswaldi* was living on the open shores of the East African lakes. This was the largest baboon of all time. Having the dimensions of a present-day gorilla, its limbs were completely adapted to life on the ground, and according to its dental structure it fed on grass seeds (Martin 1990). Despite its size, it may have been exterminated by the early humans who lived by the lakes and hunted its young. Today the once thriving genus *Theropithecus* is represented by only a single species, *Theropithecus gelada*. It has withdrawn to the high mountains of Ethiopia, living at altitudes up to 9,000 feet or more and eating mainly the seeds and roots of grasses. The gelada groups, with about 150 members on average, are the largest among the baboon species (figs. 3 and 4). This progressive enlargement of the groups probably results from the increasing danger of predation. Large groups are likely to detect predators more reliably, and in any case they can intimidate approaching enemies by screaming and mock attacks.

Fig. 3. A male gelada in the high Semien Mountains walks protectively on the flank of his troop. At this altitude, 12,300 feet, it freezes almost every night. The males' brown mantles and blond mustaches grow to an extraordinary length.

Group size, of course, is a crude characteristic of a species. In order to understand it, the species comparison has to be extended over a broad circle of related forms. In contrast, to investigate the internal refinements of the social system as it relates to the environment, one must limit the comparison to closely related species, which live in different environments at the present time. Closely related species offer two advantages for such comparisons. First, they have not been separate for very long in evolutionary terms. Therefore the differences between them probably arose in the environments they inhabit now. Second, closely related species still share a large proportion of their genetic material and hence are likely to respond to a given environmental change in the same way. Sets of species that have been separate for an extremely long time, such as primates and carnivores, have become so disparate in their whole structure and behavior that they are totally unable to respond similarly to a given environmental challenge; their abilities are now too different. For instance, higher primates protect their infants from predators by carrying them wherever they go. They can do this because they have only one infant at a time; since the infant has hands and feet to hold on to the mother, the latter keeps *her* hands and mouth free. In contrast, carnivores have many young, who cannot cling; so the mother must either carry them singly in her jaws, or, a bit less time-consuming, tuck them away in a den. Ungulates can do neither; their long legs can neither grasp nor dig efficiently, so the infant's protection must be to hide, or to be able to

Fig. 4. Gelada habitat in Semien, with alpine meadows and lobelia plants. Here the high mountains plunge 4,200 feet down toward the north. The geladas spend the night on the cliff faces.

excape within the first hours. Few environmental changes would evoke comparable adaptations in animals of such diverse construction.

The closest relatives of the hamadryas baboons are the other subspecies of the genus *Papio*, the savanna baboons. According to Shotake's (1981) calculations based on the mutation rates of blood-serum antigens, the subspecies *hamadryas* split off from the savanna baboons only 340,000 years ago. This was about the time when the first archaic *Homo sapiens* emerged in Africa and Europe. The genus *Papio* as a whole is older. Bone fossils indicate that it existed two million years ago, by which time it had spread out from the tropical forest, where it presumably had already been living on the ground, into the more open savannas, consisting of grasslands with scattered trees. It arose from the genus *Parapapio*, which has since become extinct.

Thus the savanna baboons provide the background for comparison with the hamadryas (fig. 5). Like the latter, they are strongly built and have squared-off, doglike muzzles. Although they usually sleep in the crowns of trees, their body form is particularly suitable for traveling on the ground. The males of both savanna and desert baboons have strong, pointed canine teeth with sharp back edges, and both sexes have well-

Fig. 5. Anubis baboons at the Awash River. This is a subspecies of savanna baboon. At the Awash their distribution range makes contact with that of the hamadryas, which live to the east of them in the hot lowlands. The hamadryas subspecies originally split off from savanna baboons such as these.

developed calluses on their bottoms, which protect the skin when they are sitting on rough rocks and bark. In all *Papio* females, the skin around the vaginal opening swells up to form a taut funnel a few days before and after ovulation (figs. 18, bottom, and 35). At this time they are eager to copulate and conception is possible. This period of swelling is called "estrus." As long as a female is not pregnant, the swelling recurs every month. Menstruation occurs halfway between these periods.

The male savanna baboons, like the male hamadryas, are considerably larger than the females but have the same coloration as females and lack a mantle. The glowing red posterior areas (plate 5, bottom) are also a special feature of hamadryas males. In the savanna baboons, these areas are also naked but dark, dull, and smaller.

The four species of savanna baboons are familiar to those who have visited the most popular African national parks. The regions they inhabit are mostly wetter and have more trees than the home of the hamadryas. Their typical habitat is tree-covered savanna. The savanna baboon species lives in a different part of the continent from the hamadryas baboons (fig. 6.) At the boundaries between their ranges, hybrids are not uncommon. The range of the hamadryas baboon in Africa is bounded on the

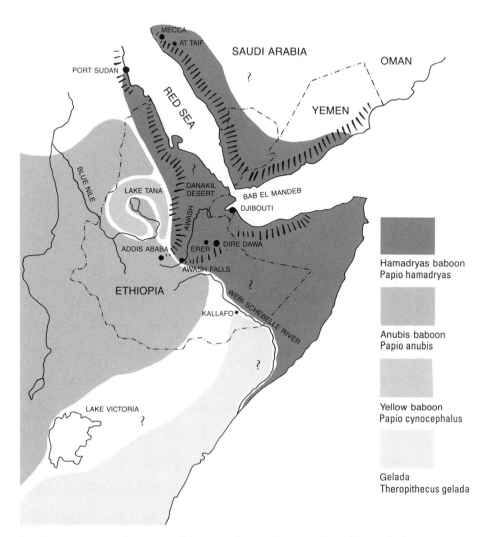

Fig. 6. Approximate distribution of the hamadryas baboon and neighboring baboon species. The boundaries have been precisely determined at only a few places. West of the Danakil Desert (the Afar triangle) the hamadryas baboons sometimes ascend into the mountains. They probably venture into the Danakil and the interior of the Arabian desert as far as they can find a daily supply of water.

south and east by that of the more slender yellow baboon (*Papio cyno-cephalus cynocephalus*), and on the south and west by that of the anubis baboon (*Papio cynocephalus anubis*), which is dark olive in color with a dense pelt and is distributed along a belt that crosses Africa south of the Sahara. A few thousand years ago, or perhaps not as long as that, the advancing Sahara isolated a small population of anubis baboons in the rocky Tibesti Mountains, and they still survive there in the middle of the desert, thanks to a few meager springs in the rocky cliffs. Huard (1962) saw them there as recently as 1952. According to him, some simi-larly isolated groups also still exist in the Sahara mountain ranges of Aïr and Ennedi. Western Africa is the home of another yellowish species, the Guinea baboon (*Papio cynocephalus papio*). In South Africa, finally, lives the gigantic, dark chacma baboon (*Papio cynocephalus ursinus*), males of which weigh almost sixty pounds. The chacma is characterized by the multimale groups typical of the other savanna baboons, but on the bare heights of the Drakensberge they are reduced to families with only one male, like those always formed by the hamadryas of the semidesert. The social life of savanna baboons has been thoroughly studied particularly by Jeanne and Stuart Altmann (yellow baboons, e.g., 1980), Shirley Strum (anubis baboons, e.g., 1987), and Barbara Smuts (anubis baboons, e.g., 1985). The society of geladas is well described by Robin Dunbar (1988), who has also reviewed results of other savanna baboon studies.

The hamadryas baboons live in the semideserts on the horn of Africa. Vegetation maps show that the semideserts in this region are separated from those at the southern edge of the Sahara by the Ethiopian moun-tains. This isolation may have played a crucial role in the evolution of a specialized desert form. Everywhere else in Africa the semideserts are bor-dered by savanna along a broad front, and if they are inhabited by ba-boons at all, it is by savanna baboons.

In making its transition to life as a desert baboon, the hamadryas al-tered a number of features of its savanna ancestors. The closed groups averaging forty to seventy members were replaced by a flexible fusion-fission system, which we have interpreted as an adaptation to the semi-desert. It is harder to understand the more delicate adjustments of social structure. Within groups of savanna baboons, friendships do develop be-tween a male and a female, but not stable pair bonds (Smuts 1985). Each female can choose to mate with any male, and each male with as many females as his current rank and his tactical skills permit. Among hama-dryas baboons these loose friendships have consolidated into permanent marriages between one male and several females. This is probably related to the fact that the male hamadryas, with his light mantle and red-and-white posterior, has become so conspicuous. Sexual dimorphism gener-ally goes with polygyny. Another change has occurred in the way the two sexes are bonded to their native groups. The females of all savanna baboons spend their whole lives in the group in which they were born. The males leave it and move to other groups. But in the social structure of the hamadryas baboons the reverse applies: the males stay with their birth clan, but the females shift to different clans and bands during their lifetimes.

This complex of changes should be understood as a process by which the former savanna baboon was converted for life in the semidesert. At the end of the book we shall review all of these specializations to understand at what stages in evolution they could have developed.

In the very recent past the hamadryas must have been subjected to events that caused it to settle on both sides of the Red Sea, which had come into being long before the hamadryas split off from the savanna baboons. This is a puzzling situation. It is unlikely that two populations of savanna baboons would have evolved independently into identical hamadryas baboons, one on the horn of Africa and the other in Arabia. Therefore the hamadryas must have originated on one side or the other—as yet we do not know which—and eventually moved from some place on that coast to the opposite coast. One place that suggests itself in the south is the strait of Bab el Mandeb, which at present is only 360 feet deep. The geologist Peter Burek kindly informed me that this land bridge was last above water about 10,000 years ago, but in his opinion it was a saline desert that primates would hardly have been able to cross. This salt-desert bridge had also been exposed earlier, at intervals of about 50,000 years. Now, I do not believe that the hamadryas populations on the two coasts have been separated for even as long as 10,000 years. In general, the longer two populations are separated, the more they differ in appearance and behavior. But during my studies in Saudi Arabia I could find no obvious differences in external form between the Arabian and the Ethiopian hamadryas baboons; the animals from various parts of Ethiopia differ from one another more than from the quite average, uniform hamadryas baboons of Arabia. Furthermore, the behavior of the animals to the west and east of the Red Sea differed only with respect to a very few gestures. The friendly behavior called lip-smacking, for example, is rarely performed in Arabia, and then in only a weak version. Biochemical comparisons of the enzymes and the DNA (genetic material) of the two populations could measure the genetic distance between them. Meanwhile, the behavioral comparison gives preliminary evidence that the separation between the east and west coast populations occurred only a few thousand years ago.

Instead of the link by way of the Bab el Mandeb, it is more likely that the two populations were originally joined by way of Suez, which did not become a desert until about 5,000 years ago. In that case, the Nile would have been the boundary between the anubis baboons of the Sahara, remnants of which may still be imprisoned in the mountains, and the hamadryas baboons, which would have advanced along the Red Sea coast as far as the Mediterranean.

This brings us up to historic times and another encounter with the ancient Egyptians. They gave the hamadryas baboons a second chance to cross the Red Sea. As recently as 1500 B.C. Queen Hatshepsut sent out a great expedition to bring back shiploads of incense, myrrh, gold, and precious woods from the "divine land" Punt, situated somewhere in the south on one or both coasts of the Red Sea. Among the living animals that were imported, according to pictorial representations, there were male hamadryas baboons. The journeys to Punt were first mentioned during the Old Kingdom, around 2400 B.C., at the same time that the construction of marine ships was first reported. The earliest pictures of the hamadryas also date from about 2400 B.C. and were at first more rare than pictures of the anubis. The Egyptologist B. Peters in Cologne wrote to me that from the time between 2665 and 2135 B.C. only three representations of the hamadryas baboon are known, but about fifteen of the anubis. Whereas illustrations of other animal species were very true to life at this time, the hamadryas was drawn rather ineptly, with the ears wrongly pointed and the mantle more like a transparent shawl than a mass of hair, as though the artists had never seen a real specimen. Later pictures and sculptures of the hamadryas, dating from about 1500 B.C., are eminently realistic. The hamadryas drawings in the hieroglyphs also derive from this period, the Middle Kingdom.

It might be, then, that at the time of the ancient Egyptians the hamadryas were no longer living in their country but were imported from the south, beginning about 2400 B.C. I have seen maps of their sailing routes: the ships crossed between the ports on the two coasts. Wherever they may have been captured, if I know my hamadryas baboons, it is very likely that over the many hundreds of years some of them escaped on the other coast during a scheduled landing or shipwreck. This could explain why today the African and Arabian hamadryas are so extraordinarily similar to one another, much more so than, for example, the colorful African oryx antelope to its smaller, paler equivalent in Arabia.

If molecular biologists analyzed the DNA of the Egyptian mummies of sacred baboons along with that of the two living populations, it might just be possible to localize the legendary land of Punt. At present, however, it is still not clear whether hamadryas baboons originated on the African or the Arabian coast. I am inclined toward the African origin. If they had come from Arabia, they would probably have colonized the mountains of Oman as well, because the land between these and the present range in the western Arabian mountains has not always been desert over the last 340,000 years (31). It became impassable only a few thousand years ago, at about the time when the hamadryas were crossing the Red Sea. Coming from Africa, they would have found the way to Oman closed.

Now that we have an outline of the likely history of the hamadryas baboons, which has raised the question of the functions of their special adaptations for life in the semidesert, we must clarify the third approach of modern behavioral research: we will interpret our observations in the light of evolutionary theory. Here we are not merely concerned with the history of the species, but with obtaining a convincing insight into the causes of the individual steps by which it changed. The evolutionary theory of behavior can be found in its most fully developed and accurate form in two disciplines that originated in the seventies: sociobiology and behavioral ecology. Sociobiology deals with social behavior within a species, and behavioral ecology with the behavior of animals with respect to food, parasites, and predators. However, researchers in the two fields think in similar ways. A sociobiologist, seeing an important situation in an animal's life, wonders what forms of behavior or "strategies" the animal could use in that situation. For instance, a female might have a choice between a strong male that already has a partner and a male that is weaker but still a bachelor. The question then is, what alternative behaviors are available to the female herself, to each of the two males, and to the rival female? There will be various consequences for the choosing female, depending on her choice. With the stronger male she would have access to better feeding places, but she would risk the enmity of his first mate. If the latter is higher-ranking than the female herself, to choose the stronger male could bring more problems than advantages. All these so-called costs and benefits are estimated as realistically as possible for each of the two options in terms of their effects on the number of offspring the female will be able to bear—which is also called her "fitness."

Why is the number of future offspring so important? We have good reasons to assume that animal behavior is always to some degree genetically determined and hence is passed on to the young through heredity. Therefore the genetic behavioral programs of individuals with more descendants will be more common in the next generation than the programs of individuals with fewer descendants. After many generations the more common programs can eventually eliminate the others. As applied to our female baboon, this means that fitness actually determines which of the behavioral programs governing female choice will eventually become dominant: those that favor monogamy, those that favor polygamy, or those that allow flexibility, so that her preference depends on circumstance. A computer can then be used to calculate which strategy on the part of the female, given which strategies used by the partner, will produce the best cost/benefit ratio for the female. The hereditary factors that ought to have survived are those that, in a given life situation, help to activate the most advantageous response to the strategies of a partner. With animals that have sufficiently simple behavior, these analyses and predictions can be tested.

It is not hard to see that this approach incorporates modern economic considerations of cost versus benefit, which will surely arouse some skepticism. Have the biologists been so imbued with this cultural attitude that they automatically apply it in their own field? Or is the cost/benefit ratio—even though it takes no account of several aspects of life—indeed a basic factor in the survival of both humans and animals, a fundamental determinant of evolutionary as well as economic success? I suspect that it is. Like any model, of course, sociobiological models simplify reality to such an extent that they are mostly inapplicable to complex animals. Furthermore, in the case of a long-lived animal the consequences of a particular strategy for the number of children it might have in all the rest of its life are practically impossible to measure. Nevertheless, sociobiologists have been able to provide solid support for some of their theorems; the latter have sharpened the thinking of behavioral scientists and focused their observations. Sociobiological considerations have directed the attention of the behavioral researcher to things no one had thought about before, with very exciting results. It seems worthwhile to go on looking at things from the cost/benefit perspective, as long as we preserve our skepticism and try a different view from time to time.

Our hamadryas studies were not begun with the efficiency ideas of sociobiology in mind, because the field didn't exist then. I was trained in developmental biology, the field of Spemann, Baltzer, and my teacher Ernst Hadorn. I learned to do experimental research on embryonic processes, in which the various parts of an organism interact to produce differentiation and development of the organism as a whole. Later, watching the social life of the hamadryas baboons, I was interested to find that the groups are like marvelously transparent organisms, the parts of which communicate visibly and audibly with one another—unlike the cells of the body. Groups can also change their form more freely and can even divide and later become reunited. I saw social structure. Our later interpretations of hamadryas baboon behavior, however, were nourished by the sociobiological efficiency concepts, which focus not on the group but on the individual as propagator of its genes. Viewed in this light, social behavior is not the behavior of a group organism, whose members act in the interest of the group. The group comes into being only because its members obtain advantages from cooperating with other individuals and thereby increase their own fitness.

It seems obvious to most of us today that this is the right approach to an understanding of why groups arose at all in evolution. But it is not the only one; having recognized a strategy as optimal, we still do not know *how* the animal implements it—with which sensory abilities, motivations, and thought processes—and under what conditions the strategy sometimes fails after all. The reality of the individual resides in the immediate or proximate causes: the internal factors that drive it to act, and the events going on momentarily in the world around it. Individuals live and experience their *behavior*, and not the distant, ultimate causes that in the course of evolution selected the behavior's hereditary basis.

The efficiency hypotheses predict how organisms that have evolved to optimality *should* behave. This way of thinking attracts my fascinated interest, but my love belongs to what organisms actually *do*. Here we see the concrete solutions that a species evolved as a response to an environmental pressure. The responses are often awkward or laborious, but often they are ingenious. No animal species can be efficient to perfection because, like us, it is limited by the apparatus handed down to it from the past—its bodily apparatus and the apparatus of its society. Each species is a temporary station in an ongoing history that makes its often obscure way between the harsh demands of new niches and the restrictive "I can do no other" of its preexisting dispositions. History is always constrained by what has happened before; it is fate. Species, too, have one.

In our studies we have tried to find out what lies behind the survival of the hamadryas. For hundreds of days we wandered along with backpacks and field glasses, between the clans and in the bands. For some thousands of evenings and mornings we sat, with notebook or dictaphone, at the feet of the baboons on their sleeping cliffs. In the State Museum of Berlin I later found an Egyptian statue from about 1370 B.C., which shows a

Fig. 7. An Egyptian scribe takes down the words of the sacred baboon. In the course of the centuries, the scribe lost his stylus. Statuette of wood and serpentine, eighteenth dynasty. (State Museum of Berlin)

scribe similarly at the feet of a hamadryas, the latter enlarged and elevated as befits its divine significance (fig. 7). Both the ancient and I wrote down what the hamadryas told us. The scribe probably wrote the words of the god. We described the doings of an animal that, like us, is trying to make a living in this world. For me, these are also words out of an alluring and deep mystery: the evolution of living beings on our planet.

The Zoo Baboons

Individuals and Gestures

One morning in the early summer of 1955, my professor, Heini Hediger, took me on a tour of the Zurich Zoo, of which he had just become the director. As we walked, he stopped from time to time to suggest possible topics for the research I would do toward my Master's degree. For example: Why can geckos walk up vertical panes of glass? Are boas and pythons really unable to hear? Perhaps something about the chemistry of aquarium water? All zoological research questions, each of them promising a journey to the frontier of the unknown. It would be a feast after semesters of listening to lectures!

Once again Hediger paused, this time by the rocky primate pit next to the carnivore house. "I can't tell you much about hamadryas baboons, but I am quite certain that interesting things are going on down there, things we have never thought of." Pasha, the gray-maned leader of the baboons, peered up at us over his shoulder. His females sat close to him; farther away a youngster screeched. They didn't look very attractive, with their squared-off muzzles, their dull hair, and their red hindquarters. That hamadryas baboons can be beautiful I experienced only later in Ethiopia when, after hesitating at length, a hundred of them descended from their sleeping rock in the morning. The great troop flowed down over the ridges and slopes, the large silver males striding in long paces and absorbing the force of each landing with their powerful shoulders, the young ones tumbling playfully from one level to another like balls, all of them finally in agreement about the direction of their departure.

During the days after that tour of the zoo, I would often gaze down at the baboons, completely intrigued. Although it was incomprehensible to me, a kind of sign language seemed to be in use, accompanied by visits, gatherings, and departures. Here was the promise of something absorbing: social structure. My research subject had found me, and the hamadryas baboons had found their biographer—thanks, above all, to Heini Hediger.

My decision was also influenced by the memory of my favorite reading when I was eight years old: Lofting's books about Dr. Dolittle, the little country doctor who had learned the animals' language and was thus able to know what they were thinking and feeling. If only one could experience what it is like to be an animal: that was also the secret wish of my high school biology teacher Konrad Escher, as he admitted to me much later. He and I both thought it could never come true. By research we can learn what animals know, and that in itself is exciting enough. To feel what a bat feels, though, we would have to become one in every respect—in body, in sensations, and in thinking—as the philosopher Thomas Nagel wrote in 1981. The most that my efforts to imagine the bat experience can tell me is what it woud be like for me if *I* were a bat.

My studies, then, began in the zoo (2). The advantage of this approach is that no precious time is wasted in jungle or steppe for learning the "language" of one's animals; after all, provident people who move to another country learn its language before they leave home. However, the first task was to learn to distinguish the fifteen baboons, an art in which some people are more skilled than others. My colleague during later work in Ethiopia, Walter Angst, is undoubtedly among the talented ones. When we were trapping female anubis baboons at the Awash River in Ethiopia, he very soon became personally acquainted with all the males in the group as well, even though they were entirely irrelevant to our project. By contrast, in the Zurich Zoo in 1955 I needed a whole Sunday afternoon to learn to tell my baboons apart, although they were well separated in age. Pasha, the only adult male, was easily recognized by his fog-gray mantle and conspicuously large size. Among the smaller, brown-haired members of the group I had to search painstakingly for some clear identifying feature, however tiny: a tail tuft curled in a particular way, a small white scar just under the right eye, two notches at the top of the left ear. The big worry at the outset was that there might be two animals identical in appearance, and this concern was amplified later on, when we were observing the huge troops of baboons in Ethiopia. In the first days of the zoo study it could take minutes until a baboon turned so that the critical feature became visible. After a few weeks, though, I was able to recognize individuals merely by facial expression or even from behind, by the way they were sitting, just as we identify members of our own families at a distance by their gait and posture. This "I just know" reaction is quite reliable; it makes scientists uneasy only because we cannot be sure *why* we recognize the animal. Hence we feel bound to search again and again for the small white scar or the notched ear. One of the basics of science is the need to know why one knows.

The baboons themselves seem to recognize one another by details of shape. In Ethiopia we once tried to mark wild hamadryas baboons so that we could identify them from a distance by dyeing their fur a conspicuous red or green. Their family members were not confused for a moment. Only the vultures responded, by diving low over the brightly colored column of baboons on the march. Perhaps they expected such discolored baboons to be seriously ill and a likely source of food in the near future.

By the evening of my first zoo day each baboon had a name, in most cases an abbreviation standing for the particular physical imperfection that set it apart from the crowd. The young Wiffel, for example, was so called because of the "white fleck at the left" on his face. The group was a family with the following composition:

Pasha	The sole adult male, object of fascination and fear for all the others.
Sora *Ofe* *Vecchia* *Nacha*	The adult females, Pasha's harem, in descending order of rank. The wizened, submissive Vecchia still had a belated career ahead of her, as we shall see. Nacha was the whipping girl for all the group members, even the adolescents. Her tail always bore open bite wounds.
Ulysses *Kalos* *Wiffel*	The three subadult, sexually mature young males; the five-year-old Ulysses already had the beginnings of a gray mane, though it didn't yet reach his elbows.
Liba *Nina* *Intora*	The three juvenile females, about three years old; in the course of the study they passed through puberty and entered the subadult category.
Glumo *Remo*	The two-year-old boys.
Proka *Seka*	The small girls, just one year old.

Superior to the whole group, a sort of "superalpha," was their keeper, Mr. Rehm. In greeting Rehm, even Pasha behaved like a subordinate, presenting his hindquarters.

Once I was able to identify the baboons and had named them, I wanted to learn to understand their sounds and gestures. Here it is best to start with the more dramatic activities, the meanings of which are immediately apparent: biting, hitting, vigorous chasing, fleeing, and mating. These forms of behavior, familiar in ourselves as in most mammalian species, provide a point of departure for further understanding. Whatever is done just before an attack is presumably a threatening gesture: before they bite, hamadryas baboons raise the skin of the forehead and stare at the opponent. I called this facial expression "brow-raising." When a bitten animal takes flight and, in so doing, bares its closed teeth, this expression is probably one of fear, comparable to submissive grinning in humans. At first, of course, such interpretations are hypotheses to be tested and refined each time the gestures appear, and if necessary they are corroborated with statistical methods.

A second aid to learning the animal dictionary is the "language" of approach and withdrawal, common to all higher animals including ourselves. A skilled puppeteer can demonstrate this kind of communication by casting the beams of two flashlights onto the ceiling. Suppose one of the two spots of light regularly "goes ahead" and then "waits" for the other; then, when the distance becomes "too large," the first spot actually moves back a bit to "meet" the second one, only to proceed forward as soon as the second has "caught up." An observer of this scene unhesitatingly interprets it as an interaction between a caring leader and a follower needing protection, even though the spots of light have not made a single gesture or sound. Now, if the following spot were to hum whenever it fell very far behind, and the leading spot then usually waited or hurried back, the general meaning of the humming would become obvious.

I believe that this interplay involving distances is the most general form in which mutual intentions are communicated, a kind of Esperanto. It also functions between species: between cat and sparrow, oryx and hamadryas baboon, and even between humans and animals. We often hear of "body language," based on the spatial relations between various parts of the body; this is more specialized, varying from one species to another, but it too communicates generally understandable messages based on posture and muscle tone. A mime can be disguised as a limbless being with a faceless head and nevertheless express shyness, cautious hope, determination, and finally resignation—merely by posture and movement. The scientist studying behavior can also learn to understand these signs. But then he may soon find himself seeing through his own conspecifics more often than he desires and deems decent.

In the zoo, I was now spending several hours a day standing with a notebook at the railing around the baboon area. At first it was hard to cope with the shrieking of frightened females and persecuted juveniles, for it set off an internal alarm trying to convince me that something dreadful was happening. The reason was that I am a primate, like the baboons, and we share this signal. I had to learn to suppress my agitation enough to be able to observe events rationally. In the first few days it became clear that the baboons also, occasionally, control their own excitement. One day, a young female baboon flouted convention by going to drink ahead of an old female and the nearly adult Ulysses. The two of them responded immediately, the old female by giving the young one a small bite, and Ulysses by pulling her hair. Nevertheless, the young female first drank her fill, then ran away, and began screaming only when she was at a safe distance. I enjoyed the way she had temporarily restrained herself as the situation demanded. It reminded me of the time when my little sister, with a bloody knee, had climbed the stairs in fiercely contained silence, and burst into tears only when she opened the door to our

Table 1. Examples from an ethogram of the hamadryas baboons.
(P = performer, R = receiver)

Abbrev.	Name	Definition	Message, Freely Translated
br	Brow-raising	P stares at R and raises eyebrows	I don't like what I see: watch out
gb	Ground-beating	P stares at R and beats palms against the ground	Stop or I'll attack you
gr	Grooming (skin care)	P uses hands to investigate R's hair and skin	I want to be near you; your nearness interests and soothes me
ipo	Interposition	P places him/herself precisely between two Rs	Stop paying attention to one another
ke	Kecking	Staccato sound, ca. four pulses per sound	I'm beginning to be afraid of you
ls	Lip-smacking	Audible, rapid opening and closing of the lips	Your hindquarters, your hair makes me feel friendly/ erotic
nb	Neck bite	P pinches R's neck between incisors	That's too much
pg	Possession grip	P, a male, holds R, a female, firmly by her sides or back	I claim this female for myself
pi	Piggyback invitation	P turns hindquarters to R and bends knees	Climb onto my back
pre	Presenting	P turns the hind parts to R and remains so more than a second	
	Variants of presenting	Head lowered onto hands, female to male	Invitation to copulate
		Knees bent, with ke, to threatening superior	Submission; I'm afraid of you but want to stay with you
		In passing, male to male	Notifying; come or go in peace

apartment. I didn't yet know how important such control of one's own motivation is for the social life of all higher primates.

My list of the signals in hamadryish, the so-called ethogram, finally contained seventy gestures and sounds, each with a name and a description that distinguished it from every other one. Table 1 gives some important examples. Being used for communication, these signals have evolved to be conspicuous. In addition to these signals, the hamadryas baboons give more subtle cues, probably hundreds of them, that imply to their conspecifics what they are about to do or what they know—hesitating briefly while walking, perhaps, or emphatically looking away. These behavioral nuances are not evolved signals but merely small, revealing undertones of ordinary activities. When a baboon sits with its elbows between its knees, it may be cold, but the posture can also mean that it has retreated from an insoluble social situation.

It can happen that an animal's gesture is indecipherable, either by its connection with fighting or sex or by the "Distance Esperanto" described above. An example was the circle-wiping of the Zurich baboons, in which they moved one hand in a vertical circle in front of the nose. This was no ordinary nose-cleaning, for which the hand rubs the nostrils vigorously back and forth several times, each time slightly differently. "Circle-wiping" was just the one movement, always the same, and often did not even touch the nose. It looked like an attempt to catch a fly and was not coupled with sex or grooming or attack and flight. Still more puzzling was that juvenile baboons were never observed making the movement; it first appeared shortly before sexual maturity and among the adults it became almost a fad, whereas real nose-rubbing, after drinking, was performed by young and old. Many protocols were scrutinized, and a pattern finally crystallized: circle-wiping occurs only when a baboon wants very much to do something but does not dare to. Its motivations are then in conflict. It can also make this gesture when an event does not proceed as expected—for instance, when a partner in play or grooming suddenly runs away. Once, the three-year-old Intora was playing with the small Seka so vigorously that the latter cried out. Immediately Intora looked around at Pasha, who sometimes intervened in such cases. This time he did not, and Intora made a circle-wiping movement. The movement apparently occurs when the normal progression of motivations is interrupted because the situation has become ambiguous. It seems as though the confused baboon then has to do *something*. This something, in many animals and in humans, is usually a gesture of body care such as scratching. Circle-wiping was revealed as such a gesture, just one step removed from nose-wiping.

But why then does circle-wiping become more common as the baboon grows older? Young animals are still permitted to behave foolishly. An infant can climb onto an adult male's head. A two-year-old male can dare to play at mating with an adult female and go unpunished. Once he has reached sexual maturity, however, such a thing is no longer tolerated by his superiors, and infractions provoke severer responses. He becomes unsure about more and more kinds of behavior, not knowing who will tolerate them or not and under what circumstances. A conflict arises between desires and expectations of punishment, and this, contrary to prejudices about uninhibited monkeys, suppresses many impulses. The marked increase in circle-wiping reflects this development.

Circle-wiping was the hardest nut in my ethogram. In contrast, gestures that higher animals have evolved as signals for communication are soon understood by a sympathetic, unprejudiced observer—sooner, in fact, than the symbol-laden rites of foreign cultures within our own species. Sometimes I happened to hear the zoo visitors on either side talking about what the monkeys were doing. The remarks made by small children were often right on target. Adults frequently pulled judgments out of their drawers of cliches, and completely missed the point. It was amusing when these adults tried to fob off their much more observant progeny with the idea that the observed sexual behavior was only play.

Among animals, the gestures and their effects on the partner are largely genetically determined, so that they are the same for all members of a species, just as they all have the same physical characteristics such as paws and ears. Once I was able to understand the zoo baboons in Zurich, I could understand hamadryas baboons all over the world, whether in the Cologne Zoo, in Ethiopia, or in Saudi Arabia. The gestures and sounds of the hamadryas on the Ethiopian and Arabian coasts, after probably several thousand years of separation, are still 98 percent the same. However, the humans on the two coasts speak different languages despite the active shipping traffic.

Every animal has the genes of its parents and hence its gestures. Its great-grandchildren will still have them, because a gene mutates only every thousand generations or even more rarely. Genetic evolution is slow. The words of humans change at the express speed of cultural evolution, genetically constrained only by the basic structures for sound production. Words and their combinations are nearly free from control by genes. They can change at a whim, and if a new word or saying finds approval it propagates itself from mouth to ear over hundreds of miles within a generation. By contrast, no baboon can learn from another one a gesture that is not programmed in its own hereditary material. The gene-bound evolution of gestures proceeds so slowly that when a rare novelty does arise, wandering animals have carried it to every corner of the species' area by the time the genes are altered again. For baboons there is no Babel. But human innovations follow one another so rapidly that migrations have never produced a homogeneous mixture of language throughout our species.

Animal gestures and sounds are something fundamentally different from human words. Usually they express a mood, an inclination toward a particular activity, whereas typical human words are symbols and designate mostly things. Animal gestures can be loosely grouped according to mood and situation but have no grammar; human words are arranged in sentences.

Many signaling gestures of animals have arisen from movements with a practical, material function. In the hamadryas baboon the piggyback invitation simply makes it easier for the child to climb on, and ground-beating is the first, barely arrested leap in an attack. Lip-smacking is presumably derived from the lip movements with which a baboon cleans another's hair. These gestures are not very difficult to interpret because they hint at an imminent behavior. Most human words, on the other hand, are different from one language to another, arbitrary symbols that do not in any way imitate the object they represent. From the sequence of sounds in "tree," it is impossible for the uninitiated to guess what the word means.

There is no known animal gesture that signifies an object, such as "tree" or "water." The primate signals closest to such object identifiers are the three different alarm calls of vervet monkeys (*Cercopithecus aethiops*). One is given when the danger is associated with a snake, one for predatory birds, and one for terrestrial predatory mammals. But even these "words" fail one test of speech: the monkeys do not combine them in sentences.

Pasha's Harem

The first scientific observer of the behavior of the hamadryas baboon was the English physiologist Sir (later Lord) Solly Zuckerman. His studies of the hamadryas colony in the London Zoo, brief visits to other zoos, and a trip to the free-living chacmas in South Africa showed him that sex and male sexual jealousy are the factors that dominate the social behavior of primates. In his book *The Social Life of Monkeys and Apes* (1932, reissued 1981), probably the first book published on this topic, Zuckerman pointed out that primates—including humans—are interested in sex not only in certain seasons of the year but all the time. Therefore every male primate tries to collect a harem, and his rank determines his success. Only sexual attraction keeps these one-male families together, and it is the diversion offered by sexual stimuli that keeps aggression among their members more or less in check. Only primates practice this "prostitution."

Zuckerman's observations were basically correct, except that his interpretation ascribed the society-forming functions too exclusively to sex and rank. He had seen how the large colony of male hamadryas in London was first kept without females; then suddenly a few females were added—not enough to go around. This situation hopelessly overburdened the mechanisms for peacekeeping that we now know exist among the hamadryas. The frustrated males fought so violently over the new females that Zuckerman could well have been misled to his oversimplified interpretation. What I cannot comprehend is why this highly respected scientist, feared in England for his sharp criticism, so rapidly decided that the harem structure of hamadryas baboons is *the* form of organization of all primates and maintained: "There are no loosely organized or sexually promiscuous bands of monkeys and apes." Here he was wrong.

When I first observed the hamadryas colony in the Zurich Zoo, it had two unequally strong poles (2): Pasha and the oldest of the young males, Ulysses. Pasha was the stronger of the two; he was followed by the "harem" of four adult females and the two girls Liba and Nina, who were just entering puberty. All were Pasha's wives and under his sexual monopoly. The rest—the group of juveniles plus the not yet mature Intora—gathered around Ulysses. In the movements of the two groups I soon noticed a regularity: when Pasha was leading his females toward the east in his rocky enclosure, Ulysses got up and wandered to the west, and the juveniles followed him a little later. Pasha positioned himself so that he could see Ulysses, who then sauntered to a place where the central towers of rock interrupted his line of sight. Ulysses never retreated hastily but arose quite casually, as it appeared, after one or two minutes and strolled out of sight. Other primate researchers have also observed adult males, in particular, playing down their actions in this way. One must not jump to the conclusion that they are being intentionally secretive. Maybe the males have simply found out that in general they become involved in fights less often when they move gently. It could also be that responding in an unconcerned manner is one way for a male to maintain his status—think of John Wayne. I could have tested the first hypothesis back then, but I wasn't thinking of it at the time. I merely marked down the positions of the males on a map of the enclosure at regular intervals, and I found that Ulysses' places were concentrated around the central rock towers whereas Pasha preferred the edge of the enclosure, as though the younger male were looking for cover and the older for a place from which he had a good view.

The most time-consuming activity in the harem consisted in a female busily searching through the hair of Pasha's mantle with both hands. There was rarely anything to find there, because Pasha was not fully employed like his conspecifics in Africa. He never had to force his way through dry thickets where bark could rub off and stick in his hair, nor was he exposed to ticks waiting on blades of grass to creep under his mane. The need for cleaning, which had once fixed grooming behavior in their genes, was absent here, but the motivation for it was now programmed and could not be turned off merely because the behavior happened to be useless. The sight of even a clean coat of hair suffices to arouse a desire for grooming. In classical ethology this was recognized as a fundamental characteristic of animal behavior: the desire to act is first anchored by evolution in the genes because the action promotes fitness; but once the desire is there, it takes little heed of necessity.

Among baboons, macaques, and chimpanzees, grooming the hair of group members has assumed an added social function that is independent of whether the hair is dirty or clean. An evolutionary process, called "change of function" in comparative anatomy (e.g., jawbones that become ossicles in the ear) and "ritualization" in ethology, has endowed grooming behavior with the new, additional function of appeasement. This is illustrated by the fact that the high-ranking group members are most often groomed, especially when the one doing the grooming needs their support in a dispute or has reason to feel threatened by them. In the next sections we shall see how intensively the Zurich baboons had recourse to hair in their conflicts.

Sometimes two females were grooming Pasha at the same time; then they scolded one another surreptitiously behind his back until he threatened or bit one of them, or until the lower-ranking female gave up of her own accord. From my notes it could be seen that Sora dealt out aggression most often and received it the least (1). The balance of aggression given minus aggression received decreased continuously down the rank order, from Sora to Ofe, then to Vecchia, and from her to Nacha, the victim of all. As a beginner, I was satisfied with this "dominance order," but the proper approach would have been to draw up a balance for each pair of females separately. As calculated by my method, the second to the bottom one could have seemed to be the highest if she increased her score by a large enough number of attacks on the lowest-ranking one—to which the latter, of course, would not reply. But in this case my mistake did not alter the result.

The rank order of the four females had nothing to do with body size: Nacha, the lowest, was large and massive, while Sora, the highest, was slender and small. Was it Pasha's support that had raised the elegant Sora to the rank of leading lady? There was no evidence of this. When a lower-ranking female had her monthly genital swelling and aroused Pasha's sexual interest, she never ascended in rank as a result. He clearly preferred Nacha, the lowest-ranking, as sexual partner; but being his favorite did not bring her any advantages. In fact, Pasha allowed the other females to turn him against Nacha particularly often. Apparently the females had worked their ranks out among themselves.

Vecchia and Nacha almost always found that the place next to Pasha was already taken, so they were rarely able to groom his mantle. Both were threatened daily by the others, chased, and slightly bitten; in turn they themselves were remarkably impatient toward their own young. Sora and Ofe played with their children, which the two lower-ranking mothers never did; indeed, they sometimes gave them serious neck bites. Once Vecchia bit her daughter Proka merely because when presenting before Pasha the little one had taken fright and fled into her mother's arms—and the bite was on the neck, the severest discipline there is among hamadryas baboons. There was a special, mild form of bite that the adults in the group used in dealing with troublesome children. The young one was grasped by the forearm or foot, which was then raised to the adult's mouth and gently bitten. This reined in the youngsters but, unlike the neck bite, never made them scream. I never saw this kindly admonition in other zoos or in the wild troops. It was a special invention of the Zurich group.

After a few weeks director Hediger and keeper Rehm allowed me to visit the baboons at night as well. Surrounded by the now-familiar odor and the rustling of mice, I sat in the monkey house until, in the weak, red light, I could discern the rows of baboons seated on shelves along the walls. During the second night I noticed that Vecchia moved every few minutes, without waking up, and out of curiosity I counted how often each of the four females stirred while she was presumably sleeping, as her eyes were closed (1). The totals for eight nights were: Sora, 27; Ofe, 45; Vecchia, 70; Nacha, 95! When Sora later fell sharply in rank, the number of her sleep movements shot up almost to the level of Nacha's. On several occasions I saw Nacha, and only Nacha, while closing her eyes and apparently asleep, raise her brows—the threat expression, a signal she hardly ever had a chance to give in her daytime life. A disturbance of socially oppressed animals so profound that it extends into their nighttime sleep has not, to my knowledge, been studied in detail. I would be skeptical about it if other researchers had not since then described still more astonishing psychosomatic effects of social position among primates. For instance, Jeanne Altmann and her colleagues (1986) found that in their group of yellow baboons in the Amboseli Park, the lower-ranking females bore distinctly more male babies and the high-ranking bore more females. In other species the opposite effect of rank was observed. One way or another, life at a particular rank level seems to influence even the details of reproductive physiology. The decisive test here would be to see whether a given female changes the sex ratio of her offspring after falling or rising in rank. However, this test is probably impossible, because in both savanna baboons and macaques the females acquire their rank from their mothers and usually keep it all their lives.

Pasha's grooming sessions with an adult harem female proceeded according to a little ritual. They began when the female returned from a short excursion, perhaps to groom one of the subadult males, a time at which she was in an anxious mood. The first point in the program was a mixture of timid appeasement and a sexual offer: the female positioned herself close in front of Pasha and presented her naked, bright red hindquarters. The greater her anxiety, the deeper she bent her knees, looking over her shoulder into his face and making the sound called "kecking."

But if she had her monthly swelling and could fearlessly issue a genuine sexual invitation, she would bend over with knees straight, her head on her hands and her swelling displayed high before him.

When a female is not in estrus her hindquarters are flat, and copulation is almost impossible mechanically. Even then, though, the female initiates the meeting with a small sexual advance. Just as grooming has acquired an additional function, baboons have adopted movement patterns from the sexual sphere to use as friendly signals in general, even between members of the same sex and when they are not disposed toward sex at the moment.

The second step in the ritual, Pasha's response, would normally be copulation. If the female is not estrous, he would simply mount her politely, so to speak, keeping his feet on the ground instead of grasping the backs of her knees. However, Pasha's many mates approached him in this way dozens of times a day, so he often gave only the merest trace of a polite response. Remaining seated, he grasped the female briefly by her hips and cast a glance at her hindquarters, or he touched the vulva lightly with the back of his hand and didn't even bother to check the olfactory message it had picked up.

As soon as Pasha had acknowledged the presentation, the female scurried around him in a semicircle, sat down behind his back, and began throwing the hair of his mantle back and forth with both hands. The more anxious she was, the more hectically she groomed. But within seconds she would stop kecking and instead start the eager, friendly signal of lip-smacking, in which the lips are audibly opened and closed in rapid succession. Soon, too, her hands would push and pick in a more organized way, and her mouth would occasionally catch a bit of dandruff. The act of searching through the mantle seemed visibly to calm the females.

At this point I must explain the monthly sexual swellings of the female baboons. These are extremely striking structures, often even larger in zoo animals than in the wild. Many a lady visitor has run horrified to Rehm, the keeper, to tell him that a female with a swelling was sick. The swellings appear only in the days before and after ovulation. Between these times, and during the fourteen months of pregnancy and nursing, the females are "flat." The swelling is evidently a signal for the male waiting to copulate. However, male monkeys, like the males of other mammals, can also detect the sexual state of a female by means of special odor substances called pheromones. Although pheromones are perceptible only at a short distance, this would be quite enough for the leader of a hamadryas family, since he is near his females day and night. Why, then, do female hamadryas baboons make the same display as do savanna baboons, chimpanzees, and mangabeys, producing these obviously highly attractive, but tender-skinned and no doubt troublesome swellings every month? On the knife-sharp, hot lava rocks in Ethiopia, a female with the swelling sits so that her weight is on the side edge of the hind area, like an uneasy penitent in the confessional. And such a female forcing her way through the branches of a sharp-thorned *Acacia longispina*, in search of the edible pods, is a pitiful sight.

Swellings occur in those primate species in which many males live in the same group and compete for the females. They are a sign visible from afar, with which a female can attract more suitors than she could with the sexual odor alone. From this greater selection she might find a better partner than she would among the few males she already knows well. Among the savanna-dwelling relatives of the hamadryas baboons, this situation might also benefit the males, but it is certainly not in the interest of a hamadryas male for his females to advertise their sexual receptiveness to all the males in the troop. When hamadryas females made the transition to the closed harem society, they evidently did not change in accordance with the interests of their males but rather kept the stimulatory organ, even though it is so vulnerable. The sight of a retinue of three or more magnificently swollen females following the same older "pasha" might well give all the males in the troop that had no females, or too few, urges for a change that could be very much in the interest of the females.

Hamadryas females have the peculiar tendency to synchronize their cycles with other females of their family, but not with those of neighboring harems (6), a tendency also known in human females. The testes of hamadryas males are relatively small and thus, not surprisingly, females have a lower chance of conceiving when in synchrony with others than females who had their swelling alone (Zinner et al. 1994). Why, then should females synchronize? If the tendency were at all adaptive, should we understand it as a means to occupy and satiate the harem leader to such a degree that it would be a little less difficult for a female to seek out another male? That females in estrus keep farther away from their regular male than at other times (6) is a hint in this direction.

As it happened, while I was observing Pasha in Zurich he really was in this situation: all his females had swellings at once, as none of them were pregnant, but the three bachelors were not at all up to challenging him. The most they could do was snatch whatever opportunity they had behind a rock tower. It turned out then that the swellings can be attractive even to other females. Ofe maintained certain sexual relations with Nacha and Liba. When all three were swollen at the same time, what happened was something like this: Ofe steps up to Nacha, briefly lays a hand on her swelling and mounts her from the flank. Immediately Liba hurries up and interrupts them. Liba and Ofe now present to one another simultaneously, each touches the swelling of the other, and they look into each other's eyes. On the same day Ofe allows herself to be mounted by Liba several times, pulling the latter to her with one hand. When Ofe mounts Nacha, she holds Nacha's swelling with both hands and moves her pelvis back and forth. In the wild we never saw such explicit sexual activity between females. It belongs to the "luxury" phenomena that I shall describe in the section "The Hothouse of Social Behavior."

The females did not merely show interest in a feminine sexual stimulus, then, but actually reacted with male copulatory movements, although their behavior toward males was entirely feminine. Male baboons also mount one another with copulatory movements. In contrast to female hamadryas homosexual behavior, such behavior occurs among males even in the wild, where it has the important function of appeasement in situations that require coordinated behavior. We never observed intromission or orgasm between individuals of the same sex, and I know of no case in which a primate rejected heterosexual behavior in favor of homosexual.

None of the seventy gestures and sounds in my ethogram were associated with only one sex. Both males and females carried the young against their abdomens, even though this is primarily a protective behavior of a mother toward her own infant. It was as if two workmen were using the same toolbox in different ways: the mothers carried the infants in routine transport and while fleeing, and the males carried them as a form of lively play.

Embracing also evolved primarily in the mother-child relationship: mothers hold their infant when it is suckling, sleeping, or afraid. The sexually mature subadults in the Zurich group would hug others when they themselves were afraid, especially when they were meeting for secret sex out of Pasha's sight. A rendezvous lasts several minutes, because baboons mate with serial copulations, only the last of which results in ejaculation. During such a meeting, during each pause the young female rushed to a place where she could see Pasha, then hurried back to her partner and presented herself to him for the next round. Sometimes her lover accompanied her to the point where they could be seen. Then if Pasha's gaze turned on them, they fell terrified into each other's arms and clawed their hands into each other's hair again and again, kecking, with their faces turned toward the patriarch. Often the young female would actually leap onto her lover's back, and he would flee with the precious load in great agitation, as though he were trying to save her from a leopard. Now, a reader who thinks that this flight was toward the farthest, most secluded niche in the rocks would be entirely sensible, but utterly wrong. This commonly happens to ethologists, because although behavioral systems have evolved to an overall state of improved adaptation, in their individual manifestations they can be about as unreasonable as a screw in a jeep door. When vibration has loosened it a little bit, it becomes even looser instead of screwing itself tighter. Both a behavioral system and a screw have characteristics besides those for which they were designed. In fact, the young pair would dash *toward* Pasha for salvation and embrace in front of him, clutching at each other with great urgency, while he usually looked mildly on. Then, separately and somewhat more calmly, they returned to their love nest.

Fleeing toward Danger, and Triangular Maneuvers

On summer evenings back then, I would walk home through the Dolder forest, along the brook where we had found newts as boys, and as I strolled along I meditated on the intricate doings of my baboons, trying to work out the order underlying what they did. I was feeling my way by intuition as much as by intellect; it was my first taste of the joy of research. It was during this period that I had a dream: I was about to pass the gate of the zoo one morning as usual, when the ticket seller called to me, "You have visitors, waiting in the zoo restaurant." Entering the restaurant, I saw my fifteen baboons sitting on chairs at a long table, Pasha at its head. He looked at me and spoke: "We have seen that you are trying to understand, and you are not too far off the mark. But listen: we want to explain to you how things really are." Unfortunately, everything the baboons then told me vanished from my mind the moment I woke up. I'm afraid their world, as they knew it, was too foreign to my understanding. The reader will have to be content with my version of it.

At first I was most fascinated with the "social structure" of the group. But what that actually was, and how it could be studied, neither my zoology teachers nor the ethological textbooks could tell me. I worried for weeks about this question. The one thing that was clear was that primates—monkeys and apes—treat one another as individuals and not as interchangeable members of a class, as happens among ants or termites, in schools of fish, or in enormous bird colonies. Eventually I thought I had found a solution: by diagramming how often each group member directed a particular signal at each other member, and by doing that for every signal, whether aggressive, caring, sexual, or playful, I must ultimately obtain a picture of the network of social relationships in the group. The complete diagram would then show, for instance, whether Pasha had a sexual preference for one female and whether lower-ranking mothers really punished their children more often than higher-ranking ones. Friendships and enmities would surely be revealed in the graphic network. So that is what I did (2). I was unaware then that this exact sociographic method had already been used in human sociology to document preferences among group members; however, it was new to ethology. With it, I acquired a measure of (unearned) renown, and the method was taken up by others, although it has serious deficiencies.

The main problem with this approach is that it is based on the implicit assumption that the more often A signals to B, the closer and more intimate their relationship is. But is this true? An example suggests otherwise. In my time, at least, when shy people fell in love with each other, they would often barely speak, and they even suppressed nonverbal signals. Such a relationship is still far from being intimate. Once the partners admit their attraction, a phase of very intense communication follows, during which they gradually become more intimate. But it can happen that sixty years later the same two people again speak very little, because now they know each other so well that there is no need for much talking. That is, there are cases in which signal density is no indicator of how close partners are to one another. Purely communicative signals often serve to *alter* something in the relationship. For instance, courtship is intended to put the partner in a sexually receptive mood. Regardless of the outcome, after a while courtship signals will disappear; the signaler who is ignored will give up, the one who has been satisfied will have no reason to continue, and the uninterested will never have begun in the first place. The three cases are completely different, and yet the signal density is zero in all of them. The actual information provided by signal frequency, then, is different for each stage of a relationship. The same applies to threats and fights over rank. We shall return later to the origin and history of a social relationship (see chapter 7).

A second deficiency of the signal-frequency method was that it usually reduced the network of relationships to one-to-one interactions, so that the complex signaling had to be sampled from one pair of individuals at a time. The study in the Zurich Zoo soon showed that this simplification can be misleading. The hamadryas baboons turned out to be specialists in three-way maneuvering, one using another as a tool against a third. Later research confirmed that primates in general use such tripartite (or "triadic") tactics. That is why Frans de Waal, publishing in 1982, entitled his book *Chimpanzee Politics*. In 1955 a zoologist choosing such a title would have endangered his career: in zoological circles no one was entertaining the notion that animals could actually be tacticians. Now, on the contrary, it is necessary to caution against uncritical acceptance of seemingly clever behavior as a sign of intelligence.

The first examples of triangular maneuvers known to primate research came from Pasha's group in the Zurich Zoo (2, 5) and I am glad that they did, precisely *because* the baboons thus revealed a blind side of my sociographic two-individual method. As long as the animals say "no" to some of our assumptions and hypotheses, we are learning—and on the right track. On the other hand, when they seem to be confirming every one of our hypotheses in a research project, it is time to start feeling uncomfortable. We are either being exceptionally perceptive and astute or—more likely—we are no longer in dialogue with nature, and there could be no worse failure than that.

At the end of the book we shall return to the triangle as a component of social networks. Now, though, we are concerned with the particular triangular maneuvers in Pasha's group. They are closely related to the mysterious effect of Pasha's mantle.

Disagreements among baboons follow a logic different from our own. For example, while Ulysses and the smaller Wiffel are playfully wrestling, the lighthearted panting suddenly stops and Wiffel screams. The panting means, "This chasing and fighting is only a game." Now Ulysses has apparently gripped Wiffel too hard; Wiffel looks straight over to Pasha, who then begins a sham attack—but toward Wiffel, not toward Ulysses. Or: little Proka presents to mighty Pasha, but kecks more and more rapidly as she does so, and she finally leaps into mother Vecchia's arms—but her mother bites her in the neck. Or: Glumo is scuffling with the much larger Ulysses and loses a few hairs; he flees immediately, but when he is only a yard away he turns and hurls himself, kecking, against the breast—of Ulysses. These all seem paradoxical: sometimes Pasha's lightning bolt strikes the smaller, "innocent" one; fear rather than audacity is "punished"; and a "fleeing" baboon rushes into the midst of danger. Let's try to decipher this paradoxical flight.

A frightened baboon not only strives to escape the external danger of bodily injury, it also tries to regain its inner equilibrium, which may be an even more urgent need. While an infant, it can still find both external and internal security at the same place, in its mother's arms. When it becomes older and a younger sibling has taken its place at the mother's breast, it looks elsewhere. The older juveniles in Pasha's group, in literally hair-raising situations, simply ran to the largest baboon around, whoever that might be, and clung to its hair. Usually that baboon was Ulysses, with whom the little ones liked to play, or in his absence it was Kalos. Baboons are observant and, if they are not too excited, they learn rapidly. A small one clinging to the breast of a large one may become aware that sometimes the one to whom it has run for refuge will attack the opponent from whom it has just fled. It will dawn on the young baboon that its flight can bring it a further, previously unsought advantage: it can use the large one as a tool in the conflict. A triangle of refugee, protector, and opponent comes into being (5).

Triangles are difficult for all young primates. As long as the mother is their protector, the little ones at least know where they stand. If she takes sides at all, it will be her child's side. But a young male like Ulysses is not their mother, and after infancy they can never again take things for granted; maybe he will side with the opponent. The large one has become a double-faced figure, and now can turn into a protector or an attacker, a source of inner stability or of fear. Perhaps we are beginning to see why the nervous circle-wiping behavior becomes more common as a baboon grows up. As a little one, should I flee to Ulysses the protector or away from Ulysses the menace? If I run away, I may gain safety but will forfeit reassurance. The latter might seem the less important benefit of flight, but for the baboons it was not. In moments of great fear they always chose to flee *toward* the larger animal, even if no third party was involved and the large one was itself the source of the terror.

I often underestimated the baboons. They first made this clear to me when I saw that the growing juveniles were not simply accepting the dilemma imposed by the triangle. They learned ways to deal with it. From a certain age on, whoever arrived first when fleeing to a large individual immediately took precautions by presenting. No large baboon will bite one who is presenting. By age two they had already developed this tactic, and females entering puberty developed it further: their "great one" was neither their mother nor Ulysses, the boss of the subadult males, but rather the harem chief Pasha, and their opponents were usually the other females. They, too, presented to him, but in doing so they also looked at the opponent and screamed. This "scolding" stigmatized the opponent, as far as Pasha was concerned; when the uproar finally enraged him, he directed his rage toward the baboon that was being scolded. The trick failed to work only when the targeted individual took no notice, not even glancing toward Pasha and his screaming companion. Then Pasha did not attack. Later, in Ethiopia, I successfully employed the tactic of the scolded one for my own protection. A person faced with a threatening baboon is relatively safe if he pretends not to notice and casually blows the dust from his binoculars. This is a demonstration of innocence that every male respects, even if the person is actually guilty of having startled the baboon's females.

But the really impressive behavior is "protected threatening," the most highly developed tactic of the adult harem female. It consists in preventing a female opponent from fleeing to the dominant figure (fig. 8). She takes up a position such that she is blocking the way to Pasha at all times, and enhances the effect by threatening the other female instead of merely screaming at her. Simultaneously she presents to the male. She positions the "sex end" and the "biting end" suitably between the two other individuals, and is submissive in back and furious in front. Her genuine internal attitude remains a puzzle; in any case, brow-raising and presenting are

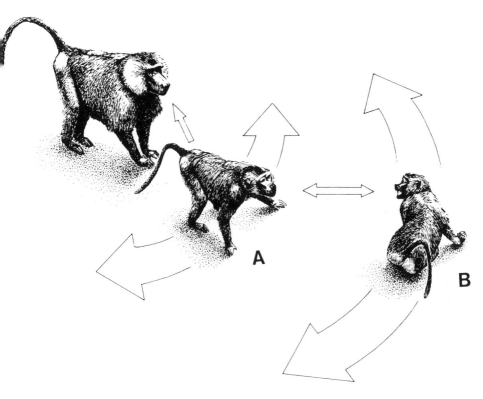

Fig. 8. The tactic of protected threatening. The female A in the middle threatens her opponent B on the right, blocking the latter's access to the male while appeasing the male by presenting. A always keeps herself between the male and B, so that any threat expressed by B would also be directed toward the male.

never performed simultaneously with *the same* partner. Either the female engaged in protected threatening is merely simulating one of the two motivations, or she can actually experience both simultaneously and transmit two incompatible signals, each of which is directed toward and activated by one of the partners. I would guess the latter. This remarkably high-level but rarely appreciated behavior is inevitably required of a species living in an individualized social structure. It is not enough to recognize the others as individuals; one must also approach them with different motivations, according to the status of the mutual relationship and to current conditions. What is so special about protected threatening is that two contrasting motivations are active at the very same time. Would you find that easy?

The female A, the one who first presented to Pasha, had all the advantages on her side. She was safe from Pasha; if he attacked, he would attack the more distant B. The latter tried to protect herself by screaming against the earlier arrival, A, while sitting with her body twisted so that she could simultaneously present her hindquarters to Pasha. Because A was occupying a position directly in front of Pasha, B had to send both her signals in the same direction. Therefore she could not actually threaten A, because Pasha might have taken the threat to be directed at him. When she tried to rush past the entrenched A, the latter needed merely to shift over a smaller arc in order to continue blocking the way to Pasha.

The only effective behavior available to the one who was blocked out has been mentioned above: to take no notice. But even when a female had the nerve to do this, the threatening female near Pasha could try another ploy, if she was higher ranking. She would make a sudden dash forward, bite or tug the tail of female *B* who was ostensibly ignoring her, and immediately return to her central position. Now the victim was certain to scream, marking herself as Pasha's target. However, this trick was risky. For female B, this was the moment to flit past her attacker to Pasha and reverse their positions. Adult females were not outmaneuvered in this way, but the young Liba and Nina were less skilled. They had their first swellings that summer and were trying to gain position and rank in the harem. In the process, they performed protected threatening from the A position against the four adult females, for no apparent reason. During the first weeks they would recklessly make sorties against their B and thereby promptly lose their position, finding themselves in the excluded position of the B female. A few weeks later they were no longer making this mistake.

A female cannot perform the offensive maneuvers of protected threatening if her primary aim in staying near the highest-ranking baboon is to obtain reassurance. Low-ranking and thoroughly fearful females could merely cling to Pasha's mantle, shrieking. After a few seconds, when they could stop screaming, they switched from this childish way of regaining composure to the adult technique: instead of holding on to the hair of the great one, they groomed it. As I have explained, hair care is a form of soothing behavior widespread among primates, which calms both the groomer and the one being groomed, although its primary function is to clean the skin by removing ticks, grass husks, and other foreign bodies. When two male gibbons are chasing and striking each other at the boundary between their territories, they occasionally pause and for a while each lets himself be groomed by his female—presumably not for the purpose of cleaning. At the Delta Primate Center near New Orleans I was once able to prevent a rowdy young male chimpanzee from biting the shoe off my foot by beginning to "groom" him. As if surprised, he stopped abruptly—head down, for he was hanging from the shirt on my chest by his feet. For a while he remained still as I gently ran my fingers through his hair, and then he trotted away.

All sexually mature members of the Zurich baboon group seemed almost compulsively drawn to Pasha's mantle after frightening events. (It was only during the field studies that we learned that the cohesion of the harem depends on this attraction.) Usually the hairy giant himself had caused the fright, but he carried the antidote with him. The adult females calmed themselves by rummaging through his mantle, but the younger ones did not dare do that. Their fascination with the long hair was overcome by fear. Once, when Pasha's mantle brushed past him, Kalos did not fix his gaze on the old one's face but rather on the magnificent hair, first lip-smacking briefly and then kecking. With these nuances of behavior he revealed that he was both attracted *and* anxious.

The degree to which a group member feared Pasha ought to have been discernible on the basis of the average distance that individual maintained from him. I estimated these distances every fifteen minutes and found an average of seven feet for the adult females, ten and a half feet for the sexually mature, subadult females, and almost twenty-two feet for Ulysses. I had no time to collect data for Kalos and Wiffel, but I estimated their mean distances from Pasha at about twelve to sixteen feet. Grooming of Pasha's mantle was progressively inhibited in the same order. Whereas the adult females plunged both hands into the mantle, the young females did not dare use both hands but approached with poignant hesitancy. Once they had finished kecking, they would extend one index finger and gently use it to move the tips of the hairs on Pasha's back. Sometimes the finger would first scratch the ground lightly near Pasha's tail and only gradually move over to the tail itself (fig. 9). The three subadult males did not touch Pasha at all. When he merely appeared suddenly, they lost all composure. They would stand facing him with knees deeply bent, their short capes of hair standing on end, screaming and often even passing water. The males never used the tactics of scolding or protected threatening.

Whoever is too much afraid of one higher in rank does not dare seek reassurance by touching his hair; he is doubly disadvantaged. The three subadult males also hurried behind Pasha's back when they were scared, but they did not touch him. Their extreme fear prevented them from calming themselves with his mantle. They merely scrutinized the mane, bending over to peer at it from a distance of twenty inches or so, hands between their knees, heads jerking toward one spot and then another, smacking their lips or making slow chewing movements with empty mouths, just like baboons actually engaged in grooming. This examination of the mantle could last for many minutes and occasionally occurred with no preceding fear. In figure 10, Sora and Ofe are grooming the re-

Fig. 9. Nina, here sitting behind Pasha, is just reaching puberty. She still does not dare groom Pasha's mantle except at a distance and with the tip of her index finger; here she is doing that at the safest place, the tip of his tail.

clining Pasha while all three subadult males watch, chewing; the youngest stands close to Pasha, Kalos sits next to him, and Ulysses, the oldest, cautiously keeps his distance. Such gatherings gave the impression of small cult meetings. The group was celebrating the mantle of Pasha. In no other circumstances did I ever see a baboon pay unwavering attention to anything for so long without touching it. Here I am using "cult" in the loose sense of a fan club. A real human cult is also much like this assembly of hamadryas baboons in its obsession with a particular object, but it goes beyond that into a world of symbols, an animal equivalent of which is still unknown.

It should be added here that neither the young females' touches with the index finger nor the subadult males' contemplation of the mantle has as complete a calming effect as the hectic grooming activity of the adult harem members. After a minute the young ones might suddenly get up, step aside, and, still standing, sweep the ground wildly with the flat of their hands. What they didn't dare to do to Pasha, they took out on the ground. The principle is not foreign to humans and also fairly common in other animals. Ethologists call it "redirected behavior." The adult fe-

Fig. 10. The Zurich group participating in the "mantle cult." Pasha is surrounded by grooming females and watching young males, so that only his right hand and mantle are visible.

males never did such sweeping. After all, they were able to sweep their hands through Pasha's mantle.

In their Ethiopian homeland, wild hamadryas baboons do not engage in protected threatening. Their triangular maneuvers have not developed beyond scolding without presenting, for example when two rival females scream at one another behind the male's back and both try to groom him. In the wild, young females do not touch with the index finger, nor do young males scrutinize the mantle; there is no discernible "mantle cult." Many readers will conclude from this that Pasha's group was behaving abnormally in captivity, and that studies of zoo animals are therefore of dubious value. I do not share this view. We should remember something fundamental. The hereditary predisposition for certain forms of behavior is not a fixed instruction to do a particular thing under all circumstances; it tells the animal how it should behave in a particular environment—for instance, "When you find a lot of food, play and explore; when food is scarce, move only a little and don't waste energy." Hereditary predispositions give if-then instructions, which the developmental biologist calls the "reaction norm."

Because a given animal inherits such instructions for many environments, every substantially different social and ecological situation will elicit different behavior although the genetic material remains the same. No single one of the many possible environments develops the animal's full potential. The kind of thornbush steppe in which we studied the hamadryas in Ethiopia is only one of the natural environments that have contributed to selecting the genetic makeup of these baboons. Their behavior in captivity, where they experience neither predators nor hunger, shows that the behavioral system is capable of things that are rarely revealed in the wild. The full potential even includes forms of behavior that have probably never been realized in evolution; astonishingly, these too occasionally turn out to be adaptive. A flexible apparatus can almost always achieve more than it was built to do. Our own brain offers a dramatic example. Having evolved as the brain of a hunter and gatherer during 99 percent of the history of the species, in virtually a moment it was capable of serving a farmer or horse breeder, then a bronze worker and, in ever more rapid succession, the philosopher, the mathematician, and the computer specialist.

Everything animals do teaches us something about the potential of the species, which we can never see in its entirety. Our research is concerned with this full complement of latent possibilities and the ways it responds to the environment, not just with the behavior that occurs in the wild, although the latter is particularly important to those interested in evolution. Behavior under zoo conditions deserves close attention because we civilized people also live in a kind of zoo, which we have constructed for ourselves.

Because of its rather biased concentration on "natural" behavior, ecology has not contributed much fundamental insight into two important questions. The first relates to the environmentally induced pathology of behavior, examples of which confront those involved in intensive animal husbandry; the second concerns ways in which the behavioral repertoire is enriched by artificial environments. That is, when we stop looking through ethology-tinted glasses we can see that "unnatural" environments may facilitate certain kinds of development considerably better than "natural" ones. Just raise your eyes from this book, for example, and consider your immediate "unnatural" surroundings. The ethologist Paul Ingold in Bern is pursuing this idea experimentally to learn whether endangered species of wild animals can be adapted to life in the civilized world by raising them in specially designed unnatural environments.

The special forms of behavior that blossomed from the social life in Pasha's zoo group were an enrichment, and not at all pathological. The cult of the mantle revolved around a species-specific feature for male display that is also characteristic of wild hamadryas and has not evolved in any other baboon species. It allows us to spot the adult males in a troop at first glance. When the subadult males in the zoo contemplated this mantle for a quarter of an hour, they confirmed what we had suspected— that it also impresses the baboons themselves, and not only us humans.

The fact that such behavior is never so obvious in the field is irrelevant. We can even learn what kind of impression the mantle makes on the others: they find it attractive. Groups in the field are routinely observed to close ranks when danger threatens. The bearers of the mantle may well serve as the banners about which the agitated animals assemble.

The development by females in the zoo of signaling and positioning maneuvers in which they used Pasha as a tool against their competitors was an inventive achievement. As they matured, they adapted the archaic triangle of protector-protegé-opponent, which stemmed from the relationship between mother and infant, by replacing the mother with new and more powerful figures.

Animals kept in zoos can develop the potential of their species to a degree unknown in the wild for certain areas of behavior, though other abilities may atrophy. For primates, the zoo can easily serve as a hothouse for social behavior (see p. 132), but it also creates animals that know as little about foraging and predators in their native habitat as a human city dweller knows about deer hunting or raising sheep. So if a critical reader is still convinced that Pasha's group was behaving abnormally, I would ask: How normal is it for *us* to play and explore beyond our basic needs?

Old and Young Marriages

From 1957 to 1959 I worked in the laboratory of the Zoological Institute in Zurich, preparing a dissertation about the physiological conditions under which the fruit fly *Drosophila* can have a long life span. Every now and then there would be a phone call from the zoo, summoning me to take off my white coat and pay a visit to those gray-coats on the Zürichberg. The zookeeper Rehm stood with me at the monkey pit and told me about the signs of changes that had occurred and portents of changes to come. For a few days I belonged to the baboons again. My observations on these visits are published for the first time in this and the following section.

It gradually became apparent that Pasha's dominance was coming to an end. Ulysses and Kalos, the former now as large as Pasha, were no longer uneasy in Pasha's vicinity; Pasha moved from one place to another more frequently than before, glancing over his shoulder to check if his retinue of females was following. The following January, Rehm saw Ulysses threatening Pasha to prevent him from climbing onto the sleeping shelf for the night. Ulysses and Kalos often fought, and at such times Pasha and his harem withdrew into a corner. In April, Pasha lost much of the hair from his mantle, so that his thin body could be seen and his head appeared disproportionately large (fig. 11). At night he rested his head on

Fig. 11. Old Pasha (*left*), with almost all of his mantle hair gone, sits unnoticed amid all the activity. (Photo: Bruno Sulzer)

the nape of one of his females; until then he had held it erect while sleeping. In the evening Pasha waited until last to to be fed, which Rehm did not recall ever happening before.

In December 1958 I found Vecchia with Ulysses and Nacha with Kalos. The two low-ranking females had left Pasha. It was probably not by chance that the lowest-ranking ones were the first to desert him, because their bonding with Pasha had been impeded by the continual intervention of the higher-ranking females. In the chapter on the anatomy of the partner relationship, we shall learn from experiments on geladas that the "loyalty" of a female depends on how much she has to lose.

No one saw how Pasha lost his two lowest-ranking females. But he was not injured, so I believe that Vecchia and Nacha changed partners on their own initiative. In so doing, each of them acquired a position with unrestricted access to a male. A few months later Ofe, who had become the lowest-ranking adult female once the others had departed, also left him.

The males seem somehow to know that harems are most likely to break up beginning with the lowest-ranking females, because they take action against this danger. In her Master's degree research on the rules governing relationships in the Munich hamadryas colony, Marietta Fritz also observed that the low-ranking females have the fewest chances to groom their male. The Munich males compensated for this disadvantage by preferentially grooming their low-ranking females. Hamadryas males have several techniques for bonding a female to themselves. One is to groom a female of whom they are not yet or no longer certain. Once they have a mate on whom they can rely, they stop being so attentive and let themselves be groomed by her. Marietta Fritz also noted that the females of high-ranking males have better access to food than those of low-ranking males. Therefore, by changing partners a female may move up to the position of alpha female, but at the cost of being relegated to poorer feeding places. Whether to be the second spouse of a high-ranking male or the only spouse of a lower-ranking one—this is a genuine optimization problem of the kind investigated in sociobiology.

Readers will hardly have failed to notice that Pasha in his prime was a rather colorless figure. Though he had uncanny influence, he actually did very little. With the gradual loss of his harem, quite unexpected sides of his character surfaced. As soon as Vecchia and Nacha had left, the small baboons began to play near him. He had ignored them before, or driven them away with a stern glance. Now he looked on with friendly lip-smacking. Once, Glumo and Pfiff had a scuffle close by and Glumo playfully grabbed Pasha's hindquarters. I could hardly believe my eyes when the old one responded by presenting to the youngster, whereupon the latter boldly mounted him. Pasha no longer terrified the others, and the gatherings around his mantle were forgotten. The young males became Pasha's companions. Glumo, now as old as Wiffel had been in the discussion in the previous section, calmly used both hands to groom the few pitiful, female-brown bristles the old male still had left, and when the young ones were wrestling near him Pasha playfully shoved his open, toothless jaws into the rough-and-tumble youngsters. Sometimes he even initiated the game. The following incident serves as an example.

Little Pfiff, about two years old, trots up to Pasha several times. Each time, the old baboon begins a remarkably slow biting match with him. Then he walks a few steps away, looks over his shoulder at Pfiff while lip-smacking, and makes the gesture with which mothers invite their infants to ride piggyback: he bends his knees with his rear end toward the young one. But Pfiff responds impudently and inappropriately, with the back-bite of a mating male, after which he flees and lures Pasha on with a scrap of paper that he carries in his mouth. Pasha runs after him and the two engage in a biting contest that is now clearly playful. Finally Pfiff jumps down onto Pasha from a rock, and the latter wards him off with open mouth.

In his "best" period Pasha had never played with the young males. If he had tried it, the youngsters would probably have urinated in sheer terror. Now, however, he was practically assuming the role of boss of the boys, and he played the part with greater gusto than Ulysses ever had. It looked to me as though Pasha was simply amusing himself.

I put "best" in quotation marks above. From a sociobiological viewpoint, that period was good, because Pasha kept a harem and propagated his genes. Now he was no longer concerned with reproduction. This situation did not appear to bother him. On the contrary, he gave the impression of having been released from a chore. His games with the little ones were hardly a matter of senile regression into childish behavior. He continued to lead his females energetically. Yet in his choice of partners and activities Pasha had partly returned to the life-style of a young bachelor. Later we shall see that something similar happens to old deposed harem leaders in wild troops, once they have overcome the trauma of the loss.

In July 1959 Pasha was deserted even by Sora, the highest ranking of his wives. His harem had shrunk down to one—the young Liba. He was remarkably indulgent toward the last of his females. If she hesitated to follow him, he waited or even went back to her. In his prime he had never groomed a female for very long, but now he did so with Liba. By our human standards all this makes him a more sympathetic character. But so that we do not misunderstand the former Pasha, I should mention that an average harem in Ethiopia comprises barely two females. By this measure, Pasha at the height of his powers had too many mates, so that often he did not pay much attention to their advances. Unfortunately, it is a common practice in zoos to keep only one sexually mature male, even in the case of species that naturally live in groups with several adults of both sexes. The idea is to avoid fights, but the sole male—and the visitor—pays for it with boredom. The hamadryas colonies at the zoos in Frankfurt-am-Main, Madrid, and Munich are now kept in larger areas that accommodate several males and their harems.

The young marriage of Nacha and Kalos was turbulent in comparison with Pasha's marriage in old age. Kalos wanted to have everything at once. An experienced male keeps his female with him by walking ahead, then turning to check up on her, and, if necessary, raising his brows. He waits for sex until she is in the swelling phase. He mounts when she presents to him and afterward she grooms him. Kalos and Nacha mixed all that up into an eager jumble. For example, Kalos tried to lead Nacha by walking backward, so he could see her, while smacking his lips. She kecked and slipped timidly after him on her hindquarters. She then pressed herself to the ground under (not in front of) Kalos. Awkwardly Kalos attempted copulation, but Nacha's flat hindquarters defeated him. At the same time he bent forward to look her in the eyes, intermingling friendly lip-smacking with threatening brow-raising. When she presented, he kept grasping her over and over, and pressed his wide-open mouth against her back as if he wanted to devour her.

However inept this kaleidoscopic behavior may appear to the amused observer, it does not necessarily imply that the previously unmated young male did not know the correct sequence. Kalos had spent more than four years without a mate since puberty, and he was visibly suffering from a huge motivational backlog; the stored-up motivations for leading, copulating, and grooming all broke through at once. A new female excites even experienced males in a similar way, though to a lesser extent. In Ethiopia, when a harem leader had acquired an additional female he eagerly guided her on tours around the sleeping cliffs, embellishing the excursion with hasty mounting, while his older females dawdled along far behind them.

I inferred that Nacha and Kalos often did not know what their partner would do next, because they kept watch on one another with really extraordinary intensity. When they separated, the one who remained behind fixed his or her gaze on the spot from which the other had disappeared. If it was Kalos who departed, at practically every step he looked around at Nacha. While they were resting, she looked into his eyes in suspense whenever he made the slightest move. During attempts to mate, he bent forward at her side and tried to see her face. Baboons know only one copulatory position, in which the male mounts the female from behind. Only the anthropoid apes occasionally copulate facing one another. We may suspect that they need to see the face of the partner. While seated, Nacha and Kalos often looked into one another's eyes for a long time. Ordinarily baboons do this only for a fraction of a second. Eye contact has the effect of a threat if it is at all prolonged. Indeed, after these long exchanges of gazing, Nacha often became frightened.

I do not know for certain what this mutual gazing conveyed between the two partners, but we know that one characteristic of a social relationship is to know what the other will do next. Now Nacha and Kalos had known each other since Kalos's birth, and each must have long been familiar with who the other was in general and in relation to the rest of the group. But what they were to each other was something they could not know before their marriage.

Is a baboon something special to each of its companions? Isn't Nacha the same Nacha for all of them? Years later we pursued this question with our hamadryas colony in Zurich. We reasoned as follows: When A frequently grooms B, there can be three reasons: (1) A spends a lot of time grooming everyone, without regard for the individual, because he just likes to groom; (2) B is an attractive individual to groom for all the others as well as for A; (3) A often grooms B in particular and at length, even though he grooms others only rarely and B is not especially sought out by the others to be groomed. Only the third pattern is the expression of a *personal* relationship as we humans understand it. A mathematical procedure, the analysis of variance, was used to distinguish the relative trends toward these three explanations. The result confirmed that hamadryas baboons do indeed maintain personal relationships; that is, they do not merely follow their own general urges or respond to the general attractiveness of others. Therefore the relationship between Nacha and Kalos was unique to themselves; they could not know what it would be like if they had observed each other only in interactions with third parties. That, perhaps, was why they scrutinized each other's faces so intensely.

Half a year after they had become partners, Nacha and Kalos led a quiet, orderly married life and no longer sought each other's eyes.

At the time of these marital rearrangements, Rehm gave me an example of his intuitive understanding of the baboons. Kalos had killed the last infants that Pasha had managed to father. Rehm said hesitantly, "I believe he did it because the babies weren't his own." A zoologist who had raised such a hypothesis in those days would have been frowned on, but twenty years later it was discovered that among wild langurs, an Indian species of leaf monkey, when males drive away the previous leader of a group of females, the first thing they do is bite to death the infants their predecessor had fathered. The proposed explanation was the subject of lively dispute among primatologists. The reasoning was that when the mothers lose their babies, their hormone balance is altered so that they can conceive again. If a new male kills the infants of the females he has just acquired, he can impregnate them sooner and therefore have more descendants of his own than if he allows them to live and simply waits out the cycle. Therefore the genes for "infant killing" would have become relatively more abundant in successive generations. Opponents of this hypothesis claimed that infant killing was a pathological trait. Complex computer models finally showed that, under certain assumptions, infant killing is indeed an advantageous strategy for successor males, as Rehm had once surmised.

A Female as Harem Chief

In December 1958 Vecchia, the wizened old female who had previously been persecuted by Sora and Ofe, became the alpha female of Ulysses. Until then the sole companion of Ulysses had been Zippa, a sexually immature female. She groomed and followed him but was not yet ready for sexual interactions. Vecchia became Ulysses' first mature spouse. When I first saw them, they already had the turbulent phase behind them. Vecchia groomed the young male, and Zippa now stayed a short distance away. After one month Vecchia had a swelling, and Ulysses experienced his first undisturbed copulations. Like Kalos, he could hardly get used to it. Instead of sitting down quietly afterward and letting himself be groomed, he flung himself off Vecchia's rump, turned away, and swept the ground for minutes at a time. There was no question of his being afraid of Vecchia; he gave her unmitigated bites in the neck, to which she responded by crying out and grooming him. His nervousness was exclusively associated with full sex, which he had had to suppress for years because Pasha would not tolerate it. After seven months, when Sora also joined him, he swept the ground after mating with her. It was only after several more months had passed that he could take sex with more equanimity.

Meanwhile Ulysses had become full grown and was now the largest male in the group. Pasha's sparse remnants of hair no longer drew the group together in a mantle cult. Nevertheless, in February 1959 Kalos and Glumo still spent long periods watching Liba groom Pasha. This kind of attention was never paid to the splendid mantle of Ulysses, even though he was now Pasha's superior.

Among hamadryas baboons, as with others, power and ability are not always united in the same individual. It was still only Pasha, scrawny as he now was, who would intervene in group disputes, while the two strong young males contented themselves with embracing their new females protectively.

Even though Ulysses looked like a Pasha, he wasn't one, and his new, elderly alpha female Vecchia took advantage of that. In April 1959 I heard that new fights had broken out among the males. The next day it seemed as though Ofe, the former Number Two in Pasha's harem, had also joined Ulysses. Ulysses responded to her shy presenting by softly nibbling at her lower back. Little Zippa tried in vain to keep Ofe away from him by protected threatening. Vecchia, however, took no half measures; she charged at Ofe, who once had been her superior in rank, bit her in the neck, and shook her, as only a very angry male would normally do with a female. This was clearly the behavior of a harem leader. Ulysses did not intervene, then or later. When Ofe fled to him after being bitten by Vecchia, he ran away. Eventually Ofe gave him up and returned to Pasha.

Vecchia continued to develop her position. First, she continued to deal out neck bites. When Ulysses gave someone such a bite in a ramifying quarrel, Vecchia might follow at his heels and top it off with a bite of her own. Occasionally Sora, once the head wife in the harem but now lower in rank, came over from Pasha and presented to Ulysses at a distance. He would then smack his lips in a friendly way but do nothing to keep her. At first Vecchia was satisfied with barring Sora's attempts to flee to Ulysses during quarrels. But I soon noticed that during the rest periods around noon, Sora continually groomed Vecchia and never Ulysses, as would have been customary. When Sora lowered her hands, Vecchia would induce her to continue grooming with a rather pathetic-looking gesture that hamadryas use in this situation. She raised one arm toward the sky, exposing her flank—the gesture that may have been interpreted by the Egyptians as a greeting to the sun. If Sora still wanted to approach Ulysses, Vecchia casually stepped into her way and blocked all of Sora's attempts to go around her. Ulysses did nothing. Sora learned that she would not be allowed to groom her new spouse.

Sora progressively became Vecchia's female rather than Ulysses'. The process began with Sora devoting all her grooming to the senior female, and then it extended to other marital interactions. Soon it was only from Vecchia that Sora received the punishing neck bite used for pacification. One day Sora tried to present her swelling to Ulysses but, to be on the safe side, did it halfway in Vecchia's direction. Ulysses responded and copulated with Sora. Immediately afterward she hurried around behind Ulysses' back, as usual. However, Vecchia was already sitting there and demanded for herself the grooming that was the male's due. This now became a regular occurrence. A little later Vecchia took over the final element of the male's role: she mounted Sora and bit her gently in the back, as males sometimes do while mating. Now Vecchia controlled all Sora's interactions, both within the family and outside it. Only full copulation was denied the old female, for obvious reasons—though when Ulysses was performing this last of his functions, she participated to the extent of biting Sora in the leg. Of course, Vecchia also lacked the mantle of a family leader. She seemed to compensate for this lack by positioning herself just in front of Ulysses after each of her attacks, as though using his mantle as a theatrical prop. She herself hardly groomed Ulysses at all. In her everyday life she had virtually changed sex; she had taken the place of the ineffectual harem leader in everything but reproduction.

Vecchia had not become chief of the harem because of any superiority to Ulysses in rank or strength. She had simply learned to do what Ulysses—incomprehensibly to me—left undone, and had estimated correctly the extent to which he would let her play leader in his place. She made her own way to the top, from low-ranking harem female, disdained and chased by all, to executive officer of the family. It is remarkable that this position, otherwise exclusively the province of males, was one to which a female would aspire. I was even more surprised that her years of being persecuted had not extinguished either the abilities or the self-confidence she needed in her leading role. Perhaps a feeling for one's identity can only be destroyed if one has an identity to begin with. No such thing has been documented in primates below the intelligence level of the chimpanzees.

Eduard Stammbach (20), who worked in our laboratory later on, found that all-female groups also form "one-male" units, in the sense that the alpha female is the main object of sexual and grooming behavior, as a male ordinarily is. This structure was developed by the low-ranking females themselves; each was eager for interaction with the alpha female and tried to keep the others away. Higher-ranking females were better at this than lower-ranking ones, so that a general rule could be formulated: the sum of the durations of grooming between two females was greater, the greater the sum of their ranks. Alpha and Beta groomed one another most often, and the two lowest ranking, least often. The innovative American primate researcher R. M. Seyfarth had previously found that this rule applies to other primate species (Seyfarth 1983). However, Edi Stammbach showed that grooming is not influenced by rank alone. In his experiments, one female was released into an enclosure where two other females were present, each in a cage, at a considerable distance from one another. He then watched to see how much time the free baboon would spend with each of her two companions. The one who was free to choose had entire control of the situation, and she chose not the higher-ranking female but the one with whom she had always been more friendly, although we could not tell what it was that made the latter more attractive. In the everyday life of the group, both aspects—rank and friendship, or tactics and inclination—resulted in frequent grooming.

The small cult centered on Pasha's mantle faded away when he grew very old. I never saw such a thing in another zoo or in the wild, perhaps because all those groups included several adult males. In the world of the Zurich baboons, there was only one mantle. Can it be that whatever is unique in the world—like the sun or the moon—carries within it the seeds of a cult?

In the zoo I learned to understand the baboons' language and their elaborate social tactics, developed well beyond those we later observed in the severe natural habitat of the hamadryas. What I could not learn in the zoo was the social structure of large congregations of baboons, and its ecological significance. For that I had to see them in their native land.

CHAPTER TWO

On to Ethiopia

Compass Setting: Southeast

A deeply rooted desire—*and* good luck—can achieve a great deal. Even when I was a boy, my internal wish-compass was set to the southeast. I loved the language of the ancient Greeks, the stories Herodotus had written about the Nile country, and the wild animals of eastern Africa long before I ever left Switzerland. Whenever I dreamed of lands of happiness, even in my dream I knew that they were located in the "hallowed southeast."

The good luck involved a bottle of Kaiserstühler wine. It opened the door for me to go to the wild hamadryas baboons in Africa. It was 1957, in the German town of Freiburg in Breisgau. My professor, Heini Hediger, had suggested that I present my work on the zoo baboons at the International Ethology Conference held there that year. This was a rather intimate club, in comparison with the mega-congresses now held under that name. There were just eighty participants, all of us spoke German, and in the front row the great ethologists sat together: Niko Tinbergen, Konrad Lorenz, G. P. Baerends, and the psychologist Daniel Lehrman, who with his two students constituted the American contingent. The sessions lasted from eight in the morning to ten at night. In the intermissions even a student could talk to Tinbergen about motivation analysis without having to stand in line.

As I was giving my talk about "fleeing toward the highest ranking" and the inhibited forms of grooming that result from the associated conflict, I noticed that Konrad Lorenz was amusing himself by imitating, on the tabletop, the way young females touched the male with one finger. In all my experience I never had a more enthusiastic audience than he was. When he was listening to a vivid presentation, making small sounds of agreement and delight, I found it almost impossible not to talk directly to him. Moreover, late at night after a particularly difficult lecture, he could still stand up and, beginning with the words "If I understand you correctly," summarize the lecturer's ideas precisely in a few pithy sentences.

Ethological research on primates was something new at that time. A common view was that ethology was the study of instincts and therefore could not be profitably used on mammals, which were thought to *learn* their behavior. The hamadryas study had now shown that ethological methods could usefully be applied to primates, the mammalian order most like humans. To celebrate, Heini Hediger invited me to supper in an excellent Freiburg restaurant. I think it is fair to say that both of us are a bit shy with people; in any case, I had never heard my professor tell such stories about his experiences in Africa as he did then over our glasses of wine. I am sure that it was only the wine that eventually gave me the courage to ask, "How do people actually manage to get to Africa?" From then on things moved unbelievably fast. Hediger simply asked where I wanted to go, and without hesitation I replied, "To Abyssinia, to the hamadryas baboons." The Swiss National Science Foundation had just been established, and Hediger promised to speak to my doctoral supervisor, Professor Ernst Hadorn, about it as soon as we returned. On the way home in the overnight train, I saw the rocky landscape of Abyssinia before me as in a dream. Later on, while preparing for the trip, I was suffused with incredulous joy whenever I reminded myself that I would really see Africa.

Hediger kept his word, and Hadorn helped. While I was still working on my dissertation, the inquiries were begun. At a meeting of the Swiss Zoological Society, Professor Adolf Portmann gave me the names of two anatomists in Frankfurt, Professors Starck and Frick, who had just come back from a primatological study in Ethiopia. What I learned from them made clear to me, for the first time, what I had undertaken. I needed an all-terrain vehicle and someone to go with me. The latter, to my amazement, was not easy to find. There was no shortage of colleagues who congratulated me effusively on my African horizons, but when I pointed out that there was room for someone to accompany me, all found several very plausible reasons not to accept, ranging from their wives to their health.

And I too now had a wife, but mine was a help rather than a hindrance. She wanted to come along to Ethiopia, but half a year before departure a newborn daughter canceled that plan. Nevertheless, Verena was quite convinced that I should go, and she assumed a heavy burden for the sake of this Ethiopia year. "When the dahlias have withered again, you will still be gone," she wrote to me in November 1960, after I had left.

But I am getting ahead of my story. I found my companion for the expedition in a young, inventive zoology student named Fred Kurt, who later made his reputation as an elephant researcher in India as well as through his studies of deer and his appearances on television. Our network of informants about the unknown land of Ethiopia expanded. My father gave me addresses and kept his worries to himself. We were soon to realize that my reluctant colleagues had had a good nose for trouble. I remember a visit with an Ethiopian ophthalmologist who belonged to the ruling group of the population, the Amhara, and was working in Zurich. He spent an evening telling us about the mutilations customarily carried out by the Afar nomads, called Danakil by the Amhara, his face pale and expressionless under the light of a green floor lamp. Fred Kurt and I were silent on the way home. We did not yet know that an Amhara at that time had every reason not to go for a walk in the subjugated nomad territory without an armed guard. However, the horror stories turned out to be longer-lived than the danger itself.

In 1960 there was no need to compose a voluminous, precisely organized application for funds as there is today. In January of that year I wrote a simple, four-page letter to the Science Foundation setting out our goals: "Ethology, the comparative study of species-specific behavior patterns, has previously concentrated primarily on insects, fishes and birds. Primates have been studied mainly with respect to their ability to learn, and mainly in the laboratory. Innate behavior has been neglected, although it should be a prerequisite for these studies. Only for a few New World monkeys is the structure of free-living groups and their relation to demarcated territories known. To obtain reliable data, it is necessary to observe the animals without interruption for at least one year. In very few cases have individuals and groups been identified. Observations of anthropoid apes have not been very successful because the tropical rainforest makes the work extremely difficult." (In the same year Jane Goodall began a study in the Gombe Reservation at Lake Tanganyika that would render this sentence obsolete.) "Our intention is to study *one* carefully selected troop of hamadryas baboons during a period of about eleven months. Comparisons with other troops are planned, but with a low priority. The troop under study should be of an average size and composition, have been influenced as little as possible by humans, and live in terrain favorable for observation." There followed a list of aims and methods. Among the justifications for the project was the following: "Students of early humans would be glad to have detailed information about the controversial questions of the use of tools and the hunting of prey by wild primates. Among psychologists and psychiatrists there is also a growing demand for information about the natural behavior of higher mammals, especially primates."

Today, thirty years later, the social structures and ecological strategies of many primate species have been investigated in the field; cooperative hunting, "fishing" for termites, and the use of natural hammers by wild chimpanzees have even been observed and filmed in dense forest. The hamadryas baboon stands out among the other species with respect to three characteristics: the rigid, hierarchical, multilayered social structure, the perfection with which the males lead their harems, and the decision process by which they jointly determine the direction of the daily march each morning.

My application was approved. The Georges and Antoine Claraz Donation was willing to provide the material necessities. In an attic at the Zurich Zoo, in summer of 1960, we collected the supplies for our expedition. We had bought a secondhand Willys jeep, our "Emma." Every Saturday afternoon we visited her in the garage owned by a mechanic friend of ours and familiarized ourselves with her idiosyncrasies. Müller, the mechanic, whom Fred Kurt referred to as Little Ferret because of his agility, was a gifted teacher. He would send us behind the garage, remove some critical piece or contact from Emma's internal organs, close her up again and, enjoying himself, call us back in: "Now, doctor, get under her, look her over, and then the diagnosis!" He explained to us the logic of diagnosis *per exclusionem*, and as we sat over our coffee with brandy he would go into raptures about some trick or other that could be used to make an old wreck keep on running. Little Ferret also knew how to shift gears without using the clutch. He would really have liked to come along with us, but publicly funded research does not extend to such luxuries. The field biologist has to be his own jack-of-all-trades. In fact, I found a use for almost everything I had learned: languages, fixing things, cooking, mending socks, diplomacy, climbing, and trying to cure sick babies. The only thing that did not come in handy was playing the violin. We owed it to Little Ferret that in spite of Emma's caprices we always got her to the "nearest" garage, even if we had to replace the broken axle springs by tying acacia branches to the chassis.

I passed my driving test with difficulty, a week before our departure. The examiner let me slip through with the rationalization that I couldn't do much damage in the bush. He would not have said that if he had shared our crossing of the dilapidated Awash bridge, when I maneuvered Emma over the ravine along a slanting strip of rubble without knowing at what angle she would tip over.

Despite the helpful bits of advice from Starck and Frick, we were not sure whether we would find "our" hamadryas troop in the hot semidesert or in the mountains, so our equipment was correspondingly varied. We took an old stovepipe from my parents' house along. It was supposed to serve as a chimney for a stove we would build for ourselves in our tent if we were in the highlands or, following the recommendation of an American army regulation for tropical hygiene, to be used as a urinal.

On October 18, 1960, we set out. Emma, loaded up to the roof inside and on top of it outside, was sagging alarmingly low on her rear springs, like a gray toad. We had reservations for her and ourselves on a ship leaving Naples on October 25 and sailing to Massawa on the Red Sea. Before we reached Ancona we had our first problem with Emma: her engine began to roar, so that she sounded like a tank. I thought our expedition was already finished, but it turned out that the exhaust pipe had merely broken off, close to the engine. We wired it together and had it welded in Ancona.

Fred Kurt and I had hardly ever been outside Switzerland, and we devoured the novel scenes before us. Naples. A nun rushes through the city park at a gallop. A man selling hot chestnuts has a steam whistle on his kettle that he operates by pulling on a string. Two small boys are riding behind a streetcar, on the bumper. A dented bus overflows with young men who are bellowing offers of love at a woman driver two lanes away. At one and the same intersection, three traffic policemen are whistling, waving, and shouting, one of them in plain clothes; remarkably, they do all of this in coordination.

On November 1 the Italian ship *Diana* sailed, a week late. As the freight came on board we leaned on the railing, and watched our four-hundred-pound crate come crashing down a mountain of other boxes into the loading hatch and split open. Some kitchenware that rolled out of the gaping wound was pushed back by an indifferent stevedore. Cared for by a white-haired waiter with great skill and grace, we dined in style for ten days, six superb courses at every meal. Less competence was evident, though, in the drills with life-saving apparatus and pumps.

Catania. Fishing boats on the sand, their bows brightly painted with saints, mermaids, and proud mottoes: "Guarda mi bene se non voi mio caro sei nemico" ("Watch me with a good eye, my friend, if you do not want to be my enemy"). Another: "Let God take care of the sea; I'll take care of the crew." And on each side of the bow, a painted eye.

We spent every day on deck, writing detailed research programs, doing exercises in order to build up the strength for whatever might lie ahead, and, from an Italian textbook, learning Amharic, the language of the ruling tribe and the official language of Ethiopia. According to our little book, for example, the Amharic word for "leg" was "Sh'sh'kltm"—but no one understood this word in Ethiopia.

The nights on the sea gave us time. The water was purplish black and smooth. Now and again rustling patches of foam were pushed aside by the prow and drifted along the ship in the moonlight. The light in these clouds! Layer upon layer, they extended far into the distance and sank behind the globe of water. Distance here was not a continuous dimension but a link connecting disparate worlds. Each with a different light and different beings, these worlds lay one after another before the inner eye. So far I'd had to assemble them painstakingly out of all times and spaces. I was happy, felt completely at home, and saw more clearly what this trip, crazy as it appeared to some, meant to me—not only in terms of research, but also the question of how someone from the ivy halls would cope with a more primitive life. And then, at sea on the night of my thirtieth birthday, it became clear. I needed to experience the world as it would be almost without people: an existence before humans had appeared and begun to change everything. That I really did have this profound Adam experience has been one of the deepest joys of my life. Fundamentally, perhaps, many field biologists are happy when alone.

As we approached Port Said and I was on deck watching the flying fish, I struck up a conversation with Vangeli Halaris, an Italian-speaking Greek whose beautiful wife enthralled young Fred. Halaris had an automobile workshop in Dire Dawa, the small town in eastern Ethiopia that a German doctor in Harar had recommended to us, by letter, as a good place to find hamadryas baboons. I asked Halaris about it and soon realized that he knew what he was talking about. He imitated the contact rumbling of the hamadryas, lowering his round chin into his shirt collar and humming a bass tone, about one and a half brief notes per second. At first he kept his lips pressed together; then he opened them to form a round hole so that the final tones in the series had an "O" sound. He told me that the hamadryas spent the night near Dire Dawa on vertical walls of rock, lived in troops of two hundred, and often allowed humans to come to within about thirty yards of them. This was good news indeed and, as it turned out, correct. Vangeli Halaris later showed us "his" sleeping cliffs on many a morning and evening, and he took care of Emma on the frequent occasions when we had demanded too much of her.

November 8. We have left the Suez Canal behind. Veiled by dust, the vertically fissured, bare coastal mountains of the Red Sea stand all day in reddish light. We make the acquaintance of a pipe-smoking English doctor who gives us a friendly warning about schistosomiasis and offers two suggestions: we should add a spoonful of rum to the local tobacco, and at least once a month we should visit the nearest town "with collar and tie."

Almost all those on board, from lady diplomat to doctor, have one thing in common: prejudice against the Africans. Those who go there with a positive attitude come back with a negative one, or at least are disappointed. These whites considered their moral rules to be the generally applicable minimum. They recognized no qualitatively different scales.

The bay at Massawa. A triangular shark fin glides by; a coal-black man with a turban nevertheless leaves his leg dangling from his tiny fishing boat.

The quiet friendliness of the Ethiopian customs officials would have been a good example for their ranting counterparts in Naples. After hours of negotiation, and thanks to letters that had been received from the Ethiopian Foreign Ministry, we finally got everything through customs without paying the thousands of francs they had at first demanded, which we could not have afforded in any case. We got a nice lesson in the notorious practice of tipping from a young soldier at the customs station. He had found the letters mentioned above by looking in the files under "Philipp," where indeed they were. In Amharic a person's first name is the most important, and in my passport the title "Dr." was followed by "phil." for "philosophy." When I tried to reward this ingenuity with ten Ethiopian dollars, he refused politely, taking two steps backward and bowing. But in the evening, after we had loaded the last box, he said candidly, "You may now give me the ten dollars."

While I was negotiating, Fred watched our fully loaded Emma being taken off the ship. Thirty feet above the pier a tear opened up in one of the four decaying nets suspended from a crane to support the wheels of the jeep. Our expedition nearly fell to its death. Calmly, Fred took pictures of Emma hanging there askew; my coworker clearly had strong nerves.

We spent the night in the heat of Massawa, in an old, airy hotel in the ancient Arab quarter. Through its windows, topped by pointed arches, no traffic noise could be heard, but all night there was the sound of quiet conversations in the packed-earth alleys and behind the nearby white wooden lattices in the windows of the neighboring houses. It was so hot that we drenched our shirts to stay cool while sleeping.

It takes us three days to travel to Addis Ababa. Emperor Haile Selassie is still ruling his feudal realm. The road is full of pedestrians, porters, and beasts of burden. While one of us drives, the other's hand flies over the notebook pages, writing and drawing: local costumes and hair styles, forms of greeting, races of humans and domestic animals, hut architecture, wooden plows, beehives in the trees, vultures, viverrids. Naples had no such wealth of images! Fred Kurt quotes continually from Brehm's natural history of animals, which he had studied as a boy. At the top of the embankment at the side of the road, a man whirls a sling like the one used by David, a rope doubled back with a patch of leather in the middle, as long as a man's body. He is driving monkeys out of the fields. His ammunition consists of round stones about two inches in diameter, which whistle as they fly. A fat dignitary in the toga-like white shamma wobbles hastily past us on a mule, a form of transport preferred to the horse in the highlands. Next to him, barefoot and erect, trots a tall, slender, white-bearded man with mouth closed, holding a thin twig in his fingertips.

Emma creeps over steep, winding passes up to alpine pastures. Some slopes are so steep that the shepherd boys hold onto the grass with their hands. At the top, instead of descending on the other side, the road continues horizontally into the distance, just below the gleaming clouds. Here the cultivated areas are on the high plateau, and the rock walls and dense brush are down in the canyons. We are on the roof of Africa. An hour later we are going down again through tricky gravel curves until, more than three thousand feet below, we are among darker people and lighter huts. The pictures in our diary, drawn in shaky lines as we bump along the road, show faraway canyon rims on which stand eucalyptus groves, tiny in the distance, which mark the sites of the invisibly small groups of round huts where the highland farmers live.

I must tear myself away from the intoxicating effect of these early impressions; the memories are strong, and far too numerous to relate here. For us, after all, Haile Selassie's realm was supposed to be the land of the hamadryas. One evening in Eritrea, we saw them. On the right of the road to Asmara they were moving in a leisurely way through an acacia grove, in a small group. The pasha at the end of the file glanced at us over his shoulder. I leaned back and took a deep breath.

The Highlands

November 21, in the highland city of Addis Ababa (nearly a mile and a half above sea level). Spotted hyenas wander laughing through the city at night, taking the dead donkeys for themselves. We lie in our tents for the first time, in the garden of the Swiss airplane mechanic Zimmermann, and listen; it already sounds like the wilderness. But we still have a labyrinth ahead of us. We need letters of introduction to the provincial governors, work permits, gun licenses. Thanks to the preparations made by the Swiss chargé d'affaires Jean de Stoutz, who takes a fatherly interest in us, and the tactical knowledge of his Ethiopian coworker Bagashu, we manage all that in the incredibly short time of three weeks.

Emma weaves back and forth between the ministries, giving way to two-wheeled horse-drawn taxis and laden donkeys and finding a route between potholes in the asphalt and the hundreds of pedestrians. A street scene. On the left: in front of the modern offices of Ethiopian Airlines, elegant Ethiopians in blue European suits step out of expensive cars. On the right: a "hut" little more than two feet high made of loosely layered plates of rusty tin. An old man sits on the ground in front of it and mends his trousers. Next to it, about thirty shabby men are standing in a meadow, cutting the sparse, dry grass with sickles. On average, only about four are working at any given time—there are not enough sickles. The area they mowed yesterday could have been cut with a scythe in two hours by my friend Paul Zinsli in the Swiss mountains. Is it laziness, inefficiency? Westerners would have hired the most industrious and sent the others away to join the ranks of the unemployed. In the Ethiopian method the money is shared more directly, without bureaucratic middlemen. Even these reapers are working too hard for the one Ethiopian dollar they earn in a day, but it is enough for them to survive.

An official in the ministry has employed his brother, not the best-qual-
ified candidate. He notices that I am critical, and is surprised: "Well, can
the ministry be more important to you than your own brother?" Now it
is I who am surprised. What he says is so reasonable that I can only
wonder how we ever broke free of this natural way of seeing things, so
that we could construct a more efficient economy. Today, though, I think
I understand better. To favor one's relatives is the most ancient biological form of helping, observable in species as diverse as ants, birds,
ground squirrels, humans, and elephants. In the large human states nepo-
tism is disruptive because work groups here consist not of relatives but of
specialists complementary to one another who have come from all over.
The typical human form of help is mutual assistance based not on blood
kinship but on the ability of one person to provide what the other lacks,
in the expectation that the recipient will return the favor when necessary. For this to succeed, people have to know their partners and be
able to estimate accurately whether they will be able to keep their end
of the bargain in the years to come. It may be because such estimation
is so difficult that only a few animal species are yet known in which unrelated individuals help one another entirely on the basis of calculated
reciprocity.

Near Addis Ababa we are involved in a slight collision with another
vehicle. The "fault" lies with the other party, an old Ethiopian truck
driver. In the end, though, we pay up, partly because during the hour of
argument our antagonist slowly makes a graphic throat-cutting gesture.
The police officer passes judgment as follows: "He is older, and you are
the only ones with money." He's got a point there.

Between two office visits there is time for a first excursion to see the
baboons in the highlands. As a guide familiar with both the animals and
the language, an elderly Prussian baron living in Addis Ababa had been
recommended. The baron is a thin, cheerful, and talkative man who
strides through the bush in short pants, footless knee socks, and low cloth
shoes. He always carries with him a rifle and a permit to hunt "noxious
animals," which includes warthogs and baboons. From him we learn ru-
diments of the Amharic vocabulary, beginning—as we stumble among
the boulders—with curses. When there are words he does not know, he
fluently fills the gaps with Italian or German equivalents. When a boy at
the edge of the highway offers us eggs for sale, the baron turns him away
with the sentence: "In Arussi ager busu nkulal fare schon kikeriki." Only
the middle three words are Amharic. In translation, he has said, "In the
Arussi land too many eggs are already saying cock-a-doodle-doo." What
we learn from the baron is in any case more useful than "sh'sh'kltm." He
himself is called in Amharic by the appropriate-sounding "shumagerli,"
or old man.

The baron guides us northeast for thirty-four miles, toward Dessie, then eastward along farm tracks through the grain fields on the high plateau of Aliltú. From a distance, the countryside looks like the pleasant, fertile Abyssinia described in travel books around 1930, when there still was unused land for agriculture. Suddenly we are standing at the edge of a canyon. Up here, on the bright plain, the Amhara are walking among their fields of ripe grain, robed in white like biblical figures. Oxen are treading out the grain and two men shovel it up into the air so that the highland wind can drive the chaff away. It shines in the sunny air. Nearby is an eight-cornered, tin-roofed Coptic church under tall, windblown eucalyptus trees. At the edge of the chasm, our gaze falls from the quiet plateau down to colorful basins filled with rocks and bushes, and onto terraces lively with smoke and shouts. At this level there are still groups of grass-covered conical roofs; then the cliff plunges down and disappears into thickets in the depths of the canyon. Twelve miles away, on the other side, the plateau reappears as a yellow streak on the horizon. Here in Shoa, the home of the Amhara, the wilderness is again below and home is above it.

The baron calls to a boy and asks him about the "nedj djindjero" or white monkeys, the hamadryas baboons. The youth leads us through a fissure in the rock wall, down to the highest terrace, and questions the farmers working there. Each of them bows low, lays his sickle on the ground, and leads us in the right direction to the boundary of his land. There he hands us over to his neighbor, bows again, and goes back to his field.

Then the young boy begins to "telephone." He raises his hands to his mouth and, in a high, monotonous voice, calls long sentences out into the valley. Where to? Far away, on the other side of the upper canyon, a tiny white streak responds. Amazing that they understand each other! The man on the other side sees the baboons on our side of the canyon and can direct us.

First we find the "tokur djindjero," the geladas—brown-mantled, beautiful highland baboons with a red-shielded breast—which now live only in the Ethiopian highlands. For the first time we take out our field glasses and waterproof notepads. This species, too, had not yet been studied in the field. It was not until a few years later that John Crook, the first to investigate them, would spent the night in a tent in our garden in Switzerland on his way to Ethiopia.

The social structure of almost all mammals is reflected directly in the way they distribute themselves in space. Suppose you see seven geladas together, fifty yards away from some others; you can be nearly certain that the seven have close, permanent relationships with one another. Among civilized humans it is not so simple. To be in the same bedroom has some social significance, but to sit in the same streetcar or airplane means essentially nothing. We made notes of the composition of groups of geladas that were at least fifty yards apart, while they grazed on the slope below the uppermost walls and in the harvested grain fields. In seven out of eleven groups we found only one adult male. A few years later John Crook found that geladas do indeed live in one-male groups.

On one of the following evenings we saw the hamadryas baboons. We stood on the rim of a deep basin in the canyon wall. Opposite us and three hundred feet lower down, the steep slope gave way to a vertical cliff almost a hundred feet high (fig. 12).

They stepped out of the dense shrubbery at the top of the cliff and sat down on the bare edge, next to the abyss. Almost all of them sat quietly, wrists on knees and hands hanging down, looking straight ahead into the depths, in the symmetrical, centered posture in which they are represented in ancient Egyptian sculpture. Before twilight they moved, one after another, to the chimney of rock on the left in figure 12, climbed slowly down, feet first, to a ledge barely a foot wide that slanted across the wall. They proceeded along this ledge in an extended line until they reached a place where part of a softer layer of rock had broken away, leaving a shallow cavity. It was worrying to see mothers with young clinging to their backs on this precarious climb. One of the subadult males went directly from the large bush at the top of the cliff down to the hollow, lowering himself hand over hand along a swaying tree root. In this inaccessible refuge they settled down for the night. Black strands of feces marked the wall below the sleeping hollow. Now we knew how to identify regularly used hamadryas sleeping places, even from miles away.

We stopped for the night in a farmyard at the edge of the canyon, enclosed by dry-stone walls. In the evening the Amharas taught us their language amid much laughter. They were masters of innuendo. A thirty-year-old woman in front of her whole family told us the words for man ("wand") and woman ("ssyeet") and let her eyes flash. "Aiii!" sang the others in high, soft tones—an exclamation of delighted disapproval. Fred Kurt and I spent the night in the one-roomed hut of a young married couple. None of the four of us slept very much.

In the canyon of Aliltú, geladas and hamadryas slept on the same cliff, but apart from one another. During the day they mingled. The geladas gave priority to the hamadryas, even though the latter were less numerous (55 against 80) and, as we soon noticed, were only guests here. At the vacated threshing sites the hamadryas, on average, fed closer to the middle where more grain had been left. When the baboons were traveling in the same direction, the hamadryas went ahead in a closed group and the geladas followed them. During a midday drinking stop, the geladas waited for an hour and a half two hundred yards away, until the nedj

Fig. 12. Sleeping cliff of the hamadryas in Aliltù.

djindjero had had plenty of rest and left the drinking site free for them (6). Instead of waiting, the geladas could easily have used the brook farther upstream or downstream. I do not know for sure why the geladas were so remarkably respectful, but I can guess. As already mentioned, all geladas have a bare, pink field on their chests. That of full-grown males is surrounded by a finger-wide border of white hairs, in the otherwise chocolate-brown coat. Face and hindquarters of geladas are not red but almost black. Let us make the reasonable assumption that the white-bordered red chest field of the gelada males acts as an impressive stimulus to their conspecifics; such a stimulus is called a "releaser" in ethological terminology. The geladas would then view the hamadryas as supermales, because their red field, although located posteriorly, is three times as large and is also surrounded by a ring of white hairs. In the front the hamadryas displays yet another, similar feature, the reddish face with cheeks wreathed in a broad, white beard. In general, larger, more intense, or more numerous releasers are known to have a stronger effect than small, pale ones with few elements. This is plausible from an evolutionary perspective. The early precursors of releasers take a relatively weak form; more pronounced characteristics occasionally appear by chance, but they can become established only if they have a stronger effect on the partner. It follows that the responsiveness of the receiver must increase in advance of the development of the releaser. In some animal species, supernormal releasers have indeed been shown to be more effective than normal ones. For example, when the Swedish biologist Malte Andersson (1982) made the long, decorative tail feathers of male widow birds even longer by inserting pieces from other individuals, the birds with the superlong tails attracted extra females into their territories. Some features of human fashion illustrate the principle.

That hamadryas and geladas lived there in a socially and ecologically interesting relationship counted as a plus for the Aliltú highlands when we were choosing which troop to study. But there were also disadvantages. The terrain was very steep, and 40 percent of it was covered by bush, which slowed us down and interfered with observation. The baboons plundered the fields and were therefore shot and caught in snares, which must surely affect their behavior and the structure of the population. Before we made a final decision, we wanted to make a survey of the living conditions of hamadryas baboons along a west-east line running a few hundred miles into the eastern lowlands, which would also show us whether Aliltú was typical. Apart from the mantles of the adult males, the coats of the hamadryas are not very thick, and here, where the altitude was 7,500 feet and the nights were often cold, they did not seem to be in their element. When we were in Aliltú for the second time, we saw the hamadryas group marching away one morning; they trekked down the canyon in long strides, across the lower terraces, and vanished in the east, toward the Danakil Desert. In the following days they did not reappear. Perhaps they ascended into the relatively wet highlands only at harvest time, when the lowlands are in the grip of the dry season.

Choosing a Troop

After spending a few days in the Aliltú canyon we knew what kind of data we should collect on our survey trip, in order to pick the best place for our study. On December 6, 1960, we drove Emma eastward onto the highway from Addis Ababa to Djidjiga, toward the thornbush steppe and the Awash River, which dries away to nothing in the Danakil Desert. Included in our party was the baron as well as two young Ethiopian helpers. Now Emma was really put to the test: staircases of rock, erosion gullies two feet deep running across the track, rivers to cross. We soon found the most effective schedule. We traveled during the day. After 3 o'clock in the afternoon we asked in a village whether anyone knew of a djindjero byed, a "baboon house." Usually a boy would lead us to a sleeping cliff that was used regularly by the baboons. Toward evening, when the columns of hamadryas appeared, I reported to Fred the age and sex of each arrival at the speed of a football announcer, and he wrote them down. All this did not escape the attention of the local children, and even after we had not been there for weeks, they would call out "Weibli, Weibli" (Swiss for "female") when they saw us coming again. After this census taking, we observed individual subgroups, especially while they were climbing into the sleeping places, because that was the best time to see which individuals belonged together. When they had settled down, we described the racial characteristics of the local population. We found that toward the east the faces were redder, the hair of the females blonder, and the mantles of the males whiter. At twilight we set up our tents, usually near the village in order to be a little safer from the shiftas, the bandits, about whom we had repeatedly been warned. Once, however, in Ursu, we broke camp in the middle of the night because of the incessant howling and barking of the feuding hyenas and dogs. Without headlights we drove out into the thorn thickets, so that no one could see from a distance where we were sleeping.

In the early morning we counted the troop again as it left the cliff, and then we followed it. As we did so, we measured the tolerance distance— that is, the shortest distance to which we could approach quietly while still being tolerated by the seated hamadryas; if we attempted to come closer, they would get up and move off. If the tolerance distance was small, the implication was that the baboons here had not learned to be wary of humans; it also meant that we would probably be able to observe them at close range. At about eight o'clock we let them go on and turned our attention to the habitat, estimating the relative areas of cultivated land, grassland, and bush of various densities and describing the contours of the ground. Flat land overgrown with vegetation is worst for visibility, while rolling hills with their tops separated by distances about double the tolerance distance make it easiest to see the animals. From a hilltop one can observe the troop in the valley or on the opposite slope. We soon realized that it was especially important to have the most complete short-range view possible of the sleeping cliff and the resting places above or below it. It was here that the social behavior of the hamadryas could be observed for several hours on ordinary days, with no need to climb up after them. When all this had been fully recorded, we drove on to the next troop.

Before long we found out what it means to climb after the baboons. At a cattle ford across the Arba River we had discovered a small group. We rapidly made camp in the shade of the tall umbrella acacias with the help of our young Ethiopian helpers: Muhammad of the Gurage tribe, which did not enjoy high status but was said to provide good workers; and Melkessa, who claimed to be an Amhara. After noon Fred and I took leave of the baron, who made a great point of telling us not to get lost. On foot we went through the thornbush plain toward the northern wall of the valley, where the baboons had disappeared from our sight. Soon we saw a gray-mantled male sitting on a boulder on the steep slope above our heads and looking at us. We were on our way! Forcing ourselves through the thorns, we clambered up the hot rocky stairway at what I thought was a respectable pace. But the male never let us come closer than about one hundred yards. Bringing up the rear of his group, with long highlander's steps, he climbed deliberately and without effort over the blocks of stone. He even had time to sit down occasionally and wait for us. We puffed and sweated as he considered us calmly. Then I became afraid that we might never be able to follow hamadryas baboons. The sun sank; we had to turn homeward.

In camp Muhammad announced that the baron had gone toward the south to hunt in the thorn-bush plain. As night fell, our companion had not returned. Could this be the shiftas? After a big supper we novices had to organize a search party. There was no moon. Fred Kurt kept watch at the camp, and Melkessa was stationed on an acacia at the southern edge of the gallery woods to flash a light once per minute as a signal, so that the searchers could orient themselves. Muhammad, an intimidating sight with our long bush knife, and I set out into the bush at a constant compass angle, in the direction from which we had heard shots hours ago. But Melkessa had misunderstood what he was supposed to do with the light. He flashed it in all directions except ours. I went back and had him change places with Fred, muttering "stupid" in my annoyance. That he understood. After ten minutes we could no longer see Fred's light. There was no response to my pistol shot, but after another half hour we let off another shot and heard the baron call out an answer. We found him sitting on the ground, leaning against a bush; in his blood-soaked backpack was the head of a male bushbuck, the trophy of his hunt. There was no way to get through these thorn bushes, he declared. He had not fired in response to my shots because he needed his ammunition for better purposes. The most irritating thing, however, was the dead bushbuck, which his Noxious Animals License did not allow him to shoot, and certainly not here on a wildlife reservation. When he had dropped hints earlier, I had made clear to him that we would not carry any trophies of ungulates in Emma. A field researcher in a foreign country can easily become suspect, wandering around in unlikely places with strange-looking equipment. In such situations the law must be obeyed to the letter.

On the way back we were guided approximately by the compass and more precisely by Muhammad's excellent sense of direction, then finally by Fred's light. A shot sounded in the woods next to the camp. Again the thought of the shiftas chilled us. We ran forward and bumped into Melkessa, who was holding the baron's second gun, smoking, in his hands. Before we understood what had happened, the baron had started to beat him. Then I cast politeness to the winds and stopped the beating by locking the aristocratic neck under my arm, the only close-combat technique I ever learned. We finally calmed down and I apologized. Melkessa, who after all was twenty-five years old, was still lying on the ground and whimpering. It turned out that he had lost his nerve when he was alone in the camp and a hyena had rattled our pans. The baron maintained that one must behave as master toward the Africans, and anyone who made the mistake of laying hands on the master's weapon should be beaten. Well, it takes all kinds.

Unfortunately, the story was not yet over. From the very beginning we had wanted to have only one Ethiopian helper in the long term, so we had agreed with the two young men that they would be hired on probation for a week. The next morning, at the Awash train station, I paid Melkessa a rounded-up week's salary and bought him a ticket back to Addis Ababa. He protested in vain but finally went off, whining. The rest of us walked under the arbored roof of the station restaurant. At the entrance sat the ice-gray, melancholic father of the Greek proprietor, drinking a glass of ouzo. When he caught sight of the seat of the baronial trousers, which had also been soaked with blood from the contents of the backpack, he leaped up as though bitten by a tarantula: we must get out of there immediately. But disaster was already approaching: two policemen, in khaki and armed, escorted by Melkessa. We were led away. For the first time we learned of the polite and yet unsettling Ethiopian custom of leading strangers not by the hand, but by grasping them around the wrist.

The police chief of Awash questioned us for a long time, with the baron as translator, and entered everything by hand in a large book. The accusations, truthful enough, were as follows:

· that Doctor Hanis Kumari had illegally photographed a Soemmering's gazelle and an oryx, his papers having mentioned only monkeys in this regard,
· that the same person had called Melkessa stupid,
· that Baron von X had beaten Melkessa,
· that the same person had killed a bushbuck without permit at the Arba River.

The camera, the bushbuck head, and the gun were confiscated.

As further punishment we were detained overnight but were kindly allowed to spend the night under guard in the hotel rather than in jail. I was standing thoughtfully at the door, considering our plight and smoking my pipe when a small boy begged for a gursha, a tip. He did it so charmingly that the gursha turned out to be a little larger than usual. The boy acknowledged my generosity by another archaic gesture: he stepped back, threw himself to the ground, and crawled up to me to kiss my feet. I hope he was not insulted that I interrupted him. At that time in Ethiopia there still survived several formulas by which affection was expressed between highly placed and more lowly people, because the days of the feudal order—based on the ideal of a bond between lord and vassal—were not long gone.

Friendships involving a vertical protective relationship were not so unusual or even frowned upon as among us Westerners; on the contrary, they were desired, and they had their rules. When Jean-Jacques and Helga Abegglen, who later lived for a year in the village Erer-Gota, introduced me to an old Ethiopian with whom they had made friends, such tangible sympathy developed between him and me that shortly thereafter he pronounced me his son. He sealed this with a present that must have cost half a month's pay: a bottle of Italian whiskey. I decided to give my new father a fine present in return, but Jean-Jacques explained that it would be entirely unacceptable for me as son to offer something more valuable than the father's present. We agreed on a simple, pretty pillow for my new mother, and the warmth with which it was received showed that Jean-Jacques had been right. Age went before wealth. Even in my relationship with a beggar in Dire Dawa, the superior dignity of age was perceptible. The old man customarily sat in the roadside ditch at the gate of the Omedla Hotel, frequented by Greeks and Italians, where we stayed during our trips to Dire Dawa for shopping, medical care and jeep repairs. Under his worn brown robe he held lightly in his hand the stick without which no Ethiopian walked the roads. His encrusted feet were shod in sandals made of pieces of old automobile tires. Whenever I came, I gave him his samuni (a 25-cent coin) and sat with him for a while to find out how he was getting along. The ancient radiated such peace that the meager conversations with him became priceless to me. Perhaps he sensed this need; in any case, he accepted a younger man's small donation without the usual subservience.

To return to Awash. On the next day we were supposed to drive back west under police guard to the police station in a larger town, all of us on and in Emma: a total of seven men and their baggage. With a sigh I pointed to Emma's rear axle, where the springs were sagging, but no one took pity on them except that the police escort was cut in half. Go like that or stay here, they said. All day we rumbled westward along the potholed track. In Nazareth-Adama lived a police captain who knew English, so that finally we, too, had a chance to say something. Fred put a pamphlet from the recently established Ethiopian Board of Tourism on the desk before the captain and placed his finger on the sentence, "Ethiopia is the photographer's paradise." As I added my colorful comparison of the paradise I had just experienced with the way I had imagined it, the captain became amused to the extent that we were given back our camera. Melkessa, Muhammad, Fred, and I were released. The poor baron, however, was sent to jail. From our limited funds we left him some money for food, because after all it was for our sake that he was here, but that was the limit of our loyalty.

We had now come so far west that we would do better to return straight to Addis Ababa to replenish our provisions. On the way back, Fred's verbal caricatures of the cast in the drama we had just left behind were a delight. On the rocky trail west we turned the whole thing into an operatic duet for tenor and basso buffo, with obligato claps of thunder from the sheet of iron that shielded Emma's oil sump from the rocks projecting from the middle of the road. In the pauses Muhammad improvised an Amharic song; we understood just enough to know that it recounted his version of our experiences.

In Addis Ababa we steered poor tired Emma to our base quarters, the Swiss Embassy. With sweat-darkened shirts and hair white with dust, we stepped into the subdued light of the reception room. It was teatime, and the conversation concerned the best way to cut the tip off a cigar. A British diplomat resting indolently against the cushions said, with perfect diction, something like, "Continentals may use those little steel scissors. British smokers nibble the tips with their fingernails." He inspected the thread of smoke rising from his cigar. Figures emerged from the dimness as our eyes slowly adjusted to this incredible world. Madame de Stoutz, the wife of the Swiss chargé d'affaires, drew us into the circle as we were, and handed us tea. We looked forward to the long evening conversation at this table, even though it was in French; Jean de Stoutz was widely traveled and an idealist who put his ideals into action. He called Fred and me "le petit et le grand Papio."

The baron was kept in jail for ten days, and then released without his gun. For us, too, the next few days were depressing; in Addis Ababa an uprising of the emperor's bodyguard broke out the night after our return. On the radio Crown Prince Asfa Wossen was forced to read out a statement prepared by the revolutionaries. The emperor, however, returned from Brazil immediately and landed in the embattled capital. The news was spread by women in high-pitched ululation, and the revolution collapsed. After the fighting was over we went with members of the embassy to check on our compatriots in the city, and we saw the general of the bodyguard hanged in the market square.

I spoke to Haile Selassie only once, in 1968. The cool, narrow hand

and the soft voice of the emperor betrayed nothing of the bold decisiveness with which, fifty years earlier, he had ended the fights over succession after Menelik's death and granted his people one of the longer periods of peace in their history.

The second trip into the eastern lowlands, this time with only Muhammad, was a success. We reached Dire Dawa, the Arab city of Harar, and Djidjiga. In Awash Station we succumbed to malaria, and after returning to Addis Ababa I was confined to my camp bed—under the care of Madame de Stoutz, to my surprise and gratitude. Then, at last, we had the final stumbling block behind us.

We had now gathered data on twenty-three troops, distributed over 220 miles from Aliltú in the west to Djidjiga in the east (6). According to our exploration, two regions were particularly suitable for intensive study. The rolling plain at the southern edge of the Danakil Desert near Erer-Gota offered good conditions for observation, as its vegetation consisted only of scattered bushes. The sleeping cliffs here were accessible, there were many troops of baboons, and human interference was minimal. The land was too arid for agriculture; its inhabitants were nomads, and they were indifferent to baboons. However, the canyon at Aliltú was also tempting, with its double population of geladas and hamadryas. We went to inspect it again. The Amhara farmers promised us a house if we wanted to stay, and accommodated us as guests with a nobility unique to themselves. A brother of our first host was a minister in the capital. While the grandfather was still entertaining us politely from his leather-sprung bed, a white-robed young man bowed at the door and invited us into the neighboring farmyard. In the evening we climbed up the gullies in the canyon, tipsy from drinking t'alla.

The choice between Aliltú and Erer came down to a simple question: here the Amhara farmers hunted the baboons, whereas rumor had it that the Afar and Somali nomads around Erer would be more likely to hunt us. According to credible reports (Thesiger 1988, pp. 122ff), as late as the 1930s the status of an Afar warrior depended on how many male genitalia he wore or possessed. It did not matter how he killed his victims; to shoot a river bather in the back was as good as open battle. The participants in the three expeditions of Munzinger Pasha, Giulietti, and Bianchi met their deaths in the Danakil Desert. From several people we heard the same stories about the warlike Issa Somali at the southern edge of the desert; like the Afar, they wore in front of their stomachs the djile, a knife with a curved blade over a foot long, sharpened on both edges, and across their shoulders they carried a spear or gun. It was said that the number of leather cords on the sheath of the dagger stood for the number of people the owner had killed, but we were also told that Europeans did not count as trophies.

I lay awake in the tent and weighed the advantages and disadvantages. In the end, the decision was taken away from us. On our fourth morning in Aliltú a group of men appeared high above on the rim of the canyon and "telephoned" to have us brought up to them. A governor with military escort politely checked our papers and then ordered us to leave the region. After the aborted coup, the rebellious bodyguards of the emperor had become dangerous fugitives; yesterday they had robbed a church and killed two men. We were unsafe here, and therefore unwanted. The die had been cast for the land of the nomads in the east, about a hundred miles south of Hadar, where the famous australopithecene Lucy was later found. Under acacias we raised our tents by the mineral springs of Erer, close to the Hotel Erer run by Signor Andrea from Naples. He was understanding about our chronic shortage of funds, allowed us to camp by the hotel for our safety, let us use a storeroom for our equipment free of charge, and was satisfied, in return, to have us at his table. Anyone who follows monkeys through thorns in the heat cannot be after money, and anyone that crazy surely needs help. So he seemed to think, at least, as did others in Ethiopia who extended a friendly welcome to us as curiosities and guests.

At the Ravine

In the morning before and in the evening after their daily march, wild hamadryas baboons sit for a few hours near their cliff, especially on the slopes above it. Almost all of the fights and games, the entire gamut of sexual behavior, and most grooming are concentrated within these sociable rest periods. Therefore the sleeping cliffs are first-class places to observe them, and a lot depends on finding a site where both the sleeping ledges and the rest areas are in view from a single observation point. Our job now was to find the best cliff in the area we had chosen—the place where our troop dwelled and the ultimate goal of our journey.

Every day we traveled from hill to hill and scanned the countryside from the tops, searching for rock walls as far as our binoculars would reach. From the forested mountains of the Ahmar Range in the south, the river valleys ran down toward us. In only two of them did water flow all year—the Erer and one we called the Hammerhead River after the many *Scopus* birds that lived there. The others wound between the hills as bright ribbons of sand and vanished in the north behind veils of dust, running through the flat land toward the yellow stripe that marked the southern edge of the Danakil Desert. All this was hamadryas country, descending toward the east as far as the Red Sea, and extending westward into the canyons of the Amharic highlands and northward as far as there was water to drink, into the region of Port Sudan. We were closest to the southwestern boundary of their range. Somewhere in the wetter Ahmar Mountains, the dark anubis baboon took the place of the hamadryas baboon.

It was February and the dry season. The leaves of the umbrella acacias along the larger wadis were still green, but the scanty tufts of grass on the stony slopes looked bleached and the sparse thornbushes on the higher levels stood bare and gray. In some places the earth was empty or covered with nothing but stones. Only a few manganese-red rocks and bald hills added color to the picture, because the sky was white with dust. We found most of the potential sleeping places in the sheer cliffs along loops in the river, where the high water had undercut the bank. To me there is something primeval about rock walls. Throughout human history they have provided us, too, with a refuge in caves, and their tops have been lookout points from where we watched for enemies and prey. Their colors and the often enigmatic runes of their faces have always attracted me. On some of them it is virtually impossible for a human to set foot. They are shrouded in loneliness. I was glad that "my" animals lived among rocks.

About once a day we would hear the distant whimpering cry of a young baboon, or we could distinguish a gray form on an acacia umbrella. Sometimes the figure was a vulture, but if we were lucky it was an adult male hamadryas. Knowing that a baboon is almost never alone, we would then struggle toward it as quickly as possible and try to follow the troop until evening, so that it would lead us to its cliff. What we learned we entered on our homemade map, establishing the troop's position by primitive magnetic-compass triangulation with reference to characteristic mountain peaks. The "World Map 1:1 million," which had guided us so far, would no longer do.

During one of these searches we had our first encounter with the Issa-Somali, who the year before were said to have held up the Addis Ababa–Djibouti train in this area, robbed the passengers at gunpoint, and killed a passenger who refused to hand over his watch. This was mere hearsay, yet it began to affect us. On one of the highest hills, two lean, dark men waited for us, motionless. We greeted them, scanned the surrounding area with the binoculars, and then gave each of them an orange—also to the little girl who was with them and who was terribly afraid of us. Now the older man came up to us, gray-haired, glowering, with silver bracelets around his thin arms and only three fingers on his right hand. Along with the loincloth and the djile, he wore a faded English pinstripe vest, which reminded us unpleasantly of the Djibouti train incident. As though it were a matter of course he looked through our backpacks. Bedouin-style, he seemed to regard anything moving in his land as his own property. Only

Fred's extra underpants aroused his interest; he held them up against the sun for examination. We said good-bye and, an hour later, found a troop of hamadryas. We followed it toward the mountains in the hope of finally finding a good cliff.

Suddenly the old man reappeared before us as if he had sprung from the ground, without the little girl but with five young men, also equipped with knives. We could not understand a single word of the harsh-sounding Somali language. "Probably want money," I muttered. We gave them the two birr (an Ethiopian dollar, then worth about a U.S. quarter) we had with us, in order to get away quickly and not lose our troop. Now, however, they became pushy and began to feel our shirt pockets. We showed what we had: packet of bandages, signal whistle, and a suction cup in case we were bitten by a poisonous snake. They waved all that scornfully away. Eyeing my long knife with the black-ribbed metal handle suspiciously, they tried to pull us along by our wrists. In the meantime, our precious troop disappeared toward the mountains. This made me really angry, despite my pounding heart. I sent Fred ahead to the road and to Emma, rapped the fingers of one of the men crowding in on me, enouncing deeply felt curses in my own idiom, and finally followed Fred at a measured pace without looking around. When afraid, don't run. Distrustful after all the shifta stories, I listened tensely for the swish of a spear. I was thinking of the Frenchman who was said to have been answering a call of nature outside Djibouti when a spear plunged into the ground just in front of him, and for the first time I was glad to have a pack on my back. The grim ancient wanted to keep us there, but his young companions were not as determined as he, and they finally let us go.

Later we understood what we had done wrong. We had presented our papers only to the Amharic governor, who was part of the central administration, and at the police station, but had not greeted the chieftains of the Afar and Somali nomads who had once been subjugated by the emperor Menelik. Therefore they knew nothing about us, were right to be suspicious of what we were doing, and had no reason to respect us.

A few days later a hamadryas troop led us up the river we knew by the yellow boulder in its left bank, to a place at the foot of the Ahmar Mountains where the water had cut through a rocky ridge. The narrow gorge was flanked on both sides by rock walls sixty feet high, and the baboons were climbing down onto one of them for the night. Next morning, in the early dawn light, we lay down cautiously at the top of the other wall, only fifty yards away from them, and they tolerated our presence. Evidently they had correctly judged the protection afforded by the chasm between us. Looking down over the edge we could see all the sleeping ledges (fig. 13). On the slope above them, at our eye level, the baboons carried on their social life. This ravine seemed to be the right spot for us.

Fig. 13. At Ravine Rock, the observers on one side could look down to the base of the cliff on the other. The troop is climbing up to its sleeping places.

Every afternoon at three o'clock we man our observation post and wait for the troop. The sleeping cliff is still empty except for some marmot-sized animals, the rock hyraxes, which shriek from time to time. At the bottom of the ravine a thin stream of water trickles invisibly, and sometimes a warthog splashes through a puddle. We wait. Occasionally one of us misinterprets the distant cry of a bird or a hyrax as the eagerly awaited scream of a young baboon, and we dissect the rocky horizon with our eyes, trying to pick out something other than the small acacias that curve up as they grow out from the steep slopes, spreading their umbrellas horizontally like mushroom caps. Then, finally! This time they must be coming. Only an infant baboon modulates its fretful whining in that way.

Now, from just behind the spur of rock down at the mouth of the ravine, we hear the cozy contact-rumbling used by the adults to keep track of one another in the bush. Then the first family appears on the ridge above it. Their leader sits down and acknowledges our visit with a deep, resonant "baahu." This is the call with which the hamadryas announce everything unfamiliar that they discern at a considerable distance: nomads, hyenas, us during our first months—and also a group of conspecifics unknown to the troop, for these too can be dangerous. After pausing to inspect the territory, the male traverses the nearly vertical rock, bracing his tail against the wall in difficult places. On a block of stone he stops, hands and feet all together on a single point, muzzle lowered to peer down into the ravine and tail curving upward, still as a statue. After him comes a female, who now hurries to sit by him and begins grooming him. Then their youngsters whirl over the cornice to join them. Two more females climb onto the wall, knocking loose a few stones that bound into the depths unnoticed. This could be a family. The last to arrive is a subadult male, who seats himself several feet away from the others. Many one-male groups include such a companion-at-a-distance; these are always young males, at all stages of mantle development—that is, six to nine years of age. We call them "followers" (plate 6, bottom).

More columns now arrive, groups of thirty or more animals. Some come up to the ridge from the riverbed, others through the bush. When all have settled to rest, Fred counts them; there are eighty-two. The one- and two-year-olds romp on the scree slope, but the others are quiet. Infants less than eight months old, still in a coat of black hair, hang tiredly in their mothers' arms, their eyes closed and often with a nipple in their mouths. A half-grown female grooms her mother. On one ledge is a row of two- to five-year-old males, already drawing apart from their parental families. Before it grows dark, one group after another climbs down further onto the rock, and they arrange themselves on the sleeping ledges.

The cavity under the overhanging block at the top of the cliff seems to be the favorite place; the early arrivals stop here, although they may eventually turn this shelter over to later ones. Finally they are all accommodated on sleeping ledges and their eyelids droop. Families sleep huddled close together, sitting up with their snouts lowered onto their chests. To be closer to her family, a female will often cling uncomfortably to a tiny projection on the wall. In such cases the muscles do not relax even during sleep (fig. 14 and plate 2, bottom right). Infants coming from the playgrounds just before dark try to force themselves between the mothers and whimper if they do not succeed right away. The followers usually sleep alone, so they often enjoy a degree of comfort denied to the males that have females clustered around them: they can stretch out on their sides.

There are twelve hours of night in the tropics. Because baboons, like all higher primates except the night monkeys of South America, are day animals dependent on their eyes, they are incapacitated by darkness for many hours, just as our ancestors were before they had control of fire. The baboons do not sleep straight through. Several times during a night a scolding sound is heard here or there, as though someone were jostling for a better place, or there are one or two "baahu" calls, perhaps in response to a hyena or leopard near the cliff. On each such occasion the excitement subsides with a chorus of deep contact-rumbling, which is also used to mark the end of a fight and to greet the sun after a storm and seems to mean something like "it is over now, we are all peaceful together."

Even today we do not know whether individual baboons do secret, significant things during the night—in particular, whether followers slink up to receptive females. With modern night-vision devices that amplify starlight, it would be possible to find out. In those days, however, when the cliff was wrapped in darkness, we too went home to our tents.

In the early morning, when the silhouettes of the now-familiar boulders and bushes take shape against the first yellow shimmer in the sky, we climb back to our observation post. On the cliff opposite us, occasional shadows move up the wall to the rest area. In the dry season the nights are cold, often no more than 50°F. Early in the morning the buttocks of the baboons are pale and bluish. As the light grows stronger they crowd together in small groups and wait motionless for the sun. Each huddled group includes only one adult male. Our advisers in Frankfurt, Starck and Frick, suspected that hamadryas form "families" or one-male groups, but before we can be certain that that is what we are seeing, we have to prove that each such group always consists of the same individuals. The followers cower alone a few steps away from their families, holding their elbows clamped between knees and flanks. Their social separation also means that they must be colder than the others.

The sun finally reaches the upper ridge of the sleeping cliff, which faces

Fig. 14. After long marches, the baboons already fall asleep in the early twilight. The female to the right of the male has to anchor herself in a fissure even while she sleeps.

west. The troop now comes alive, with grooming, playing, and a little sex. In these first days we are writing down what the whole gathering and certain recognizable small groups are doing, without a fixed program of data collection. The idea is to keep our minds open for any sign of order, large-scale or small; none of the many thoughts that occur to us is rejected and none is firmly recorded. Two males are chasing one another along the top of the cliff, between the bushes; they change roles several times, never touch one another, and end the chase with neither one victorious as far as I can tell. "Did you see that?" I want to whisper to Fred Kurt, but I restrain myself. I had suggested to Fred that during the first weeks we should not share our impressions and ideas. Each new coworker in a project brings the chance of a new way of seeing things, and I did not want to bury this opportunity under a cascade of my earlier thoughts. Over there, now and again a small group of baboons moves farther up toward the ridge and sits down again. Not until the sun has been up for one or two hours does this movement extend to the whole troop. This is the sign of general departure. Against the sunlight, their mantles fringed in silver, the last males disappear over the horizon.

Hurriedly we pack up our notebooks and backpacks, run between bushes and over rocks into the cold ravine, and climb the steep slope opposite on all fours. If we are lucky we see the troop one ridge ahead of us. It marches continually; we stand still on each ridge, scribble a few notes about the marching formation, and then rush down after them, unseen, until we reach the next ridge. Whenever they can see us, we move slowly. Sooner or later we lose them, because during their rapid morning march their tolerance distance increases to about 600 feet, several times as great as that on the cliff.

At this distance and speed the efforts we were making to record the events during travel were far out of proportion to the results. We could not go on this way; a behavioral scientist should surely be able to think of something better. Our evening discussions increasingly revolved about the question of how the baboons were likely to be observing and evaluating *us*, and how we could use these insights to get closer to them.

Getting Close to Animals

The zoologist's dream of being accepted by wild animals, nourished by Kipling's Mowgli and Lofting's Dr. Dolittle, is actually a prerequisite for a primate ethologist in the field. An entomologist, by contrast, can crouch at the nest of a mason bee or by the transport route of an ant colony without disturbing the objects of his attention; if he just holds still he soon becomes part of the landscape. This makes his work easier, but he will never have the pleasure of being regarded as a conspecific by his animals.

On the other hand, alert large mammals with sharp senses and an ability to distinguish inanimate objects from living beings are not taken in by mere motionlessness. They soon detect the observer, classify him as alive, and become suspicious. Even if he could hide, that would be no use when the animals travel long distances. But with the right kind of behavior he can induce these wild animals to tolerate him as at least a passive member of their community. He can look into the bed of a wild boar, be snuffled by an elephant cow, or have an infant chimpanzee peer into his shirt pocket.

There are two ways to get close to wild animals. Konrad Lorenz brought them into his own house and garden. They eventually became accustomed to him or even imprinted on him, which means that they regarded him as a conspecific and voluntarily stayed with him. He once told me the story that when a concerned visitor objected to his keeping a sand martin captive in his room, he sympathetically threw the bird out the window to freedom. One minute later he did the same thing with a second martin that had just landed on his shoulder. It took a while for the visitor to realize that it was always the same bird.

Niko Tinbergen visited his animals outdoors in their natural liberty; from a sufficient distance he watched them engaging in their ordinary pursuits and confronting experimental situations he had arranged. The two great ethologists represent two ancient forms of the animal-human relationship. One tamed the animals like a herdsman, the other spied on them like a hunter.

Among the younger ethologists, field study is preferred, but even here there are hunters and tamers. Some stay in blinds, camouflaged tents, or elevated platforms; or they drive slowly past in cars, which many animals do not associate with the dreaded two-legged creatures; or they attach small radio transmitters to the animals to locate them from a distance and sometimes even determine whether the individual is resting or moving around. These are the hunters, trying not to be there at all from the animals' point of view. Ornithologists and those who study game animals almost always choose this method, and some of them even use hunter's jargon. Others are the tamers, who want to get close to their animals in the field and are willing to spend months on achieving this goal. Strictly speaking, taming means making an animal so accustomed to you that you can touch it. But field researchers do not go that far, because they too want to influence the animals' behavior as little as possible. Among primate researchers, the pioneers of this "habituation" method have been the Japanese, the chimpanzee specialist Jane Goodall, and George Schaller, who studied gorillas and later tigers and lions.

Primates have superb eyesight. Even seemingly hidden things do not easily escape their scrutiny. One late afternoon near Erer, when I had just discovered Cone Rock, I waited under an overhanging thornbush for the troop that lived there. I was dressed in khaki and sat half-covered by the branches of the acacia, and I did not move as the first baboons appeared on the ridge 1,500 feet in front of me. Nevertheless, they instantly sat down, and the sonorous "baahu" of the leading male was carried to me on the hot air. He had spotted me in less than two seconds. To be even moderately concealed, a person would have to construct some kind of camouflage at a fixed site and therefore would have to know in advance just where the baboons would pass by.

Only once did we try to hide ourselves completely from the baboons. In 1964, working with a team led by the Basel film director August Kern, we dug a six-foot-deep hole next to a wadi. Then we carefully drilled a tunnel through the vertical earthen wall between the hole and the wadi so that the camera objective could have a view into the riverbed. At dawn the cameraman took up his post and was covered with dry branches. From the wadi, along which we hoped the troop would march down from White Rock, all that could be seen was the hand-sized opening in the wall, which we had unwisely made rectangular, next to many round holes that had been left by small animals and roots. The troop did come along the wadi, but hardly had it rounded the bend in the river when two subadult males ran to our viewing hole; one looked in and the other climbed onto the pile of branches covering the cameraman. The latter, fortunately, kept his nerve and stayed motionless. It is not advisable to startle a male baboon at arm's length.

The hunter method is obviously not very promising when monkeys are involved, because anything that looks peculiar is not only noticed immediately but also investigated. The best way here is just the opposite: instead of hiding, show yourself as often and openly as possible. Forget the green camouflage, and wear conspicuous clothing (or even perfume) that makes you distinctive; the animals can then learn to tell you apart from humans who may not have such friendly intentions. Fred suggested yellow sou'westers—certainly unique in the Somali bush, but not very comfortable under the tropical sun. The young biologist Laudo Albrecht showed that the chamois in the Aletsch reservation could learn to distinguish an unusually dressed observer from tourists and doubtless also from hunters. For weeks he stayed in view of the chamois, talking softly to himself and wearing a black-and-white costume that attracted puzzled looks from the tourists. In the final tests the chamois allowed him to come significantly closer when he wore his black-and-white outfit than when he was in normal tourist dress.

Even more important than clothing in gaining the acceptance of animals is the "correct" behavior. Wild animals become restless when a human behaves in an unaccustomed manner—for instance, stands still longer than usual or leaves the path that others usually follow. They draw the logical conclusion, interpreting a departure from routine as a sign that the human has something unpredictable up his sleeve. Clearly, what a tamer must do in the field is to make his animals trust him by letting them learn as quickly as possible how he looks and what he does in each situation. He must draw up his own simple rules of behavior and follow them consistently, even if an infringement might bring him some temporary advantage. The temporary advantage gained by deception or a smart trick suffices for the first shot of a hunter, but it is of no help in the long labors of the behavioral scientist.

This was the plan we decided on in 1960, encouraged by the first experiences of George Schaller with mountain gorillas and of Jane Goodall with the chimpanzees at Gombe. Whenever possible, we approached so that the baboons could see us clearly, with nothing in the way. As soon as they stood up, we ostentatiously took a few steps back, sat down, and turned our attention to our shoelaces, our notebooks, or the sunrise. Our baboons were supposed to learn that we respected their tolerance distance. Within just a few weeks the troops treated in this way had become so used to us that we could approach to a distance of 120 feet rather than 600.

The method of building confidence through predictability worked. It ultimately enabled us to move quite freely near our animals. Apart from its usefulness, this approach appeals to me because it is based on politeness and respect. An ethnologist trying to study a human tribal community from hiding places, using night-vision apparatus and concealed microphones, would seem boorish to a Westerner. After some time with the baboons, I felt a similar consideration. It has long become a matter of course for field primatologists to use the method of confidence building or habituation, because once the animals have become habituated, the benefits of wandering along with them all day and observing them at close range more than compensate for the months of effort required to get that close. In the early eighties, Christophe and Hédwige Boesch spent five years with chimpanzees in the dense rain forest of the Ivory Coast before the mothers with infants would let them come within 30 feet. Under the forest conditions, observation would have been impossible from farther away.

By the end of the first year the hamadryas baboons tolerated Fred and me at a distance of 90 feet by the sleeping cliff and 180 feet during the daily march. The reader may wonder why there should be such a difference, since the "enemy" is the same in each case. One possibility might be that the tolerance distance is shorter at the cliff because there the baboons are objectively safer. That is probably true, but when we systematically measured tolerance distances we found other differences indicating that the hamadryas take additional factors into account. The same troops would allow us to approach them at the same cliff to within 90 feet in the evening but only to 150 feet in the morning. At a given water hole, we could come as close as forty-three yards before they had drunk, but afterward they would flee when we were about 150 feet away. These differences were statistically significant; that is, they were not explainable by random variation. Apparently the baboons not only estimate the objective safety of the terrain but also decide on the basis of their momentary subjective need for a secure place to spend the night or for water to drink. As is often true, these subjective needs closely reflect the objective advantages and disadvantages. For example, if a troop had left their cliff in the evening because we were nearby, they would have had to find another one in the twilight or darkness at the risk of being attacked by a leopard. If they had given up drinking at a water hole, they would have had to make a long detour in the midday heat.

In our longer studies during the following years, the tolerance distance gradually fell to 15 to 30 feet. My doctoral students Abegglen, Sigg, and Stolba were actually able to walk between a hamadryas male and his females from the time of the third field study on. The baboons would hardly have allowed another hamadryas male to do that; they had obviously learned that a human observer presented no challenge to their possession of a harem. In general our baboons allowed women to come closer than men.

I have already said that the observer must not betray the animals' trust by changing his routine when it happens to be convenient. Years later, the baboons impressed me by relaxing this requirement themselves. We captured dozens of members of the Cone Rock troop in cage traps in order to mark their ears. This was a clear breach of confidence, even though at least initially the baboons did not understand that *we* triggered the traps, by pulling on a string from a distance. Being caught and carried away agitated the prisoners, which all the baboons in the vicinity could see. Adult males threatened us just 5 feet away as never before. Nevertheless, the next day the troop again tolerated us at a distance of five to ten yards. They became intolerant only if we captured too many at short intervals. I suppose that the Cone Rock baboons by that time permitted us a certain amount of bad behavior, as they did their companions in the troop. Only the most intense fighting can cause companions to separate, and then only temporarily.

Once achieved, the tolerance persists for years. In 1964 I returned to White Rock for the first time, with the people from the Kern-Film company, to revisit the troop that Fred Kurt and I had finally chosen as our study troop three years earlier. We were incredulous when the adults remained quietly seated while watching us and let us come as close as though we had seen one another just yesterday. Only the youngsters less than three years old, who had never seen Fred and me, fidgeted excitedly and looked alternately down to us and at the stolid adults. Troops habituated to us also tolerated our bringing strange visitors along, though we do not know whether they were merely extending their trust to similarly dressed people or whether the strangers were accepted simply because they were with us, like guests in an exclusive club. This point deserves further study, because if the animals transfer their trust to everyone who looks similar, they will also tolerate a disguised poacher. In that case they would have to be prevented from doing so by deterrent training, and by secret clues given only by the observers.

Having been accepted by the group, the observer must resist the temptation to become an active member. It is crucial not to join in, not to play with a young animal however appealing it may be, but to try to remain an unobtrusive traveler who just happens to be going the same way. Interference with the animals' behavior should be avoided on scientific grounds, of course, but healthy self-interest also urges restraint, in view of the trials a person would have to endure as a full-fledged member of a baboon group. The baboons themselves drew us into their affairs in later years, especially when it appeared to be useful to them. The nomads in this region dig water holes for themselves in the sandy riverbeds, and they try to protect these sites from baboons by surrounding them with thorny hedges and by throwing stones. When Alex Stolba and Hans Sigg first came to such drinking places with their baboons, the stones flew and the animals fled. Then Alex and Hans would discuss the matter with the defenders of the hole, explaining to them that the hamadryas were their own herds, just as goats were those of the nomads. This seemed plausible to the Somalis. In most cases the stone throwing stopped, and the baboons soon noticed. Before long they would hide in the bush nearby while the negotiations were going on, even keeping the youngsters as quiet as mice by some mysterious means. On one occasion they were so well hidden that their ethologist shepherds could not detect them when the parley with the nomads was concluded and hurried off under the impression that the baboons had run away after all. Still later the baboons did not even bother to hide; they waited in full sight but beyond throwing distance until the humans had finished talking, and then they came to the water.

In one respect the observer causes unavoidable interference: he keeps the predators away from his group, because predators have not become habituated to him. Years later, Hans Sigg noted the following occurrence as he was following the Red Clan of the Cone Rock troop.

All members of the Red Clan suddenly stop still at the edge of a plateau, the males in front at the brink, females and young behind them. The males line up facing a particular place in the bush, where a hyena soon emerges and runs away. The male baboons have arranged themselves in such a way that Hans Sigg is included in their front line, although he has not moved at all. Three minutes later they march off at right angles to the direction in which the hyena has escaped.

This sequence of events could easily lead one to think that the males used Sigg as a means of scaring off the hyena, but the report of a single incident—"anecdotal evidence" in scientific jargon—is not sufficient to demonstrate a planned strategy. Chance circumstances can combine to give the impression of intentional actions; in this case, for instance, human and baboons could have been standing in a line merely because it was natural for all those who arrived first to position themselves at the edge of the drop, where they had the best view. However, considering what we know about protected threatening, I think that after a few repetitions of such scenes the males *could* learn how to incorporate the observer actively into their front line. Our baboons also seemed to exploit the advantage of their relationship with us when they confronted a hostile troop of conspecifics. Then they closed ranks, not just anywhere, but around "their" observer. Perhaps they had really learned to use the human to whom they were habituated as an ally against opponents who were more afraid of humans, and in whose eyes we towered above the troop like Hannibal's elephants above his army.

Very rarely, hamadryas males really treated us like their peers even when there was no emergency. Our animal caretaker Ruedi Wey, who participated in one of the later projects, once encountered the old male of Band I, called Admiral, all alone far to the south of his sleeping cliff, while Band I itself was farther north. When they first noticed one another, Admiral stooped down to the ground. But once Ruedi had approached to within 70 feet, Admiral seemed to recognize him. In any case, the old baboon trotted up to him with the greeting sound, which resembles the play sound made by the youngsters, greeted him with the quick presentation swing used by males, and then proceeded on his solitary way in the original direction.

In spite of their much greater toughness, their dangerous canine teeth, and their incredibly swift reactions, the hamadryas males never injured us. Maybe they were fooled by the same misconception we had at first: they thought that body size meant fighting power. When my wife and our small children were visiting the White Rock troop with me in 1968 and I happened to be busy elsewhere, a large male hamadryas—a "hunk," as the children called him—sat down 30 feet away and eyed them. "Mommy, does that hunk know he's stronger than we?" asked our eight-year-old daughter Kathrin. "No, he doesn't," answered my wife. Satisfied, Kathrin returned to the twisted root on which her toy animals were waiting.

A Day in the Field

In March of 1961, at the beginning of the first field study, we had not even dreamed that our relationship with the monkeys would develop to such an extent. Every day, whenever possible, we wandered along with one of the six troops we knew about in the Erer region, and carefully observed our rules for habituating the baboons to our presence. Our days had taken shape.

They begin at five o'clock, with the jangling of the alarm on the tin box where I keep letters from home. I awaken from dreams about lonely journeys through the world. Salomo, the new "boy," is already busy at the wood fire next to the grass hut that serves as kitchen. It is still dark, but at least the moon is out. The dogs and the last hyenas are howling. Under the acacia, by the light of the petroleum lamp, Salomo puts bread, hot water, Ovaltine, and powdered milk on the wobbly table. Then we fill the pockets of our shirts and pants. The backpack gets stuffed with bread, sardines, and tea (cheap rations, because we were spending more on Emma than we had budgeted for), the ridiculously large straw hats go into Emma's belly, and we're off. The beams of the headlights dance along the bumpy road ahead of us, and, as we pass the cone-roofed dwellings of Canteras, sweep over the village men answering the morning's first call of nature and the women starting fires in front of their mud huts. We turn into the "Chemin du Bonheur," which runs through the emperor's plantation. The scent of orange blossoms arouses tender memories even on a workday morning. But we have no desire for oranges now, because our guts are churning once again with dysentery, practically unavoidable here. When we ask the villagers for medicine, we indicate this frequent problem with the appropriate-sounding Amharic word "chigge-chig?" ("difficulties") and point to their stomachs. They understand.

The governor of Erer has meanwhile decreed that for our own safety we must be accompanied on our daily excursions by two armed policemen, here still called "askaris" as they once were in the Near East. The governor does not trust the Issa nomads. Therefore we must first drive down to the police station. The guard in the sentry box pulls a yellow woollen blanket from his shoulders. Well-wrapped sleepers are lying here and there, but in the little padlocked building with walls of branches, the prisoners are already chatting and laughing. Evidently their wives are somewhere nearby, or they would have nothing to laugh about—or to eat. Now we have to wait until the sergeant comes, and then a while longer until the two askaris are ready, with large hats, U.S. cartridge pouches, guns, shorts, and nailed sandals, water bottles at their belts and their indshera, a kind of flat, moist bread, in a cloth-wrapped, colorful enamel pot. They crawl into Emma's belly and we jolt back onto the road, through the ford across the Erer River and on eastward. Dawn is approaching. After half an hour we leave Emma behind, with one of the policemen as a guard, and trudge north in the sandy riverbed, toward the Danakil Desert. The red sun rises behind veils of dust, the air is soft and cool, and a wood dove calls in gentle tones that come faster near the end of each verse, as precisely as a ping-pong ball tapping out its last bounces on the floor. From a crevice in the ground, two magnificent striped hyenas, almost completely white, flee at our approach.

It is still the dry season. Our riverbed meanders along between rocky humps. Tufts of pale, withered grass are scattered over the slopes of brownish-red sandstone. Here and there stands a short, gnarled dobera tree with green leathery leaves. Under a rocky barrier in the river, a puddle of water remains, in a hollow shiny with mud. As we jump over it, the water turtles hastily paddle under the black projection of basalt. Further on are rows of miniature volcanoes along the banks of the wadi, cones of fine sand about five inches high, each perfectly formed with a crater and central opening. Once in a while jets of dust shoot out: these volcanoes are made by colonies of naked mole rats (*Heterocephalus glaber*) as they dig out their systems of tunnels. Like termite colonies, they consist of one queen, a couple of fertile males, and masses of sterile workers.

In the distance, the Red Rock glows in the morning sun. We feel relieved: the hamadryas are there. High up, on the left and middle domes, the silver males are sunning themselves. According to ancient Egyptian beliefs they ought now to raise their hands in a greeting to the sun. But they do not; they merely begin a chorus of comfortable rumbling as the warmth begins to envelop them.

We climb up a side ridge over rattling stones and settle down on the rocks with our binoculars. A couple of young baboons appear at the top of the ridge above us and peer down, alternating threats against us with side glances toward the adults. The adults, however, know us already and continue to groom one another undisturbed. Only when a bird gives a warning call or a stone falls do the adults, too, give us a quick look, as though we were to blame for everything unusual that might happen today. Not illogical.

At eight o'clock the troop leaves for the day, streaming down over the ridge of rock to a clump of acacias on the wadi's bank. Then one band branches off and ascends the steep slope on the other side. Soon they are far ahead and disappear into a bushy gully. We jump down onto the sand in its cool bed and pull ourselves up the opposite wall of earth by clinging to a dobera root, not having observed the more convenient route that the baboons had used to leave the gully.

The pace is demanding even for our askari; during the hour after the baboons' departure we must sometimes trot at five miles an hour to keep up with them. Once, we lose the troop because our bodyguard cannot climb a rocky slope in his wide sandals. On several occasions we have to venture out again at night to look for a lost policeman. We share our bread with the askaris, but sometimes they decline the offer; later we learned that those were days of fasting for Muslims. No wonder then that they run out of energy. But to us they say nothing, and none ever complains of exhaustion. As the demands of the work become clearer, more and more often Muhammad is sent with us, a small wiry man with aquiline nose and mustache. On account of his agility, Fred calls him Rumpelstiltskin. He soon became a good companion, taught us pidgin Amharic, and loyally berated the baboons when yet again they got away from us: "Yet abat djindjero?" ("Baboon, where is your father?"), a great insult in Amharic terms.

It is growing hot and the daily battle against thirst begins. If we drink while moving at this rate we routinely become weak kneed, perhaps because we haven't thought of taking salt as well. At about ten o'clock the pace slows down; the baboons climb into the acacias and gorge on dry pods left from the previous year, or they gather the hard pits of the dobera fruits lying on the ground. Every half hour one of us stays back and takes compass bearings on two electricity pylons, to determine the troop's position. From these measurements we make maps of the daily marches, which document the home range covered by the bands of baboons. Each pylon is individually identified by a number; when we began, we mapped the course of the line, which follows the railway and the road to Djibouti. We take notes about the animals' social behavior (which is quite sparse when they are on the march), about the initiatives that lead to changes of direction, about the kinds of plants they are eating, about everything. As yet, we know hardly anything at all.

Around noon the baboons allow us to rest. If we are unlucky they occupy the few spots of scanty shade under the lacy umbrellas of the acacias, leaving us to roast on the hot stones. Of course, we mustn't displace them from their shelter. If they stop in the denser gallery forests we are better off, but here we have to watch out. While we are emptying our sardine cans, one baboon after another quietly vanishes from the crowns of the trees. Time to go—or can we wait a while? We'd better get up, or we'll lose them again.

To my own astonishment, I find myself throwing an empty sardine can into the thorny shrubbery. Why on earth have I done that, when at home in the mountains I always carry my rubbish home with me? As we walk on, I realize why. In this land, nature is stronger than I—and we tend to protect only what is weaker than ourselves.

The heat makes our heads feel full of wool. At times I believe I can see in the distance the snowy mountains of home, and Fred hallucinates the ringing of church bells. We are traveling over a high, nearly bare plateau. The baboons are digging for the tiny but tasty carrots of *Boerhavia repens*. We cannot spot these roots, because the above-ground leaves have dried up and were carried away by the wind. The plant may protect itself in this way, but the baboons remember the root fields. With powerful sweeps of their arms, alternating right and left, they tear up the stony ground. The older ones proceed with steady sureness, while the young rush back and forth and apparently have less success. Now, in the afternoon, the ground is often so hot that the animals squat while digging rather than sit down as usual. Even we, with our thick-soled shoes, avoid black rocks, and I learned not to sit on hot stones after they gave me a temporary case of piles.

It is one o'clock. We are in luck: our part of the troop is resting again, this time to drink. Only a few water holes within the home range of a band provide water all year round. During the dry season the baboons must drink at least once a day, because the food they eat contains hardly any water. On the rocky outcrops over the few pools remaining in the riverbed, the families gather around their males in the shade. Two males that have no females are grooming each other, while others sit alone. The young are playing. In the next two hours, parts of the widely scattered band arrive at the water hole, one after another. After resting a while, the families go to the water in turn and drink, long muzzles lowered to the brown, motionless mirror and tails raised in a high arch or curled around a block of stone as an anchor. Some dig their own drinking holes in the sand at the edge of an alga-bedecked pool, sit back to watch the clear water filtering into the hole, and then drink it. The baboons also know places where no open pools remain on the riverbed, and water can be obtained only by digging.

Traveling through the semidesert with baboons is like taking a survival course. A human following their example could, in an emergency, stay alive for a few days with nonpoisonous berries, roots, pods, and water. But close attention to the baboons would be essential; there are no domesticated vegetables here but only wild plants, which defend themselves against hungry animals with thorns, poison, and bitterness. Of the lance-like leaves of the knee-high *Sanseveria*, baboons eat only the somewhat softer, white base, and even this tastes repulsively bitter to us. We would have trouble climbing the dense thorn trees, and our thin fingernails would split after a few sweeps of root digging. We could not manage without a primitive stone tool.

The baboons are superior to both humans and the ungulates of the thorn steppe in that they can reach both fruits and leaves high above ground and roots and water underground. The ruminants make up for it with their special stomachs, in which hordes of microorganisms convert the cellulose of woody plant parts, which we primates cannot digest, into a digestible form. In the nomad culture a primate brain and a ruminant stomach join forces to produce a successful team. The nomads find out from one another where rain has fallen, dig wells, and cut off the crowns of small trees to feed their cattle; the stomachs of the latter serve as factories in which microorganisms turn the ligneous parts, which human stomachs cannot break down, into food for both. Pumping underground water up to the surface, as has been done in the name of assisting development in the Sahel, can easily make the team all too successful; the herds become too populous for the sparse grass growing there, and the steppes turn into deserts.

The rest at the water has come to an end. The baboons get up and start back toward their sleeping cliff, pausing to forage here and there. Where food is abundant they fill their cheek pouches; like quids of chewing tobacco, the two balls of food make their cheeks bulge. They chew on them while marching through the next barren zone.

Fig. 15. Nomad women at the market. (Photo: Walter Angst)

The heat is abating. We pass some nomad graves, earthen mounds covered with raw stones, the whole area surrounded by a rectangular row of stones. At the entrance to the rectangle stands a squared stone with an engraved X.

From behind a solitary kraal of tangled thorn branches, smoke is rising. Inside it are round huts made of bent poles and matting, with women milking cattle in front of them. The man calls to us: "Woreá, kale, werrr bijihi erb." In the rough sounds of the Somali language, it is an invitation: you, come, drink a little milk. From the clay-lined grass pail we gratefully drink the smoky-smelling milk, which the women also churn into butter and bring to market (fig. 15). The container is cleaned with a firebrand; water is too precious. We give the nomads an orange, if we have one left, or we let them look through our binoculars. They laugh at the amazement of one man who, when the world suddenly springs so close to him, jumps back startled. Sometimes they also need simple medicines, especially malaria tablets.

At about four-thirty the hamadryas band finally heads for the sleeping cliff. There Fred and I share the work of taking notes. Each of us devotes himself to one of the five data programs, but after an hour the social behavior gradually dies out. The adult baboons sit almost motionless on the cliff face, centered and symmetrical, wrists on their knees, as though meditating. None leans back, supports himself on one side, or crosses his legs, as chimpanzees and humans do. As they doze, some heads sink back so that the snouts are pointing toward the sky. The contact rumbling becomes less frequent, and silence spreads over the hills. When the baboons are indistinguishable from the rock wall in the last light, we leave the cliff and walk without speaking to the road, along the darkening wadi. We have given these rocks and rivers names, and most of the narrow, winding paths are familiar to us. The hilly steppe is slowly becoming our land as almost no other has been. Property is not what one owns, but what one knows.

Rainy Season

March 15, 1961, a rest day. I am squatting in the entrance to the tent, smoking a pipe and listening to the first rain since November as it drums on the roof. The wet dust smells like freshly washed linen towels, but more astringent. My tent has already acquired domestic animals. Along the ropes, columns of small black ants walk up to the sugary drops of acacia gum on the awning. In the corner to the right of the entrance there lives a cricket, now chirping away in spite of the rain. And this morning, as I saw the graceful black silhouette on the tent wall facing the sun, I knew that the lizard would also stay. It lives between the ceiling and the outer roof. When it isn't flitting about it sits on the gable just above the small petroleum lamp. The lamp appeared last week from the tin box of supplies Verena had sent along with me. In it she had packed little presents for me, one for each Sunday of the year.

It is like home in the tent. Wherever we may be, in beautiful places or weird ones, we create our own familiar place: the cot along the left wall, the books on the right, the petroleum lamp hanging from the ridge, and the shoes in the entrance. The floor serves as a table just as it did for the little boy when the adults' table was out of reach. At night the soft, flat ticks come to visit. They force their way through the seams in the sleeping bag and crawl along my leg. I try to squash them between thumb and index finger, but the twenty pounds of pressure means nothing to them; they easily slip out and stroll on toward my body.

Home it may be, but some things have gone wrong. I am worried. Time is passing, the little money we had is steadily diminishing, and our work keeps running into difficulties. I did have a couple of hours blessed by fortune at the ravine cliff, during which I came to understand the system the males in a band use to decide among themselves the direction of the morning departure for the day's march (chapter 6). But then the ravine troop disappeared. For ten days we have waited in vain for them each evening. They must have a second home elsewhere. To speed things up, Fred and I look for them separately, but with no success. The police refuse to accompany us into the Issa region, across the railway tracks to the north. We go alone.

The sick people in the village have established the habit of coming to us in the evenings, bringing ampules they have been given in the hospital at Dire Dawa so that we can give them their intramuscular injections. I have just bent my needle on the buttocks of a thin old man with skin as tough as leather; I close the nickel box containing the syringe, and light my pipe. In the twilight a slender, pretty woman slips into my tent, entering head-first without stopping, and undresses on the cot. Then, smiling, she hands me her ampule. I swear to myself in frustration, and the pipe stem cracks between my teeth. There is no danger of the needle bending this time.

Fred has developed creeping malaria. When he comes into the field anyhow, he is tormented by the bumps as Emma rolls over roads eroded by rain. As he walks, his vision is disturbed. Later the doctor in Addis laughed when we told him the dose of Nivaquine that had been recommended to us in Switzerland; he prescribed twice as much. I drive Fred to Dire Dawa to see the doctor of the Greek colony. We learn nothing new. On the way home, night falls. The road is soft, and Emma slithers left and right like a sleigh. Our two policemen bought chat-weed (*Catta edulis*) at the market in Dire Dawa and are slightly intoxicated by it, but one of them nevertheless holds Fred's rolling head. On a spare tire in the back of the jeep crouches a little old Galla woman from the Ahmar Mountains, on the way home from the market.

Nearly home. Carefully, I let Emma slide down to the ford across the Erer River. The headlights shine on brown waves shooting by, our first high water. I stick a branch into the mud at the edge of the river. After half an hour it shows that the water has receded six inches. The flood is sub-siding, and we are ready to risk the crossing. On the right, below the ford, the river roars over a three-foot high waterfall. To avoid it and lessen the sideways pressure of the water, I aim a little to the left and upstream. Unfortunately, it is deeper there. Stones crash against the wheels, one headlight disappears under the brown, churning surface, and a liquid looking like milky coffee pours through the cracks around the doors. In the middle of the river, a warning light goes on, and the engine stops, though we don't hear it over the noise of the waves and stones. The water must have entered the engine too. Surrounded by grinding rubble, Emma slowly drifts sideways like a crab, toward the waterfall. We strain to open the doors to relieve the pressure, and water flows through the interior.

Now everything depends on bringing Emma to a standstill before we reach the waterfall. Fred comes alive. He takes one end of our rope and works his way to the bank, while I hold the rope as a safety line. Then I dive with the other end and tie it to the front leaf-spring on the left. That done, I send the two askaris along the rope to the bank. The Galla woman, however, does not want to be "saved" and clings to the spare wheel, surrounded by whirling water. So I go, leaving Emma attached to the rope. Damn! The rope barely reaches the bank, and there is nothing to tie it to. Luckily, one headlight is still shining above the waves; it beams onto a fallen tree trunk higher up the slope. We retrieve it and drag it to the bank a little way upstream from Emma, lay it down perpendicular to the direction in which the jeep is pulling on the rope, knot the rope to the middle of it, and roll boulders against the trunk. Emma stops moving. Time for everyone to have a cigarette. There we are, with our project hanging on an old rope. Emma is worth nine thousand francs, nine months' pay. Fred departs for the hotel to get help from Signor Andrea. I go out to the jeep again and try starting the engine, in vain. Now headlight beams appear at the top of the slope. On the way, Fred met the police colonel, who has been well disposed toward us since we spent an evening drinking whiskey together. He had thought he had a wire cable in his car; now he found he was wrong. It is our askari's turn to go to the hotel, and *tolo*, fast. We cannot rely on our rope. Cursing, I take another bath and turn the ignition key, over and over. A miracle: Emma, wonderful girl, begins to turn over her engine perceptibly, and the warning light flickers. The exhaust pipe is probably above the current now. The engine had not been drowned, just choked off. Gas pedal to the floor, clutch gradually engaged, the jeep moves. On the bank, Fred, in his fog of malaria, thinks Emma is going to be swept away for good. He dances about in despair, unable to hear the engine anymore than I can. But Emma is pulling herself toward the bank, until she bumps into an underwater boulder. I have to back up twice more before we finally have our girl on dry land, covered in mud but bravely humming. The Galla granny hurries away into the dark Erer ravine. I take a deep breath: that was magnificent! A couple weeks of hard but quiet work, then an event in which something is really at stake—*that* is what our nervous system is made for, not for day-to-day nuisances with no real significance.

Later someone told us how to drive across rivers. A length of closely fitting hose should be pushed onto the exhaust pipe, with its other end tied to the roof rack, and the fan belt should be taken off so that the fan stays still and does not spray water over the distributor. The battery can manage that long without charging. You might wonder where a hose of just the right size can be obtained: from the rows of boxes full of old things in the Arab market in Dire Dawa. After rooting through them for hours, Vangeli Halaris even found a particular cogwheel for Emma's transmission.

Fig. 16. Emma crosses the swollen Ursu River. (Photo: Fred Kurt)

So in the days to come, we drove through water up to the headlights with no problems (fig. 16). If it was an unfamiliar ford, one of us first waded through with a stick, probing for holes and large rocks.

Two more tips. Worn spots in the gas tank can be filled in with a mixture of dust and soap, and small leaks in the radiator can be stopped with chewing gum. The soap worked perfectly for us, but we never needed to use the chewing-gum trick.

CHAPTER
THREE

The One-Sided Marriage

Guardians of the Harems

You are probably wondering, When do they get any work done? We were worried about that ourselves.

But one evening our luck turned. A new hamadryas troop led me northward in the Brown Pool wadi and there, in a bend, was the perfect sleeping cliff, fifty feet high and curving inward like an amphitheater. From its stage in the gravelly riverbed one could see all the seats in the wall and the gallery above, the resting slope. Only the positions of actors and audience were reversed. The White Rock baboons did not let us down; they became our chosen study troop.

White Rock was situated only a few hundred feet south of the railway gang's house at Garbellucu. The French railway director at Dire Dawa invited us to live in part of the house. This saved us the daily drive from the Erer Hotel, but deprived us of the nutritious suppers with Signor Andrea. No Ethiopian helper except for the valiant askari Muhammad was willing to live out here with us, so we had to cook our own evening meal outdoors over a wood fire. The house was a sturdy structure of natural stone, like a fortress, and our compartment was a small, unfurnished room with a square window opening and a lean-to roof of corrugated iron. The other compartments were occupied by the Gurgure men who maintained the railway, and their families. To judge by their culture, they were obviously nomads; outside the stone wall that protected the house, there was a thorn-branch kraal with a few cattle.

We soon found that we were no longer able to follow the baboons from starlight to starlight more than twice a week, because after such days we were too exhausted even to cook. Furthermore, there was so little social behavior to be observed while the baboons were on the march that all our efforts were yielding little more than route maps and feeding data. The mornings and evenings at the sleeping cliff were the times for social life; or rather, it was here that the relationships between the baboons were built, relationships that during the day functioned almost "wordlessly." Here the data flowed regularly into the notebooks, according to organized programs. In addition to numbers, as the weeks passed, entire episodes and more suggestive scenes accumulated in our heads, and during the uneventful marches and the waits at the sleeping cliff some of them began to interweave. Dim ideas about the kind of order underlying what we saw began to form. The work had finally begun (6).

A hamadryas baboon never sees vast numbers of conspecifics. It knows a few hundred by sight, namely the members of its troop and a few neighboring troops. It interacts regularly with seven to ten troop members within its band, and stays together day and night with only one or two of those: the mother with her small child and the male with his female. This chapter is concerned with marriage, the latter type of bond. It is the core unit of hamadryas society and occurs in no other species of baboon.

Remember that the females of savanna baboons are bonded to their mothers, sisters, and daughters, with whom they defend a common feeding place. The females of a hamadryas family form no such alliances; in fact, they have little to do with one another. The family is produced exclusively by the marriage bond between the male and each female. Their sociogram has the shape of a star, in the center of which is the male (fig. 17).

About 20 percent of the adult males in the Erer region were bachelors. The rest lived together with one or more adult females, and rarely with as many as ten. On average there were barely two females per male. Most of the males, then, are involved in multiple, simultaneous marriages. The later long-term study at Cone Rock showed that the pair bonds last a long time. Some pairs stayed together over six years, and 70 percent of marriages lasted more than three years. However, hamadryas marriages are not life-long, because a male can maintain the status of a husband only for the brief years of his prime. The female becomes ready for marriage at puberty, when she is four to five years old, and stays married from then until she dies. The married life of a male is considerably shorter. Although he reaches puberty at six years of age, he must wait as a follower until he is ten to twelve years old. Then he can acquire his own females, but he may lose them again soon after age fifteen, to a younger male. Hence a female cannot be married to the same male all her life. She, too, has several spouses, but one after another, not simultaneously as the male does. The partners' consensus is not enough to keep them together for their whole lives; when the male is no longer capable of defending his female from competitors, the latter break up the marriage.

A zoologist can identify animals that have this lifestyle just by the external appearance of the two sexes. In permanently monogamous species such as the greylag goose or the gibbon, the male is only a little larger than his female. The hamadryas male, on the other hand, weighs almost twice as much as his female and his bushy mantle makes him look even larger. This sexual dimorphism is frequently associated with polygyny, because the number of females a male can attract and keep depends on his

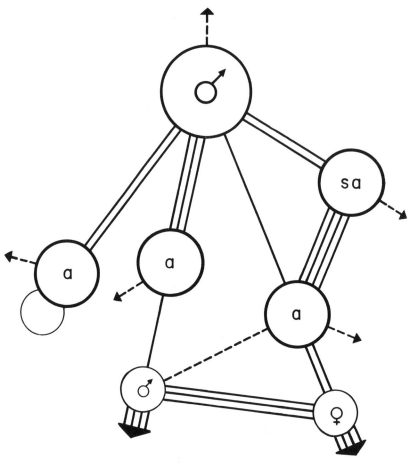

200-min observation time

Fig. 17. Sociogram of the family of the male, Circum. Each connecting line signifies that the connected individuals spent 10 percent of their time in social contacts. The male (*top*) often interacts with his four females (a = adult; sa = subadult), but the females in the hamadryas family spend hardly any time with one another. The exception on the right presumably involves a mother and her subadult daughter. The adults associate with outsiders less than 3 percent of the time (dashed arrows). Small circles represent juveniles.

display and strength in fights. But fighting strength is not at its peak for very long, so the marriage does not last.

The primary sign of pair bonding is that the partners are always together. Among anubis baboons, which have no marriage, close pair relationships are formed only during the days when a female has her swelling; then the male almost always follows in the footsteps of his sole partner.

Although among the hamadryas it is also mainly the male who is interested in the relationship with the female, he cannot simply follow his two or more females, because they are not bonded to one another and often go separate ways. A male that insists on having more than one female must thus make sure that *they* want to be near him. In fact, the female hamadryas baboons do follow the males in established marriages five times as often as the males follow them. Unfortunately, the male hamadryas achieves this seemingly elegant solution only by threatening violence. When he walks ahead, he often turns around to look at his females. Usually he simply waits when they dawdle here and there, but even a minor delay can make him issue threats (fig. 18). If the female dares to wander far away or is actually near other males, he rushes to her and gives her a neck bite (see fig. 41). And now something remarkable happens. Instead of running away from the attacker, like any "sensible" animal, the female presses herself screaming against the ground or runs straight into the jaws of the attacking male. After the bite she follows close behind him, making a quacking sound, and begins to groom him hectically as soon as he sits down. This behavior illuminates the paradoxical flight of the fearful zoo baboons to their menacing Pasha, the only one with whom they found refuge and comfort: it functions to bond the female to her male. In the zoo, this urge was absurdly taken over by the followers and juvenile males as well, and the grooming in response to attacks became exaggerated as the mantle cult. That the neck bite is a particular punishment for a female that has wandered too far away was not noticeable in the zoo, where confinement made straying impossible.

When giving a vigorous neck bite, the male hamadryas lifts the female from the ground, but she is almost never injured. It looks as though the male bites not with the long, sharp canine teeth but only with the incisors, and I could confirm this when I saw a bite at a distance of only three yards. The bite is inhibited; otherwise it would kill.

Although hamadryas males herd their females aggressively, they also take care not to desert them. Once a male waited for his limping female so often that he lost contact with the troop and remained alone with his family. Another arrived late at the sleeping cliff one evening, after all the other groups. Behind him his female was hobbling on three limbs, carrying her dead infant in one arm. An old single male was delayed even longer, reaching the sleeping cliff twenty minutes after the others, but he arrived alone; no one waits for a male.

The anubis baboons in the Nairobi National Park, on the other hand, will leave a sick female in the lurch when she can no longer follow (Washburn and DeVore 1962). In the anubis group observed by Shirley Strum and Robert Harding, near Gilgil in Kenya, I saw half a dozen male baboons flee from a few, much lighter dogs belonging to native poachers; these males watched, from a safe distance, as the dogs severely injured a

Fig. 18. *Top*: A male hamadryas brings his female back to him by threatening. *Bottom*: When the female arrives, she presents her swelling to appease him.

female cut off from the group. They left it to Robert Harding and me to save her, by beating off the dogs with a torn-off tree root and a broken exhaust pipe.

I hope you will regard this defense of hamadryas males with suitable skepticism. In the first place, our moral standards are meaningless for any other species. And second, there are exceptions. When the hamadryas female Narba, of the Cone Rock troop, was very old and had passed menopause, she arrived delayed and alone; her husband had not waited for her. Maybe she was no longer of much interest to him. The old female, in turn, would have made it hard for him to wait because she habitually wandered along at a great distance from the family. Conversely, in the Awash park a male anubis came back from his fleeing troop when two jackals were creeping around an old female that had not been able to keep up with the rest, and he chased the jackals away. In any case it is certain that every female hamadryas has a special protector, who as a rule will risk a great deal for her. Among the anubis the males' help is less consistent, and a lone female is more likely to be left by the wayside.

There are certainly also moments when a hamadryas female voluntarily stays in the vicinity of her male. In a thunderstorm the male sits with his back to the wind and the cloudbursts, and she snuggles up to his chest, on the lee side. When two males are engaged in a serious fight, during pauses in the fighting the females run to the safe side of their male, the side away from the opponent, so that they are lined up to the "leeward" of an attack (see plate 5, bottom, and fig. 22, bottom). And yet it is quite clear that it is mainly the male who insists on an exclusive marriage. I have never seen a female who had drifted apart search for her spouse in a state of utmost arousal, but I have seen it the other way around many times. A male that has lost track of his female can become dreadfully agitated. One female that had just reached sexual maturity hung farther and farther back on the march. When her young male, also just fully grown, noticed and ran back, she slipped off to the side, into the dense thornbushes. He stood up on both legs like a human and looked around, but she stayed out of sight. Now the male began to rush back and forth, called "baahu" incessantly and even suffered an attack of diarrhea. In between he hurried up to an older male with whom he was evidently well acquainted and looked into his face, as though in hope of advice and consolation. But the old one merely sat there quietly and waited. After he had been searching aimlessly and unsuccessfully for fifteen minutes, we lost the desperate young male from view, but we could still hear him calling. If a female is determined not to stay with her spouse, she can make life hard for him.

We found out how strongly rooted a male's claim to possession is a few years later, when we kept hamadryas baboons temporarily in our camp for behavioral experiments. A female had escaped from her cage, but one of our males grasped her through the wire mesh of his own cage and held her fast. All we had to do was put the traveling cage over her.

At the end of that series of experiments with captive baboons, we took each back to its home cliff and released it into its troop. One evening we had just set free the adult male Bacchus, and while driving away from his cliff onto the road I happened to glance into the rear-view mirror. I could not believe my eyes: in the cloud of dust behind the car, Bacchus was galloping after us. What on earth could he want? We stopped and got out, and already he was clambering onto the top of the jeep. In cages on the roof there were some females that we were going to return to *their* cliffs the same evening. Bacchus had become acquainted with them during the experiments and now did not want to be separated from them. We had to push the engine to its limits in order to shake him off.

This experience offers an important hint to the animal lover. Intuitively we had expected that after ten weeks of exile Bacchus would rejoin his home and troop with the same feelings we would have at such a homecoming. Bacchus certainly recognized his "homeland" when he saw it again; it was merely that in the meantime he had developed other priorities.

Affection for a creature cannot replace knowledge about it; both are necessary. This applies to animal welfare as much as to all kinds of aid to humans. *A Good Heart Is Not Enough* is the title of a book by the active philanthropist Regina Kägi-Fuchsmann. In it she tells how, in distributing aid, she allocated the first food shipments not to small children but to the truck drivers, for they could then deliver further shipments. Indeed, a good heart often leads the wrong way. When someone with the same sentimental ideas as we had on that evening "frees" animals that have lived in captivity for years, and leaves them at the mercy of their conspecifics in a wilderness unknown to them, in many cases he is abandoning them to a situation they cannot handle. This has happened, for example, to zoo chimpanzees that have been released, and it would have happened to the famous lioness Elsa raised by the Adamsons, except for the help of her foster parents. When a higher mammal, which needs to learn to survive in nature, is set at liberty without preparation, it cannot survive on its own in an unfamiliar place, and its conspecifics are more likely to be antagonistic than helpful. Anyone who frees large animals must be prepared to assist them in their adjustment to freedom—just as assistance must be given to humans released after a long term in prison. Keeping animals in captivity is a responsibility, and so is setting them free. How would you like to be turned loose with a couple of stone tools into the Ice Age home of our ancestors, into one of the magnificent natural habitats of your species, left to join the natives who would just love to feed a hungry person even though she or he would not even know how to cure a hide or to attach the tip of a spear to the shaft?

To return to the hamadryas marriage: its one-sidedness is also reflected in sexual faithfulness. An adult male never copulates with females other than his own. In eight years in the field we have seen no exception. Rarely, his gaze will follow a strange swelling; but when such a swollen female approaches, he gets out of the way. He appears to be interested in sex only within marriage. Males with few females therefore do without sex for months at a time, because their females have no swellings during the half-year of pregnancy and the months when they are nursing. (The reader may recall here the boundless sexual appetite claimed for the baboons by Gessner!) Single adult males must refrain for years on end. But not the females.

Although all sexually mature females are married, during the swelling period they readily take advantage of opportunities for quick copulation with a juvenile or subadult male—but only behind their mate's back, because if he notices, he will attack. And *she* will be the one to receive the neck bite, not the young suitor. Such escapades, which the female often initiates by presenting, do not seriously endanger her spouse's monopoly on fatherhood, because hamadryas baboons must copulate several times in rapid succession before ejaculation occurs. The male is too watchful to let things go that far. Only the young girls in his family are kept on a looser rein, and they are not very interesting to him during their swelling period. This leads to amusing scenes like those observed in the zoo, in which the girl rapidly mates with a sexually immature male behind a rock, then nervously hurries to the head of the family and presents to him or saunters with conspicuous casualness on a meandering stroll in front of him, only to rush back after a suitable interval to the lover waiting for her in hiding. Only adult males, then, respect the marriage bond. Whether this is really "faithfulness" or some kind of opportunism will be examined in the section on respect for possession (chapter 4).

Any idea that hamadryas females might be inclined toward exclusivity in marriage would also be called into doubt by the fact that they have retained the monthly swelling of the savanna baboons, which have no marriages. A swelling is a signal over long distances; it attracts many males and could be beneficial to the female because it gives her more choice. This might perhaps explain why female hamadryas have not lost this often troublesome swelling in the course of evolution: it gives them a chance of attracting a male outside marriage. On the other hand, to give up the swelling would offer the advantage that only a female herself would know her time of ovulation, by internal physiological signs, as long as she could prevent the males from checking her scent. Unhampered by courtship and fighting, an unattached female could pick out the partner she wanted at the right moment. However, this strategy is unavailable to the female hamadryas, as she is under constant guard. Therefore she has kept the swelling, a relic of her free-ranging savanna ancestors, as a call from the harem to potential abductors. The genital swelling is a flexible socio-sexual tool. When a female is actually taken over by another male, she is able to produce a swelling even while she is lactating (Colmenares and Gomendio 1988), and some young females far too small to give birth develop a little swelling when they enter their first marriage before they even have reached puberty (chapter 5).

Why, then, have male hamadryas baboons departed from the basic pattern of the baboon and macaque species—that of a sexual relationship that lasts only hours or days—and imposed a one-sided long-term marriage on their females? Is it really better for a male to herd his females year in and year out than to follow a female only during the rare days of her swelling, defeating all rivals, as male anubis do? This question could be answered satisfactorily only if there were still some nonherding hamadryas males to compete, in the same troop, with herding, marriage-forming males. We have never found such males; the strategy of herding has been universally adopted by the hamadryas. However, we obtained the next-best answers from certain natural experiments—encounters between nonherding anubis males and herding hamadryas males in the same troop.

At Stapelia Rock, a tree-filled gorge cut deep into the arid plain to the east of Awash, for some time a powerful, dark anubis male lived in the resident hamadryas troop. He had probably wandered in from the Ahmar Mountains. He was larger than his hamadryas colleagues, and they obviously respected him. Once the anubis tried to take possession of a female by fighting her relatively puny hamadryas male. After each round of the fight, the smaller hamadryas ran straight to his female and took her into his arms with the demonstrative possession embrace. The anubis was like the hare in the story about the race with the tortoise: no matter how hard he tried, his opponent always came to the finish line first. The anubis gave up. We never saw him with a female.

This observation, of course, was not entirely conclusive. The anubis might have escaped from captivity and therefore have been inexperienced, or as an outsider he might have felt insecure. Perhaps the female herself preferred the hamadryas male to one not of her own species. None of these objections apply to the participants in the second natural experiment. The story circulated among us as the "Rape of the Sabine." It happened in 1968, during the second field study, for which we had chosen the falls of the Awash River as our base of operations. The Awash plunges eastward over the falls, into a canyon crowned by rock walls at its uppermost edges. We knew that the ranges of the hamadryas and the anubis baboons met somewhere in this area. In that study my student Ueli Nagel was looking for the boundary; if he found hybrids there, he wanted to observe their marital behavior (9). After a few weeks he reported that anubis groups were living above the falls in the gallery forests, hamadryas baboons twelve miles downstream at the lower end of the canyon, and troops of hybrids in the canyon itself.

One evening at this time I visited a troop of hybrids with predominantly anubis characteristics at their sleeping cliff on the rim of the canyon. Incredulous, I saw a single hamadryas male crouching on the steep slope at the foot of the cliff and embracing an anubis female—in fact, one with a swelling, so that she was also attractive to the resident anubis males. The hamadryas was a young male and had no other females with him. He hugged the anubis female tightly and peered up into the rocks, from which a powerful anubis male was descending. Reaching the bottom, the anubis charged toward the pair with jaws wide open. The anubis seemed to be all muscle, the hamadryas half hair. But the latter was not abashed by his relative weakness. He let go of the female and did battle, but only for seconds. Then he ran back to the female, held her and showed his teeth threateningly. This sequence recurred several times, each time with the same effect, as in the scene at Stapelia Rock. The giant anubis eventually climbed back onto the cliff, where his troop had already settled on the ledges. Then the whole affair was repeated with another challenger and ended in the same way: this anubis also gave up. Now the hamadryas tried to lead the female away. He walked a couple of steps away from her, looked back over his shoulder and threatened her when he saw she was not following—but to no avail. The anubis female was not used to following, and this sequence of signals seemed to mean nothing to her. All the hamadryas could do was prevent her from escaping, by biting her neck. Whenever he did so, she pressed herself against the ground and remained motionless next to him. An attempted abduction was underway here, but the prospects did not seem rosy. In the last light I saw the two of them squatting alone on the open slope under the cliff. As a stranger, the hamadryas preferred to keep away from the troop even at the risk of being surprised by a leopard.

In the half-light of dawn the couple were still down below, a pair of gray lumps, and the female was still refusing to be led. Finally the troop departed for the day and no one bothered with the group member held prisoner by the stranger, not even the challengers from the previous night. The abductor needed only to let the troop go, preventing the female from going along by blocking her way with threats. When the last ones had disappeared up the canyon, he left his prisoner and climbed a parched tree. From the top branch he looked intently after the troop, until their calls could no longer be heard above the sound of the distant river. Only then did he climb down from the tree, in a leisurely manner, and seat himself next to his chosen one. He no longer threatened her, and gradually she straightened up. A quarter of an hour later she followed him without objecting. She evidently preferred the company of her abductor to being left entirely alone. He led her away from her troop, down the canyon. The next day my colleague Walter Götz saw a lone pair of baboons farther down in the canyon, a hamadryas male and an anubis female. She was following him out of the valley, toward the hamadryas country. The herding strategy had prevailed.

The hamadryas troop nearest the species' boundary habitually spent the night at the mouth of the canyon in a thorny ravine behind the Awash train station. The dissimilar pair had traveled in this direction, and it was in this troop that we saw, during the course of the year, more than one dark anubis female, each of which was herded and led by a hamadryas male with no conspecific females. The astonishing truth could easily be reconstructed: young adult males that could not win females in their own troop went all alone to the boundary in the canyon, eight miles away, and took a mate from there, where they were easier to get. If a male returning with his prize had encountered a strange hamadryas troop, its males would presumably in turn have stolen the female for themselves. But he could lead her without risk through the land of the hybrids and back to his home troop.

These individual observations of the success of the herding technique employed by the male hamadryas tempt me to speculate about the period in evolution during which herding behavior and long-term marriage began to be adopted by the majority of the hamadryas's ancestors, before these traits had become the norm. In the semidesert, food is scarce; that is, per square mile and per month it provides few calories that a baboon can utilize. A baboon troop with about fifty members must therefore cover a greater distance every day, to find enough food, than an equally large group of anubis in the richer savanna. However, the distance they can travel is limited by the endurance of mothers carrying infants, or at the point where more energy is consumed than the food can provide. The solution is to split up the troop for the daily excursions, because fewer baboons would have to go less far, to visit fewer woods and root fields, before they had found enough to eat. This relationship between food density and group size, which has meanwhile been proven, was discussed in the introductory chapter.

The smallest daytime group, which never splits apart, is the family unit. At Erer-Gota there is as much as twenty-four inches of rainfall per year; here completely isolated families are rarely seen. The typical foraging group is the clan, with about twenty members. On my visit in 1980 in the Wadi Hesswa in southwestern Saudi Arabia, where there is considerably less precipitation, I found that the hamadryas families were usually foraging all alone, miles apart from one another.

Now imagine a troop of hamadryas ancestors, still in the premarriage stage, that splits up every morning in a semidesert region. The females, like present-day savanna baboons, would have entered into brief sexual attachments only during estrus, and during a given estrus they would form such "consort pairs" with several males, one after another. With no families, every day a new decision had to be taken as to who forages with whom, and we know from Jane Goodall's chimpanzees how much commotion and uproar that can involve. The most intense conflicts would revolve about the females with swellings. Which males would succeed in enlisting them as companions for the day? It was probably here that the selection pressure for herding behavior first began to act. A male with even imperfect skill at attracting or herding females probably had an advantage over the others. He recruited more females into his retinue and fathered more sons with the same predisposition for herding. However, present-day hamadryas males also herd females at times when they are not in condition to mate. This extended tendency to herd must have been advantageous when the families stayed apart from one another for many days in a row. The longer a male went without rejoining the troop, the better off he probably was if he also took females with him well *before* their swelling period was due. On their long travels together, the females experienced him as their sole protector against predatory animals. (Under such conditions even the anubis female in the Awash Canyon followed the hamadryas male, a complete stranger to her.) By the time the hamadryas ancestor next encountered his troop, he may have been so familiar to his females that some of them stayed with him voluntarily. The outcome of this development was a male baboon that had more to gain from bonding to a female without a swelling than from opportunistic mating with whatever partner happened to be receptive. In a richer habitat such as Erer, where fairly large groups travel together during the day, this strategy would hardly have had a chance to develop. But once it had evolved, it was superior to the consort system even here, as the anubis males at Stapelia Rock and the Awash Canyon learned despite their greater strength.

Other baboon species also have ranges consisting partly of deserts or other barren regions, and in these areas they too split up into small groups for foraging. John Crook saw anubis baboons in such splinter groups in the vicinity of Debre Libanos in the Ethiopian highlands, a region of scarce food that is marginal for this species. However, the composition of the groups changed frequently and some even lacked an adult male, despite the importance of such a member for defense. I once saw what such aid can mean at the Awash while observing an anubis group running at full speed across a broad, treeless plain. An old female could not keep pace and fell back, exhausted. She stayed motionless on the ground, but two jackals discovered her and began to lunge at her, snapping. Far ahead, a male anubis had stopped and was looking at her from a tree. He even came some way back but then hesitated, probably deterred by my presence. So I thought I should make amends; playing substitute spouse, I escorted her back to her group.

As a specialist in barren habitats, the hamadryas has evolved small, stable foraging groups so that the troop can subdivide without fuss, "unzipping" itself along predetermined lines. The result is that at least one large male protector goes along with each small group. To forage in a small, protected group is no doubt also useful to the females, but the fact that the group takes the particular form of a polygynous family probably arose because herding turned out to be the best reproductive strategy for the male.

There are two anomalous populations of savanna baboons that support this conclusion. Both live in an environment that demands small foraging groups. In both cases these are polygynous families, and the males of both populations have evolved a herding behavior, though not the same as that of the hamadryas. The first example involves the South African chacma baboons; in barren mountain locations they form one-male units, and the male herds his females as follows. As soon as another group appears, far off on the bare, steep slope, the male chases his harem a few hundred yards in the opposite direction and then goes halfway back to observe the "strangers" (Byrne, Whiten, and Henzi 1987). That is, the male chacma herds his wives *away* from himself; he is not capable of bringing them *toward* him by threatening. The latter technique belongs exclusively to the hamadryas and is indispensable in their social system. Imagine: if a male hamadryas in the crowd assembled at the sleeping cliff were to drive his females away from a neighboring rival, he would simply be driving them toward the equally interested rivals on the other side.

The population in the second example has not yet been much studied. These are the Guinea baboons (*Papio cynocephalus papio*) living in forests with extremely dense undergrowth along the upper tributaries of the Gambia in Senegal. Because food is abundant, the troops are large, but visibility in the undergrowth is so poor that during the day the troop loses its cohesion and splits into one-male groups. The herding technique of these family leaders has been observed in the Chicago Zoo. It is different from those of both hamadryas and chacma and is fantastically varied, comprising no less than sixteen forms of herding (Boese 1975). When one of his females pays attention to a stranger, the male Guinea baboon may content himself with directing a long look at her or stepping between the two of them. If his female is threatened by another baboon, he makes a few hectic grooming movements with her and even continues them, walking on two legs, while the female goes away from his opponent. Sham attacks, blows with the hand, and neck bites are routine forms, also known among the hamadryas, but the Guinea male in addition can position himself like a table over his female, or ram her with his rear end, simultaneously kicking out like a donkey; or he jumps onto her back and shakes up and down as excited baboons sometimes do on strong branches. Whether this whole arsenal is also manifested in the field, or whether it is a matter of behavior that typically develops in zoos, remains unclear. Despite its great diversity, herding behavior among these baboons did not entirely eliminate the contact between families. Females groomed one another across family boundaries, and subadult males, instead of living for years in enforced celibacy as do the hamadryas, copulated sporadically with many married females and did not limit themselves to their spouses until they were adults.

The herding behavior of the hamadryas baboon is more concise and effective. However, we still do not know whether or how successfully the unmarried males try their luck with willing females near them on the cliff at night, and whether much of the nightly unrest is associated with such escapades. Among animals with a simpler brain, this strategy sometimes succeeds. There are certain fish species with harems, in which male followers behave and look like the much smaller females and so can release sperm onto the eggs without being detected by the large master of the harem. These little males are called "sneakers." The hamadryas follower would be well placed for a sneaker career, except that his harem leader is no fish and would never mistake the follower for a female. Nocturnal hamadryas sneakers could achieve their ends only with the utmost cleverness and discretion. This possibility may amuse us, and why not? But if such a strategy were successful, there would be profound consequences for the evolution of the family structure. The more successful that sneaker behavior had been in evolution, the more likely it would be for present-day adult hamadryas males to have specialized for the role of sneaker rather than that of husband. In the extreme case, the hereditary predisposition toward male marital behavior would not have been able to establish itself at all, and the family would not have come into being. The fact that marital behavior could persist even at the densely populated sleeping cliff near Erer supports the hypothesis that hamadryas husbands are not easy to deceive even at night. In Ethiopia I myself experienced how selectively one can learn to hear while sleeping. The droning bass choruses of the anubis baboons in the treetrops above our huts by the Awash River rarely woke me, but one night a small sound I had never heard before, a soft clicking of a male hamadryas in our enclosure, penetrated my sleep.

Wide awake, I went out of the hut and saw lions standing outside the fence. Responsibility makes it important to have this kind of filter in operation during sleep, and I credit the hamadryas with the ability to do the same thing.

Impressive evidence of this has recently come in from Saudi Arabia. Biquand and coworkers (1994) vasectomized four of the five harem leaders of an isolated group as a potential measure of population control. After nearly four years, the two females of the intact male had given birth to six infants, but none of the six females of the vasectomized males had reproduced. Such exclusivity is no longer a matter of course. Since the spread of paternity tests by DNA fingerprinting, animal ethologists find that they have deceived themselves in assuming that what appears as a pair bond is usually also an exclusive sexual relation, and some long-term observations in primates have helped to shake this assumption (Rowell 1988).

There is also a detail of male anatomy consistent with the idea that hamadryas males are successful guardians of their harems. It has long been known that male primates of different species have testes of different sizes in relation to their body weight. The British primatologist Alexander Harcourt and his coworkers made the hypothesis that large testes occur mainly in species in which females are shared by the males. When a female copulates with several males in succession, their sperm will probably mingle on the way to the egg. The more sperm a male has contributed, the more likely it is that one of his will reach the egg first. Large quantities of sperm in turn require large testes.

The situation ought to be different with species in which a male secures a monopoly of "his" females. He need not depend on competing with his rivals on the basis of the amount of sperm in the female's reproductive tract; he never lets things go that far.

Harcourt and his colleagues found that the testes are indeed larger in species with females that mate promiscuously than in those in which each female is constrained to mate exclusively with one male (Harcourt et al. 1981). This also applies to baboons. In the four savanna species with no stable marriages, the testes weigh 2.1 to 3.5‰ of the body weight, compared with only 1.3‰ for hamadryas males. Human testes are on the light side, but the tendency is very slight and will not lend itself as an argument for any kind of herding.

With the Railway Workers at Garbellucu

It was June of our first year in the field. Of the insights described in the preceding section, only fragments had so far crystallized in our minds—

occasional sparkles in the stream of our everyday lives. We were staying with a group of Gurgure people, sharing their house and water. Here are a few extracts from my diary:

2 June 1961. For a few days I have been living alone in our sandy, cell-like room in the railway workers' station. Fred picks up some permits in Addis Ababa. Back from the morning's work. For the third time a slight earthquake trembles below us. Volcanic region.

I have just realized that I am the only "ferenshi" here, the only "white" man. The wives of the Gurgure railwaymen are pounding grain in hip-high wooden mortars and kneeling to grind it on the large stone plate, by pushing a smaller millstone back and forth. As they work, they sing or hiss in rhythm. The chief is called Youssouf. This morning at five thirty, while it was still dark, he spread out his mat next to the tracks, prayed, bowed toward Mecca, and rapidly touched the joints of all his fingers with his thumb.

Mariam, the prettiest of the women, hesitantly brings me a piece of fresh butter she has just made by shaking milk in a black goatskin. To let me know what it is, she points to her hair: among these people that is where some of the butter goes. I eat, and to thank her return the little cup with some jam in it. The women laugh, wrinkle their noses, pass the cup around. Whereas we confidently try everything they give us, it is hard to convince them to do the same.

This morning Mariam, for no apparent reason, took a walk outside my window as I was looking out of it, searching for baboons with the binoculars. She stopped on a hill and twisted gently from one side to the other without moving her feet. Later, when for no apparent reason I chose the same spot to gather firewood, she stood at her window, looked at herself in a small mirror with a red wooden frame, and stroked her eyebrows with a stick of kohl, a mischievous smile on her lips.

The heat is oppressive even when I'm sitting quietly. How elegantly the girl pounds the grain in the mortar. They are shy. Only the granny, swathed in brown cloth, is as sweet and friendly as a grandmother at home—the freedom of the old woman. Noon: the shadow of the little pigeon in the dust outside the door could have been positioned with a plumb line. The cock with the scaly lump on its leg is panting. It is time to go out. Just now my program is to visit the watering sites at midday as well. Recently I had one of our rare encounters with a snake there. While I sat motionless under leafless shrubs against the rock wall opposite the water hole, a medium-sized cobra crept onto the branches above me. When I moved, it shot away like a whip. My eyes could not follow it. These won't allow themselves to be stepped on as long as it's hot.

4 P.M. At noon today observed Troop 19 from Red Rock at their drinking place ten minutes from here. Data on nearest neighbors expanded by five samples per class. It is now almost certain that the females of a given family synchronize their swellings.

The woman next door has a headache. For the sake of her unborn child, she does not want to take my Nivaquine. Instead she cuts herself on the tip of her nose and lets the blood and the headache run into the dust.

Today I was first aware that I like this bleached, overbright hill country, set off by an occasional black-speckled lava flow and the black steps in the sandy river beds. My head feels stuffed with light. Reason remains but emotions have dried up; worries no longer seem so profound or responsibilities so heavy. Grass husks pierce my sweat-dampened wool socks (wool to avoid blisters).

The dromedaries never go out of the sun. I drink for them. Of all the creatures I can see, the most normal seems to be the gigantic, steel-blue wasp constructing dome upon dome on the ceiling over my cot by rolling a shiny wet ball of soil three-sixteenths of an inch in diameter around in a circle. As the wall rises, the central opening becomes smaller, and when its diameter has been reduced to a quarter-inch, the wasp stops; a second later it has already inserted its abdomen. It stays that way for a while, probably laying eggs. Then it goes away to fetch and paralyze a caterpillar and threads it through the narrow hole into the nest. A lid is fitted onto the nice round hole, and then the next cell is begun. Time to leave for the evening's work at White Rock.

Later. We are lying on the ground in the yard, under the open sky. One of my bodyguards is holding the lamp for me, surprised that I am still writing. Next to me lie two track workers, then Youssouf, and at the end, Abidid, the head man of all the Gurgure. Wearing a toga and delicately perforated white-and-blue Muslim cap, he came this evening "perché sua gente rubare roba di doctor" ("because his people steal things from Doctor"; some of the older nomads still speak the language of Mussolini's colonists). A week ago, when we were still in Erer, the Gurgure removed the backpacks and windjackets from our possession—on the same day that our cook Salomo absconded with part of our wardrobe. He was nabbed at the train station. We asked that he be let off from prison, and that judgment was generously allowed.

The Gurgure chief now wants to spend a week here to see that right prevails. Listening to him is an artistic experience. The others talk but he declaims, sometimes slowly, tasting each sonorous syllable, and then dramatically swinging a vowel upward. Now he is sitting by the oil lamp in his red-checked shirt, with pointed beard and wire-framed glasses, and chanting aloud from the Koran. In the dim light of the fire the slender women walk up and down in the yard.

Then my policemen teach me pidgin Amharic. Recently I tried to get the word for "thinking" out of them. I pointed to my head, wrinkled my forehead, rested my chin on my bent hand à la Rodin. They were at a loss. Finally one suggested: "Angul?" I accepted this, and for a week I began telling them my ideas about where the baboons might be found each day with "Ene (I) angul." Until I found out that this "angul" means "numb-skull." And the fellows didn't even laugh!

Today Mueddin, who knows as little Amharic as I do, shows me an Italian magazine advertisement for vermouth, with a color picture of an Italian port city around 1780. Soldiers, sailing ships. Mueddin asks: "What here?" I reply: "Foreign land, Italia, here Askari, here large animal [I don't know the word for ship] go water Africa, China-land." Mueddin: "China-land where?" I: "There, far, people yellow [laughter], eyes so." He: "You nigigirr?" It takes a while for me to understand. That means language! "Nagara," to speak, is a word I already know. "No, I China language not." Now they probably think that the Italy of today looks like the picture. I say: "Now not so, 200 years finish. Large animal now not dress [I mean the sails and point to my shirt], have auto behind, brrr." So it goes for an hour, with much laughter.

A few months later: The great rainy season is in full sway. Every day or two, raging downpours fill the riverbeds to the rim with brown, thick water. The baboons graze in the tall grass as though in a Swiss hayfield. They cross the rivers at the shallowest places, in long leaps, and when they splash down the rushing water closes over the heads of the smaller ones. The nomads drink a lot of milk and their spirits rise, sometimes too far. Yesterday one of them kidnapped a Gurgure woman from the neighboring kraal, a daughter of Youssouf's friend. All the men have disappeared and are following the young couple. Muhammad explains it to me: when the man asks to buy the woman, he is put off with excuses from year to year and has to keep giving more cows in payment. That is why he has taken her. "Oggi lui fare bum con lei. Suo padre non volere più" ("today he making bum with her. Her father not more want"). Once the bridegroom has devalued her, the price will fall.

Malaria is going around; almost every day someone comes to us for pills. One evening the Gurgure ask about the causes of the disease. Their guess is that it comes from the oranges. Making drawings on the floor, I explain how the parasite circulates, and finally Muhammad also tries to draw a mosquito. He puts the wings on the head. The others suppress their laughter, which bursts out only when he sits up with an earnest expression, absorbed in his creation.

Exchange of Females between Species:
What We Learned from the Hybrids

In our second field study, in the years 1967 and 1968, we wanted to find out what kinds of behavior bring about the specific form of marriage practiced by the hamadryas. If the males impose marriage on their females onesidedly, as we speculated in a preceding section, then the herding behavior of the male would suffice to establish the marriage. The female hamadryas would not make a specific contribution. Our question was: Is flight to the attacking husband, which appears so unnatural, an inherited predisposition of the female of all baboon species, or is it a form of compulsive obedience evolved solely by hamadryas females?

The question could not be answered by observing only hamadryas marriages. We would have been able to record hundreds of tiny signals, but we would never have been able to figure out which of them were critical for maintaining the marriage. I decided to risk an experiment. The idea was to transfer both anubis and hamadryas females into hamadryas troops unknown to them, and then to compare the marriages they made with the resident hamadryas males (8). It may seem odd that we would also release hamadryas females into strange hamadryas troops. These control experiments were necessary for a valid comparison. That is, we needed the females of the two species to show us their marital behavior under identical conditions: while forming a new marriage with a new male.

Because this experiment required hamadryas and anubis baboons, I chose the newly established Awash National Park as the location for our work. It is on the highway that runs eastward from Addis Ababa, halfway to Erer-Gota. In the vicinity of the Awash Falls there, during the first field year, Fred Kurt and I had seen remarkably colored baboons that we thought were hybrids of the two species. Ueli Nagel then found the boundary between the species. To the east of Awash, down toward the Red Sea, was the range of the hamadryas; to the west of it, toward the interior of Africa, was that of the anubis.

It was 1967. I was research associate at the Delta Primate Research Center near New Orleans, and this time my financial situation allowed my wife Verena and our three children to come to Ethiopia with me. I had acquired two coworkers for the project: Walter Götz, a high school biology teacher in Zurich and a man with great physical and intellectual strengths; and Walter Angst, the perceptive observer of the macaques in the Basel Zoo. When confronted with Götz, every obstacle collapsed, and sometimes also a Land Rover axle or a dictaphone. One Walter Götz was crucial to our project; two would have overwhelmed it. Verena often watched with amusement as he and I got together first thing in the morning and cautiously tried to reconcile our ideas about how to overcome the latest setback. She said that during these tentative approaches we scratched our heads as often as male baboons in a conflict situation. Walter Angst was an ideal counterpart to the other Walter—a peacemaker, imperturbable, friendly, and relaxed. If both of them had been like him, the project might have flowed along a bit too slowly; as it was, he was indispensable.

The Ethiopian Wildlife Conservation Department and the Scottish director of the Awash park, Peter Hay, welcomed us to the Awash Falls. Walter Götz and his wife Dali traveled with me ahead of the others, this time by air. While we were looking for troops, testing traps, and working out detailed plans, a group of talented native workers provided by Peter Hay built a pretty tukul for my family, a small round house with red earthen walls and conical roof of grass. It stood under shady trees in the gallery forest on the bank of the Awash River. Peter Hay helped us by word and deed, and I was already the proud possessor of a house in Africa when Verena arrived two months later with the children and Walter Angst.

The idea of the transplantation experiments with the two species originated in my training as a developmental biologist. There one of the classic techniques is to transplant a developing organ into another organism and later compare it with a control organ, one which has not been transplanted, to see what its final form and function owes to itself and what to its surroundings. If the hamadryas marriage were entirely the work of its male component, then a hamadryas male should form a hamadryas marriage even with an anubis female. The female transplant would not contribute anything, because neither she nor her ancestors had lived in long-term marriages for several million years. She was used to mating with one or another male in her group every time she had her swelling. As we already know, female savanna baboons do have special friends—males that protect their children more than others and also have more chances to mate—but a long-term marriage with strict sexual exclusivity is unknown to them.

Therefore we planned to trap single anubis females and transplant each one into a hamadryas troop. As a control, we would also transplant into each of these recipient troops a hamadryas female from a strange troop.

It was a risky experiment. In the first place, we were not sure whether the anubis female and the hamadryas males could even communicate with one another. We knew that the two species have nearly identical sounds and gestures. The partners in a mixed marriage ought to understand one another in general, but they should have different expectations with respect to their married life. In this planning phase we had not yet observed the "Rape of the Sabine," with its encouraging evidence that whatever communication difficulties there are can be overcome. Our second worry was that the experiment would be pointless if members of the two species had no sexual interest in one another. The existence of hybrids in the field is evidence of such interest—but again, we did not know about hybrids in the planning stage. The third question was whether anubis baboons would be able to live in the relatively dry habitat of our hamadryas troops. The presence of male and female anubis visitors in the hamadryas troops east of Awash showed that anubis baboons can indeed cope if they can profit from the local knowledge of the resident hamadryas.

In my application for support that had been approved by the American National Science Foundation, I had described the experiments I intended to do. Now, together, we discussed their logic in detail. Once satisfied, we set up simple prototype cages of wood and wire netting, to find out the regions in which baboons would dare to enter traps and how large the traps had to be. A locksmith in Addis Ababa constructed the definitive model for us. The traps were made so that they could fit inside one another in sets of three; we had two such sets plus the necessary transport cages. The next step was to make a way for a vehicle to reach the sleeping cliffs. I went ahead and looked for a passable track between the erosion ditches. Behind me, Walter Götz used his bearlike strength to roll the boulders aside, and finally Walter Angst steered one of our two Land Rovers between the acacia shrubs to the accompaniment of the shrill scraping of the hard thorns across its paint.

When we were finally ready, an individual experiment proceeded as follows. We lured the females into the traps with corn, and when they were inside we lowered the doors from a distance by pulling gently on a string. We gave the trapped female time to get used to the cage and identified her by marking her with a special dye. On the first evening we set the cage in front of the sleeping cliff of the recipient troop so that the female was easily visible, before the troop arrived. This was to allow her to take a look at the new area, and also to give the members of the troop and the female an opportunity—of which they took full advantage—to strike up a preliminary acquaintance through the netting. Overnight we took the female in her cage away again, to keep her safe in our camp. In the dawn twilight the next day she was returned to the cliff. After a certain time, from a distance of about thirty yards, we pulled the sliding door up with a string and set her free.

What happened during the eight successful experiments with anubis females was so impressive that at the end of the series we captured it on film (see the Film section in the Bibliography). In each case, as soon as the males of the hamadryas troop had discovered the anubis female in her cage on the first evening, one of them approached the cage. It was rare for several males to start out at the same time, and when it happened, remarkably, all but one immediately drew back. After at most a minute only one male still took an interest in the dark-haired, black-faced guest, but he was eager indeed. The foreign appearance of the female did not seem to bother the males. While the troop watched from their seats higher up on the cliff, the presumptive spouse tried to lead the anubis female to the rocks by going away from the cage and looking back every few paces. None of the suitors understood that the cage was preventing her from following him. Therefore the male proceeded in what for a hamadryas was the logical manner, trying to herd the female with brow-raising and sham attacks and even sometimes shaking the cage with a misplaced neck bite. In between he would seat himself peacefully next to the chosen one, who occasionally presented to him. The rest of the males no longer took any part in all this; for them, the new arrival already belonged to her suitor.

When we raised the sliding door and freed the anubis female, two things became apparent very soon: the two partners were quite capable of communicating with each other, but the anubis female was by no means inclined to follow the hamadryas male. As would be expected, the male responded with herding attacks, from which at first she fled. From now on there were visible differences in the tactics employed by the hamadryas recipients. Some repeated their attacks more or less at random, while others threatened when the female first refused to follow and resorted to harsher measures only when that failed. With such precise training, some anubis females learned after only twenty minutes that they should approach the male in response to his intense gaze and at least look cautiously back when they moved away from him. Some hamadryas males began to handle their disobedient females more subtly. One did not threaten his female immediately when she left him; instead, he moved away in the opposite direction. If even then she did not turn and drift along in his wake, he himself would turn and walk around her in a circle until she sat down or even followed him. But if she really tried to get away, he too would attack. The cleverest herder, however, simply went ahead of the departing female, looked back with the "follow me" gaze as if checking on her, but then made a hardly noticeable correction in his marching direction so that it matched hers!

For comparison, on other days we released a strange hamadryas female into each of the test troops. These females, too, were taken over and led by a resident male. As an objective measure of the tendency of a female to follow, we noted how often she sought out the male after one of the partners had briefly gone some distance away from the other. During the first twenty minutes after the beginning of an experiment, anubis females restored the partner proximity after only 37 percent of the separations; in the remaining 63 percent the male had to do so. In contrast, the hamadryas females during these first twenty minutes were responsible for restoring proximity 62 percent of the time. At the end of the first hour, however, the anubis females had caught up; now they restored proximity 57 percent of the time and the hamadryas females 63 percent. Therefore, on average for all experiments, the hamadryas males had succeeded in training the females to follow (fig. 19). They had been more successful than their conspecific in the Awash Canyon during his spontaneous abduction of the anubis-Sabine.

This result seemed to show that the herding behavior of the hamadryas male can indeed establish a marriage all by itself. There was no need for the hamadryas females to evolve a genetically fixed tendency to run toward an attacker. Whatever the anubis females had not acquired in the way of genetic predisposition for married life, in the 340,000 years since their species had split off from the hamadryas, and whatever experience with permanent mates they had missed during their own lives, they seemed to make up for in one hour of learning.

But this was not the end of the story. Whereas the hamadryas females in the control series stayed with their new males and caused no trouble except for small disputes with the other females in the harem, the anubis females made life hard for their husbands. After days together they still had to be herded so often that their males finally gave up and let them go. As a result, we experienced the unusual sight of a female going wherever she pleased in the middle of a hamadryas troop. The experiment had shown that hamadryas males can enforce a marital relationship with threats but cannot maintain it permanently. The anubis females mastered the difficult task of learning to avoid threats and neck bites by staying near the attacker, but in the long term they were not motivated to do so.

Phillips-Conroy and her coworkers (1992) made a detailed study of individual hamadryas males that migrated across the species border at Awash Falls and settled in anubis groups for periods up to five years. These males temporarily succeeded in bonding with anubis females, but these bonds were not as close nor did they last as long as those of the all-hamadryas troops at Erer. Some of the females even left their harem when they were in estrus and mated with group males of their own species.

Therefore, contrary to our hypothesis, the females' behavior has also been altered in the evolution of hamadryas marriage. The hamadryas females we trapped became habituated to our presence considerably more quickly than the trapped anubis females, and in the experiments they fled

Fig. 19. A male hamadryas leads his conspecific female down onto the sleeping cliff, along with a female anubis we had introduced to the troop; he looks back to make sure both are following. The female anubis, by nature unacquainted with marriage, learned all the externally apparent customs of the hamadryas harem in an hour.

less often. Hence it is easy to imagine how the difference in marital behavior developed since the two species went their separate ways in evolution: by simple selection. Hamadryas females with a strong tendency to flee from herding attacks left the periphery of the troop more often and were more likely to be killed by predators. The transplanted anubis females may have met the same fate. As time passed, most of them wandered away from the recipient troops. Hans Sigg later saw one of them in another hamadryas troop.

This outcome of our experiments makes me feel guilty even today. It is all very well for me to tell myself many things: that just such misfortunes must have happened countless times while the hamadryas marriage was evolving out of the promiscuity of the savanna baboons over more than 300,000 years; that hamadryas males abduct anubis females at the natural boundary between the species, which satisfied my ethical principle that I should not impose on the animals anything other than what they encounter in daily life, for which they ought therefore to be equipped; that the transplanted animals were used to life in the wild state and that in the recipient troop they benefited from the guidance and protection of baboons that knew the locality. What no one appreciated at that time, however, was the bonding of female savanna baboons to their female relatives. It is also true that almost every baboon—indeed, every wild animal—is fated sooner or later to be left behind and caught by a predator. So I had "only" made it happen sooner. Nevertheless, now that I know their outcome, I would not repeat these experiments.

Human society is a small island of ethical principles in the sea of implacable harshness that is the rest of the living world. When we visit that world, should we act according to its rules or according to ours? Is transferring animals to strange surroundings justified when it is a matter of preserving their species, but not when we wish only to increase our own knowledge? Such knowledge, after all, did lead to the development in Australia of a system of keeping hamadryas baboons that does justice to their multilayered organization. But how ethically acceptable are zoos? After all, they are intended primarily for the curiosity and entertainment of humans, and although the animals are spared the harshness of life in the wild, they are left with the relatively empty life of an inmate.

There are probably no strict, clear lines for such decisions. However, it seems to me essential that the person who decides should have an inkling of the suffering she or he may cause. That suffering should stay with him forever, as it has with me.

Back to our experiments. In Awash we also carried out the reverse transplantations, releasing single hamadryas females into anubis groups. Although no male took possession of them, each of them attached herself to a particular anubis male and groomed him. But when the female noticed that she was neither herded by the selected male nor protected from other group members by him, she behaved as freely as her savanna baboon ancestors must have done before the evolution of marriage. In one case a hamadryas female stayed with an anubis male who did not herd her but who was very interested in her and followed her loyally, by his presence protecting her from the sexual molestations of the young males, and continued to do so even when she was no longer sexually attractive. Not a bad choice, it would seem. But she finally left this male too and lived unmarried. She accomplished this return to the behavior of savanna baboons in only a few hours.

It seems obvious that the bond of marriage of hamadryas baboons evolved on the basis of a lasting possessive attachment of males to individual females. But we must be cautious. Evolution is a change in the genetic material. If the bond had evolved, the hamadryas males' possessiveness would be inherited, and as yet we cannot be sure that the marital behavior of hamadryas is not a mere habit, a modification induced in a standard savanna baboon genotype in every generation anew by the environment. The hybrid zone was an invitation to find out which was the correct, inheritance or the transmitted habit.

If the hamadryas still had the same genetic disposition as the savanna baboons, a young male might acquire his attitude toward females by copying the behavior of the adult males around him. In that case, the behavior of the two subspecies would spread like a custom into the hybrid zone from both sides, and in the middle there would be a balanced mixture. A male would then behave according to where he lives in the hybrid zone. Hansueli Müller (25) refuted this explanation. Each hybrid group was composed of males of very diverse appearance, some almost purely anubis or hamadryas, others more intermediate. Each male behaved according to his own physical subspecies characters (which can only be genetically determined), not according to what his group mates did. In a thorough study at Awash, Sugawara (1988) confirmed and differentiated these results, showing, for example, that males morphologically close to pure hamadryas had more females than anubis-like males.

If, as this suggests, male marital behavior is indeed genetically inherited, a second prediction must be true. Hybrids of intermediate appearance must also show intermediate behavior. Ueli Nagel (9, 12) and Hansueli Müller (25) therefore investigated the marital behavior of the hybrids in comparison with the pure subspecies.

Hamadryas males threatened and attacked females more often than did anubis males. However, they also groomed their females much more than did the anubis; obviously, they bonded their wives not only by threatening force. In anubis consort pairs, the male follows the female, whereas the hamadryas female mostly follows the male. As predicted, the hybrids were intermediate in all three measures. The duration of hybrid pair bonds was also intermediate—five months on average.

Looking at the buildup of progressively well-developed marital behavior of males with an increasing proportion of hamadryas genes, one could even guess how the marital inclination of the hamadryas first began. Males with only a slight admixture of anubis characters merely showed a more intense interest in females, characterized by friendly behavior toward all females, even those currently without sex appeal. Herding was added only in males of more hamadryas-like appearance.

In the present state of our knowledge, we must take it as probable that the tendency to live in exclusive marriage can be codetermined by genetic factors, even in a primate.

The Magic of Grooming

I had driven from Awash Station north into the oasis called Fil-Oha, which in Amharic means "hot water." In the evening I had observed the troops of hamadryas baboons there and then bathed in the moonlight under the palms, in the cool air and the hot mineral water of the oasis spring, which flows in smooth rivulets out of a clear, cobalt-blue crater in the ground. It was an enchanted night in complete solitude. The next day, after the morning's work, I sat at the wobbly camp table in front of my tent, set the portable typewriter on it, and began tabulating data. I had spread my rations for several days out in the sun, on a tarpaulin, because they had been drenched by an unexpected night rain.

Then two young nomads approached in their gray loincloths and shoulder capes, as usual with spears laid horizontally over their shoulders behind the neck and their arms hung over them. A sudden intrusion of humans into a completely deserted place always seems slightly terrifying to me. When confronted by a wild animal I can estimate fairly well what it will do, but not so well in the case of a person of a foreign culture. On more than one occasion in the broad expanse of desert at Erer-Gota I was amused to see that when a person appeared in the distance, looking like a tiny black streak, as we approached one another we would both soon divert our courses slightly, so that we would pass each other a few hundred yards apart.

This time no avoidance was possible. We greeted one another. Then the two strangers sat down at my bountifully laid tablecloth and dug in. I was in quite a hospitable mood and gave them a friendly nod, but when my first day's rations had been consumed I attempted a mild protest. It was dismissed with high-pitched laughter. Not knowing what to do next, I simply kept on typing. After a while one of my guests came over and looked at my typewriter. I did not respond, but out of the corner of my eye I saw on his ankles suppurating wounds caused by the stones that lay everywhere around; we had often treated sores like these. I relied on my ethologically nourished intuition. "Grooming," it said: skin care. The first rule of grooming is not to look eye to eye. "Go to water, wash. You sick, need medicine," I commanded in my horrible Amharic. The thin black legs in the broad sandals remained standing for a few seconds as though bewildered, and then, on the double, they departed toward the well. I brought out the medicine kit and went on writing. After a short time the young man came back. He had washed not only his feet, but everything from head to toe. I ordered him abruptly to put a foot on the edge of my chair and, still without looking him in the face, put salve on the sores, bandaged them and released him. After another minute four legs were standing next to my little table and their possessors said good-bye—to my surprise, very politely, almost reverentially.

A person of culture with an instinct for psychology who has read this passage may not share my surprise, thinking that goodness can achieve precisely such things. However, I did not have goodness in mind. What surprised me was the resemblance between my action, with its effect, and the grooming performed by animal primates. In never looking my guest in the eyes and bending over his feet, I rendered myself entirely defenseless. No nonhuman primate injures someone who is in the act of taking care of it. My food did not appease them, but my medical, caring activity did. From what gray time in the distant past can this root of respect for the physician have arisen? It is certainly only *one* root. On the long road of human evolution, cultures have reinterpreted the role of the physician, elevated it by symbols, and incorporated it into a new worldview by acquiring knowledge about illness and death. But like many another profoundly human behavior, *one* of its roots extends back into prehuman times.

The Family as a Team on the March

Hamadryas marriage is brought about by the male's demand for exclusivity, to which the females conform. My students and coworkers in later projects were naturally tempted by the challenge of proving that the females are not merely obedient, but also have an active role.

Edi Stammbach, as I've already mentioned, showed that when pure female groups are set up artificially, they are not at all helpless and disorganized (20). Instead, they transfer to the highest-ranking female the preeminent central position ordinarily occupied by the male. The highest-ranking is involved in more than 80 percent of all the presenting, mounting, and grooming that goes on in the group; the rest of the females have little to do with one another, but they drive one another away from the central female. Even without a male, then, female hamadryas form copies of one-male families. Their first contribution to marriage is fleeing to the aggressor, and the second is the tendency to be concerned almost exclusively with the highest-ranking member of the group.

Not much of this can be seen during the daytime marches. The family usually travels in an open formation. Here a female suddenly jumps to the side and catches an insect. Over there a male is examining a treetop to see if it offers anything to eat; he climbs up, and those trailing behind him follow into the branches. Minutes later the family wanders over a bare field of stones with cheek pockets full, making spherical bulges in their cheeks. On this unproductive section of their journey, they gradually chew up the food stored in their cheek pockets, until the balls disappear. An infant rides upright on the lower back of its mother, strips a dry leaf from a bush in passing, and gnaws on it for a while in apparent self-forgetfulness. Then it lets the leaf drop as it regards, wide-eyed, a gerenuk grazing while standing on its hind legs. The family rests in the dense shade of a small dobera tree. The mother grasps her infant by its back and begins to pick the grass husks out of its hair, but it twists free, hops like a flea to an older sibling, and starts a little wrestling match. The male dozes a while, his snout sunk onto his chest. Once, twice he moves his hand to shoo a fly away from his face, then lowers his head again with a small shake. From the distance comes a baahu call. The male becomes more lively, scratches himself behind the ear with his foot, and gets up. With a brief glance toward the females, he begins to climb down with long paces over the sliding sand on the red laterite slope to the riverbed. The family wanders farther in the warmth of the declining afternoon.

For his dissertation, Hans Sigg looked for the rules that govern these family travels, especially the role of the females in foraging and avoiding enemies (24). He traveled along with certain families of the Cone Rock troop, in the midst of the baboons, and observed what each of the females personally known to him did in particular situations.

A family is often found all together in the crown of one of the small acacia or dobera trees, gathering fruit. For a medium-sized family, such a tree provides just enough room that the baboons do not get in each other's way. The outer, weaker branches can hold only females and juveniles and hence reserve for them a share of the food that the heavier male cannot take over. The male also hesitates to force himself through the thorns in very dense treetops. Often he can be seen gathering from the ground whatever his family above has unintentionally knocked off the branches.

However, when they are gathered around smaller bushes to pick berries or pods, the family members can get into disputes. Then occasionally something remarkable happens: after a brief squabble *all* of them hurry away and leave the pods hanging, as though peace were worth more to them than those few mouthfuls.

Hans Sigg went beyond the mere avoidance of competition and looked for specializations and divisions of labor in the family. During the pilot phase he made some general observations and formulated his hypotheses.

Then he chose three families, each of which contained only two adult females. The specialization he suspected among the females should be most clearly detectable in such a group.

A family finds itself in particular, definable situations again and again. For example, it approaches the ridge of a hill, behind which it might suddenly discover an as yet invisible enemy. Or it encounters or separates from a larger group belonging to its own troop. Or a water hole comes into view. In such cases, who does what? Sigg defined ten important situations and the forms of behavior that are available to individuals in them. Then he collected the relevant data for the three families. Later he trapped three different two-female families and kept them in an enclosure on a piece of land we rented in the village of Erer, so that he could present them with ecological problems to solve.

That the females of a family do not occupy completely identical occupational niches first becomes apparent in the social sphere. That is, in each family one of the two females routinely stays closer to the male. These "central" harem members are socially active. They groom the male much more frequently than the "peripheral" females do. Furthermore, the central female is accompanied not only by her own children but also by the children of the peripheral ones. The central female also extends her social efforts to neighboring groups. She almost always goes in front when her family's route leads them toward other families, and she is the last to leave the other families when hers starts out on its own again. She behaves as though she is seeking not only contact but also the safety provided by the proximity of her own male and of larger groups.

The peripheral females behave differently. As one might think, they are less socially interested and less obedient to the male, but that is not all. To this independence is added a marked interest in the nonsocial environment—in ecological matters. When one of the three adults is feeding on its own tree or doing anything different from the rest of the family, it is usually the peripheral female. And she is often the first to feed at a new site. As she does so, the male appears to be watching her, as the following scene illustrates.

When the very old Narba, a peripheral female, trailed behind the family and then stopped and stared at a spot on the ground, her own male came back to her and inspected the same spot. When Narba went on, he followed. The males do not pay such attention to their central females.

So now Sigg wanted to know whether the peripheral female learns and knows more about roots, fungi, and fruits. To test that idea with the temporarily captive animals, he would hide ten bananas, ten oranges, and ten vegetables every morning in the grass and bushes of the enclosure. Then he would let one of the two-female families in for two hours. In thirteen experiments the central females found nine of the thirty baits on average, and the peripheral ones eleven. These numbers are not significantly different. Evidently peripheral females do not find more food when finding it is merely a matter of chance and they cannot know where to look.

It was only when Sigg set them tasks in which observing, learning, and remembering were required that differences appeared. For the next series of experiments he made artificial root plants by sticking pieces of carrot onto the tips of painted nails. Before each experiment he buried 150 nails in five different colors in the sand so that only the colored heads of the nails showed. Only the thirty nails in one color had pieces of carrot on them, and the "correct" color was different every day. In each experiment the baboons could learn, after a few mistakes, which color was to be harvested that day. All three peripheral females were significantly more successful than the central females of their families: together they pulled up 204 nails, of which 128 were the right ones. The central females pulled up only 58 correct nails out of 221; this is not many more than if they had learned nothing at all.

Still more important for the baboons than knowing individual kinds of food is to be able to find water every day. Here again, searching is not enough; knowledge is needed, especially when the water table has sunk below the sand and the water has become invisible. Hans Sigg buried six barrels in the enclosures, so that their open tops were flush with the ground. The barrels could be half-filled with water and then topped up with dry sand, so that from the surface it was impossible to see which barrel contained "groundwater" lower down. Preliminary tests showed that the hamadryas could not smell the water. They had to depend on knowledge.

In the actual experiment, Sigg put the water into a different barrel every day, in random order. At nine-thirty in the morning he allowed one female into the enclosure, where the water-containing barrel was open to her view without its sand. Once the female had sniffed at it or drunk some of the water, he filled it with sand before her eyes. Then she was sent back to her family, which had seen nothing of all this. At ten o'clock he let the whole family into the enclosure. There was no water for them apart from what was hidden. Toward noon they began to search for it.

The peripheral females did distinctly better than the others in these experiments. In every trial for which they had prior information, they dug for water, and in twenty-one out of twenty-two trials they dug in the right place. In so doing, they showed the water source to the other members of their family. The central females, on the other hand, rarely dug for water, even if they had seen where it was buried. Overall they found the water in only six out of twenty-four trials. Either they had learned nothing from the demonstration or they lacked the motivation to make use of their knowledge. The second explanation is supported by the observation that they so rarely began to dig at all. But why were the central females not motivated? Could it be that the central females, unlike those in the zoo, were lower-ranking than the peripheral ones and therefore too intimidated to learn? Sigg refuted this idea. Most of the central females were younger than their peripheral counterparts, to judge by their dental development, but they were higher in rank. The explanation is probably that central females are more interested in social life than in knowing about resources. They obtain their security and access to good food from their stronger bonding to the male, which they demonstrate by grooming his mantle. They are able to maintain their status against challenges from the peripheral female by virtue of their higher rank. The peripheral female, however, stakes everything on her greater ecological attentiveness and experience and makes the best of her marginal social position, in which she must leave easily detectable food to the male and his younger spouse. She has emancipated herself and dares to stay alone and apart, exploiting her knowledge about water, vegetables, hidden roots, and subterranean fungi.

In a captive group, where food is clumped and its trivial whereabouts are obvious even to the inattentive, the low-ranking female loses the assets of her potential ecological skills. Her energy balance is poor because she is kept away from the food by the dominant, central female, who sits close to the male at the feeding place he occupies in accordance with his dominance (Zinner 1993).

The wild families Hans Sigg observed also divided their roles when in danger. When a baboon family has discovered nomads or their dogs, it gathers itself together and walks faster. The male routinely positions himself on the side toward the danger. A female rarely walks on the threatened side, and if one does, it is the peripheral female. In such situations the youngsters are carried on their mothers' backs or bellies, holding onto the mothers' hair. The male takes action when a young one apart from the group is startled and cries out. He runs there immediately, even if the little one is shrieking about a harmless bird, a hyrax, or a camel. If something more serious seems to be going on, he carries the young one to safety.

For some time we observers were favorite "dangers." Once I was sitting down, leaning against a small tree and looking through the binoculars, when a tiny hand touched my knee. Without moving, I squinted past the eyepiece and recognized a small female baboon named Cascasa who was known for her curiosity. I would gladly have entertained myself with her, but was worried about the inevitable attack by her father, so I stuck to the well-tried recipe and acted as though I was unaware, continuing to reconnoiter through the glasses. The father stayed away.

Females could provoke their males into wonderful sham attacks on us. Frieda, who belonged to one of Sigg's families, played at creating these inflammatory arrangements herself for a while. As the group was marching she made a wide detour, so that Sigg was between her and her male as they walked; then for no other reason, fixing her gaze on Hans, she screamed. Two or three times she managed to incite her spouse to charge at Hans. Then the male tired of the game and only glanced up briefly when Frieda tried to make trouble.

Once the enemy has been discovered, if the male is up to the challenge he goes to meet it. But when a danger is merely suspected, the peripheral female often goes into action. Sigg found that the peripheral females are twice as likely as the central females, and just as likely as the male, to scrutinize an area of the countryside not occupied by baboons. However, in doing so they keep themselves inconspicuous. It is almost exclusively the male who positions himself so that he is easily visible on the high ground and looks around the area for minutes at a time, evidently not only to see what is there but also to be seen, as the center of a family and a reference point in the coordinated movements of the whole clan.

Behind every visual horizon danger can lurk only yards away. When Sigg's families approached a bend in the bed of a wadi or the ridge of a hill, the one who went ahead of the rest was most often the peripheral female. On the horizon she sat down unpretentiously, often near bushes, and waited for the others, looking into the next valley. If something was wrong there, she would have to be the first to notice it. The peripheral female is obviously the scout in the family team. She is suited to the job by virtue of her experience and her willingness to take risks. Furthermore, being female she is small and brown, much less conspicuous than the male.

If a female were to have the choice, would she choose the central or the peripheral role? Sigg thought of an experiment to test this: he wanted to put a remote-controlled collar on the central female in the enclosure so that he could give her a slight electric shock to punish her whenever she came between the male and the peripheral female. I wasn't happy with this experiment on grounds of animal welfare, and asked Sigg not to try it until I was visiting Erer. To find out how bad the tingling stimulus to the skin was for a hamadryas, we proceeded as follows. Sigg put the collar on a half-grown male and by giving punishment stimuli taught him not to enter a particular square area of the enclosure, marked by four posts. The young male learned this remarkably quickly. Now came the test: the baboon had breakfasted on corn, of which he was very fond, and so was not hungry. I asked Sigg to offer him a banana—which he liked even better—for dessert by placing it in the square while the male was watching. We waited in suspense. The male went toward the banana, but stopped at the boundary of the forbidden square. Then he pulled in his head, ran in, promptly received his punishment, and rushed out again with the banana in his hand. When we tried the experiment again with carrots, he refused to enter the square; they were evidently not enough of a reward.

A punishment that a hamadryas who has eaten his fill will voluntarily endure for the sake of a sweet dessert is certainly acceptable. I gave Hans Sigg a green light—for exactly this stimulus strength. Once more we had learned that our subjective empathy is not adequate as a guideline for ethical decisions regarding animal welfare. What seems tolerable to us can torture an animal; this category, according to my intuition, includes primarily fear-inducing situations. Conversely, an animal can obviously not be much bothered by sensations we would find hard to tolerate; in my experience, certain kinds of peripheral pain are in this category. There are good reasons why our animal welfare laws call for research in this area.

Now Sigg planned to use the three enclosure families to investigate whether the central female could be deposed from her central position by the punishment stimulus. If so, he could then see whether the peripheral female would choose the position near the male, which would now be available, or would remain peripheral of her own accord. In one of the three families the central female did not understand what was forbidden; that is, she evidently did not notice that she was punished only when she moved between her two partners. When she received the stimulus, she ran to her husband as if *he* had punished her. In the other two families, the experiment worked. The central females gave up their central position, and, yes indeed, both peripherals now stayed closer to the male and the juveniles than before or after the test. The formerly central females kept apart and engaged more often in nonsocial activities. However, they were no more successful at solving Sigg's ecological problems. These few experiments are not conclusive, but they indicate that some peripheral females may not adopt their exposed position because they prefer it. Their lower rank forces them to avoid competing for food with the central family members, so they exploit and enhance their ecological experience because they must.

To be sure, not all families are the same. In one of Sigg's three field families the two females were close friends and often groomed each other. In most families, though, such a thing is rare, and females in the same harem can behave as though the others did not exist. The ancient network of kinship alliances among females, which has been found in other species of baboons and macaques, is evidently unknown to hamadryas females. Did the hamadryas males cut the females' net apart when they began to segregate their harems? It is hard to believe that they could have done so against the will of the females. If on average no more than two adult females live in the same family, why shouldn't at least these be allies? We shall need some insight into the strategies of the males to help solve this puzzle.

The Hothouse of Social Behavior

Have you noticed how matter-of-fact and concise the behavior described in the last section was? The signals wild baboons use for communication are the same as we saw in the zoo, but in captivity they are given in more rapid succession and the style is more florid. Wild baboons on their daily march merely keep one another in view for hours at a time, taking up certain positions with respect to one another as the situation demands. They are efficient in the sense of economy, not of haste.

The ways of desert baboons are so parsimonious and those of their zoo conspecifics so extravagant that the comparison as such is delightful. But it is still more important in the questions it raises. How does being cared for in captivity change an animal? Is the animal's behavior deformed in this situation to such an extent that it is meaningless to the ethologist, as many field zoologists believe? Or is something new being brought out here? If so, in what comparable situation do we ourselves live? In the discussions of the zoo baboons' fascination with Pasha's mantle and of protected threatening, we noted that in captivity, where predators and hunger are no problem, forms of behavior can develop that are never seen in the wild but nevertheless are not pathological. On the contrary, they are richer manifestations of a natural disposition within the innate reaction norm; they are not "abnormal" but supernormal. In this section I should like to pursue the question of how this blossoming of natural dispositions in unnatural surroundings, so astounding to the evolutionary biologist, could come about.

Let us begin with a few examples to illustrate the contrast. First, zoo animals not uncommonly invent ways to *use tools*. Something of the sort happened in the Zurich Zoo. Liba, the female who had just passed puberty, and Kalos, the middle one of the three young males, both still single, discovered an unorthodox way to use their tails. During a spell of hot weather the water level in the ditch between the gelada enclosure and their own occasionally fell so low that the baboons could no longer reach it from the edge, with mouth or hand. Then the two half-grown hamadryas lowered themselves backward into the ditch, hanging from the top of the vertical wall by their hands, dipped the tip of the tail into the water, pulled it up, guided the end of the tail to the mouth with one hand and sucked water out of the tuft. While they did this time and again, other thirsty individuals gathered around them, watched intently at close range, and licked the drops from the ground, but none of them learned the technique (Schönholzer 1958).

We are used to dismissing imitations with the disparaging phrase "monkey see, monkey do," but for animals genuine imitation is a highly cognitive ability, which only the anthropoid apes among all mammals have really mastered. In this case, the baboons would have to know that "my tail corresponds to your tail," which would mean that they had the beginnings of an objective image of their own bodies. As yet there is no evidence that baboons have such a body image.

Using the tail to drink has never been observed in the wild. The invention of new movement patterns may seem trivial to us, since we can quickly learn the manipulations necessary for any new activity. Animals, however, at all levels up to the primates are restricted to a small inventory of behavioral elements. A baboon "caresses" another only in searching through the partner's hair. Its hands could also stroke, fondle, or tickle but, surprisingly, it never does such things. Even among chimpanzees, which are much more flexible in their postures and movements, the movement inventory is limited. My colleague Christophe Boesch, while observing chimpanzees in the rain forest of Tai on the Ivory Coast, saw them break up the basketball-sized *Treculia* fruits, with their tough green rinds, by pounding them against a thick branch or root. One day he challenged me jokingly to try it myself. After a few unsuccessful attempts my feeling for tools said to me: "There must be a better way to do this." I looked around and discovered a thin, rough, upright board-shaped root. By pulling the fruit across its edge a few times, I sawed through the tough outer layer and then easily broke the fruit in two. I have too much respect for the chimpanzees to take it for granted that my technique is better than theirs—but maybe it is. In that case the wild chimpanzees' inventory would be relatively meager, containing only the hammering movement and not the sawing movement.

A second example of behavior that can develop in zoos includes *new forms of social interaction.* The technical inventions of captive animals, such as using the tail to drink, can derive from the presence in their enclosures of new situations and materials that are unknown in the field. Social developments in the zoo, however, cannot be explained in this way; conspecifics are present in the wilderness as well. Nevertheless, the Zurich baboons also developed their social life beyond what is customary in the field, as follows (2).

In the semidesert, when two baboons travel together, they usually walk one behind the other; the most convenient passage through rocks and thorns is often narrow. In the Zurich Zoo, when two baboons interrupted their friendly grooming or playing to move to a different place, they would often stroll side by side, in contact with one another, and one would lay its tail across the back of the other. When they were in an anxious hurry it could also be the arm rather than the tail, so that the embracing partner had to hobble on three legs. These are gestures with which we can easily sympathize. But we never saw them in Ethiopia, nor any traces or preliminary forms from which the "tail embrace" could have been derived. It was a genuinely new invention.

Another was the carrying dance. While playing, the subadult males of the Zurich group sometimes placed a younger baboon across their arms, straightened up and rotated, standing on two legs, so that they were swinging the young one around themselves. Among the desert baboons, males at this age had almost stopped playing. The carrying dance of the zoo baboons was never observed in the field.

The gentle biting of hand or foot with which adults in the zoo restrained bothersome youngsters was also not used in Erer.

The tactic of protected threatening, so highly perfected in the Zurich Zoo, existed only in elementary components in the natural environment. Remember that in Zurich a female would simultaneously threaten the opponent she was facing and pacify Pasha, who was behind her, by presenting. This behavior could induce Pasha to attack her opponent. The threatening female prevented the opponent herself from reaching Pasha by maintaining a position exactly between the two of them. At the sleeping cliffs of Erer and Saudi Arabia, we never saw this perfect combination of threatening, ensuring one's own safety, inciting an ally, and blocking an opponent's way. Usually an adult female merely pressed herself against her male, screaming; at most she placed herself in front of him and screamed at her opponent (fig. 20). These primitive stages were equivalent to the behavior of youngsters barely two years old in the zoo group. The protected threatening in the Zurich Zoo was the combination and perfection of behavioral elements that occurred only in infantile forms in the wild. The ritual is so tactically perfect and effective that any observer would be likely to regard it as a fully developed, adaptive product of evolution and assume as a matter of course that it was part of the natural behavior of the species. Nevertheless, it is a product of civilization.

Embracing and carrying were also elaborated in the zoo. In Ethiopia a male hamadryas will embrace his female protectively when neighbors are fighting, and mothers will embrace fearful infants. In Pasha's group the subadults turned this into a role-playing activity, by fear-embracing one another in front of Pasha. Ulysses, who was already sexually mature, could press himself to the ground with no expressions of fear, take little

Plate 1. *Top*: My Bedouin driver Osayis. *Bottom*: The hamadryas and an Egyptian priestess pray to the rising sun. (Reproduced by permission of the British Museum)

Plate 2. *Top*: Hamadryas males with large harems sun themselves in the early morning near Al Hada in Saudi Arabia. *Bottom, left*: A long offshoot of a band before departure, viewed from the tip of Cone Rock. *Bottom, right*: At night, safety has priority: uncomfortable sleeping places on Cone Rock.

Plate 3. Hamadryas country. *Top*: Sparse thorn bushland at a crater of the Fantalle Volcano by the Awash River in the dry season. *Bottom*: A dry valley near Erer in the rainy season.

Plate 4. *Top, left*: An adult male hugs an infant protectively and threatens the photographer. *Top, right*: An infant seeks protection with its mother. *Bottom, left*: Obviously relatives: Rosso and Rossini of the Red Clan (photo: Alex Stolba). *Bottom, right*: A female hamadryas digs for water in the sand of a wadi. Her infant has anchored itself to her tail. (Photos top and bottom right: Walter Götz)

Plate 5. *Top*: The "notifying" male is about to turn to his right, displaying his hindquarters to the other male, and then rapidly depart. *Bottom*: Two harem leaders have come into conflict. The females of the male on the right line up behind him, in his "attack shadow." (Photos: Walter Götz)

Plate 6. *Top*: The Arabian desert at Wadi Ranyah; our camp is just left of center. The baboons survive here only because there is a stretch of open wadi water. *Bottom*: A family on Cone Rock before departure. The follower on the right is looking in the same departure direction as the family leader, while the females are concerned with themselves.

Plate 7. *Top, left*: On the way to Dire Dawa: flute players at the Ursu River. *Top, right*: An Arabian trader leaves his house. *Bottom, left*: Nomad with decorative scars. *Bottom, right*: Karaju nomads amused by our flat tire. (Photos top right and bottom left: Walter Angst; photo bottom right: Verena Kummer)

Plate 8. *Top*: A young nomad woman waters her sheep and goats at a permanent water hole. Here the baboons must give way to the nomads. *Bottom*: Drawings scratched out by our children during a pause in the trip. Left, the portrait of a hippo.

Fig. 20. The females' ways of fighting one another in the wild never attain the perfection of the protected threatening tactic seen in the zoo. In the picture on top, the female cuddles up to her male, screaming and childlike, while her opponent grooms him from the other side. In the bottom picture, the female on the right presents to the male and threatens her opponent, but she doesn't have the knack of driving the other female away from the male and directing his attack toward her. (Photos: Walter Götz)

Seka onto his back, and then playfully enact a rescue scene, fleeing from
the far subordinate and younger Glumo. In Erer there were no such carrying games. In the zoo, fighting and scuffling games took up 19 percent of
the morning time of a male even after he had grown to subadulthood; in
Erer baboons at that age no longer played at all.

Why did the zoo act as a hothouse for social inventions as well? And
why, among the wild hamadryas baboons, do these seeds within the potential of the species never germinate?

One answer lies in the harshness of living conditions in the field. When
the Caribbean Primate Center at Punta Santiago in Puerto Rico released
a group of rhesus monkeys on the uninhabited, predator-free Caribbean
island of Desecheo, my colleague Emil Menzel found that the young ones
in the group stopped playing altogether during their first days in the new
surroundings, and played only rarely after that, which is very unusual for
monkeys. Social grooming was reduced for months. Mothers left their
infants to themselves without supervision, and the infants soon behaved
as independently as they would otherwise have done only after they were
a year old (Morrison and Menzel 1972). Presumably food was in short
supply while the monkeys were converting to a schedule of long daily
marches and learning about new food plants, and as a result the nonur-
gent forms of behavior were reduced from lack of energy. Among the
rhesus monkeys on the island Cayo Santiago of the same Primate Center,
the rate of aggression *fell* when the food supplies were not replenished for
a few days. An extreme withering of social behavior was observed when
the Cariba Dam was constructed. As the water backed up behind it to
form a lake, a few groups of chacma baboons were unintentionally
stranded on an island with an area of about eight square miles; food
became scarce. The primatologist K.R.L. Hall (1963) observed that the
baboons gave up almost all social interaction and usually wandered
around foraging alone or in pairs. In two weeks Hall saw no play, no
sexual behavior, no threatening. Social life can be postponed more easily
than searching for food. We do not know what would become of the
social life of a group in which such a situation lasted indefinitely.

Harsh conditions are evidently the icehouse of social behavior. In the
Zurich Zoo, with abundant food and very little need for physical exertion, social life grew luxuriantly, developed new forms of behavior and
took up 70 percent of the time. In the intermediate food conditions at
Erer-Gota, the baboons devoted only 50 percent of their rest time to social behavior, and a negligible proportion of their traveling time. The
baroque behavioral adjuncts were neglected (4). In the still more barren
region of the Wadi Hesswa in Saudi Arabia, finally, I saw hardly any play
and only a little social grooming, even in the rainy season (26), though

this last difference is not backed up by numerical data. The zoo, then, does not always impoverish animal behavior; in rare cases, and without training by humans, it can develop social behavior above what is seen in the wild. In the next section we shall look for an explanation of this. If you dislike speculation, I'd advise you to skip it.

The Fateful Freedom to Play

What is often so impressive about the evolved genetic system of a species is that it works in such a flexible way. It is not simply a rigid program for the construction and behavior of the organism; instead, it can initiate various programs of development, and this program selection is itself genetically programmed. The genetic system often causes the developing organism to respond to its particular environment by forming characters that are adaptive in that environment. With the same genes, a hamadryas baboon can grow thick hair in the cold mountains of Asir or sparse hair on the hot coast. Biologists call such variants "modifications." Not all modifications are adaptive, but the one affecting hair growth is, and so, probably, is modification that causes primates facing a severe food shortage to reduce their social behavior, especially the energy-devouring games, as described above. Social behavior is no less important than eating, but it can be postponed for a longer time. That seems clear enough.

It is a much more puzzling question why social behavior can *luxuriate* so remarkably at the other end of the prosperity scale. Two possible explanations come to mind: either this is also due to adaptive modification, or it results from the development of free play, which emancipates itself from control by the genetic system. Before considering these possibilities, we must make a short excursion.

The word "captivity" denotes only one facet of the altered environment to which animals in a zoo are exposed: the fact that they are locked up. However, as Heini Hediger made clear, not all animal species in the wild use their freedom to travel widely and have all kinds of interesting experiences, as we may like to imagine them doing. Wild animals are not tourists. Birds and mammals, at least, do have a moderate preference for novelty—or, more accurately, for the right mixture of much that is familiar plus a little excitement. But erratic wanderings are too expensive and risky for them. Even the urge for something new must subserve the most important thing—staying alive. Only desperados, like lemmings in a region where everything has been eaten up, emigrate without a goal.

For many animals being imprisoned is probably not the crucial aspect of life in the zoo. What the word "captivity" does not convey is that zoo and, to a great extent, domestic animals are cut off or shielded from their natural world of finding food and avoiding danger. This provision for their physical needs makes them more like the inmates of a nursing home. Almost all their inherited programs for dealing with elements in their surroundings other than their conspecifics are irrelevant—programs for knowing about paths and places, food and poisons, home and danger, and for activities such as selecting, harvesting, and processing food, hunting, fleeing, and defending themselves. Zoo animals have been forced into retirement and deprived of their occupations. No longer does the environment summon up these *ecological* programs and polish them through learning, apart from a few remnants that are used in eating and in choosing the best sleeping shelf. Everything else lies fallow.

Nowadays social species such as baboons are, rightly, kept in groups. Therefore the *social* part of the hereditary program, which organizes intraspecific interactions, is employed to more or less the natural degree. This brings us to the first of the two possible explanations: luxuriant social behavior as an adaptive modification. That is, if the genetic system could program an adaptive behavioral variant in response to the shutting down of the ecological side of life—a situation that had never previously existed—this response would have to consist in using all this newfound time and energy for social things that ultimately function to produce and raise as many progeny as possible. This explanation is implausible in principle. According to the theory of evolution, the genetic material *cannot* have evolved any modifying adaptations to an environment that never existed in the phylogenetic history of the species. An excess of food obtained with no effort, such as a zoo offers, was certainly never available during the history of the hamadryas species for long enough to have the slightest influence on their evolution. Therefore the zoo animal, with its environment truncated to only the social element, is in danger. If its modification system reacts, it will do so in an uninformed, blind manner and may let the animal slip into macabre practices such as infanticide. Konrad Lorenz and others have repeatedly sounded the equivalent warning for humans. Calhoun (1973) demonstrated the same thing experimentally, as follows. Mice kept in a limited space with an unlimited supply of food ultimately died due to a complex, stepwise breakdown of their social behavior; they were well nourished, but socially incompetent.

And indeed, of the social developments and inventions of the Zurich baboons, only one appears to be adaptive in the sense of furthering the survival and reproduction of its practitioners: protected threatening. This is a weapon in the battle for the central position near the male and hence for the best feeding place, and it is adaptive because in the zoo only the position of the central female is rewarding. All the food is set out in full view, so that no female can use her greater ecological knowledge and sharper powers of observation to turn a peripheral position into an advantage for obtaining food.

In the hamadryas colony at the Cologne Zoo, Werner Kaumanns (1983) found a social behavior that was clearly maladaptive: subadult males mistreated and killed infants. Particularly crass behavior was exhibited by the young adult male M6 at the time when he was taking over females from the older harem leaders. He kidnapped a total of ten infants, in three cases snatching them from the mother's body, carried them off, and mistreated them. Eight of the ten kidnapped infants died of shock or of having been bitten through the top of the skull by canine teeth.

At the baboon rocks in Ethiopia we saw no young baboons killed, apart from one doubtful exception. We regularly observed half-grown males carrying infants away, but they mothered the little ones, embracing and carrying them—although often despite the youngsters' vigorous resistance. The half-grown males in Cologne usually also began their kidnappings in the same way, but their embraces were more violent and mostly turned into abuse. M6 showed no sign of maternal behavior. Infants appear not only to attract tender responses, but they evidently also stimulate responses that may harm them.

In the langur population at Dharwar in India, the first thing a newly established group leader does is kill the infants of the females he has just acquired, that is, the offspring of his predecessor. A few weeks later, the females are again in estrus. In this case, infanticide can be adaptive for the killer. M6 in Cologne, however, killed at least three of his own children. Furthermore, he guarded and herded his new females so aggressively that their health suffered. Both forms of behavior reduced his own reproductive success. Kaumanns suspected that the females and infants were victims of an extremely intensified aggressiveness on the part of the male, which resulted from uncertainties about the possession of females and was unleashed almost at random.

In the Zurich group most social elaborations, such as the mantle cult, the carrying dance, or walking in pairs with a tail embrace, have no discernible adaptive value. The explanation based on adaptive modification is obviously false.

We must turn to the second, more likely and more interesting explanation: that conditions of luxury allow free play to develop by emancipating the organism from its genetic programs. The point of departure here is the following. The strategies of an animal can be evaluated by two different criteria. The first is the *survival value for the genes*: using strategy A, how well can the organism in the given environment preserve its own life, produce and raise children, and take care of relatives that also have genes for strategy A? Survival value is the criterion for evolution.

The second criterion is the *gratification value for the individual*. What strategy will the animal prefer to another if it has the choice? In other words: What forms of behavior and which of their immediate effects act as rewards and are the end and goal of a search?

The greatest importance now attaches to the relationship between survival value and gratification value. From many experiments with artificially varied environmental conditions, we know that animals select their behavior on the basis not of its survival value, but its gratification value. Sex is motivated by affection and lust, not by an understanding of its reproductive effect—which animals are very unlikely to have in any case. This rule applies to all animal species and to a considerable extent also to humans, though for the latter "gratification" must be considered as including the feeling that a behavior or way of life has a personal, social, or metaphysical meaning. In animals it is entirely the short-term gratification value that points the way to long-term survival value.

It is astonishing that gratification in this sense really should be a reliable pointer to long-term survival. This highly improbable correlation in animals under natural environmental conditions is the achievement of evolution. In the long run, selection does not permit any organization of behavior in which actions with high gratification value have a low survival value. The match between gratification and survival value is the result of an evolutionary "search process" associated with high costs and losses, the process of selection. We shall return later to the weakness of this indirect coupling between behavior and its survival value.

A more reliable principle would no doubt be for the choice of behavior to depend directly on its survival value, but that would require brains capable of a degree of insight that not even humans possess, to say nothing of more primitive life forms. The evolution of life began with microorganisms having no brain at all and therefore could not have proceeded according to the exacting principle of insight.

The principle of substituting gratification value for survival value has proved to operate surprisingly well as organisms evolved up to the highest level, but only with one clear prerequisite: the organism must not be transferred into an environment for which its behavior system has not been prepared in the process of evolution. The two values correspond to one another only in the range of conditions in which there has been a long enough series of generations to develop useful behavioral strategies and couple them to high gratification values. A robin drives other robins out of its territory, but it will occasionally also attack red tufts of feathers that an ethologist has attached to branches as part of an experiment. The behavior system cannot cope with such environmental counterfeits, which include all the artificial baits invented by humans. The gratification value for the individual and the survival value for its genes become separated. Zoo animals and to some extent we ourselves live in such an alien environment.

People tend to resist the idea that the criterion for adaptedness in the evolutionary process is number of offspring—that is, the survival value for the individual's genetic program. It is natural that we should, for the reason just discussed: we humans, too, as active individuals very rarely let our actions be guided by survival value, and when we do act for the sake of unknown future generations it is due to considerable insight and self-lessness. Survival value, the propagation of our genes, means little to us. The goal of our activities is short-term and long-term gratification, including that in relation to the higher meaning of life. Wherever we can improve gratification, we do it—even at the price of survival value.

Richard Dawkins once described us as machines that the genes have evolved to help with their own propagation. The analogy is good, but it does not mention that the most highly evolved gene machines are beginning to emancipate themselves from their original purpose. Gratification value, an accessory added during evolution to improve the machine's function, is taking its toll; it is allowing the machines to pursue their own ends even when these are of no use whatever to the genes.

The particular alienation from the environment experienced by zoo animals takes the form of giving them more spare time and spare energy than their species ever had when living free. Under these conditions higher animals begin to play with their gratification system, the word "play" being meant here in its broadest sense. Our zoo baboons not only took more interest in one another, engaging in more sex and grooming, they also invented novelties—social games and new expressions of tenderness. They played at fleeing, rescuing, and mothering in roles completely unrealistic for the individual. Females responded to the swellings of other females. Half-grown males, which in the field keep their distance from adult males, gathered around Pasha's mantle, which had become excessively attractive and fear inspiring. The evolved gratification systems developed their own dynamics and went their own way, regardless of its survival value. This is play in the broadest sense, because the animal released from the pressure to survive can choose more freely than a wild animal how much exertion, excitement, uncertainty, security, and reassurance it wants to experience. It can learn how to maximize gratification in many areas. When humans invent games for their free time and free energy, they establish the rules so that the influence of chance, ability, risk, and comfort correspond optimally to the gratification system. The game should involve tension, but not too much. It is in this respect that a football match differs from a battle, boxing practice from a deadly duel, a marriage for love from a marriage of convenience, a tourist safari from the migrations of a nomad clan. On safari we play in a precisely measured manner with our need for travel and (a very limited amount of) adventure. The Land Rover has radio communication; a real nomad is in a quite different situation. In his travels, the departure time, duration, route, risk, and success are codetermined by external forces, and what happens is often well outside the optimal range of his gratification system. Play is the enjoyment of the inherited gratification system without the striving for a gain in survival value.

A special part of the gratification system is the need for an optimal amount of piquant novelty. This is manifest in animals and humans by investigative or curiosity behavior—by exploration. Like every other part of the evolved gratification system, it has survival value in the wild. The exploring creature can discover new or previously disregarded opportunities for survival, a better hiding place, a new way of processing food. To explore is to leave the familiar for the sake of the unknown. It was only by attending to a novel and superficially quite useless object that, for example, birds in England discovered they could open the lids of milk bottles standing outside the houses and take a sip of cream.

The Zurich baboons picked at the cracks in the ground of their enclosure for hours. Even after sexual maturity, males spent 20 percent of their time examining cracks—for no other reward than the exploration itself. At the sleeping cliffs of Erer only the infants did this, and even they did it for less than 3 percent of their time. Ulysses would devote his whole attention to rolling a flat stone, and each time let it tip over to thump against the ground. If edible beetles had been living in the cracks in the ground, and if the thump had caused them to come scrambling out, he would have made a discovery. However, under stable and meager environmental conditions, exploration usually does not reveal anything new; everything that can be discovered already has been. Drinking with the tail was therefore the only technical invention of the zoo baboons. The baboons probably discovered it while they were playfully climbing around on the edge of the ditch or trying to fish a piece of food out of the water with their hands, and a tail tuft accidentally got wet.

The hypothesis of emancipative development of free play seems plausible to me. If it is correct, it implies something astonishing about the gratification system of the baboons. That is, the carrying dance, the act of walking side by side in a tail embrace, and the acting out of the role of rescuer are regarded as gratifying although these inventions do not exist in the animals' natural life. The system looks for novelties, for further elaborations, even when they offer no material benefits. Is this an elementary component of a tendency toward social culture, even though under the harsh natural conditions it has not yet been able to make any impression on the millennia-old social life of these animals?

I believe that the zoo can become a hothouse of social behavior, because an animal with free time and energy to spare begins to play with its gratification system, as a human does. The zoo baboons had only their conspecifics for that purpose. The luxuriant social and play behavior of well cared-for primates has two sides: a flowering of social life and the chance that something new will be invented, but also the danger of exceeding the bounds of adaptive modification in the alien environment. Our own species has managed both, to an extreme degree.

CHAPTER FOUR

Tensions, Conventions, and Alliances among Males

A Society with Seams

Morning after morning the troop descends from the safety of its cliff and, as it departs for the day, splits up into groups of forty to eighty baboons that set off in different directions. In the hills and wadis, these further dissolve into small foraging groups that meet around noon at the water hole and in the evening reassemble as a troop at the cliff. At first we could see no pattern in these separations and meetings. No leader commanded and organized them. No one hurried indecisively between the groups. It was simply that we gradually had fewer and fewer baboons in sight. It took years and a personal acquaintance with the members of large parts of the troop before we understood what a troop is: the largest group in a multilayered hierarchy of which the family is the smallest unit. Several families form a clan, and several clans make a band (30), and it takes several bands to make up a troop (6). The troop subdivides along the seams between these organizational units (fig. 21). Even juveniles know to which band they belong, and at the sleeping cliff they bring the still-ignorant infants back into the confines of the band (29). The males that together confront a hyena, forming a shield that protects the retreating smaller baboons, are not a random crowd. They belong to the same clan. The horde of baboons that gathers at the water hole around noon, and occasionally marches defensively toward foreign conspecifics approaching the home cliff, is a band. At the cliff and in the feeding areas, each band occupies its special region (27). The troop, finally, is merely a sleeping community based on nothing more than tolerance. It arises wherever a region can feed more bands than there are rock walls. Of all these units, the band is the phylogenetic equivalent of what is called a "group" in the case of savanna baboons, and it probably evolved from the savanna group. The other units are created by subdivision ("fission") and fusion.

This plan, in which units are progressively packed inside larger units, is organized by the males. So far we have learned to know the adult male hamadryas only as herder and defender of his females. Now it is time to

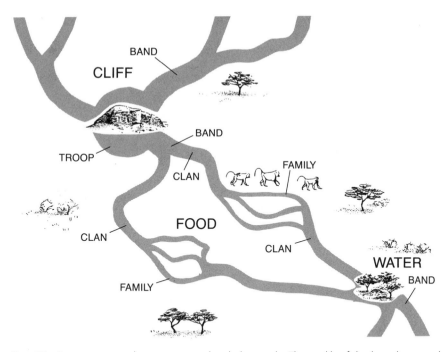

Fig. 21. Separations and rejoinings on the daily march. The width of the line showing the route corresponds to the size of the marching group. The troop, which spent the night together at the cliff, breaks up into bands during departure in the morning. Soon afterward the bands split into clans, and then the clans divide into families. At noon the band reassembles by the water. The return to the cliff, during which the groups again separate and reunite, is omitted here for clarity.

inquire into the ways the family leaders relate to one another and how their interactions give rise to clans, bands, and troops. We first ask how we can tell that these higher units exist. The second question, how the hamadryas baboons manage to create this layered organization, is the most difficult and will occupy much of the rest of the chapter, because the organization is not simply imposed by those highest in rank.

Quantitative studies, especially those by Jean-Jacques and Helga Abegglen at Cone Rock, have shown how clear the boundaries between the units are (29). They can be determined, first, by repeatedly estimating the distances between single individuals and the members of the various units. Within the clan, the members of a family usually travel side by side. The clan members in turn are not scattered throughout the band, but stay together within it, though without maintaining really strict lines of demarcation. On the sleeping cliff, the band occupies its own area within the troop. A second way to determine the boundaries is in terms of frequency of communication. A baboon directs about ten times fewer gestures toward a member of its clan than toward a family member, and there is a further reduction of approximately a factor of ten in this frequency across band boundaries, so that members of different bands almost never "address" themselves to one another. That is, there is no gradual decrease in social interactions from the closest neighbors to those more widely separated, as in a group of savanna baboons that stays together all day. Instead, there are abrupt steps between levels of membership. A baboon either belongs to the Red Clan or it does not. For this reason, the units separate rapidly and with no indecisiveness.

The organization of the hamadryas, with units nested inside other units, resembles the organization of an army. It is also similar to the social order among the Somali nomads, who live in the same habitat. The nomads' "segmentary lineage" system comprises six levels (Mirreh 1976). Here, again, the smallest unit is the polygynous nuclear family. The higher units, like the clans of the hamadryas baboons, are patrilineal kinship groups. The members of each nomad group are descended from the same male ancestor, who may have lived three to six generations ago in the case of the next-to-lowest level, or fifteen to twenty generations at the level next to the top. The functions of the different levels are largely social in nature; they dictate which groups will stand by one another in internal conflicts and for defense against outsiders. Economically, the nuclear family is largely independent. The "primary tribal groups" at the level third from the top are the groups between which marriage is permitted. The large units function chiefly in defense. The Afar tribes around Erer-Gota were apparently subdivided in this way (Saleh 1984), but we were never even able to communicate to them that we wanted to learn their language and therefore could not inquire.

Humans and animal primates in the Somali regions both live in a hierarchical system of groups. Its ecological function was probably originally similar for both: to be able to separate and rejoin one another, in groups of whatever size can best exploit the widely scattered grazing areas, without tedious fussing about who goes with whom. In both cases separations are necessary for the sake of finding food—the nomads for their cattle, and the baboons for themselves. And in both cases the main reason for assembling is defense against conspecifics and, for the baboons, against predators as well. Here, however, the similarity ends. The humans have a genuine language and hence can negotiate with distant groups about use of the grazing lands, and they can load the components of their huts onto camels. Both of these enable them to travel long distances. The baboons can neither build nor transport their cliffs, and because they do not speak in words about distant and future things, they cannot communicate with one another across the band boundaries about how to make use of their range. This ties them to a small range and a few cliffs. They are nomads only within narrow limits. Band I of Cone Rock had a home range of eleven square miles, with five sleeping cliffs (27). However, almost every square mile and all the cliffs were occasionally used by seven other bands, so that the bands of the same range came into conflict on about two out of a hundred nights, as the next section describes. An understanding of the organizational relationships between the males begins with an understanding of their conflicts.

Fights between Bands

Fights between bands usually break out in the evening when a band that does not ordinarily sleep at a particular cliff suddenly appears there (6). In most such cases the strange band can be identified by its members' uncertain demeanor. They first sit down on a distant ridge and observe the cliff. When baahu calls start going back and forth between the strangers and the baboons already in residence, that is not a good sign. Sometimes the strangers will then retreat and go on to another cliff in a forced evening march. Or they may finally, with some hesitation, proceed to climb onto the cliff, as in the following example.

The Red Rock troop had split up on the way home. Part of it marched to Red Rock, and I followed them, while the other part turned off toward White Rock. When I arrived at White Rock at about five-thirty in the evening, the rather small cliff was overflowing with both resident and foreign baboons, but calm still prevailed. A little before six o'clock, on the ledges of the right part of the cliff, two males began to fight, and soon there were three. Normally the troop would respond to such a thing only with deep uuhu calls, and the strife would not last even a minute. Now, however, screams and baahu calls began to be heard everywhere. All the baboons left the sleeping ledges. One of the fighters lost his footing on the wall and fell twenty feet onto the river sand. Immediately five other males jumped after him. More and more baboons threw themselves into the tumult on the riverbed. Some males leaned protectively over their females, whom other males were trying to snatch. Then again they would chase one another with mantle hair standing on end and mouth wide open, or they would whirl in a circle, holding one another and fencing with their mouths. The noise was deafening.

For several minutes the sandy riverbed seemed to be in chaos, with groups flowing back and forth and brief duels occasionally occurring like whirlpools in their midst (fig. 22). Then, gradually, larger units closed up and moved apart, only to advance again immediately, now in distinct fronts; these were the bands. The main line of a band front consisted of

Fig. 22. *Top*: During a fight between bands, the male on the right tries to chase down one of the females (far right) of the male in the middle, but the latter attacks him in time. *Bottom*: The female joins the end of the row of females in the lee of their male, away from the attacker; the former refuses to engage in battle.

Fig. 23. The band at the front of the picture advances toward the band occupying the slope in the rear. A fight has broken out on the right.

the adult, full-mantled males, standing next to one another a few yards apart in an irregular phalanx and threatening their opponents. In front of and between these males, followers scurried about and, screaming like juveniles, looked around repeatedly toward their adult males. Behind the males' front moved the females, their infants holding tight to their bellies or backs. Sometimes a female would dash screeching ahead of the front and then fall back immediately. The opposing band fronts surged back and forth almost in parallel, so that the distance between them was always approximately fifteen to twenty-five feet. Apart from a few isolated sorties, the two lines never came together (fig. 23). It was not until we examined the films that we realized that the "fighters" hardly ever touched one another.

Soon individual males began to lead their crowded-together families away from the battleground as though in retreat, and sat apart with them. There the females lined up close behind the family leader, on the safe side—that is, the side away from the foreign males (plate 5, bottom). By about 6:20 P.M. the battleground had been vacated. Whole bands departed and made camp far away from one another, each on a hill to the north of the cliff. The fight was over.

It now was 6:45 P.M. In the fading light, band after band returned to the cliff. There were four bands, with thirty to ninety members each. As they moved in, the third band turned again to face the final band and drove it back. Then a female suddenly broke away from the midst of the attackers and rushed across the space between the fronts, into the arms of a male of the retreating band. She had probably been abducted and was now fleeing back to her own male. By the time darkness had fallen, all the bands were on the cliff. However, in the twilight of the next dawn the tumult broke loose again. Even before it was light, long before the customary departure time, the invading band fled to its original overnight cliff, Red Rock. I knew this because they had left traces of liquid feces, which are always produced in the excitement of pitched battles between bands and which marked the route along which the Red Rock group had withdrawn. The White Rock troop, however, fled in the opposite direction, into the slopes of Table Mountain to the north. We had rarely seen them there before.

In five years of observation, we saw a dozen of such fights between bands. We filmed some of them. They all proceeded in about the same way: first *individual fights* between males over females, then *formation of a front* between the bands with the males concentrated in the advance line, followed by *separation* of the bands, and finally a headlong *departure* from the cliff, either the same night or the next morning. We could never see that one band was the "winner." After the dreadful excitement of the first fight, which gripped us as well, we looked for severely injured or dead baboons but found none, then or on later occasions. Apart from the attempts to steal females, the fights had merely been screaming and threatening contests.

It is still not clear whether the fighting was primarily over the sleeping cliff and then, for certain males, turned into a fight over females. There are two arguments against a battle for the cliff. First, by the time the dispute broke out the strangers had already been settled on the sleeping ledges for quite a while; and second, at the end of the fight the cliff was sometimes abandoned by both bands rather than occupied by the victorious baboons. It certainly looked as though it was all about possession of females. The less familiar the bands are with one another, probably, the more likely they are to attempt reciprocal abduction of females, and the more they fear it. The fights usually break out near and on the cliff, only because here the stranger bands must dare to come closer together than they ever do on the day's march.

The abduction of a female is difficult to observe closely in the turmoil.

The one certain thing is that a particular male repeatedly rushes at a particular female of another male and tries to take hold of her. Usually the husband can throw himself between them and engage the would-be abductor in a duel. When a male has several females to defend at once, he bends over across all of them, holds them fast, and whets his canine teeth threateningly against the attacker. While this is going on, the females press themselves screaming against the ground.

Once a hamadryas fight has progressed to the point at which the bands form fronts, abduction becomes essentially impossible. The abductor would have to penetrate the opposing advance line of males and then bring the female back through it. Most successful abductions probably occur when a female becomes separated from her male in the confusion and finds herself in a strange band—where she is immediately seized.

Individual observations also confirm that cooperative defense of the females is effective: a single male in a strange band can neither acquire nor keep a female. While we were among the hamadryas baboons in Erer, we never saw a male conquer and lead away a female from a strange band. If such a thing occurs, it might be in the dense bush. The male hamadryas in the Awash Canyon was able to abduct his Sabine from the hybrid troop not only because he embraced her after each round of the fight, but because her only defender received no support at all from his troop. Very rarely did we see adult hamadryas males traveling alone over the countryside in Erer, and only two or three of them joined our troops. Our males tolerated this, but none of the immigrants made any attempt to come into contact with a resident female; in contrast, an anubis male that immigrates into a group of his conspecifics is usually able to strike up a relationship with a female if he is patient enough.

Whereas invading bands of strangers can take their females away with them after the fights, a single male hamadryas in a strange troop cannot even keep the females he brings with him. Twice during the first study we trapped a family and transported it into a strange troop, so that we could film a fight with known contestants. The first male immediately led his females away from the strangers and fled with them. The second did not manage to do this; he lost his wives in barely an hour of fierce fighting. After that, the residents left him in peace. They merely seated themselves around him, in a ring about twelve yards in diameter, and looked at him sitting alone in the middle of the empty circle. After a quarter of an hour he got up and moved away, through the circle and off toward his own cliff. They did nothing to stop him.

At that time we did not yet know how severely a male is affected by the loss of his females and what little chance he has of acquiring new ones. Although this fate eventually catches up with every family leader, who will then have his turn to wander alone, I still feel sorry for that male. I am reporting the experiment so that no one will repeat it, and also because it shows us what returning a zoo animal to "freedom" can mean to it. When a captive is set free in a region where wild members of its own species are still living, the outcome is probably worst for the animal if conspecifics are already living there, and it is also least useful for the conservation of the species. Our defeated hamadryas, under the gaze of the conspecifics impassively surrounding him, is a haunting illustration.

The fights between bands showed that a troop is not merely an anonymous crowd defined by the supply of and demand for sleeping cliffs. It can consist only of bands that know and trust one another sufficiently. A band probably goes to a strange cliff for the night when it intends to forage the next day in an area that would otherwise be too far away, or if something unpredictable has prevented it from getting back to its own cliff.

We have seen that forming a front is an effective way of defending the females, but that does not tell us how the front is formed. At the beginning of a battle, males belonging to the same band can also face off against one another, but after a mere quarter of an hour their belligerence is directed only toward outsiders; the comrades they were just fighting are now standing side by side with them and threatening those who are not part of the band. This "reorientation of aggression," in which the attack on a friend is redirected toward the enemy, is an important mechanism for animal species that live in closed groups. It is also not unknown to humans. The tendency to stamp someone as *entirely* friend or *entirely* enemy for a fairly long time, often on the basis of a minor difference in degree of familiarity, gives closed groups their stability and perhaps even makes it possible for them to exist (cf. p. 294). If two males were taken from different bands and brought together far from their cliffs, it is likely that they would be no more hostile toward each other than two males from the same band. The polarization is probably the reason for the abrupt drop in communication density at the borders of clans and bands. It enables the males of a band to close ranks and cooperate successfully against another band.

If this interpretation is correct, the males of a given band, although they stand together when necessary, would also be inclined to take one another's females. In one artificial environmental situation these inclinations were indeed revealed. We came upon it unintentionally when we were trying to lure hamadryas baboons into traps so that we could mark them, using corn as bait. When several pounds of loose corn were poured in a heap near the sleeping cliff, members of the same band crowded around it, so that they were much closer together than usual. Two families were suddenly feeding within an area of barely twenty square feet and intermingling. This was more than even males in the same band could tolerate. They grabbed their females and pulled them aside, dealt out neck bites, threatened and chased one another, and finally each led his closely packed harem away from the feeding site—a picture in miniature of the large band fights.

Distance, familiarity, and careful avoidance of fights, if necessary by the retreat of both parties, are the ingredients that make it possible for harem leaders to live side by side. Polarization of the relationships to enemies and friends is probably the mechanism that unites a group for concerted defense against another.

> I against my brother
> I and my brother against our cousin
> I, my brother and our cousin against the neighbors
> All of us against the stranger.
> —Bedouin proverb (Chatwin 1987, p. 224)

Enemies Stand by One Another

Competition and cooperation are the two faces of the social relationship of animals that live in groups. The young male baboon, newly adult and still a bachelor, that stands by the side of a harem leader to confront another band may be the same baboon that robs the leader of his females in a duel a couple of years later.

Conspecifics are always competitors, because they need the same resources. No other creature in the semidesert requires precisely the same food and lodging as a hamadryas baboon, except for another hamadryas baboon. And no other creature requires the hamadryas females, which as such are certainly only of interest to the male hamadryas. "Lupus est homo homini, non homo," said Plautus of our own species: man is a wolf to man, not a man.

Why, then, do social animals come together with their conspecifics, their fiercest competitors? Why does a male hamadryas not try to live alone with his family? One widespread reason for group life among animal species is communal defense. However, it would seem that communities for warning and protection could be more usefully formed with other species, which have requirements different from one's own. Such communities do in fact exist. According to Washburn and DeVore, anubis baboons in Nairobi National Park keep company with impalas and bushbucks. This cooperation seems ideal, because the baboons have sharp eyesight and the ungulates have an excellent sense of smell. The vervet monkeys in Amboseli National Park, according to Cheney and Seyfarth, pay attention to the warning calls of a particular bird, the superb starling (*Spreo superbus*), and can even tell the difference between its warning calls for ground predators and for those in the air. But species so unlike one another cannot travel as a group for very long, precisely because their needs are so different and therefore must be satisfied in different places. Only conspecifics can stay together permanently. Identical requirements are the basis of competition and at the same time they are the cause for traveling together.

There is one way for conspecifics to live together without competition. The sterile workers in a colony of ants or bees are entirely peaceful and helpful *to one another*, and this is because they can have no descendants of their own. Only their mother, the queen, can pass on her genes; the best thing an ant worker can do in the evolutionary sense is to take care of the mother and her other children, including the future queens. All workers in the colony are programmed for this task. If each of them had her own brood, they would automatically become one another's competitors. As it is, they all want the same thing: to care for the siblings they have in common.

The "higher" animals are very much younger, on the geological scale, and have not achieved the often-admired social perfection of the old hymenopteran and termite societies. At our "higher" level, every individual can reproduce itself in principle and also has the inclination to do so. Anyone unwilling to win in the competition for reproduction will not propagate the genes that produce such defeatist behavior. The many social species of mammals, including humans, must form groups with their competitors, creating societies inherently full of conflict. The psychologist Donald Campbell called this "cooperation among competitors." Such a relationship encompasses both enmity and assistance, and it shows one face or the other depending on circumstances. The hamadryas males are not alone here; they have merely taken the polarity to an extreme. Competition among males for females is especially intense in harem-forming species; nevertheless, the hamadryas males have managed to overcome it so that closely associated competitors can form fighting groups to oppose more distant competitors.

If my readers think this insight into the dual nature of the social relationship is really not new, they are right. Even our generation, however, was still haunted by the naive attitude that saw friends as only friends and enemies as only enemies.

The Bonding of Males to Their Clan

Beginning in 1970, the second generation of Zurich hamadryas researchers went to Ethiopia. Having finished the experimental field study and spent several years at the Delta Primate Research Center near New Orleans, I had returned to the University of Zurich as an assistant professor. Now it was my turn to encourage young people, to discuss with them their draft applications to the Swiss National Foundation, to sign the applications as the person in charge, and finally to provide critical evaluation of their dissertations. Paperwork. But it was interesting to see how differently my young colleagues tackled hamadryas society and life in the field. Jean-Jacques Abegglen approached it as an integrator, making friends with many inhabitants of Erer; Hansueli Müller was a tenacious perfectionist; Hans Sigg continually thought of new, fascinating experiments and pressed on even when the old ones should have been repeated a few more times, and he was an excellent car mechanic to boot; and Alex Stolba had an imagination and a wealth of ideas that could hardly be contained, and like Sigg he was an excellent observer. I visited each team for a month in Awash or Erer, but not until they had been there for a few months, because all young researchers bring the chance of a new way of seeing things and should not have the old way imposed on them before they begin. Although I was only a guest out there and had to learn the names of the baboons from the young people, there were rewards: at my desk at home, I could see the picture of the hamadryas becoming more complete and expanding in directions I would not have explored.

The young group, with their often highly critical boss, had it worse than I did in my time, when I could follow my own ideas freely. On the other hand, many things were easier than in 1960. My young people lived in their own earthen houses. There was also enough money for a wife to come along as assistant, so that occasionally—after carefully selecting the next doctoral student for Ethiopia and settling the details of the project— I was suddenly introduced to a nice young lady who was going to join the party and about whom I knew nothing except that my new student found her a suitable partner. In the event, the loyalty and industry of these young women exceeded my skeptical expectations, even as they had briefly set aside other occupations to take on something for which—with the exception of Helga Abegglen—they had no training at all. There were some little surprises, of course. On one visit to Awash I was amazed to find a genuine porcelain toilet. At least this is some progress, I thought, for our pretty round tukul had meanwhile been set on fire by a Russian team that was laying down trails in the park.

We no longer carried out transplantation experiments. Sigg's experiments on the varying ecological competence of family members took place in an enclosure built on the land that came with our rented house in the village of Erer; the families were trapped as a whole and later returned to their troops. The main work now was concerned with the organization of the higher units. Cone Rock was chosen for this research (fig. 24).

Jean-Jacques and Helga Abegglen, Alex and Vreni Stolba, Hans and Leonie Sigg, and our animal caretaker Ruedi Wey were able to study the Cone Rock troop at Erer for five and a half consecutive years (28, 30).

Fig. 24. Cone Rock near Erer, site of the five-year study.

The troop numbered around 240 baboons and lived at the same cliff—sugarloaf-shaped and visible from far away—where in 1960 the hamadryas baboons had instantly discovered me under my acacia bush from a distance of several hundred yards. The Abegglens learned to know individually the adult members of Band I and eventually also some members of other bands in the troop. Band I became our main study group. Its composition was regularly recorded; in the January censuses of the years 1972 to 1977 it comprised 59, 51, 66, 67, and 69 members.

When Helga and Jean-Jacques first drove to Cone Rock and onto the grassy terrace where we had once set up our traps, the baboons came to meet them. The young zoologists were understandably rather taken aback, and without getting out of their cross-country car they reversed for some distance. The baboons followed and began to examine the place where the car had just stood. The Abegglens supposed, probably correctly, that the Cone Rock baboons remembered the gifts of corn that Walter Götz, Walter Angst, and I had brought as bait two years before in a similar vehicle. It would obviously not have surprised the baboons if the Toyota had dropped some corn for them from its belly before backing off.

It was early in the Cone Rock study that the Abegglens discovered the existence of clans. Helga was the first to notice that males that regularly spent the night in the same part of Cone Rock resembled one another. Fortunately, she did not simply dismiss this impression as a figment of her imagination. The males spending the night on the outer right part of the cliff—Rosso, Rossini, Bub, Bishop, and Pepsi—all had very reddish faces, white cheek beards, and light gray mantles. The Abegglens called them the Reds. Rosso and the somewhat younger Rossini both had unmistakable curving brow ridges and looked as much alike as twins (plate 4, bottom left). In the same Band I were two further groups of males that slept in neighboring places and looked similar to one another; on the basis of their facial hues, they were called the Browns and the Violets. Neighborhood groups of males of similar appearance were later found in Band II as well. The Abegglens chose the term "clans" for such groups of similar-looking males, plus their females and young. Some females also resembled one another, but in their case the similarities were not so strikingly correlated with clan membership.

Naturally, degrees of resemblance are not easy to establish objectively, but Helga Abegglen's impression was confirmed by all subsequent observers and, in time, was supported by data on the relationships between the clan members. The males of a clan stayed closer to one another on the sleeping cliff (22), and clan members groomed one another more frequently (29), than did baboons in the band without this association. Two years later, when Stolba and Sigg were regularly accompanying the Cone Rock baboons on their daily marches, they found that the clans are also marching groups, which often look for food out of sight of one another (27).

The similarity among adult males in a given clan could have only one plausible cause: these males were related, and they remained in their birth clan into adulthood. If they ever left it, they returned later. This finding was a departure from all that was known about savanna baboons; the females of those species stay permanently in the group in which they were born, whereas the males migrate and join other groups, either as they grow up or later, and either permanently or eventually to return, depending on the population. The same applies to the macaques and to most other Old World primate species. The chimpanzees of Gombe in Tanzania are an exception; here the males remain and the females change groups instead. Some members *must* leave the group before reaching the age for reproduction to avoid a harmful degree of inbreeding. In Band I, then, did the females emigrate? And if so, how—since they, like the females in all other bands in the study region, are guarded and herded by their males?

During the five and a half years they were observed, nine of the initial nineteen adult females in Band I did indeed transfer to another clan or even to another band of the Cone Rock troop (28). Four others vanished from Cone Rock without a trace during this time; perhaps they died, or they may have moved to another troop that we were not observing. The often dramatic events associated with these female transfers will be related in the section on overthrow by force. Here we are concerned with the males' tendency to stay in place.

In the same five and a half observation years, none of the initial eight adult males of Band I shifted to another clan, though two of them disappeared. Again, there is no way to decide whether the lost ones had died or moved to distant troops. If such long-distance emigrations were the rule, however, we ought to have seen emigrants arriving regularly in our clans, but of these there were only two in the five and a half years—relatively old bachelor males, to whom we shall return later.

Including the band members that reached adulthood during the observation period, we observed a total of nineteen clan changes by adult females and only one transfer by an adult male. The contrast with the savanna baboons is obvious. There the males go to females of strange groups; among the hamadryas, they stay in the clan of their male relatives. We can only presume that the same thing happens in other hamadryas troops.

Occasionally the Cone Rock males also sought outside company (28); juvenile males would leave clan and band and go to visit neighboring bands. On May 10, 1972, late in the evening, Jean-Jacques Abegglen observed Mango, a small three-year-old male of Band I, sitting in the riverbed at the foot of Cone Rock with his family and letting his mother groom his hair (29). Slowly Band I ascended the steep gravelly slope to the cliff. At first Mango went along, then he suddenly turned around together with a male of his own age who was at his side. The two youngsters left their band, crossed the valley alone, and climbed up the opposite cliff, where Band IV had already moved into its quarters for the night. Mango sat down by a young bachelor belonging to the strange band and groomed him, while his fellow runaway sat at his side. After a few minutes Mango dared to go further into the strange band. A young resident male threatened him but was chased away by another one. The visitors ran past them. Mango groomed a resident bachelor. When it grew dark, the two youngsters withdrew into a niche in the rock occupied by Band IV. They probably spent the night there. On the morning of the 15th, Mango's companion turned up at home again, in Band I, but Mango himself departed for the day's march with Band IV. In the evening he played exuberantly with one of its juvenile males. On the 23rd, the Abegglens again observed him in his own Band I.

Over the years, all thirteen juvenile and subadult males of Band I were observed sleeping and traveling with other clans or bands for short periods. Sometimes the residents examined them curiously, but they were never maliciously attacked or driven away. Four of them extended their visits for weeks or months, if only because the band they were visiting happened not to reencounter the home band at the same cliff for weeks at a time. But none of them stayed permanently. The birth clan was known for seven males, and all of them ultimately returned to that clan. We do not know whether these visits are a vestige of the emigrations that were customary for males among the ancestral savanna baboons. In any case, the young males probably acquired a general familiarity with the home range of the host band, which could be useful to them later on.

The most surprising demonstration of clan loyalty was provided by two juvenile males whose mothers were abducted by males belonging to another clan in the same band (29). One of them was Ishi. When his mother was taken away, he was only two years old. He did not follow his mother into the new clan but stayed with his father, Admiral; the two of them often groomed one another. Twice Ishi was seen to visit his mother, groom her a little, and then return to his father.

The other case involved little Maybe of the Violet Clan. He was still an infant when his mother was abducted, so he depended on her for his own survival. He lived with her for almost two years, as part of the abductor's family in the Red Clan. Only occasionally did he visit his own clan, the Violets. But then, when he was about three years old, he returned to his father and brothers and stayed there, giving his mother up. Bonding to male relatives, a new specialty of the hamadryas, had conquered the ancient bond with the mother, which is far more powerful in other primate societies. The hamadryas is the only species in all the genera of macaques and baboons that has invented bonding between father and son. And it was the mother who paid the price. Why?

Primate groups are not anonymous swarms like those of birds and fishes. All forms of primate society are based on organized, closed, and usually small groups, the members of which know one another individually. The phylogenetic root of this type of group in mammals is very likely the family comprising mother and children. Fish families can also consist of father and children, but among us mammals the mother is always the center. This difference is related to the fact that mammals may be less sure who the father is, because of the way the eggs are fertilized. Some fish fertilize them externally; the female deposits unfertilized eggs at the spawning site and the male swims over them, discharging sperm. He can make sure that no other male contributes sperm, so that his paternity is guaranteed. Because mammalian eggs are fertilized internally, a male cannot be sure when the egg is ready to receive sperm and whether the female might have mated with another at the critical time. When a mother gives birth, however, she can be certain that the infant is her own. Of course, an animal parent presumably does not "know" about parenthood as we understand it. All that is needed for parental care to evolve—but this is an absolute prerequisite—is for the process of reproduction to ensure that the newborn with which a parent is presented is in fact its own. Caring for the young is a costly activity, and it takes energy that might otherwise be spent on producing the next offspring. Genetic predispositions toward parental care would soon die out if they were not coupled to inherited behaviors that practically guarantee that the caring individual is really the parent. A mammalian mother is in no doubt of this, so she suckles and protects her young, and the maternal family is created. The more highly differentiated the mammalian brain becomes in evolution, the greater is the mother's store of knowledge and ability in comparison with that of her small child, and the longer is the period during which she can usefully protect and guide it while it learns from her. Ultimately even an adult daughter continues to live with her mother, who is still the more experienced and can still, as matriarch, offer guidance to her daughters and grandchildren. Grandmother families of this sort are found, for instance, among deer and elephants and also in most of the higher primate species where females remain in the group. The permanent core of these groups, as the years pass, consists of the related females. They can assist a relative even at some cost to themselves because they are certain of their kinship, and in so doing they tend to propagate in the relatives their own predisposition to provide assistance to kin.

This is the theory of "kin selection" formulated by William Hamilton; it is the best explanation to date of the evolution of altruistic behavior— that is, helping others at the expense of one's own reproductive success. At the simplest level, it would be impossible for a genetic character to propagate itself in a population if that character caused the individuals carrying it to help others, and thereby sacrifice their own genes for the sake of the others' genes. The predisposition to behave egotistically and not offer such help would be more likely to pass to the next generation, so that helpfulness would die out. However, if a helpful individual knows who its relatives are and helps only them, the genes for helping have a chance, because being related means having many genes in common. Someone who helps her sister thereby assists the propagation of whatever genetic component of her own helpfulness her sister may share. The predisposition to helpfulness can propagate itself if the kinship is close enough and if the help is of more benefit to the recipient than it is damaging to the donor. This relationship can be expressed as follows: $C < r \times B$. Here C is the cost, the amount by which the helper reduces her own reproductive success as a result of helping. B is the benefit, the amount by which helping increases the reproductive success of the recipient. The degree of kinship of donor and recipient is given by r; r is 0 for unrelated individuals, 1 for identical twins, and ½ for full siblings, that is, sisters or brothers with the same mother and father. The formula therefore says that for help between full siblings to be genetically viable, it should benefit the receiver at least twice as much as it costs the donor. A more detailed explanation can be found in Richard Dawkins's book, *The Selfish Gene*.

Kin selection really is not the selection of kin, but the selection of genes that program for supporting one's kin. A prerequisite for kin selection is that the helper be able to distinguish his relatives from other conspecifics. Mammals, having developed internal fertilization with all its consequences, have had only one way to evolve a system in which a male cares for his partner's young: he must prevent his partner from mating with another male throughout her fertile period and then keep her with him until the child is born. Under these conditions, the child she bears must be his genetically, so that it is worthwhile for him to act as its father socially. This is the route the hamadryas males seem to have followed in developing their herding behavior, and that is why I said that the bonding between father and son has been at the mother's expense; she has paid for it with her sexual freedom and even her freedom of movement. In this situation the males, secure in their paternity, could cooperate with their sons, and father and son could help one another at some cost to themselves. It would then be understandable that hamadryas sons stay with their fathers, just as in other species the daughters stay with their mothers.

In a previous chapter the possibility was raised that even at night, while the troop is asleep, a harem leader may have to be ready to discover and prevent secretive affairs between his wives and other males. It may have seemed amusing, but we see now that the evolution of the clan could depend on the husband's vigilance.

Two characteristics of hamadryas society, unique among baboons, support the idea that the clans defined by their male members were evolved by kin selection. First, males could be particularly sure of being the fathers of their females' offspring, and second, the sons remained with them rather than emigrating. As further evidence, however, we should demonstrate that fathers and sons actually do cooperate with or even help one another to such an extent that it is worthwhile for the son to stay and for the father to tolerate his son "at home." Our project came to an end before we could collect the necessary data.

We do not know whether hamadryas males make a greater effort to care for their offspring than do male savanna baboons, as must be predicted from their assured paternity. Once we saw a hamadryas male hobbling all alone behind his troop. He was bringing a dead infant with him, alternately carrying and dragging it. Was it his child, and had a predator killed the mother? Isolated scenes such as this, mere anecdotal evidence, get us nowhere.

The males in the population of yellow baboons that Jeanne and Stuart Altmann studied in Amboseli National Park also protect the young in their group. Most mothers have a couple of special friends among the males, and these of their own accord take on the role of "godfather" to the infants. They visit the mother and child often, and when they are there they protect the little one from larger juveniles trying to pull it around. Soon an infant knows its godfather and chooses him as a refuge when afraid, lets the older male carry it, and is allowed to share its guardian's food. According to Jeanne Altmann's studies (1980), the child's godfather is always also a friend of the mother and, as such, is more likely than others to be the father of her child. Yet the male does all this without being certain of his fatherhood.

What should be studied now, in both species, is the amount of effort a male expends on child care and his actual kinship with the child. The latter can now be determined from blood samples by the method of DNA fingerprinting. If it turned out that male savanna baboons take just as much care of certain infants as hamadryas fathers do of their offspring, one possibility would remain: perhaps strictly guarding a female is not the only way for a male to be sure that he is the father of her child. Maybe there is some criterion by which male baboons can recognize their own offspring. Experiments have shown that when animals of some other species meet blood relatives for the first time in their lives, they treat them differently from individuals to whom they are not related. There has been one report of this "kin recognition" in rhesus monkeys, but it was not confirmed in later studies.

Back to cooperation in the hamadryas clan. The most obvious form of cooperation among adult males is their joining forces to defend their female "property." If kin selection were operating here, males belonging to the same clan ought to form the closest defense force. But it is not clear that they do so; in the fights observed at the sleeping cliffs, the opponents aligned themselves in bands. The next step is to look more closely, to see whether the males of a clan within the band risk more for one another than the males of different clans. An intriguing question, but not an easy one to answer.

For the time being, then, the hypothesis that the male clan has arisen by kin selection is not convincing, in the absence of documentation that males within a clan cooperate especially closely. If it turned out that they do not, there would still be another possibility to investigate. It could be that although the males of a clan do not actively assist one another more than others, they compete less. There is a kind of trusting friendship among males in the same clan that points in this direction. I shall give the following examples, not to save the theory—which they cannot do in any case—but because they show the males involved in an unexpectedly carefree relationship with one another. This highest degree of trust was observed by Sigg and Stolba in three cases, each time between males of the same clan. The first pair comprised Spot and his friend in the Brown Clan. When they traveled side by side, with the line of their females strung out between them, one of them might leave his position on the flank and go out of sight for ten minutes to inspect something. His females then drew together into a pack near his colleague, who never took advantage of the opportunity. In the Red Clan the relationship between Rosso and Rossini was so relaxed that one of them gradually, and without fighting, relinquished Rosa, his female, to the other. This peaceful transfer of a female was also observed among other members of a clan. The third example again involves Rossini. In 1976, after he had lost all his females to Band IV, he went into a physical decline and his movements became slow and apathetic. A year previously, he had lost one of his females to his younger clanmate Bub. Now, after Rossini's complete defeat, Bub allowed this female, though she remained his own, to groom her downcast former mate several times, before his very eyes! This was extraordinary. A human observer is almost compelled to interpret Bub's permissiveness as an act of pity. Once again, however, the scientist must exert his skepticism and also point out a simpler explanation: Rossini, in his present condition, was less of a threat than a young follower, and some family leaders allow even young followers to be groomed by one of their females. Both explanations are possible. Jane Goodall is convinced that chimpanzees experience sympathy; I am less certain for our baboons.

Sympathy, in which one is not simply infected by another's emotions but can appreciate them as distinct from one's own, is something that only humans have evolved, according to all the evidence so far. This is illustrated by one event Jane Goodall observed among the chimpanzees at Gombe. There had been an outbreak of polio, and the old male chimpanzee McGregor was completely paralyzed in both legs; he could move around only by pushing himself back with his arms, a few inches at a time, while sitting down. The males in the group that had been close companions of the healthy McGregor at first threatened and attacked him once he was paralyzed, and later they simply avoided him. The old male lay abandoned for days in his sleeping nest. One morning eight of his former companions had assembled for social grooming in a tree, two hundred feet from McGregor's nest. The invalid kept his gaze fixed on this convivial group, and finally he started out on his agonizing way toward them. When he finally reached two males grooming each other, he made a deep sound of satisfaction and extended an arm in greeting. But before he could touch them, they swung away from him and continued their grooming on the other side of the tree trunk, not acknowledging his presence with a single glance. The crippled male looked at them for two minutes, and then laboriously climbed back down to the ground (van Lawick-Goodall 1971).

I must admit that in the case of the Red Clan I, too, would rather believe in Bub's sympathy. I'd like the island of humanity to which we owe allegiance to extend as far as possible beyond the boundaries of our culture and species; then it would not seem so much in danger.

Showdown

Above the snow-covered slopes of the mountain valley in which I am writing this book, the snowflakes are flying almost horizontally. The massive rock stove—our sleeping cliff—radiates heat, and my skull is buzzing from concentrating so long. Field work was different: there the science was nicely interspersed with silly, irritating, instructive, or critical incidents. On the chance that you also need a refreshing change by now, I'll tell you the story of the showdown. It illustrates how much I was able to learn from baboons.

At one stage during the experimental field study in 1968, Walter Götz, Walter Angst, and I had moved from Awash into the Erer Hotel, and for a while I worked alone at White Rock. We had had a cordial reunion with the Gurgure of Garbellucu. My special friend Muhammad roasted a sheep, and I distributed the presents we had brought. One long evening I sat on the ground within a Gurgure thorn enclosure, leaning against the wooden box my host had brought out of the branch hut and covered with a cowskin. I drank quantities of smoky milk and with some effort, to top it off, a wooden cupful of golden melted butter. The enormous horns of the cattle hung close above me like black crescent moons, and between them the slender women strolled calmly back and forth.

At White Rock, though, there was trouble. One evening I sat at my observation point on the large, yellow boulder in the loop the wadi made opposite the cliff, dictating notes into the tape recorder. Suddenly something frightened the resting troop away from the gravel slope above the cliff. The baboons hastily left the rock and dived behind the upper edge of the slope. From the left, stones flew after them, and a "mushroom head" came into view on the horizon. All nomad men, whether Karaju, Gurgure, or Issa, proudly wore their hair in the same style: a large, dense crinkly ball truncated by a cut perpendicular to the slender neck (plate 7, bottom). The ball of hair was combed with a small wooden fork and oiled with butter, often bound with a strip of hide and occasionally admired in our car mirror by its fascinated owner. During our first two years in the field, the mushroom silhouette had presaged something unpleasant too often for me to welcome its appearance now. Recently one of these men had snatched away Walter Angst's watch and got away with it, because while chasing him Walter stumbled and fell. We had become conditioned to seeing the mushroom head of a stranger as a symbol of hostility.

The one approaching now over the horizon was new to me. Most of the nomads were wiry, but this was a sturdy man, about twenty years old. He looked down at me provocatively from the cliff, continuing to throw stones after the invisible baboons. My evening of observation had been destroyed. I picked up my things, to keep them away from any of his comrades who might appear, and climbed up to him. In my fractured syntax I asked him to leave the monkeys alone, and I gave him a tip in compensation. We seemed to be in agreement; he departed.

Next evening, however, he drove the baboons away again. Then he stood on top of the rock and flung out his open hand with rough arm movements, demanding tribute. I have never seen such an arrogant expression and gesture. Back at the hotel I held a council of war with Walter Götz. We were unanimous: I had to show my teeth now too. At least this fellow wasn't carrying a gun, as so many of the nomads did. I was not happy with the situation, but I had no choice. On the third evening, when he once again scared away the baboons and demanded money, I shouldered the backpack, climbed up the gravelly slope in a fury while conserving my strength, and hit him in the face with my fist. Surprised, he jumped back and whipped out his curved knife; I drew my pistol. He immediately withdrew to a distance of twenty yards and bombarded me with stones. Every one was aimed straight at my head, and every one flew past as I leaned out of the way, laughing furiously. Now I could understand, however, how horrid punishment by stoning must be; if several people *were* throwing in concert, there could be no escape.

As happened often, more men appeared as if by magic, one of them with a gun. Now I was worried. They listened calmly, however, to my attempts at explanation, and one of them even gave the stone thrower a symbolic stroke across his calves with a little stick. When I ran through the scene in my mind on the way home, I remembered with bitter regret that I had not really landed a proper blow. My fist had slid off his cheekbone. Boxing was another skill I should have acquired.

In the following days my enemy no longer came to White Rock, but I sometimes shivered on my boulder. I had no idea what social implications my hitting him might have—for example, whether he would feel bound to take revenge in order to save face. He could easily have shot at me from the bushes.

After a week I described the man to my Gurgure host Muhammad and asked him to make inquiries. On my next visit I learned that my challenger was an Issa, belonging to a group that had recently set up camp to the north of us. Muhammad had seen him, and said his cheek was still very swollen. I was delighted at this news, to a degree that I now find hard to understand. I had become easily angered and roused to action as a result of the physical exertion needed for our work in the field and the daily difficulties that had to be overcome. Soon after I had returned from the first year in Ethiopia, my dear wife was horrified when I abruptly seized by the collar a young man who had pushed in front of us at a market stall. But civilization rapidly cured me.

After this dispute we had no more major disturbances at Erer. The story was still circulating in the region years later. However, the escalation could probably have been avoided if we had known about the recent arrival of the Issa and had introduced ourselves to them through an interpreter.

The incident made one thing clear to me: I was no warrior. My handling of wrath and weaponry was poorly controlled. We shall now see that male hamadryas handle their weapons more judiciously.

Discretion with Weapons

The upper canine teeth of a male baboon are terrible weapons, almost as long as those of a leopard and whetted knife-sharp at the back edge by the chewing movement made by furious males during pauses in their fights, as a visible and audible threat. The wound made by the full bite of a fighting male is a deep, long incision. In South Africa chacma baboons have mutilated and killed attacking dogs, and there are tales from zoos of severe injuries inflicted on humans. To the effectiveness of these weapons is added a factor we don't often think of: a tooth, like a horn or a pointed beak, is firmly attached. This can be a problem, one with which humans are not encumbered. Since our earliest ancestors began to use tools as weapons instead of parts of their bodies, we have been able to lay down our clubs, swords, or guns and approach one another unarmed, in a convincing gesture of peace. Animals cannot do that. In the most friendly and the most peaceful situations, they carry their weapons with them, unsheathed and ready for instant use. The canine teeth of female hamadryas are so small that they are not really dangerous to anyone, but for two males the potential danger each presents to the other is an almost visible burden, with a profound influence on the males' relationships.

Even before it was entirely clear to us how risky cooperation really is between such violent competitors as hamadryas males, in some of our observations we thought we could sense the scrupulous effort they were making to avoid a serious biting fight, even when the two males were strangers to one another.

Animals have more than one way to ensure peace. The simplest and most ancient is to avoid crossing each other's paths. In hundreds of species that have been investigated, including the savanna baboons, the macaques, and the chimpanzees, to name but a few, it is always only one of two that gives way, and always the same one, the lower-ranking. Among male hamadryas baboons, astonishingly, the yielding is mutual. When two males and their families are in a tree too small for everyone and the males come into conflict, *both* of them run away together with their families, leaving the fruit unpicked. If a fight between bands becomes too severe, *all* the bands flee into the hills, and the cliff is abandoned. Hamadryas baboons behave as though no one could be victorious.

This is extremely strange. When two fighting fish, cocks, or rhesus monkeys are doing battle, one emerges the clear victor and takes over the territory, female, or higher rank. The males in an anubis group can readily be classified according to their rank on the basis of the one-sided signals of submission. The social life of macaques is so saturated with knowledge and maneuvers about rank order that hardly anything happens without reference to rank. Among free-living hamadryas males we could discern no rank order. If it exists, the males must actually camouflage it, whereas other monkeys assert it at every meeting. Signs of subordinacy such as pulling back the lips to bare the teeth, or even screaming, are the rule in fights between male savanna baboons; they are never seen in even the fiercest fight between hamadryas males. At first I thought this was impossible and doubted Fred Kurt's and my own talent for observation, until I first watched a group of rhesus monkeys on Cayo Santiago near Puerto Rico. Within minutes I knew we had observed correctly. The alpha male of the rhesus group was identifiable at first sight by his raised tail. Where a high-ranking individual, male or female, approached feeding subordinates, the latter got out of the way with bared teeth. In Band I at Cone Rock, even after five and a half years of observation, none of us could have picked out an "alpha male"; here the expression seemed meaningless. Later, at White Rock, Walter Götz was able to measure a feeding rank order among the adult males by throwing a bait between two of them, in various combinations. Whichever grabbed it was counted as the higher-ranking or dominant one; this male would also be expected to acquire more females than the other. However, Götz found no significant correlation between feeding rank and harem size. Alex Stolba also tried to establish the existence of a rank order later on at Cone Rock, by taking notes of subtle submissive behavior. Such behavior was so rare between males encountering one another that for some sets of two males it did not occur for months. He was unable to collect enough data. It was only in the Munich Zoo that Marietta Fritz succeeded in documenting a rank order among the five males there, taking instances of presenting as a measure of subordinacy (21).

Why do male hamadryas avoid rank disputes so scrupulously—or, more precisely, why does none of them try to be the acknowledged alpha male? What causes the remarkable fleeing of both parties, so that neither is victorious? The most plausible explanation, and one that will be confirmed in the section on inhibition of fighting, is that a family leader with several females should fear nothing more than to engage in battle in the presence of several other males. He might vanquish his opponent and at the same time hold on to one of his females, but while he is fighting, the males not involved in the fight might try to take over his other mates. Fleeing from them, the females could be dispersed in all directions and caught by males while far away from him. Once they have become distributed among several other males, his prospects of reconquering them are poor. Property owners have everything to lose and nothing to gain by social unrest, and the male hamadryas seem to know that.

In contrast, a male anubis or rhesus monkey has no females as long-term possessions. For him his acknowledged rank is one of the instruments with which he can win one female or another for a short time, without risking an escalated fight on each occasion. While in the company of a consort female, he, too, does not try to add another but stays apart with the one he has.

Possession of females also seems to affect the friendly relationships between hamadryas males, as becomes apparent when they embark on their first marriage. As youngsters, the males play enthusiastically with one another. Half-grown males from several families often sleep close together on a ledge apart from their families, which young females never do. Young bachelors preferentially groom one another, sometimes even across the boundaries of the bands. As soon as one acquires his first female, however, this intimacy comes to an end. Once married, the same males cautiously maintain several feet of distance. If one wants to greet or appease another, he approaches no closer than an arm's length, rapidly presents his hindquarters, and then hurries away again (plate 5, top). As long as the male is married, his male friendships are frozen at the level of presenting. There is no more friendly body contact with other males, no grooming or playing, until he has been defeated by rivals and deprived of his females. Then, solitude is usually all that remains for him (p. 238).

This extreme circumspection with regard to fighting was once vividly illustrated when what was at stake was not females but rather the males' own safety. We had completed some experiments in the Awash camp and were taking the males back to be released at their sleeping cliff. There was a long way to go and not much room in the Land Rovers, so we took a chance: relying on what we had learned in the experiments, we put two grown males from the same band together, in a cage five feet long. The first male was already sitting in the cage when the second entered, hesitantly. Without sparing the new arrival a glance, the first male immediately turned his back on him. The second paused just inside the entrance, then also turned aside and sat down very slowly. For the whole trip the two sat facing away from each other at opposite ends of the cage; neither looked at the other. I am convinced that each of them could sense how dangerous the situation was.

A fight in such a confined space would have been murderous; we would have had to open the cage immediately. The danger that aggression will break out between aroused males is greatest when their eyes meet. Therefore the seating arrangement the two males adopted was the safest there could have been. What impressed us most was not the fact that they sensed this, but that both *dared* to make themselves vulnerable by turning away, as though each was confident that the other would also adhere to the only sensible solution. If either had breached this confidence, it might have been fatal for the other one, defenselessly looking the other way. The two males had solved a problem in game theory that often defeats the environmentalist movement. It would be possible to agree on a position that would not cost any of the participants too much, but with a risk that someone might break the agreement and have an advantage over those who keep it. If no one is willing to run this risk, the costs become insupportable for all.

Observations and thoughts like these made me decide to test experimentally the discretion of hamadryas males in handling their weapons.

Experiments on the Inhibition of Attack

If male hamadryas baboons avoid fights when they possess harems that are difficult to defend, they must have some sense of tactics, and this is quite plausible for such a circumspect animal. However, not all their competitors are also leaders of harems. A band includes many young males in prime condition for fighting who have never had a female in the years since they reached puberty. Since they have no females to lose, it would be remarkable if they too refrained from using their weapons. Yet even in the first field study we saw signs that all males, even the bachelors, respect the marriages of males in their own band. The most important evidence was as follows.

First: The customary peace among males in a band cannot be explained as indifference. A mere heap of corn that brings the families closer together than usual can destroy it, as fights over females break out on all sides. A dangerous aggressiveness really does exist among the males in a hamadryas band.

Second: Although females are such objects of desire, an unattached female is taken over by only *one* male; there is no fighting over her. As early as 1961, when we were first trying out female transplantation experiments, we saw that although it was common for several males to advance in the first second, all but one then immediately held back.

Third: When we released various females to the same recipient troop at intervals of several days, each of them was taken over by a different male. However, when we placed the same female in a cage repeatedly in front of the troop, she was always approached by the same male. It was as though the slightest exchange of gestures between the female and a male inhibited all the other males from then on.

All three observations were confirmed by the transplantation experiments (p. 119) in the second, experimental field study with Walter Götz and Walter Angst. Let us now return to it, and to the Awash Falls. The plan was to investigate the two processes on which the family structure of the hamadryas seemed to be based: the herding behavior of the male, which ensures the family's internal cohesion, and the inhibition of fighting among males, which protects it from external attack. Here we are concerned with the second project (13). It developed in a sequence of steps typical of ethological projects. In brief, for the reader interested in the research process, there were seven stages.

1. At the beginning, there gradually emerged an *intuitive* idea. The scenes described above had occurred at different places and times. The intellect, which functions chiefly as tester and critic, did not see the connection between them. I still recall vividly how intuition (I cannot really refer to it as "mine") gently and almost subconsciously flitted over the subject from time to time as I walked home from the sleeping cliff in the evening, lay on my camp bed at night, and later wrote up our findings from the first year. At first this was all below the level of understanding, but one day as I lazily watched the stream of images and fragmented concepts flowing through my mind, conscious thinking suddenly came wide awake, stared into the river, and pulled the fish out of the water. It is astounding and makes me feel grateful how unconscious intuition can select, from the huge number of scenes observed, the half dozen that go together. All the conscious, working ego can contribute is to create favorable conditions, among them an equilibrium between tense concentration and freely ranging thought.

2. The idea now had to be converted into a detailed and well-founded *project*. If an inhibition protects the families in a band from reciprocal male aggression and thereby holds the competitive component of their social life in check, this ultimately indicates a respect for property that governs even the stronger opponent. A project to study this question seemed worthwhile. The U.S. National Science Foundation financed it, and an additional contribution was made by the Wenner-Gren Foundation for Anthropological Research in New York. My hypothesis was the following: among the hamadryas, the sight of an established pair inhibits the tendency of male rivals to attack it; this inhibition operates even on

rivals with fighting ability superior to that of the male in possession, and it thereby protects the marriage bond.

3. The first step in Awash was to carry out some *pilot experiments*. The design of these is still partly intuitive; they are often used to find out whether the basic concept is on roughly the right track and where unexpected difficulties and opportunities may arise. Fifteen times, in various troops, we trapped a family leader temporarily and left him, caged, in the midst of the troop for all to see. On each occasion one or two males in the troop immediately chased down the prisoner's females and led them away. Until he was held captive, they had respected his marriages. That they would take action as soon as he was immobilized suggests that their previous respect was not altruistic. What happened when we released the captive males was even more informative. If they were released after only half an hour, they attacked the usurpers and in each case recovered their females. If they were kept in the cage, fed, and watered for twelve hours, during which time their wives had been the property of the new males, the fights were fiercer—and now the females remained with the new males in four cases out of nine.

At least these four males, then, were capable of defeating the former family leader. Why had they not taken his females earlier? Can it be that continuous proximity to and interactions with a female make a male more confident of his status as possessor, and that this confidence decreases progressively with each hour of separation from her? Can such confidence enhance his fighting powers? On the other hand, might the sight of these marital interactions make a rival a little less eager to intervene, whereas once he has taken the other male's female and kept her with him for a while, he begins to feel more secure about her? This would be the mental prerequisite for what humans call property ownership.

4. Before designing the *definitive experiment* in Awash, we had a few things to think over. A behavioral experiment of this kind has two functions. The experimental conditions should be such as to make important but rarely observed events occur more often. And second, during the experiment all disturbing influences should be excluded as far as possible, so that only the causal influence being investigated has a chance to act. In our case this influence was "the sight of the established pair." The hypothesis underlying the experiment was simple. If a rival has seen that a female and a male are companions (fig. 25), he will respect their marriage. If he has not seen this (fig. 26), he will take over the female if his strength is superior.

5. Now we had to rule out the *disturbing factors*, the undesired influences that might affect the rival's respect for possession.

For example, a rival might also be inhibited if the possessor has more allies than he himself does. To exclude this factor, in the experiments the only individuals present had to be the female, the possessor, and the rival.

Fig. 25. Test experiment on respect for possession. *Top to bottom*, Scenes 0, 1, and 2. Does a rival respect the marriage of a weaker possessor after he has seen the pair together?

Fig. 26. Control experiment on respect for possession. *Top,* Scene 1; *bottom,* Scene 2. Here respect for possession was not expected, because neither of the males had seen the other as the female's partner. Further details in text.

This could be achieved only in an enclosure away from wild troops, but the experiment had to be done in Ethiopia because we needed hamadryas baboons with all the experience, knowledge, and habits that only a free-living animal can accumulate. We had to capture such baboons ourselves. This solution also offered the advantage that we could release the animals to their troops again after the months of experimentation were over.

6. *Practical preparation and the schedule of trials.* On the bank of the Awash we constructed an enclosure measuring about twenty by thirty feet, in the light shade of two acacias. In each trial, two male and one female hamadryas would be brought together here (fig. 27). In different trials, all that would be changed was the sequence in which their relationships were established; in our terminology the preparatory phases of the experiments were called Scene 0 and Scene 1, the encounter itself being Scene 2. Each scene lasted fifteen minutes.

In the *control experiments* (fig. 26), during Scene 1 the cages containing the two males were arranged in such a way that they could not see each other, but both could see the female. In this situation, neither of the males could observe an "established pair"; each would have to assume that the lone female was unattached. In the subsequent Scene 2, when all three baboons were let loose in the enclosure for a further fifteen minutes, we therefore expected to see no evidence of respect for possession, but rather open competition. For the *test experiments* (fig. 25) we picked one of the males in advance to be the "possessor" and at the very beginning, in Scene 0, we put him together with the female in the enclosure. For Scene 1 the second male, designated the "rival," was placed next to the enclosure in his cage, so that he could observe the pair through the wire. Since he could see that the pair belonged together, he was expected in the subsequent Scene 2 to respect this relationship and not fight.

Before the experiments began, we captured all the participants and housed them in cages distributed among the small clearings in the gallery forest. In one of these, the females lived in a long cage we had built, divided into compartments by partitions made of discarded tin road signs, still bearing their Amharic lettering. In each of four other clearings we kept two males in individual cages. The two males sharing a clearing came from the same troop and could see one another continually, whereas the males in different clearings came from different troops and could not see the males from the other troops. None of the males could see the females from their clearings, nor was the enclosure visible from any of the clearings. Therefore the participants were all unknown to one another except for the males that had come from the same troop, which meant that the experiments would not be affected by preceding relationships of which we were unaware. We named the eight males after the zoology professors in our home cities, which added an amusing subtext

Fig. 27. The experimental enclosure in Awash cost only a few hundred dollars. The possessor (middle) has just left his female (left) in order to visit the rival.

to the observations we recorded with the Dictaphone. After all, in the African heat we had built fences, carried forty-five-pound monkeys down gravelly slopes in cages on our backs (fig. 28), repaired leaking car radiators for the third time and changed the experimental design for the fourth, all for a project with an uncertain outcome—without having some fun, we couldn't have managed.

7. The final *experimental design* was a little more complicated. We needed combinations of males in which the rival was truly superior to the possessor, and as we know, the fighting rank of a male hamadryas is not obvious. We solved this problem by testing each set of two males twice, in opposite roles. That is, in one test X was made the possessor and Y the rival; in a second test, with a new female, Y was the possessor and X the rival. If it was fighting ability that decided which of them won the female, the same male—the stronger one—would win in both tests. But if the inhibition hypothesis was correct, the first possessor would always keep the female.

We also wanted to know whether the excited gestures with which a threatened husband demonstrates possession can in themselves induce inhibition of the rival. Here, again, a double test was needed. In one trial

Fig. 28. Walter Götz carries a newly captured male hamadryas to the Land Rover.

the rival's cage was placed next to the enclosure in such a way that the pair could see him clearly. In the complementary trial, we made the rival invisible by letting him observe the pair from a "voyeur's booth," a box inside the darkened Land Rover with its opening covered by wire mesh painted white on the outside. Because the pair could not see him through the glaring white mesh, he would provoke no show of possession. However, he would be able to watch the pair very well from his hiding place.

Finally, it was necessary for none of the females to encounter the same male twice, because their earlier interaction might have had some aftereffect. Also, no male should be cast in the role of rival several times in a row, in case he became discouraged for later experiments. And no baboon should have to "work" in more than one experiment per day.

These variations and conditions occupied Walter Götz's organizational talent for several hot days, during which he often paced thoughtfully up and down the river bank. He finally came up with a multicolored schedule that assigned in detail the appearances of the eight males and fifteen females we were going to catch, and made allowance for all the conditions according to their importance. The plan was discussed at length and given the seal of approval—that is, from then on no change was allowed for any reason. Once the experiments have begun, an ethologist's interest is focused entirely on the answers the animals are giving to his or her questions. The complicated considerations underlying the design of the experiment are set aside. Therefore any adjustment of the plan is forbidden; one change would inevitably lead to others, and the whole planning process would have to start over.

By now it is certainly reasonable to wonder whether the baboons would go along with the whole thing at all. To be trapped and carried to a strange place by frightening beings can easily upset a wild animal's internal equilibrium. Then all it can do is try to escape or withdraw into immobility in a corner and stay there, depressed, for weeks. Vervets and anubis baboons can react in this way. The most important condition of a successful experiment is that the animals are motivated primarily for the behavior about which the experimenter is going to question them. They and the scientist must have the same priorities. In the hamadryas, luckily, we had made a good choice. Of course, we treated them more gently than the assistants of a commercial animal trapper, often untrained, did in those days. When the door of the cage trap fell shut, almost every captured baboon became terrified and tried to break out. We could do nothing about this except wait a while before approaching, without looking at the baboon, to lock the door. Most baboons calmed down on the trip to our camp. On arrival we transferred them to individual cages in the segregated, quiet clearings, gave them water and corn, and left them temporarily. When we next approached them we did it quietly, and if they were especially frightened we spoke to them softly and avoided direct eye contact. I already knew something about the character of the hamadryas, but I was nevertheless impressed to find that all the baboons would accept food within the first twenty-four hours. Even the older animals tolerated us next to their cages after three days, and did not try to flee. By that time many would take food from our hands. Dali Götz actually induced some of them to eat food unfamiliar to them by eating it herself before their eyes. Although they had become accustomed to having us close to them, we observed them from a distance of seventy feet during the experiments.

After a few days we began to habituate each male singly to the enclosure where he would be tested. We let him explore it until he gave all the following signs of restored confidence: he should make no attempt to break out; he should sit near the middle, away from the fence; he should threaten us when we came close and looked into his eyes, a good sign that he felt secure; he should come to us when we approached him with food, and to eat it he should go no more than six feet away from us.

As improbable as it may appear, all eight males reached this degree of habituation in little more than a week. But the main thing was that in the experiments themselves, their interactions with female and rival were so extensive and natural that we could detect no difference from the corresponding situations in the wild troops. I do not know where hamadryas baboons get this robust self-confidence. Maybe it comes from the fact that they have traditionally been used to leaving their own band and clan and facing the dangers of the semidesert in groups of only three or four. Around the campfire during those first weeks we kept returning to the question whether captivity is easier or harder for a human than for an animal: it is easier for humans because they can occupy themselves with thinking, but harder because in their imagination they are burdened by worrying about an uncertain future. We came to no conclusion.

The excitement of being captured seemed to bother the baboons less than we had thought, since the same individuals often entered the traps several times. One male in particular gave us a good example of the saying that a little knowledge is a dangerous thing. When the raised door fell shut behind him, he gave a start but did not look around; he merely remained seated and continued to eat. His reaction seemed to say something like: this thin wall of twigs can wait, I'll deal with it in due course. Only after several minutes, when his meal was finished, did he examine the wire door. He became visibly more unsettled, tested it by pulling the mesh twice with his hand, and then appeared suddenly to realize that there was no way out. He stormed around the cage, trying to break through, as most of the others did right away.

This false security occupied my thoughts. Animals that do not live in caves hesitate to enter a trap. A baboon, however, is adroit and ingenious and seems to be aware of that fact from experience. It will go into human huts, from which it can break out with no trouble, and hence also into traps—in some regions, without the slightest hesitation. Isn't the baboon's nonchalant entrance into a trap reminiscent of modern *Homo sapiens*? Humans, too, after several experiences with happy outcomes, will continue to try more daring adventures, believing that they can deal effectively with whatever happens. To know a lot, but not know one's limitations, is one of the problems bestowed on those with large brains.

I have rarely seen more absorbing animal behavior than in the experiments now to be described (13). First there was the immediate result: in three of the eight control experiments, the males fought over the female that belonged to neither of them. The fighting probably occurred when it was the weaker who first tried to take possession. We then carried out sixteen test experiments in which the two males were from the same troop; here, no rival who had seen the pair during Scene 1 subsequently attacked the possessor or tried to seize the female. That is, a pair bond only fifteen minutes old was regarded as unassailable. The statistical evaluation clearly refuted the notion that fighting ability might be the decisive factor in this situation. Baboons "respect" the marriages of others, even when the others are weaker than themselves, and I am certain that hamadryas families would be unable to coexist without such a protection of marriages.

This numerical result, more or less, had been predicted by our hypothesis. What we had not expected was the conduct of the individual males. The details of their behavior revealed what was actually going on in the inhibited rival and in the respected possessor. Indeed, in this artificial situation—as in the zoo—the behavior appeared in blatant clarity, with an exaggeration of natural patterns and some new inventions.

The *rivals* did not need to see full-blown demonstrations of possession in order to be inhibited. Inhibition was elicited when the pair merely sat side by side, presented, or groomed each other a little. When the rival had entered the enclosure to join the pair, he sat down separately and turned away from them, scratched himself or groomed his own hair. He avoided looking at the pair at all (figs. 29, 30). Instead, he would often examine the sky, an activity we had never seen among the baboons. The more aroused rivals peered intently into the bushes about a hundred feet away from the enclosure, as though they had detected a predator or something else important. But nothing was there, or the pair and we ourselves would have seen it. These kinds of behavior are in the category we ethologists call "redirected." Their intense interest in the female having been frustrated, the rivals redirected it toward elements in their surroundings that were entirely irrelevant at the moment, or even not there at all. Some rivals pushed little pebbles aimlessly back and forth on the ground with their index fingers, looking very much like an embarrassed human child, though in fact this behavior was redirected grooming. When the same male had the role of possessor in the next day's experiment, he paid no attention at all to sky, bushes, or stones, and devoted himself to his female rather than to grooming his own hair.

The sight of the pair, then, had more profound effects than we had

Fig. 29. An inhibited rival (front).

expected; not only the attack behavior of the rival was blocked, but *all* his social behavior with respect to the pair. No rival ever directed a gesture toward the female, even on the rare occasions when she presented to him. And when the possessor approached, the rival usually turned away and waited, motionless, until the other male went away again. The rival's exaggerated scratching, circle-wiping (p. 28), and grooming of his own hair revealed the conflict he was experiencing between tremendous social motivation and the almost complete inhibition of interactions with the pair.

We were just as surprised by the way the *possessors* responded to this inhibition. They did not preen and strut in triumph—just the opposite. A few minutes after the three baboons had been put together, the possessor typically left his female, went quietly to the rival, who was seated apart, and soothingly presented his hindquarter in the fleeting manner customary between males, which is known as "notifying." The hindquarter of the male hamadryas looks like a bizarre red mask (plate 5, bottom). In tense situations a male will give the other male a view of this "posterior face" in a conciliatory gesture (plate 5, top). The two males first look one another in the face, and then look at the penis or the mask. The recipient

Fig. 30. After one of the experiments, we put the female's cage on top of the rival's cage. The rival moved as far away as he could and turned away. The possessor, however, grabbed for the female without inhibition.

of the gesture often touches the presented hindquarter with his hand. In our experiments the possessors repeated this friendly notifying gesture many times. But it was hardly acknowledged; rarely, a rival would eventually respond with weak lip-smacking or a slight hand movement toward the presented hindquarter, but usually they did not move at all and kept their faces turned away. The possessors had emerged completely victorious from the encounter with their competitors, and yet they were the ones who tried to establish friendly relations with the losers!

One old male excelled all the others in his efforts on behalf of his inhibited rivals. He not only presented, but he spent minutes at a time walking around his inert competitors at a distance of only eight inches, bent forward until he was nearly in contact, and contemplated their faces and hindquarters. When the rival was the male from his own troop, he made an entirely novel gesture, moving one hand slowly over the rigid form, only an inch above the skin but not touching it, as though he wanted to groom him. We had not observed any such behaviors in the wild troops. They were new expressions, easily understood, of the friendly motivation that is the basis of the bonding and cooperation between the males in a hamadryas band.

Frans de Waal has shown, in his fascinating book *Peacemaking among*

Primates, that many other primates reconcile after arguments by means of peaceful gestures. The wild hamadryas males depend on peace. They need one another.

So much for encounters between males from the same troop. Having seen fights between bands, we really expected that strange males from *different* troops would fight one another too. Indeed, in four out of fifteen experiments the rivals did attack, and in two of the four they acquired the female; in two further experiments the possessor himself started the fight. There was one curious aspect, however: four of the six attacks were directed against the two males from the troop that lived in Staircase Valley, and it was from these that the two females were taken. The Staircase Valley males had not been caught with corn as bait, as all the others, nor could they be tempted by eggs or bananas or even the best products of our kitchen. As a last resort, we had put caged females into the trap as bait, and that worked. But the two males we trapped seemed, even in our own dealings with them, to be remarkably sensitive and insecure. Our other males appeared to regard these two in much the same way. It could be that by using females as bait we caught especially inept males, which had had no success with females, and it is conceivable that the inhibition that keeps rivals from attacking breaks down when they are confronted with extremely inferior possessors. In the remaining nine tests with males from different troops we observed inhibited rival behavior. Altogether, this result was equivocal. Does respect for marriage apply only to members of the same troop, or is it ultimately only opportunistic discretion in the use of weapons that serves primarily for self-protection even in conflicts with strangers? We shall return to this question later.

What was incontestable and new was that even among animals, established possession can provide a competitive advantage that supersedes the priority of higher fighting ability and thus protects the marriage of a weaker individual. If the rivals in our enclosure had encountered either the female or the possessor alone, they would certainly have made contact with them immediately—eagerly and intensely with the female, hesitantly but in general amicably with the possessor. (We had observed the latter when, to check the possibility that the first male in the enclosure felt more "at home" there, in Scene 2 we first brought the two males together in the enclosure and thereafter introduced the female.)

In summary, then, what inhibited a rival was something that existed *between the two others*: their relationship. The sight of the interacting pair probably gives the rival the experience of being excluded, an experience with which we can easily sympathize and which makes highly social beings extremely insecure. The following story of an excluded female shows that not only males are vulnerable to it. In one of the experiments the two "shy" males from the Staircase Valley troop were set against one another. They did something we would have thought impossible: they left the female alone and began eagerly to groom *one another*. The female, unaccustomed to such neglect, then threatened the rival. He took no notice. She presented to her male, the possessor. He refused to be diverted, and continued to groom the rival. The excluded female now behaved in the same perplexed manner as the rivals in the other experiments. She sat motionless for a while, then with quite inappropriate interest examined the surroundings of the enclosure and finally the sky.

The Hippopotamus Scarecrow

At this time a bull hippopotamus, not yet full-grown, was living in the brown water of the Awash in front of our camp. All day he stayed in the water, watching the men work, the women wash, the children play, the baboons crack the corn, and the vervets slip through the crowns of the trees. But his real contribution came at night, when he came ashore to graze—among doing other things (fig. 31). For example, he stepped on a water pipe newly installed by Peter Hay, the park director, and crushed it; and on August 1, the Swiss national holiday, he attended our celebration, his body glistening festively, brown on top and pink below, in the light of the bonfire. During the months of our inhibition experiments, he visited our camp as though it were a toy store. At night we could hear him amusing himself with chains, baboon traps, and gasoline drums, and once he also knocked over a bucketful of clean laundry and dragged the wet clothes through the dust.

For a while we ferried Ueli Nagel across the Awash every morning in a rowboat, because he was working with the hybrid troops down in the canyon, on the opposite side of the valley. On the trip over, the boat had usually barely reached the other side when the bull came to investigate. When it was about to return, the hippo positioned himself neatly between the boat and the dock at camp. Peter Hay had warned us about such events. In his career he had found that people were more likely to have serious encounters with hippos than with elephants. So it was sometimes necessary for the whole team to collaborate on these river crossings. Before the boat departed, everyone on shore collected a pile of stones the right size for throwing. When it was pushed off from the other bank for the return trip, everyone opened fire at once to make the hippo submerge and perhaps become disoriented in the turbid water. To the person in the boat, the hippo was no less a threat in the form of an invisible submarine, but at least he felt consoled by the fact that the missiles hailing down around him were meant for his enemy. Once it was even necessary to fire a gun into the water, with the permission of Peter Hay, to keep the hippo

Fig. 31. The grass next to our tukul at the Awash was grazed by a young hippopotamus bull, which often arrived before sunset. At the left of the tukul is our shower.

at a distance. The shot was aimed by our always helpful neighbor Ted Shatto, an American who was running the Tent Lodge at that time and owned an impressive cartridge belt.

On land the situation became more precarious. Walter Götz, who was then dreaming of having a farm in Africa, had sown a large bed with cabbage seeds. It was densely packed with hundreds of sturdy seedlings when one morning we found a clean swathe the width of a hippopotamus mouth running across it, as though a lawnmower had gone berserk. Walter was livid. This was too much. Now he spent his free time working on a mysterious sculpture, a delicately balanced tower made of barrels, beams, and iron cages. The idea was that when it collapsed, the industrious bull hippo would be scared away for a while. Meanwhile, one morning Ueli Nagel found on his tent, which was just in front of ours, an enormous imprint of lips with chewed greenery stuck to it, and the indentations made by two teeth. He decided to move elsewhere, giving us a better view of the river. The hippo continued his nighttime activities, upsetting boxes and rolling tires, and finally climbed onto the storage tent. But he never touched Götz's creation. People got used to seeing it there.

But one night we were awakened by a great uproar and a furious bass voice from the cabbage patch. Walter Götz himself had walked into the trap.

Respect for Possession: Fear or Morality?

From our point of view the willingness of hamadryas males to refrain from taking the females of weaker males, despite the importance of a harem to themselves, seems like very decent behavior. While we were doing these experiments I was pleased with the thought that we had found a functional equivalent of morality, a principle of social interactions that for once overruled that eternal, tiresome dominance by force and gave the weaker at least one right of precedence over the stronger. I was looking through egalitarian glasses. Fortunately, this optimistic interpretation of the results did not at all invalidate our experiments. What I like about empirical science is that the results stand on their own and can be interpreted differently later on.

Three years before our experiments, William D. Hamilton (1964) published his famous articles on "The Genetical Evolution of Social Behavior," which set sociobiology onto a track that brought it a long way—through brilliantly clever models, exaggerated claims, and heated debates extending into the ideological, until it attained the widely acknowledged status it enjoys today. It became necessary to rethink the rival inhibition of the hamadryas in the light of this theory. Was it really a moral renunciation in favor of a fellow member of the troop, or was it "simply" a matter of caution with respect to the use of weapons, imposed by fear in the course of evolution—a strategy in which an individual rejects aggression at just the point where, by doing so, that individual obtains for himself the best balance between costs and benefits?

We have two findings that help us decide between these alternatives. *First*: In the pilot experiments the males took over the female of another male belonging to their band, as soon as the latter had been imprisoned. That is, they ceased to respect his property at the very moment when he became powerless, so that for the time being, at least, the usurpers would not have to bear the cost of fighting.

Second: A study carried out later by Hans Sigg and Jost Falett, with hamadryas baboons that were then being kept in the Department of Ethology at the University of Zurich, gave some pertinent results (32). These captive baboons' behavior in relation to property conformed in principle to what we had seen in Awash, except that here the object of possession was not a female but rather a tin can that gradually released grains of corn through some holes. Again there was a Scene 1, during which the rival in a separate cage could watch the possessor handling the can, carrying it around, and eating the corn. Then, for Scene 2, the rival was allowed into the same cage as the possessor.

We were well acquainted with this hamadryas group and knew their rank order. In each experiment a lower-ranking possessor was confronted with a higher-ranking rival. The outcome was quite clear: males always respected another male's possession of the can, whereas females respected another female's property in only half the trials. But watch out! The males were certainly not more "moral": they hardly ever respected *females* as possessors.

Both series of experiments favor the explanation in terms of self-serving caution in employing weapons. In the pilot experiments at the sleeping cliffs, the females of the imprisoned males were taken over because the latter could not defend themselves. In the laboratory experiment with the cans of corn, the females probably lost their cans to higher-ranking females and to males, because their small canine teeth cannot cause severe wounds. Property is evidently not respected when it belongs to an individual that offers no serious threat. In contrast, males have such dangerous teeth that a fight, even against a weaker opponent, may be too costly in comparison with the benefit of the property to be gained. Sociobiological models have now demonstrated that in theory, respect for possession can be a convention when the costs resulting from an unrestrained fight count more than the value of the prize at stake (Hammerstein 1981). However, this kind of destructive fighting was something we never found among the hamadryas males. They *could* seriously injure one another, but moderately severe wounds were inflicted in only one of about a dozen escalated battles we observed. I have thoroughly tested many models of fighting strategies and found none that correctly predicts the actual respect primates have for property, so I shall say no more about theories here. The models available at present are based on assumptions still too simple to apply to our close relatives (Kummer and Cords 1991).

There is one take-home message here: the hamadryas' respect for possession has nothing to do with morality, and the same is probably true of the social behavior of animals in general. To behave morally means to obey a formulated rule of society, more or less regardless of the momentary advantages and disadvantages, because the other members of the society expect such obedience and will apply sanctions in case of infringement. In comparison, to refrain from destroying the marriage of someone a little weaker is just the mere dawn of morality. Such behavior is analogous to morality—that is, it has the same function—because it allows a problem of competition to be solved without the use of force by way of a convention to which everyone conforms. Nevertheless, it is far from human morality. The "convention" of male hamadryas baboons is unconscious, unless we are deceiving ourselves fundamentally; it is not formulated or taught, and society definitely imposes no punishment on those who break it.

As a principle by which to manage competition, however, property and respect for it are much older than our moral and legal rules that govern them. Even butterflies, fish, and birds occupy territories, within which the occupant has priority. The right of possession is certainly not an original product of human society.

The Pergola

Conventions are necessary and useful. But it would be hard to live fenced in by them forever if there were not, now and again, a piece of glorious mischief that breaks the bounds and yet hurts no one (which makes it much preferable to revolutions). I, for one, feel the need for some mischievous diversion after the last section, so I shall pull something out of my box of memories.

The last of the baboons that had participated in the inhibition experiments were back home in their troops. With three metal baboon traps on the roof rack of the Land Rover, I was coming back from the Staircase Valley cliff, where I had set the two shy males loose, and planned to take a short rest at the Omedla Hotel in Dire Dawa. I carefully turned into the unpaved courtyard, trying not to stir up any dust. The proprietor was Signor Stefano, a rotund Italian who had often helped us out. Wearing shorts, he was waiting on the guests seated at tables in the courtyard; the local Greeks and Italians often had their noon meal here. Hardly had they glanced up from their plates toward my loaded vehicle when something terrible happened. The pergola (trellis) that was suspended over the whole yard, with vines growing over it to shade the diners from the glare of the sun, fell down onto them. Now it was hanging on the guests' heads with frayed wires dangling, like a circus tent draped from one mast to the next. I had forgotten about the cages on my roof rack, and they had torn one of the suspension wires.

The buried diners were making feeble efforts to free themselves, with no hope of success. But Signor Stefano quickly overcame his dismay and shouted for his Ethiopian waiters, whom he equipped with sticks and sent under the hanging structure to act as emergency supports. To my shame, I must admit that I was no use at all in this hour of trial. I leaned helplessly against the wall and laughed. It was the last time I ever felt this crazy need to laugh at a wildly comic event, even though my embarrassing role in it called for earnest efforts to help. My repeated, sincere apologies to Signor Stefano could not have sounded very convincing, but he was not angry with me, and we remained good friends. Presumably being scatterbrained was part of his image of a monkey doctor.

I was not yet a professor then, but the portents were obviously favorable. Last week, not for the first time, I absentmindedly knocked on my own door—from inside, before leaving the office.

How Could Morality Originate?

Selection has equipped the higher primates with flexible behavior. The lower-ranking, in particular, can gain advantage by varying their tactics and their allies, as has been enthrallingly described by the Dutch ethologist Frans de Waal in his book *Chimpanzee Politics* and by the Britons Whiten and Byrne in their collection of anecdotes (1986) about the ways in which primates practice deception. Humans call this opportunism. It is not considered laudable, because it smacks of amorality, and rightly so. But opportunism is also evolutionarily successful—at least up to the threshold of hominization.

As seen by a behavioral biologist—admittedly not a qualified expert in this area—morality is quite remarkable. Its rules are extremely rigid. There is no "if" in the Ten Commandments, only "thou shalt" and "thou shalt not," under all circumstances. They prescribe the opposite of opportunism. In regard to killing, respect for property, and false witness, taken at face value they demand the same actions no matter what the situation or what other person is involved. The optimal strategies that result from sociobiological models are generally conditional.

Selection theory ought to be able to account for the emergence of morality as such (though not for the particular moral norms in the various human cultures). The only available scientific explanation for it is that it must have provided some advantage in the process of selection. The question is: Why should biological evolution produce a species with eminently flexible behavior and then permit this adaptive capacity to be suppressed by a superimposed cultural trait?

Perhaps it happened like this. Flexible behavior was an advantage, but not in every context. In their roles of hunter, setter of traps, gatherer of food, warrior, or toolmaker, it was important for humans to be as inventive and versatile as possible. Any improvement in foresight and any additional trick or skill would be beneficial. But as a member of a group, a human can be too tricky for his own good. He becomes less predictable to the others, and a person—or any other being—whose behavior cannot be predicted is dangerous, not only if he is an enemy or competitor, but even as a collaborator and friend. The fundamental disadvantage of group life is competition, and its fundamental advantage is cooperation. To succeed, cooperation requires that each participant be able to predict the other's actions. By being predictable rather than deceitful in their mutual interactions, the members of a group should be able to increase the benefit of cooperation. Somewhere along the line of human ancestors there must have been a phase in which greater guile and unpredictability were advantageous in dealing with human enemies, but a disadvantage in relation to companions during the hunt and in social relationships at the resting place. "Only what is simple works," according to a rule of cooperative tactics. The development of morality is a conceivable way to resolve this conflict. By means of simple rules, morality suppressed deviousness in the communal life of close associates (Kummer 1978). As a result, it is now considered praise rather than disparagement when a friend is described as being straightforward, having no ulterior motives.

Male Consideration of Female Preferences

By now, women readers may be feeling that they have heard enough about the males' organization. Some of my students were also not happy with the idea that the females had so little influence in the social structure of *Papio hamadryas*. I should confess that cooperation among competitors so dangerously armed as the hamadryas males has always had a special fascination for me. Also, at the beginning of a project one's attention is attracted to what is most conspicuous. In this case, that was the behavior of the males. It was not until later that we became aware of the more subtle ways in which the females under male dominance try to satisfy their own needs.

We have already learned from Eduard Stammbach's work that in the absence of males, hamadryas females form a substitute for one-male groups by conferring on the alpha female the central position of family leader (p. 55). In the Zurich Zoo, Vecchia, once persecuted by all the others, later took upon herself the functions of the incompetent family leader Ulysses (see chapter 1). Hans Sigg had shown how the peripheral females, the ones farther from the male, emancipate themselves from the male for foraging and develop an ecological competence of benefit not only to themselves but to all the family (pp. 125ff). However, no one had investigated whether, within the natural bands, the females can choose their mates at least within certain limits. Not, that is, until my student Christian Bachmann began working toward his Master's degree (23). He was reluctant to accept that the hamadryas females are merely property, herded by their mate and respected by his rivals. Their ancestors must have had minds of their own, as the female savanna baboons still obviously do; surely that could not have been completely extinguished. Bachmann raised the hypothesis that the hamadryas female knows exactly which male she wants, and that the males can discern this preference and

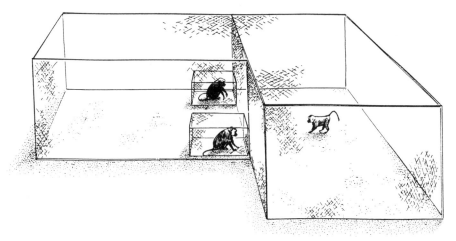

Fig. 32. In Christian Bachmann's choice experiment, the female (right) had the unrestricted opportunity to express her preference for one male or the other.

even be influenced by it. I did not think this was very likely, but Bachmann's idea and his planned experiment were interesting, so I gladly let him go ahead.

First he collaborated with Edi Stammbach on a series of choice experiments, in which each of the six females in our colony in Zurich was given a chance to express a degree of preference for the six males, so that a popularity rank order could be established (fig. 32). In each experiment the two students presented a female with two males. So that the males could not influence her choice between them by their own activities, each of them was kept in a small wire-mesh cage. The female could move freely back and forth between them and, if she wanted to, groom one or the other through the mesh. Her preference was measured by a point system in which the time she spent close to one or the other male was converted to a preference score. Even at this stage the surprises began. Although a female could compare only two males at a time, the responses of each female over a series of tests resulted in a consistent preference list, with no internal contradictions. That is, if the female preferred Winnie to Warto and Warto to Sago, in a choice between Winnie and Sago she should logically prefer Winnie, and that is what she did. The second surprise was that the preferences of the individual females varied; that is, for each of them the "best" male was different. And the third: the rank order of the males among themselves, which we knew, was irrelevant to the females. They chose according to other criteria, unknown to us even today.

According to Bachmann's hypothesis, these clear choices by the females were not merely ineffectual expressions of their own inclinations.

Its second part predicted that the greater the female partner's affection for her possessor, the more a male rival would respect a pair. This was not so easy to test, because in our possession experiments in Awash the rivals had respected *all* the marriages of other males in their troop, so that the females' preferences could make no difference. But Christian Bachmann had a plan. He repeated our possession experiments but designed them so that the rivals had an advantage over the possessor and therefore had less incentive to respect the marriage (fig. 33).

In Scene 1 the possessor moved freely in a compartment of the enclosure next to which the female had been placed in a small cage. The rival, also in a small cage, was positioned in the neighboring compartment at a considerable distance from the female. Therefore the possessor could stay close to the female, and the distant rival could observe the two as a pair. In Scene 2, the rival was released from the small cage so that he, too, could approach the female, within the limits of his compartment. In the next scenes Bachmann moved the cage containing the female progressively away from the possessor and toward the rival, in several uniform stages. Bachmann had intuitively chosen the distances so well that in about half the tests the rivals did not respect the marriage, as indicated by their either reaching toward the female through the cage or directing bites at the possessor. Now he could study what factors affected this respect, or its absence. To my surprise and delight, the results confirmed Bachmann's hypothesis. The rivals respected a marriage significantly more the higher the possessor was on the female's preference list. Furthermore, there was another feature that even Bachmann had not expected. Only the medium- and low-ranking rivals took the female's preference into account. High-ranking rivals ignored it.

Was it because the high-ranking males were unable to discern the degree to which the female was attached to her possessor? This is a conceivable explanation, since Bunnell and his coworkers (1980) have found that among rhesus monkeys, high-ranking males discriminate less well in certain learning tasks. The implication is not necessarily that high-ranking males are stupid; after all, they were once low-ranking themselves. Perhaps it is merely that they have no need to pay attention to everything, as lower-ranking individuals must. In the case of the hamadryas baboons, the situation would be as follows. If a female wants to stay with her present partner, it is less likely that a rival's attack on him will be rewarded. During the fight, the female can keep fleeing to her mate, and even if the rival should succeed in abducting her, the unwilling female would be harder for him to herd. For relatively low-ranking rivals, these factors can make a difference. High-ranking ones, with their superior fighting ability, run less risk of injury and are therefore better able to bear the extra costs of an unwilling female; hence they may not need to concern themselves with such subtleties.

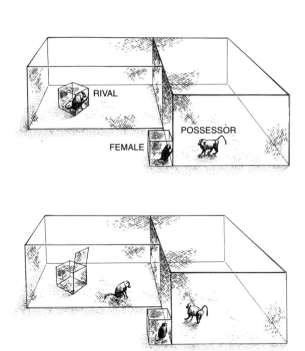

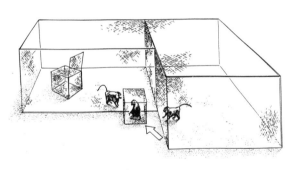

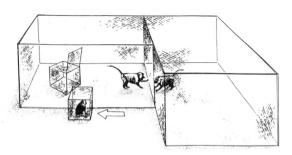

Fig. 33. In the four scenes of Christian Bachmann's experiment (top to bottom), the female in her cage is gradually moved closer to the rival (arrows). In Scene 4, about half the rivals attack rather than continuing to respect the marriage. This outcome is most likely when the possessor does not rank highly in the female's order of preferences.

In the last analysis, then, "consideration" for the females' preferences could simply benefit the males themselves. Nevertheless, the consideration displayed by Christian Bachmann's rival males is a first evolutionary step on the road to a more egalitarian society. The journey started long before humans invented the ethical principles on which to base a demand for equal rights. It began as soon as a strong individual realized that he had more to gain from cooperation with a weak one—whether his female or a lower-ranking male—than from pure dominance. And this realization becomes possible when the individual is capable of consideration for the inclinations of the weaker one. Such delicacy of perception does not necessarily mean that the strong can attribute a mental state to the weak, as humans can. In Bachmann's experiments, the rivals may have perceived only that the opposing male behaved in a more determined way when he was the partner his female wanted.

Even if consideration for another individual is just an elaborated form of selfishness, it still constitutes a real gain for that individual. The history of progress toward equal rights raises interesting questions: How much has in fact resulted from the calculated interests of those in power, and how much from an ethical ideal?

The Story of the Treasure Chest

At the time of our field study in the Awash National Park, relations between the Karaju nomads and the park personnel were strained. The government in Addis Ababa had ordered the Karaju to leave their traditional grazing grounds at the Fantalle volcano, forever. Grazing cattle were thought to have an adverse effect on the park, which from then on was supposed to be exclusively the province of wild animals. Recently an Ethiopian park guard had barely escaped being shot in the head from ambush; the bullet passed through his hat. A rumor was going around that the nomads would soon overrun the park and drive out the employees, tourists, and researchers. We devised vague plans for such an emergency, in which we would cross the Awash in the rowboat and escape downstream along a narrow trail the smugglers used.

Although the nomads were sometimes a nuisance to us—for instance, by breaking and stealing the chains that we used to secure our traps from theft—in this dispute our sympathies were with them. Their use of the park for grazing had been moderate, and there was abundant wildlife. After all, their region had been found suitable for a national park: what better evidence could there be of well-balanced ecological management? Since Emperor Menelik's troops had exterminated the buffalo and giraffes, their cattle occupied the buffalo's ecological niche and kept the grass short enough to satisfy the rare Soemmering's gazelles. The nomads should have been left in the park and compensated for not increasing their use of pasture by giving them a share of the entrance fees. The Karaju were understandably skeptical about promises of other grazing lands.

The Karaju's resentment was directed more toward the government in Addis Ababa than toward us. One morning, when the tension was at its peak, I drove up the gently rolling Kudu Valley, in the shade of the acacias, to look for hamadryas cliffs near the Fantalle. On the first rise stood a single Karaju. He aimed his gun at me and kept me in his sights until I had passed around his hill and out of sight. This did not cause me great alarm, because the nomads are warriors and for that very reason understand discretion in the use of weapons. With them escalation is calculated; they are not carried away by rage as I might be. In the experience related below, however, I learned even more. I wrote the story down as a birthday present to my wife, for lack of a better; it tells of a time when her most important possession had not been respected, and she had missed the crucial events.

Dear Verena,

Do you know that for six hours you once held in pledge one hundred and seventy eight camels (strictly speaking, dromedaries)? It was one of the days on which you keep asking yourself whether what you see is really true. Because we agreed to be economical in the treats we give each other this year, I am dedicating this story to you on your birthday in the bush. It was enacted like a well-rehearsed play on the thorny stage, with dignity but also much laughter.

The cast:

The Governor: Ato (Mr.) Mashesha Mogos, the young governor of Metahara. A tall man with a round, boyish face, wearing light pants and a black leather jacket. He is fond of climbing onto a boulder to issue his commands, and standing there with his chin and nonexisting belly thrust forward.

The Lieutenant: Ato Mogos Gebre Maskal, police lieutenant of Awash. Very young, a bit rotund, in immaculate light uniform and hat turned up at the sides. A countenance of almost bridal beauty. For the first scenes, Ato Mogos has strapped on a giant pistol and a little knife in a red sheath.

The Policemen:

Ato Wolde Selassie Idjda, police sergeant in the market town Merti. Older, rounder, quieter than the others.

The corporal: industrious, zealous; his ambition assuaged by his first promotion.

Sagay Gabru, the handsome policeman. Elegant, carrying a gun.

Dado Wolde Michael, the policeman with the sad expression, saddle nose, mustache, and also a gun.

These represent the government's forces.

Now the Karaju:

First Balabat (chieftain): Balabat Boru Fantalle, a forty-year-old giant in handmade leather sandals and a straw-colored, shabby police coat. Moderate mushroom hairdo, bold face with wide, arched nose. Remarkably yellowish eyes that gaze afar; the sun has engraved deep folds at the base of his nose. Because the coat has lost all its buttons, the balabat keeps his hands folded over his stomach, which adds a delicate, abstracted note to his bravely calm demeanor.

Second Balabat: A bizarre, lean form, always in motion, wearing a white turban, brilliant blue jacket, Somali loincloth, light short socks and European shoes.

Third Balabat: Kato Fantalle. A small, thin Karaju in the native sand-colored toga, with sandals cut from automobile tires. The right eye closed to a slit by an old wound; V-shaped scar decorating the base of his nose. Unprepossessing, intelligent.

First Shumagerli (old man): A tall, slender graybeard with dust-colored loincloth and the broad, bent nomad dagger tucked aslant into the front of his belt. Strikingly large, glowing eyes. Can burst into laughter in the midst of an outraged tirade.

First to Ninth Karaju: Wrapped in camel-colored cloths, with mushroom hairdos, tire sandals, and old guns with brass mountings that they carry horizontally across their shoulders, their arms slung over them.

The thief's group:

The Thief: A young Karaju shepherd. Stays behind the curtains throughout the performance.

The Second Shumagerli: A melancholy ancient, leader of the camel herders.

The Thief's Father: An old man with an even sadder mien.

The Hostage: A twelve-year-old shepherd boy.

The Corpus Delicti: Your red tin box with money, passport, a mysterious pair of earrings, jewelry, letters, address book. The heart of your itinerant earthly possessions.

Setting: Road from Addis Ababa to Awash in a lonely region at the Garibaldi pass, twenty-seven miles east of Metahara; the Metahara police station; the market at Merti; a Karaju kraal at the foot of the Fantalle volcano; the brickworks at Merti.

Time: November 20 to 22, 1968.

And now to the action, which was so typical of the complex yet finally effective actions of Ethiopian officials.

On the 20th of November the Kummer family left Addis Ababa to return to Awash in the heavily loaded diesel Land Rover; I was still full of smoldering anger about all the trouble we had had from the bureaucracy there. On the lonely stretch at the pass, we came upon a large herd of camels traveling in front of us along the road, driven by a group of Karaju. With their usual apparent arrogance the young Karaju shepherds demanded "k'brit" (matches), but this time they went away empty-handed. The camels began to kick out and proceeded ahead of us at an ambling trot. There were rock walls on either side of the road, so they could not get out of the way. We considerately slowed to a walking pace, surrounded by the dust of the camels and by the gesticulating Karajus. Suddenly our eight-year-old daughter Katie called out from under the canvas cover, the only place she could fit in: "Hey, Mommy, he's taking the little box." She had seen a black hand reaching under the cover from behind. You began to protest, for the box contained all the property you valued. I stopped the Land Rover abruptly, fuming, grabbed the loaded pistol, and jumped out onto the road. The mushroom-heads scattered in all directions, and your red case was gone—we did not know where. In the Land Rover everyone was howling except Urs, our youngest boy. I sent a low shot after one of the Karaju. Then I discovered the Second Shumagerli, the only one who remained standing quietly on a bare spot next to the road. I called out to him, but he said only "Ene yellem, ene yellem" (not me), whereupon he too saw a shot hitting the ground in front of his feet. He did not give way an inch. I ran toward him to take him hostage, but he raised his gun and aimed it. You were begging me to stay by the car. You were right, of course. The little round hole pointed at my face convinced me to get in again and drive on. I was now even more angry because the Karaju had maliciously exploited my courtesy in slowing down for the sake of the herdsmen, but eventually I calmed down and noted the mileage so that we could identify where it had happened.

We drove straight to the police station at the sugar plantation in Merti, but our friend, Lieutenant Alemseged Gebre Yohannes, was not there. The sergeant said we should come back at nine the next morning. In the darkness we drove along the muddy track to our tukul, with no hope of ever seeing your treasure chest again.

The next morning Walter Götz, Walter Angst, and I decided to join forces in recovering the lost prize. We still had the mistaken idea that this was a kind of cowboys-and-Indians game, with a good charge at the end.

In the morning, at nine o'clock, we indeed found the sergeant standing in front of the police station, preparing to leave. We drove with him to the police station at Metahara, a plot of bare ground roughly fenced in, with all kinds of rusty engine parts scattered around, and an earthen hut. A few policemen came out, stooping through the low door. We waited. The governor appeared and greeted us. The police recorder also arrived and sat down at the desk, and the translator announced: "First we must write." And write he did, over my objection that "First we must catch." As we went through the list of stolen items, we had more and more trouble with the English-Amharic translation. Finally, I pushed the English list toward the recorder and convinced all present that it was more important to catch the thieves than to catalog the damage. It was ten o'clock.

We stepped out into the yard. There the governor was already giving instructions to a gigantic Karaju, holding his old police coat together like a bathrobe: Balabat Boru Fantalle. The translator explained that to begin with, someone would have to go to the market at Merti to find out who was currently in charge of those camels. But first, he said, it was necessary to go to church. Indeed, from the tin-roofed, octagonal Coptic church there resounded deep drumbeats, the long-drawn-out song of the Amharic priests approached, and from the village a column of schoolchildren carrying Ethiopian flags emerged to meet the priests' procession. The populace assembled. Above their heads the white turbans of the long-frocked priests swayed in a ceremonial dance, to the constant background of the deep drum. Some Karaju watched this Christian performance, expressionless. Through the mire of the village street a third procession approached, a flock of turkeys clucking loudly with heads held high.

In a remarkably short time the ceremony was over. The governor came back. The handsome young Awash police lieutenant also popped up from somewhere. The Karaju in the police coat climbed into the back of our car, and we all drove to the market square in the nearby village of Merti. Silently, the Karaju positioned himself at the edge of the market and stood there with hands folded, peering at length into the colorful crowd with his yellow eyes. Watching him, I gradually perceived not an inconsequential market visitor but what he really was: Balabat Boru Fantalle, Karaju chieftain. Then he dived into the throng and soon reappeared with the Second Balabat, the thin, imaginatively dressed one. There followed a flurry of obscure activity; messengers slipped all around the market on various quests, ran into the village, came back, and disappeared again. Meanwhile, nomads and villagers climbed over the wide, rickety rope-and-log bridge that crossed the Awash River to the market, leading bizarrely up and down through the crown of a giant fig tree. Among the shady branches, old men could be seen walking unsteadily and supporting one another. A sheep slipped between two of the gnarled logs, and plopped down onto the river bank.

Eventually, having been joined by the Second Balabat and some Karaju picked up at the market, we drove our two Land Rovers back to Metahara. There the governor, the lieutenant, the translator, the handsome policeman, the sad policeman, the corporal and the sergeant also packed themselves into the vehicles. With sagging springs we chugged out onto the road leading to the scene of the theft. It was 11:30.

Wherever we met anyone, Boru Fantalle descended from his undignified seat on the load space of the Land Rover and asked about the herd of camels. A truck driver had encountered them on the road early that morning, but on his return trip they were no longer there. Somewhere, the thief's group had left the road. We stopped where the mileage indicator directed us. With some difficulty I found the place. Walking bent over ahead of the Land Rovers, I examined the camel tracks. They continued east about five hundred yards and then vanished. We didn't know whether the herd had turned off the road here, or whether the rain during the night had washed out the trail farther to the east. We stopped. Boru Fantalle climbed over a fence of dry thorn branches to a little shepherd girl. She had seen the camels traveling inland that morning, toward the south. We drove a little farther eastward and stopped again. The two chieftains led us through the bush to a large thorn kraal. At the dark entrance to an unusually large, hemispherical grass hut, Karaju men were seated for a ceremonial meal of meat. One of them was using his knife to cut strips of skin from the severed head of a cow. Only the two Karaju chieftains entered the sariba. The Amharic policemen stayed tactfully at a distance; representatives of the government in Addis Ababa preferred to let the Karaju settle such matters themselves, if at all possible. More Karaju appeared out of the dark grass cave, including the First Shumagerli, the tall one with the volatile moods, and the Third Balabat, Kato Fantalle. Two of the men had painted their foreheads with cow's blood, and most had the V-shaped decorative scar at the base of the nose. A long palaver began. When one spoke, the others listened attentively. No one ever interrupted another (do you hear that?). The younger men stood back a little, listening but saying nothing. The women had disappeared into the bush. Soon the men from the grass house followed them, in a closed group. The translator said they knew where the thieves were and had gone to negotiate with them.

We expected nothing to come of this except that the thieves would now have been warned and could escape more easily. In fact, we were seeing the inescapable tribal laws in action. There were no arguments or threats, merely negotiation, in the certainty that even in the unending bush the thief could not get away from his tribe. If he tried to escape into the regions occupied by the Adal or the Issa, the translator told us, he would be killed there. The Karaju chieftains, whether under coercion or voluntarily, were on the side of justice. "This is the greatest shame for them," the translator declared. Again the Amhara stayed at a distance, seated on a tree trunk. The remaining Karaju from the grass house offered to slaughter a fat sheep for them, but they declined politely. Here it is not considered necessary to eat three times a day.

It was two o'clock by the time the delegation returned. The negotiations had evidently failed. There was a short discussion, with the decision to mount a pincer movement. The grass-hut Karaju departed in the direction of the thieves. Boru Fantalle directed the motorized contingent onto a side track, which brought us close to the flank of the camel herd. As we got out, on the west side of the herd, the Karaju from the grass house were just appearing on the horizon at the opposite side of the herd. No sign of the herders; they had run away. Only the twelve-year-old boy had remained with the camels, and he too withdrew into the bush. It looked as though our efforts had been in vain. There was a lot of standing around and leisurely conversation. But suddenly the sergeant discovered the hiding herd boy, seized him by the collar, and locked him into one of our Land Rovers as a hostage. Then the lieutenant gave a command, upon which the policemen and Karaju fanned out, surrounded the camels, and began to drive the bellowing animals down to the main road. The ranking authorities carried on their casual chatting, as though the whole thing was now settled. We were skeptical. In response to my question, the translator said only, "They will come." He meant the thieves. Meanwhile, the herd boy reported having seen your little tin box. Below us, the camels were streaming out onto the highway. We strolled after them. On the hill behind us, two figures appeared, but when we looked around, they fled.

We gathered on the road by our bellowing, blubbering captives and next to a Karaju kraal, from which other striking figures emerged. These new recruits were given the job of managing the restless herd. One sixteen-year-old objected. Without formality, the handsome policeman disarmed him and locked him up in a Land Rover. The First Shumagerli lodged a vigorous protest with the governor, who responded imperiously from his elevated position on a boulder—but both of them were laughing in between their rhetoric.

Meanwhile, I tried to console the weeping hostage with a banana. The boy would not accept it until the balabat in the blue jacket had eaten a piece in front of him.

The assembly by the roadside was now so picturesque that every passing car driver slowed and looked in astonishment at the Karaju squatting along the embankment. One of the cars stopped, and our host Lieutenant Alemseged from Metahara got out. His sergeant greeted him by kissing him on the cheeks, and he responded in the same way. After asking cordially how things were proceeding, he drove on. The efficient corporal, who was recording the expedition in Amharic writing as we went along, meticulously noted that one hundred seventy-eight camels had been confiscated.

It was five-thirty in the afternoon. The thief's group had not appeared. Finally, two policemen were assigned to the camel guard and the rest got into the Land Rovers. We adjourned until morning. The engines were just beginning to growl when Boru Fantalle ordered everyone out again. A hesitant form materialized far away in the bush, indistinct in the twilight. Side by side, our Karaju advanced ceremoniously toward it, surrounded it, and vanished with it in the direction from which it had come. The Amhara stayed close to the cars and whistled at our inquisitive Ueli Nagel, to call him back: this was a matter for the Karaju. The Amhara were already congratulating us on the return of the treasure chest.

Three of our Karaju returned. Boru Fantalle had now seen the red box with his own eyes. The Shumagerli of the camel herders had described to him how the theft came about. By way of Boru, we heard his version. It was completely true to the actual events, with no retinting, excuses, or complaints about my shots.

We waited, and darkness fell. At 6:30 a light appeared in the distance, moving up and down in a walking rhythm. Our Karaju came back with an old man from the thief's group, the same one before whom I had fired into the ground. Melancholic and rather shy, he stood in front of me while, in the routine legal procedure, I was asked whether I identified him as the leader of the perpetrators. In a sense, they were putting me to the test. I replied that he must be, if he could relate the events so accurately. Laughter and palaver. Then the old man withdrew behind the hill, alone. No one was worried that he would run away with the thieves. Another wait. In the darkness, the Karaju squatted silently on their thin calves, while the Amhara gossiped happily, once interrupting themselves to stop a truck that was coming down the road without lights.

And then, incredibly, at the edge of the acacia thicket there actually appeared a red rectangle in a thin, black hand, illuminated by the beam of a flashlight. Everyone got up. The old man stepped up close to me and, without a word, laid your little box at my feet. Then he vanished in the darkness, certainly not the first elder who had to take responsibility for the impetuous young men under his authority. We crouched around the box, while everyone else chattered and laughed. In the middle of the road an eager inventory-taking began. With some embarrassment I pulled out your tangled treasures and spread them on the road in full view. Everything smelled slightly like a Karaju camp: smoke, cattle, withered grass, rancid butter, dust. The sergeant checked things off the list. The gold brooch for your mother, your earrings, letters, stamps, passport, the silver necklace from Harar, Katie's painfully missed plastic monkey—everything but the twenty Ethiopian dollars, a loss we could easily endure. Tips were handed out all around.

Under the trees on the bank of the Awash, an hour later, you were even more incredulous when your flashlight revealed the little box dangling from my hand.

Early the next morning I picked up a brand new lieutenant in Awash. Hardly had he entered the police hut in Metahara when a plaintive stammering became audible under the gate to the courtyard. A man about thirty years old, in the short pants and shirt full of holes that were typical of the Kulis, crept across the yard toward the lieutenant with his forehead in the dust, incessantly calling out "Abéd, abéd" (help). He remained face down on the ground before the lieutenant until the latter amiably helped him up. Still with dusty forehead, the man explained that his employer had behaved badly toward him; he made gestures to indicate beatings and kicks. Then the lieutenant asked some questions, and finally the man went away, evidently in the hope that justice would be done.

I frittered away the ensuing hour's wait by feeding candy to a little girl and treating a young prostitute's baby for a rash, while the dignitaries assembled for the arrest of the thief. Ato Mashesha then had to give two Kulis instructions for making the soil mixture with which to construct the wall of a hut, and finally the whole assembly drove back to the confiscated camels.

A graying forty-year-old stepped out of the sariba of the Karaju village and announced that the thief's group had run away during the night. Making an expansive gesture with his toga-draped arm, he indicated the yellow mountain ridges. No one was very eager to look for the escaped malefactor there. Instead, the governor shanghaied two young Karaju and commanded them to drive the hundred and seventy-eight camels the twenty-five miles to Metahara—a massive forfeit for the fugitive thief. One of the two recruits first had to be caught and threatened with prison before he acquiesced, sullenly, to this unwelcome assignment.

Balabat Boru Fantalle said good-bye, gathered the buttonless police coat more snugly around his stomach, and set out with folded hands toward Nazareth, almost sixty miles to the west along the dusty road, with no food or water.

The ones with the real power—the Amharic governor and the policemen—I drove back to Metahara. Here I was introduced to a young Karaju who had shaved off his mushroom hairdo and put on European clothing and a pretentious manner. In his company, by order of the governor I picked my way over the tufts of harsh grass toward a village at the foot of the volcano, to fetch the owner of the camels, another young Karaju. He had already heard what had happened and was waiting for us under an acacia.

We then had to go to the brickworks at Merti. In the arid yard I found a cool retreat between stacks of fresh, damp bricks and settled down to wait once again. The mushroomless Karaju looked for the thief's father and eventually found him. Submitting to fate, the old man crawled into the Land Rover and accompanied the camel owner and me to Metahara, while nineteen miles to the west, in a cloud of dust, the herd of camels was also approaching the seat of judgment.

As to the legal proceedings that then ensued, I know nothing. I heard rumors that the thief had been apprehended and shut up in the Metahara jail. May he be dreaming of your red box and the mysterious things that a "ferendshi" woman carries around with her.

That is the story as I wrote it then, unrevised. This was but one in a whole series of incidents with the nomads, and at times the difficulties seemed interminable and infuriating. I shall add only that in this case, and later, the nomads inspired in us respect and ultimately sympathy. Perhaps it was traditional for them to consider everything wandering about in their land as their own property and booty. But they also kept their word steadfastly. Their eventual fate under the pressure of the highlanders' hunger for land was sad, like the fate of nomads all over the world. It was reported that in that very year the Karaju chieftain at the Fantalle volcano in Awash National Park was shot by his own people because he had entered into negotiation with the Amharic rulers of the country. He had hardly had a choice.

CHAPTER FIVE

Life Histories

Childhood

So far we have been observing the life of the hamadryas baboons at Erer only in snapshots, taken as they pursue their interests during everyday activities and in critical situations. But what about the consequences of these events? Some of the things that happen to the animals and that they do will affect them for years to come. Indeed, a baboon's whole life may be determined by its behavior and skill at a particular moment. Despite the differences among individuals, the lives of most hamadryas baboons pass through the same stages. The only fundamental differences in life history are those between the two sexes.

The bands and clans outlast the lifespan of an individual baboon, and their compositions during its life place the boundary conditions on its career. The crucial developments of the latter are related to the formation and dissolution of the families in which the baboon lives at various ages.

In 1971 the Cone Rock troop numbered more than two hundred individuals. Therefore Jean-Jacques and Helga Abegglen began to identify the young baboons in Band I at Cone Rock by marking their ears; what we know about hamadryas life histories is due mainly to these two young researchers (29). To mark the baboons the Abegglens and their successors caught individuals in cage traps like those we had used at Awash. The baboons were then anesthetized, and differently colored numbered plastic tags were attached to their ears. In the evening, when they had recovered completely, they were released into the troop. After the Abegglens, the Siggs, and the Stolbas continued to observe the identified baboons and marked the new young ones. In the summer of 1974 all sixty-seven baboons of Band I could be distinguished from one another. These, plus Bands II and III, were the main contingent of the Cone Rock troop, 236 animals altogether. In February 1977 the longitudinal study of the troop had to be terminated because of the effects on the Ogaden of the war between Ethiopia and Somalia. It was not easy to accept the end of the hamadryas project when it was just in its most productive phase, especially since by then we had a simple house in Erer as well as an enclosure for experiments; each year was bringing us more insight into the order underlying the lives of the baboons. Because of this interruption there are gaps in the overall picture of their social organization, gaps that may never be filled. Since then no other researchers have taken up the study of the Ethiopian hamadryas, whose habitat was already then being progressively degraded by the humans who overexploit it. Edi Stammbach had just designed a preliminary project concerning the ecological knowledge of the hamadryas and the strategies by which they make use of their environment when the war broke out and the project had to be abandoned.

The observations of the hamadryas that we were able to carry out began with the adults, as they are the ones that shape the social organization. The childhood phase was not our prime concern, so I can give only a relatively brief description here.

Among the hamadryas, mothers usually give birth at night. Nevertheless, the Abegglens were once able to observe a birth (16). Just before twilight, at 6:15 in the evening, they found a barely adult female crouching at White Rock with her arms raised in an unusual way. Her male, also young and accompanied by a juvenile female in addition to her, sat a meter away from the crouching female, scratched himself continually, and wiped his muzzle as though in conflict. The female in labor crouched in such a way that her vulva did not touch the ground, and whenever the contractions began she raised her arms vertically. Their notes continue: At 6:20 the baby's head appears. The male casts brief, attentive glances toward his female. Now the whole family gets up and goes deeper into the troop. The baby's head disappears back into the vulva. As another family passes, the young male briefly mounts the female in labor—probably a sketchy demonstration of possession. The young mother leaves the troop on the other side and sits down ten meters away from it, at the edge of the cliff. The male follows her and sits down beside her, two meters away. At 6:30 the contractions begin again. The mother crouches, lies down. Then she steps up to the brink of the cliff, turns, and crouches so that her bottom is sticking out over the abyss. The head of the fetus reappears. The contractions become more violent, and again the female raises her arms. In the pauses she supports herself on one hand or sits on the side of her pelvis, touches her vulva and then licks her hand. 6:35: slowly the upper half of the baby's head appears; the mother is still crouching with her vulva beyond the edge of the cliff. The juvenile female comes, smells the vulva and runs away. At 6:40 the mother brings the baby into the world. It falls, and for a moment it is suspended from the umbilical cord. The male jumps forward and tries to catch it, but the mother has already turned outward and seized her newborn. The male quickly retires to a distance. The mother holds the child against her belly, bites through the cord, and licks the infant. It cries. A few minutes later the placenta emerges, but the mother does not chew it as I saw in another case; she continues to clean the child. Once again the juvenile female approaches, sniffs at the newborn, and hurries away. By now it has become too dark to see any more. . . . This mother was probably bearing her first child.

That she let it emerge above the chasm was perhaps a misguided attempt to keep the vulva off the ground.

In some monkey species the infants have conspicuously colored hair. The hair of baby baboons is black during their first half year (plate 4, top and bottom right). During the weeks after birth the infant never leaves its mother's breast; later it ventures to totter away on small excursions. The mother never lets it out of her sight and retrieves it at the slightest disturbance, or she simply keeps it near by holding on to the end of its tail. Older juveniles and neighboring females continually try to touch the little one and to embrace it, but they rarely succeed. Only looking and snuffling are allowed. Males are more privileged; it is hard for mothers to prevent them from interacting with the infants (fig. 34). In innocent ignorance the tiny black creatures climb onto the knees and heads of the gray giants, but the worst that happens is that they are squeezed in a strong embrace. A year later, a mere glance from an adult male will send them into a fit of kecking. When the troop is on the march, the little one clings with all fours to the hairs on the mother's flank and hangs under her belly; as a result, after a while some mothers develop triangular bald patches on their sides. Later the infant clings to mother's back instead, and finally, after its hair has turned brown, it often sits upright there, riding far back on her rump and leaning against the base of her tail. Thus its hands are free to pull off a leaf in passing and nibble it for a while.

More than 90 percent of the time that adult baboons spend on social activities is devoted to members of their families. The very young behave more freely in this respect, visiting children of neighboring families and sometimes going even farther afield, into neighboring bands. As we have seen, the older juveniles then try to retrieve their small companions. This is their job, because if a mother or a father transgresses the band boundaries, marital relations are endangered. The mother would risk being abducted by a male in the other band, and the father could be attacked as a potential abductor. It is probably for this reason that at the sleeping cliff each band rests in its own, defined area.

While the babies are still black, as soon as they can they crawl to neighboring children and begin scuffling with them. At first they are awkward, but gradually, especially after growing their brown hair, the young baboons wrestle with greater vigor and success. Finally they are able to slide down sandy hillsides as they romp, hang upside down among the acacia branches, or chase one another through the labyrinthine roots exposed by erosion of the steep slopes.

Here they are in danger of being struck by falling rocks. Baboons often unintentionally dislodge stones as they pass through steep regions, but none has ever appeared to be concerned about the consequences, except on one occasion. The film producer August Kern, while working with us

Fig. 34. A mother kecks anxiously while relinquishing her youngster to her male, who receives it with friendly lip-smacking.

in 1964, once saw an adult male walking down a scree-covered slope to the upper edge of the White Rock cliff. As the baboon sat down there, he disturbed a stone about two inches in diameter. Six feet directly below him, infants were playing on a ledge. The male did something quite unusual: in a flash he seized the rolling stone, and he continued to hold it in the hand resting on his knee even when a female sat down beside him and groomed him. All the time, he was watching the infants. Barely a minute later the little ones went away, the male opened his hand, and the stone fell down over the deserted playground. Otherwise we never saw a baboon sitting with a stone in its hand.

A quick eye is needed to tell the sex of these tumbling youngsters by the inconspicuous anatomical signs. In their behavior, however, Fred and I could detect a difference between the sexes even in the black-haired stage (6). The young females spend more time with their mothers than the young males do, by a factor of three; even as infants, the males play in groups with other young males. This difference becomes more pronounced as time goes on, and the inevitable result is that males have mainly males as playmates. The female juveniles soon withdraw from the wilder games. At the age of three years the males' inclination to play at fighting reaches its peak; at this stage, some of them are no longer sleeping with their family but some distance away, on a separate ledge with males of their own age or older. Three-year-old females continue to live with their mother's family; they are gradually playing less often, and then only when the game is centered around a nearly adult male who can intervene in case of a quarrel. Biting games are much more common among males than females, whereas the two sexes equally often play at chasing and tussling without bites. Conversely, female children have a greater tendency than males to spend time playfully fingering and examining pebbles, small pieces of wood, soil, or leaves. These differences reflect the males' relatively strong urge to engage in rough activity and to attack. The tendency of males toward a greater employment of force is the only behavioral difference between the sexes to have been demonstrated in the laboratory, for rhesus monkeys. These experiments showed clearly the cause of this difference; the testes of male rhesus monkeys secrete the male sex hormone testosterone for a short time while the individual is still in his mother's body. Under the control of the hormone circulating in the blood of the male fetus, the brain develops in the direction of an increased tendency toward wrestling and vigorous action. Once having been switched onto this track, it cannot change back; when males are castrated after birth, they are still different from the females in this respect, even as adults (Goy 1966). This sex difference is literally inborn.

In later childhood, from the third to the fifth year, free-living hamadryas baboons play less and less and finally stop altogether. Now the males begin visiting other bands, and these visits may keep them away from their own band and their home cliff for days or even weeks at a time (p. 159). This may be partly because the males are more adventurous, but we shall soon see that most females in this age group would be prevented from indulging a desire for adventure even if they had one. They are already being guarded by their first male. A female's freedom is greatest while she is still living in her parental family. There, when she has her first swellings she can still mate with even younger, sexually immature males, meeting them secretly behind rocks (6). Sometimes one or two other little males wait behind the pair until it is their turn (fig. 35). If they are discovered by the young female's father, the punishment will be mild; the fathers are not much interested in small daughters, and an adult male will also not seriously attack a juvenile male, but merely chases him into a bush.

The sexual freedom enjoyed by the young comes to an end at puberty and never returns. It may have been nice while it lasted, but its contribution to reproductive success is at most to provide practice for later on. Once a youth sports a little mantle, the adult males will not let him get away with such things; he is now condemned to years of enforced abstinence. There remains only one way to a female, and that is through the

Fig. 35. Before they reach adolescence and are forced to live in sexual abstinence, juvenile hamadryas males can mate with females that have just become sexually mature, without risking punishment.

marriage bond. In the next sections we shall first follow the males through the sexless transitional years and then consider the tactics they use to free a female from her parents' supervision, only to guard her more strictly themselves.

The Follower Years

After puberty, a male at first has no chance of achieving a marriage of his own. All the females are in the secure possession of adult males. With his twenty-eight pounds, a subadult cannot hope to defeat a full-grown, forty-five-pound male in battle; and even if he were equally strong, the rival-inhibition effect would keep him from fighting. The massive superiority of full-grown males is a problem for subadults in most species that form harems. "Sneaker" fish, for example, have a solution: these young males are so similar to females in size, appearance, and behavior that they can join the harem unobserved. Then they may occasionally deposit their own sperm on the newly laid eggs without being detected by the harem owner, a male twice as large as themselves, because the same movement is used to release both sperm and eggs. This elegant strategy has not been observed in any primate species. For fertilization within the female's body, the male must mount her, and that is a conspicuous and undisguisable behavior—quite apart from the fact that primates are more acute observers than fish. The direct approach is no good.

The young male hamadryas has to spend years preparing to establish his own family. The most important relationships he enters into during the five years between sexual maturity and the status of full-grown male are parts of an elaborate buildup to marriage, in which several obstacles must be overcome. I cannot believe that the strategy is planned by the individual. It is much more likely to be the product of an evolution that has equipped the subadults with the correct inclinations at every age. In the following pages, readers can have the fun of trying to see how soon they can discern the long-term function of each step in a subadult's career.

At about six years of age, when the young male reaches sexual maturity, he withdraws somewhat from the other males his age, in whose company he has been spending most of his time, and once again he joins a family. It is almost always a family belonging to the clan in which the male himself was born (29). He becomes what we call a "follower" of this family. Now he is not permitted to have sexual relations with the females. Nevertheless, for long periods he sits idly and inconspicuously one or two yards away from the family when they are resting (plate 6, bottom), and he accompanies them on the daily marches. During the pauses for rest, a young follower is sometimes groomed by adult females in the family. This grooming is the most the leader of the family will allow between his females and the follower. Here is one observation typical of many. A male we called Smoker, because of the yellowish brown hair on his lower back, watched for a while as two of his wives groomed young followers. Then Smoker fixed his gaze on the younger of the two subadults, but without threatening him, until the young male began to make small, unnecessary movements and finally left the female. She gave a contact rumble, turned to her husband, and groomed him. Now Smoker threatened the older follower. He, too, understood immediately; he abruptly turned his back to "his" female. Rather than groom it, she slowly lowered her hands. She had also understood. Both followers continued to stay with Smoker's family (6).

Scenes like this were often observed, but the next one is absolutely unique—an anecdote, as we say among fieldworkers. In Saudi Arabia during 1980 I observed a family of baboons sitting below me, on the next-lower terrace in the rocks. I noticed that one of the females, while remaining seated, was gradually inching away from her male toward a block of stone that was a little higher than her head. A follower was sitting behind the block. The female took about twenty minutes to move the six feet. Finally she was sitting so that her male could see her back and tail, but not her arms and face (fig. 36)—I could tell, because I was sitting in about the same direction as he was. However, I was higher up and so could look over the top of the block: her hands were grooming the follower! The latter had ducked down behind the block and must not have been visible to the husband. An excellent arrangement, it would seem. The husband saw that his wife was there, but not that she was doing something forbidden. It may have been entirely by chance that the rock just barely hid the female's activity. I suspected that the female was cleverly aiming at concealment only because of the very unusual, conspicuously inconspicuous way she had slipped toward it. It looked as though the female had consciously sought out the "I'm here but I'm not doing anything" position. An anecdote is interesting when several circumstances and forms of behavior, each unusual in itself, combine to give an adaptive or purposeful whole. No conclusions can be drawn from anecdotes; they merely suggest ideas for new experiments. In this case my experience told me that the inching forward, the subsequent grooming, and the position of two secretive individuals behind the block of stone *might* have been intentional, but the anecdote did not convince me of this. If the female had planned the final arrangement behind the boulder, she would have had to be able to imagine just how she and her boyfriend appeared from her husband's perspective. Even human children are incapable of such perspective until they are about four years old. This faculty is a very important step in the evolution of social understanding, for it marks the onset of an ability to put oneself in another's place. For this reason, experiments along these lines would be extremely informative. We recently did such an experiment with Javanese monkeys—but the result was negative. I have nevertheless kept the above anecdote in the text, as a warning against the infectious power of anecdotes. After giving a talk in our seminar, an internationally known young speaker was asked by a student whether monkeys knew what others thought. "This has indeed been shown," the speaker replied, and as evidence gave the anecdote of the female and the follower behind the rock, without remembering its source.

Let's return to the relationship between family leaders and followers. What the former tolerates and the latter dares hangs in a delicate balance.

Fig. 36. Female changing position in a manner that looks suspiciously tactical. Bit by bit she has maneuvered herself into a position where her male (top of picture) can see that she is still there but not that she is grooming a follower.

At about six years of age, the follower shows the first traces of the male presenting behavior called "notifying," a signal of great significance in the cooperative relations between adult hamadryas males. In the inhibition experiments, we saw that the possessor of a female uses it for reconciliation with the rival, who has been left emptyhanded. Notifying is also important in another context, when males reach an agreement about the direction in which they will set out on a march. Through this second function, the follower is gradually allowed by "his" adult male to take part in leading the family. I once watched as Sepp, a very young follower of the old, patient Roto, went through his first experiences with it. Roto, the most influential male in the North Band of White Rock, was pausing at a rivulet for his midday rest. Sepp sat three feet away from Roto. The old male turned his face toward Sepp, and the latter immediately returned the gaze. Half a minute later Roto got up, rumbled, and again the two of them looked at each other. Then Roto pointedly shifted his gaze past Sepp, downriver; that was the direction he subsequently imposed as the marching direction for the band, contrary to the inclinations of the other males. Sepp turned his head and also looked downstream. A few minutes later Sepp started to go down to the water, only twelve feet away, to drink, with Roto watching. Touchingly, he stopped halfway as though he had forgotten something, looked over his shoulder into Roto's face, came back, and presented to the old male—elaborately like a female or a young animal, not in the fleeting, ritualized way of a grown male. He acted as though the little trip to the water were a vote to start out on a march! A female with a strict male may have to give notice before going even such a short distance away, but not a follower. Roto acknowledged the boyish "notifying" in the manner of the grown male, brushing the back of his hand lightly over Sepp's testicles. Not until then did Sepp go to drink, after which he immediately seated himself again next to Roto.

Older followers, from about the time when the mantle is half grown, in the eighth year, until they are fully adult, gradually assume the role of a second protector of the family during the day's travels. The females tend increasingly to walk in a line between the follower and the family leader, defended on both flanks by the males. The latter notify to one another often, but it is the older one who decides where the family goes (p. 262). Once full-grown, the follower no longer has any contact with the females; the leader will not even tolerate grooming. The follower appears to ignore the females, and if they come close to him, he gets out of their way, like the rivals in our possession experiments.

The follower years can thus be subdivided into two phases. In the first phase, from age six to about age eight, the follower is still permitted to be groomed by the females. He takes no part in leading the family, but simply goes along with them. In the second phase, when he is between eight and about eleven years old, the females of his older partner are taboo to him, but he walks protectively at one end of the line of females and communicates with the older male about the direction in which they should go.

Has this bonding to a family brought the follower any closer to his own marriage? For the time being, it doesn't look that way. Since his boyhood, when he could mate with females in estrus without risking anything beyond being chased away, the possibility of intimate relations with a female has receded further and further.

Kidnapping

But the followers have other irons in the fire. Around the time of puberty a male develops a marked interest in mothering small baboons (fig. 37). He will draw them close and hug them, turn his hindquarters toward them as an invitation to go for a ride, and carry them around the sleeping cliff on his stomach or back. Followers do all this twice as frequently as subadult females, from whom one would tend to expect it. When we first observed such conduct, in 1961 at White Rock, the followers were usually keeping the infants with them against their will (6), and for that reason we called it kidnapping. It looked like the following example.

Fig. 37. A follower, barely full-grown, stands protectively over an orphaned child. Only young males adopt orphans.

A mother is standing in front of a bush, staring into it and screaming. Her male, named Saus, looks up and rushes to her side. Now a follower slinks out of the bush, carrying a black infant on his back. Saus chases him about the sleeping cliff. Turmoil results. Seconds later the infant is free, and the mother invites it onto her back.

Just now Saus has many mothers with black infants in his family. Only ten minutes later another one walks along the ridge of the cliff and looks down at a ledge, where a follower is carrying her infant. The little one repeatedly tries to climb up to its mother but each time the follower pulls it back by its tail. The baby makes the humming sound associated with being abandoned and finally it screams. The mother walks along helplessly above it and looks toward her male, kecking. From where he is sitting he cannot see the kidnapping scene; he merely replies with the soothing contact rumble. This seems to give the mother more courage.

She herself climbs down, but she doesn't dare accost the young male. She merely walks after him until he releases the little one of his own accord.

The kidnapped infants in Erer were never mistreated. It was this kind of behavior in the field, however, that in the Cologne Zoo degenerated into infanticide by half-grown males.

The mothering of infants in their first year of life was also a striking and common event at Cone Rock, but it rarely occurred against the infant's will. Again, it was performed only by the followers; females of the same age never did it. The systematic investigation of Band I by the Abegglens revealed an orderly pattern: in 109 out of 128 cases of kidnapping, the infant belonged to the same clan as the follower that was mothering it. The followers mothered male and female infants with about equal frequency, but in different phases of their lives. While they were five to six years old, they cuddled and carried mainly male infants, whereas followers aged six to eight years usually chose female infants; and this difference was significant—that is, it did not occur by chance.

Can this urge of subadult males to play mother have any function? The Abegglens thought about this and then calculated the difference in age between the family leaders and the followers associated with them (29); it varied only slightly and was always in the range from five to six years. This is the same age difference as that between followers and their foster sons. This arouses the suspicion that they are mothering their own future followers. Remember that we found no convincing ultimate reason for the bonding of males to their clan. Could it be that the males remain attached to the same clan for life because the older generation continually bonds to the younger on an individual basis in earliest childhood? Do the males borrow for this purpose the most strongly bonding interaction from the inventory of the mother-child relationship, the act of embracing and carrying? The Abegglens thought that this might be the causal explanation of the male network and a loyalty to the clan that in related species is found only among females. It would indicate that it is beneficial to the leader of the family to have an inhibited young male, but one that will soon be of fighting age, as an added protection for his harem.

The elegant thing about this solution would be that the older and the younger males are not father and son; although a father-son partnership might well be expected from a human perspective, it is impossible for baboons because of their relative ages. A male hamadryas is about eleven years old before he fathers his first child. By the time his son could become his partner in leading and defense, the father would no longer be the family leader or might even have died. By mothering, however, a young male could acquire a "son by bonding," with whom he could collaborate later. As a fellow clan member, the infant would be a relative—most likely a half-brother, a son of the same father.

The study at Cone Rock did not last long enough for the Abegglens' hypothesis to be tested, but complementary observations came from a zoo. Since 1972, at the Madrid Zoo, the Spanish researchers Fernando Colmenares and Helena Rivero have been following the life histories of the ninety individuals in a group of hybrids of hamadryas and yellow baboons. As mentioned earlier, the yellow baboons of East Africa are savanna baboons. Hamadryas genes are more strongly represented in the Madrid group than those of the yellow baboons and, as would be expected, the males with a hamadryas-like appearance lead closed harems, while those with a greater resemblance to yellow baboons tend to have harems that are less strictly herded and not clearly defined. Like the hamadryas-anubis hybrids in the Awash Canyon, the Madrid hybrids showed us how the ancestors of present-day hamadryas could have behaved during the transition, when they were no longer savanna baboons but not yet hamadryas baboons. The disadvantage is that we can never know whether a particular behavior pattern comes from genes that are "still" retained from the savanna ancestors or "already" evolved by the desert descendants. So much information has been provided by this Madrid study that we shall return to it several times in later sections. For the present, we are concerned with the Abegglens' hypothesis that the followers in the Cone Rock troop are brothers of their family leaders.

Colmenares (1992) distinguishes between closely and loosely associated pairs of males. Closely associated males spend more than 10 percent of their time within a distance of five feet from one another. In Madrid, when a leader and his follower lived in such close association, they were always brothers, except for one case in which they were father and son. Often the follower eventually defeated the leader and took his females from him. The deprived leaders, with the one or two females they had left, nevertheless remained associated with their rebellious young relatives. They even defended their former females—to which they themselves now had no access—against strange males. They did not protect the females of an ex-follower with whom they were not related and hence were only loosely associated. This finding confirmed the results and hypotheses from Cone Rock, but it is not altogether consonant with the kinship network of the male hamadryas. That is, the leader-follower pairs in Madrid were not sons of the same father but, instead, almost all sons of the same mother or full brothers.

Therefore we have no evidence that hamadryas males prefer one another because they are sons of the same father. And it has not been proven that the subadult males *make* the juvenile sons of their father into their future followers by mothering them. The hybrid males in Madrid, at least, have not emancipated themselves from maternal-kinship bonds. We can only say that the existence of a follower who is related to a leader and inherits his females presupposes a form of society in which the males stay at home with their fathers and brothers. Anyone who moves away will forfeit his inheritance.

The problem of a large age difference, with respect to a father's training and collaborating with his son, also exists in human societies with short life expectancy. Early humans did not live as long as we moderns, and among them the knowledge and abilities of an adult man were probably often passed on from older to younger brothers; brothers probably also formed alliances for mutual assistance. As another parallel, consider the "philoi" in ancient Greece, the older and younger friend. This bonding, too, borrowed some of its motivations from a different kind of relationship, not that of mother and child but of sexually tinged love. Here, again, the gap between the "generations" was artificially shortened to a distance more suitable for educating the younger partner and for reciprocal help than the biological age distance between father and son. According to Plato's idealized description in the *Symposion*, such pairs of friends were the strength of an army, because neither wanted to seem anything but courageous in the eyes of his friend. The education of the younger man by the older one he admired is thought to have been of great concern to both parties.

The Initial Unit: A Marriage in Reserve

To enclose a little creature in one's arms and simultaneously threaten an actual or supposed rival is a basic pattern of male social motivation from the age of kidnapping on (plate 4, top left). Here, as in protected threatening, two originally incompatible motivations are combined. In this case they are solicitude and rage, and they become fused as the male defends a social possession. At first the little creature is an infant, and later it is a female in the male's own harem. In this section we shall learn about a relationship that occurs just between these two stages.

It is evening at White Rock, shortly after sundown. The troop arrived an hour ago; many families have already retired, each to the hump in the wall on which it customarily sleeps, and are dozing. They are quiet, but something is still afoot on the loose scree of the slope above the wall. The young adult male Naso, about ten years old, is coming down through the shifting pebbles toward the upper edge of the cliff. There he turns around, clings to the overhang with his hands, and lowers himself onto the highest balcony. A small juvenile female is dawdling along a few feet behind him. Pfick is at most two years old. When she reaches the difficult spot she stops and kecks. Naso climbs farther down; she can no longer see him. She tries hanging from the edge, but it is no use. Her feet find no support, and she does not dare let go. She pulls herself back up.

Now Naso appears on a lower ledge, where Pfick can see him again. She kecks and runs along the edge, lashing her tail, until she stands directly above him. He waits, she sits down and scratches herself. When he looks at her, she fidgets but stays where she is. Finally Naso proceeds to his preferred sleeping balcony, number 8. There he meets Prince, a male of his own age, and the two begin to groom each other. Pfick dozes, still up on the edge. Suddenly an adult male sits next to her, an arm's length away. Naso looks up immediately. While Pfick kecks again, Naso descends to the foot of the wall, goes around the whole cliff, and again approaches the overhang from above. As soon as Pfick sees him, she runs kecking into his arms. For twenty minutes she stays snuggled up to his breast. Then Naso leads the little one down by another route, which she can manage, and the two of them settle on ledge 14, far from Prince, to sleep. The next evening, Naso tries to ascend to ledge 8 from below, but again Pfick's mountaineering skill is inadequate. Three times Naso offers her his lowered rump to ride on, but she does not want to be carried. Again both end up on ledge 14.

Naso and Pfick were one of four "initial units" at White Rock (6). Each consisted of a young adult male and a very young female, barely halfway to the age of puberty. I chose the term "initial units" because I guessed that they amounted to an early stage of marriage, given that no pairs were ever observed in which a male of that age was leading a young *male*. The initial unit resembles a mature marriage in that the partners are always together, which is not true of the kidnapping relationships. As in a marriage, the male usually goes ahead and often looks around after the small female, who follows close at his heels. If she goes farther away, he rarely gives her a neck bite but rather pulls her toward him with his hand, as a mother pulls her infant. Although the methods were different, this was clearly herding, the expression of a claim to an exclusive relationship with the little one. The females regularly groomed their companions, who were enormous in comparison with themselves, but they never groomed another male.

However, these are not real marriages yet. There is no sex in them at all, because the female is too young to have swellings and the size difference is absurd. Instead, the male replaces his little companion's mother, whom she would otherwise still need (fig. 38). He makes allowances for her deficient climbing skills and carries her on his back over difficult passages, whereas adult females are never carried by their spouses. When there is some disturbance in the group, the young male shelters the little female in his arms, where she may almost disappear behind the curtain of his mantle, and in the evening she usually goes to sleep nestled against his breast.

There were several indications that in the White Rock troop the initial groups were formed by a sudden abduction. Often the others were all

Fig. 38. Disputes in the band have frightened the young female of an initial unit. Seeking protection, she clasps herself to her male's back.

asleep when a young male was seen to be still leading his young female back and forth, busily looking back and herding her; surely the only function of this activity would be for her to practice staying with him. While this was going on, the mother or father of the female never took any part. The only explanation I can think of is that the follower suddenly took the female for himself and kept her at a safe distance from her parents; fathers are ordinarily not very possessive about daughters of this age, so hers presumably did not defend her strongly against the young abductor. For the little females themselves, the transition from the greater liberty they enjoyed with their parents could not have been easy. At first they screamed and tried to run away. Three of the four at White Rock bore healed scars from the ear to the top of the head; evidently the young males are sometimes carried away by excitement and do a neck bite, although it includes half of the tiny partner's head.

As when mothering male babies, the subadult male is building up a relationship with a child, and again he borrows the form of the mother-child bond. The age difference between him and his juvenile female is the same as that between a younger male and a kidnapped infant—seven to eight years. The initial-unit bonding, however, has a more obvious explanation. A young female is much easier to acquire than a sexually mature one. It is not a bad strategy for a bachelor to take over a female at that age so as to reserve her for himself, meanwhile acting as a substitute mother, until she reaches sexual maturity. Not until then will she be of interest to the established, fully adult males—and by that time respect for possession will operate in the young male's favor. Now the older males in turn will refrain from abducting his young wife. This is how males get around the barrier of rival inhibition, which stands in the way of their founding a family more directly. Even in species with considerably smaller brains, the males sometimes also guard females not yet old enough for mating, keeping them in storage until their time comes. Males of the small freshwater isopod genus *Asellus* carry their females around on their abdomens for days at a time, until the females have molted and their sexual opening is exposed (Manning 1980). Similarly, the young hamadryas male can harvest such fruits only by leading a little female, bonding her to himself, and defending her until she is mature enough to become his wife.

Courtship for the Father's Eyes

At Cone Rock the young males in different bands of the same troop used different methods to found their initial units. Those in one band abducted females, while the others patiently lured them away from their parents in small stages.

In Band III, Jean-Jacques and Helga Abegglen systematically observed four subadult males (29). Two of them, Garu and Pirate, were followers of families with small daughters, but neither male paid any attention to these females. Then, after the observations had been interrupted for a week, Pirate was suddenly seen to be leading a three-year-old female from another family. He had given up being a follower and now stayed apart with his conquest. The two other subadults, Jodok and Steward, were not even followers but lived in a coterie of other young males at the periphery of the troop. They, too, at first had no relationships with young females. But within two weeks Steward suddenly acquired a two-year-old female.

In both cases, the suddenness implied abduction, as I had inferred in the White Rock troop eight miles away. We never actually observed the abductions. The young males probably took action while hidden by bushes during the day's march, because a father is not likely to let his daughter go without at least some resistance.

The process of founding an initial group was quite different in the Cone Rock Bands I and II. There all eight subadult males were followers, and they began their marital careers by occasionally mothering female infants, still in the black-haired stage, for a quarter-hour or so. They kept this up for months and years, with no dramatic following practice. The Abegglens observed these pairs through all stages. None of the little females was abducted. At first, the seven- to eight-year-old males mothered several infant females in their neighborhood, but soon each was concentrating on a single one—in each case, a female from the family to which the young male was attached.

Two years later the followers, now about nine years old, have not made much progress. The little female, having now reached the age of two or more, still associates more with her mother than with her suitor, and at night she sleeps with her parents while he crouches alone farther away. But now the young male begins some delicate maneuvers.

Consider the Padorn family, slowly climbing up to their place on the cliff in the late afternoon, while the Abegglens on the opposite rock train field glasses on them. During one pause the two-year-old female called Girl is sitting at the end of the column just behind her friend, whom we name "Friend" and who is the Padorns' follower. Girl gets up and, casting a side glance at Friend, begins to go past him in order to keep up with the rest of the family, who have resumed the ascent. However, he quickly rises as though he intends to stand in her way. She sits down again, and so does he. The same sequence occurs again. Then *he* starts out first, looking back at her as though he were leading her, although in reality she is going after her mother who is further ahead. Girl's efforts to overtake him are frustrated by Friend's moving to the side to block her, but so gently that she does not begin kecking. Just before they reach the family's sleeping place, Friend sits down in Girl's way. She gives in and begins to groom him. Six times she lowers her hands and tries to go on to her mother, but each time he intervenes. Once she attempts a detour, and he also blocks that. On some evenings, though, Girl manages to get away from her suitor; she lulls him into relaxation by peaceful grooming, and then without warning flits away to her mother.

This ostensible leading, in which the male is not actually determining the direction but rather picking it up from the female when he looks back as though to make sure she is coming with him, is a male tactic we have seen before, when hamadryas males were trying to subdue willful anubis females (p. 119). It may be that the female eventually grows used to being led and allows appearance to become reality. Friend, in any case, was gaining ground. For instance, during grooming with Girl he would keep changing position slightly, always moving farther from the Padorns, and each time Girl came along and continued to groom him. When she made a move to return, he would sit down closer to the family. Sometimes, however, he seemed to make a point of leaving the choice between him and the family up to her, by walking a few yards to the side and—although he was quite alone—adopting a posture as though he were being groomed by a female: head lowered, tail raised in an arch, and face turned away. More and more often, she would then in fact choose him. The initial unit had finally come into being.

The follower called Cadet had an easier time of it; three little females belonging to his family stayed near him of their own accord, all at once. Another follower, our old acquaintance Rossini, urged and coaxed his Rosa away from her family with tactics like those Friend had used. Many months passed before Rosa finally followed young Rossini instead of her mother. Then this initial unit, too, had become an independent group within the clan.

Why this unusual, tender patience? Courtship among higher primates is generally a rather shabby affair. There are very few exceptions such as the capuchin monkeys, where a couple cuff, chase, caress one another's chest, sit close and seek each other's eyes before they finally mate (Visalberghi and Welker 1986). But this pleasant state of affairs is all the female's doing; before the male joins in she courts him for hours and even days by following him with the corners of the mouth drawn back, cooing and trying to catch his eye. Among most primates, however, sex is a matter of seconds. He smacks his lips or flicks his tongue in and out, she presents or not, and then either it happens or it doesn't. The male chimpanzees at Gombe, who form no pair bonds, look at the receptive female from a distance of ten or twenty yards, sit so that their erection shows, and shake a little tree back and forth with one hand in a mild threat. *She* has to come to him. Evidently, courtship is perfunctory not only among the hamadryas, with their long-term marriages, but also in primate species in which the female has opportunities to choose another male instead. Many male mammals court longer and more elaborately, and when one thinks of the intricate arbors of twigs and displays of colorful flowers or stones that male bowerbirds create exclusively to attract a female, it makes one almost ashamed to be a primate. I don't know why male primates are that way, but this is what I guess. One of the supposed functions of courtship is to demonstrate to the female how valuable the male is, so that she can make a choice. Where animals unknown to one another form new partnerships every year, the dances, display flights, and parades of the males are necessary. But primates live in the same groups all year. Day after day the female sees how the males perform in all important activities. She ought to know enough about them without any special demonstrations. Instead of trying to impress her, a male might court the female he desires by doing something useful, such as protecting her child. The observations of Shirley Strum and Barbara Smuts suggest that male anubis baboons take this approach. Anubis males do employ modest but cunning courtship behavior, though only when they have moved into a strange group. Because they are unfamiliar, the resident females are wary of them. In the following excerpt, Barbara Smuts describes how a new male and a resident female get together in such a situation:

> Thalia was an adolescent female who had not yet experienced her first pregnancy. At the moment, she was in the quiescent phase of her monthly sexual cycle, but in a few days the bare skin on her bottom would begin to swell, and for about 2 weeks she would exhibit the exuberant sexuality characteristic of adolescent female baboons. Alexander, also an adolescent, had a long, lanky body and an unusually relaxed disposition. He had transferred into EC troop just a few months earlier. Thalia, like the other females in the troop, was wary of this interloper and tended to avoid him during daily foraging. But as I watched the two of them sitting on the cliffs about 5 m apart, it was clear that, in Thalia, fear and interest were mixed in an uneasy balance.
>
> Alexander was facing west, his sharp muzzle pointing toward the setting sun, watching the rest of the troop make their way up the cliffs. Thalia was grooming herself in a perfunctory manner, her attention elsewhere. Every few seconds she glanced out of the corner of her eye at Alexander without turning her head. Her glances became longer and longer and her grooming more and more desultory until she was staring for long moments at Alexander's profile. Then, as Alexander shifted and turned his head toward Thalia, she snapped her head down and peered intently at her own foot. Alexander looked at her, then away. Thalia stole another glance in his direction, but when he again glanced her way, she resumed her involvement with her foot. For the next 15 minutes, this charade continued: Each time Alexander glanced at Thalia, she feigned indifference, but as soon as he looked away, her gaze was drawn back to his face. Then, without looking at her, Alexander began slowly to edge toward Thalia. Their glances at one another became more frequent, the intervals between them shorter, and their interest in other events less convincing. Finally, Alexander succeeded in catching Thalia's eye as she was turning away. He made a "come-hither" face—the same face Virgil

had made at Pandora—grunting as he did so . . . Thalia froze, and for a second she looked into Alexander's eyes. Then, as he began to approach her, she stood, presented her rear to him, and, looking back over her shoulder, darted nervous glances at him. Alexander grasped her hips, lip-smacking wildly, and then presented his side for grooming. Thalia, still nervous, began to groom him. Soon she calmed down, and I found them still together on the cliffs the next morning.

This event represented a triumph for Alexander who, as a newcomer, had been trying for several weeks to establish a relationship with Thalia.

As cautiously as this pair established contact, the process did not take very long. In contrast, Friend and Rossini courted their little females for many months. Their courtship took more effort, involved more obvious tactical maneuvers, and altogether was a greater elaboration of the preliminaries to marriage than is usually found in primates. Unfortunately, though, it seemed designed not so much for the female herself as for her father. In the scene described above, the anubis male Alexander had to overcome the female's fear, but Friend and Rossini also had the father's intolerance to contend with. A follower grooms a juvenile male whenever he likes without exhibiting any signs of conflict. It is much less common for him to touch a juvenile female. He often merely settles down near her, watches her playing, scratches himself, and almost incessantly wipes his muzzle or shakes himself. These are the signs of conflict the rivals displayed in our inhibition experiments. The follower courting a young female evidently regards the family leader, the possible father of the female, as her possessor. Indeed, the Abegglens found that the young male's conflict behavior is enormously diminished when he has finally persuaded the little female to stay with him rather than her parents, so that the incipient marriage has become independent. Up to that point, the father clearly has an inhibitory effect. The young female at first usually sits in the middle of the harem, where her suitor dares not approach her. During the period when Friend was weaning Girl away from her family and occasionally chased her, he immediately halted whenever she ran into the family group. Sometimes a follower would take up a post outside the family and wait like a dog, hands on the ground and jaw resting upon them, watching his female as long as her father was there. When the father began to lead the group away, the follower would rush in and take the little one in his arms until she had to go after her parents. On other occasions the conflict became too much for a suitor. He would turn away, tuck his elbows between his knees, let his head sink low onto his chest, and shut the world out of sight.

The gentle courtship is obviously intended to ensure that young females do not become frightened and start screaming while their fathers are watching. By merely running toward the family rather than walking, a follower can incite the father to attack him. However, the followers do not often make such mistakes, and the family leaders seldom intervene. The worst setback was experienced by Rossini, the follower of Rosso's family, when the Abegglens trapped his female Rosa in order to tag her. While Rosa was in the trap, a greatly agitated Rossini placed himself next to her and vigorously threatened the two humans. That probably looked too much like the behavior of a possessor from Rosso's viewpoint. In any case, when Rosa was set free there was a chase between Rossini and father Rosso. Afterward Rosa groomed her father. Rossini sat far apart, and for a whole month he had no access to her. Later, the incipient marriage was set back by another fight between the two males, but eventually Rossini was able to extract his female from Rosso's family. Even then, the young male still had to make an effort to keep her away from her mother, to whom she sometimes returned for a grooming session.

Like the other initial-unit leaders, Rossini was a good ten years old and hence full-grown. All he had gained by his struggles was a female about four years old, just approaching puberty; it would be two years more before she could bear his first child. On the plus side, it turned out that the initial units really are marriages in reserve, even if they do not last very long. For periods ranging from four to thirty months, the initial females were the only partners of their young males, until eventually the latter also acquired an adult female. Only two out of eight young females later left their first mate for good. Two others went home to their mothers when their male acquired his first adult spouse, but eventually they returned to him. Even young hamadryas males prefer a full-grown female to a juvenile one. In the excitement of his first interactions with a mature spouse—a situation in which we saw Ulysses and Kalos in the Zurich Zoo—he pays little attention to the young female, so she can easily be abducted by another young male.

All eight initial units observed in Band I remained in the native clan of both partners. It looks as though a follower cannot lure a young female out of another clan. If there is no free little daughter living in his own clan, or the family leader chases all followers away, it can happen that a young male will try his luck in a neighboring clan. There, of course, he will have to face a family leader who is unlikely to have mothered him when he was an infant. Two young males of the Cone Rock troop chose this alternative, and by the end of the Abegglens' study both were still without a young female, even though they were past the age of an initial-unit leader. One of them, Stupsi, eventually returned to his own clan, where the first daughter had meanwhile been born to a male not much older than himself. Despite that male's intolerance, after two years Stupsi finally succeeded in mothering the little one. He was now twelve years old. Unfortunately, at this time he disappeared and was never seen again.

The life histories of the young females in Band I varied widely. Seven out of fifteen entered families that already included adult females without first belonging to an initial unit. All fifteen changed families several times; they could move from mature families back to initial units or the reverse. Only one, however, returned to her parents after a brief stay outside the family in which she was born. During the following two years she had regular monthly cycles; that is, she was not made pregnant by her father. Incest might be avoided even if a female never left her parental family.

Overthrow by Force

Almost every adolescent male has a good chance of acquiring his first female by reserving her as a youngster, because established leaders do not defend juvenile females very vigorously. But the really interesting females, the adult spouses of the established males, are out of reach due to rival inhibition. In these circumstances, is there no other way for a young male to acquire a mature spouse than to get a juvenile female and wait for her to grow up? This solution was impracticable in Bands I and II. Just imagine: for every new female, the young leader would have to spend months or years in elaborate maneuvering to pry another juvenile away from her parents, at the same time guarding the adult females he already has—who themselves are objects of interest to his father-in-law and hence must be kept apart from his family. We have never seen a male going through such an ordeal.

There must be another way to gain further females. During the five and a half years of observation, almost all adult females of Band I changed husbands, in spite of rival inhibition. Many females thus have just as many marriage partners as a male during their lives, but consecutively rather than simultaneously. The question is, *how* do the established possessors lose their females while still middle-aged? Why does rival inhibition fail, and how do the other males in the clan behave when that happens?

On the day's march, baboon families often wander out of each other's sight, among the brushwood or rocks. No surprise, then, that most attempts by a rival to take over another's female occur in thick bush. A wife stealer has every reason to avoid his competitors' ganging up against him, so he is most likely to operate secretively when the band is scattered. For this reason, we were rarely witnesses at the scene. The complete sequence was seen only in our experiments. In the field, at most we heard battle cries and struggles in the bush. Not until evening at the cliff did we then see males march in with more or fewer females than they had had in the morning. Some, at least, had fought hard, as their wounds attested.

In one year of the Abegglen study the old order in Band I seemed to break down (29). According to the Abegglens' records, it all began on the evening of May 3, 1972. The oldest male in the Brown Clan—the magnificent, but no longer young family leader Padorn—sat on the cliff with blood-smeared mantle and one arm injured. His family was with him, complete. Ten yards away, prone and motionless on the ground with head toward Padorn, was Spot, an initial-group leader and Padorn's oldest follower. He had assumed the crouching-dog position usually associated with the courtship of juvenile females; hands on the ground and muzzle resting on them, he kept his eyes fixed on the family of his clan elder. The other families in the band sat around the two of them, forming a semicircle—which was also very unusual. Several times Padorn got up and "notified" to Spot at a distance, by turning around where he was rather than going over to Spot as would be customary. When he did this, one of his females moved with him, almost in contact. The whole thing seemed to be about her. Soon afterward Padorn threatened Spot with gaping jaws, and he was seconded by Rosso, a family leader who was the elder of the *Red* Clan. Admiral, elder of the Violet Clan, and his followers "yawned" in various directions, and Bishop, one of the Red Clan, notified to Spot. As the Abegglens reconstructed it, on the march Spot had attempted to take over the female that clung so close to Padorn, but Padorn beat him off. Then Padorn threatened and tried to appease the young Spot, who evidently had not yet given up. Remarkably, other older males in the band did the same, as though they too were trying to deter the attacker.

A few evenings later, Padorn was sitting alone on the cliff, with fresh cuts on his face and a wounded leg. The female that had been so attached to Padorn after the first fight was sitting by Spot, who was now also injured. Padorn's other female was with Cadet, the oldest follower of Admiral in the Violet Clan and another initial-group leader. Cadet was uninjured. Friend, Padorn's second-oldest follower, had taken over the two little daughters of the Padorn family, but Padorn's daughter Girl, whom Friend had courted so assiduously, had vanished and was never seen again. These female rearrangements resulting from the first overthrow were definitive. Three weeks later, Rossini fought with Spot, who now had his hands full with his new adult female, and took away Spot's former initial-unit partner Elisabeth (fig. 39).

Barely a year later, a similar revolution occurred in the two other clans of Band I (fig. 40). The two losers—the clan elders and the main possessors of females, Admiral and Rosso—had fresh wounds on their faces.

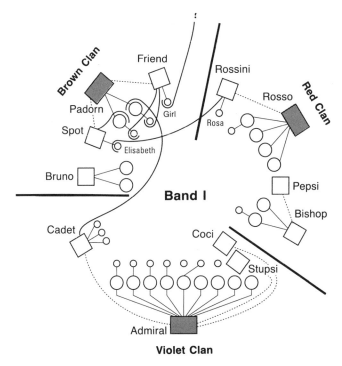

Violet Clan

Fig. 39. Revolution in the Brown Clan, May 1972. The clans of Band I are arranged in a circle. Male clan elders are represented by rectangles, other adult males by squares, their females by the connected large circles, and juvenile daughters by small circles. Juvenile males and infants are not shown. Dotted lines connect leaders and followers. The younger males have taken females away from the older ones, as shown by the hooked lines. Friend has lost his Girl to a male outside the band or through death.

Admiral lost all of his nine spouses and seven daughters; Rosso kept only one of his four females. None of the next-younger males in the band were visibly injured, but they had taken over all the adult females of the two old males except for two that disappeared altogether from the band.

The clearest rule in both overthrows was that the females were rearranged according to the ages of the males. The three old males were essentially deposed as family leaders; they had only losses, gaining nothing. The richest harvest was gathered in by Bishop, who, as the next-oldest male in the band, was already established as a family leader in the Red Clan. The other winners were the males next junior to Bishop, most of whom were initial-unit leaders and until then the oldest followers. The younger followers got hardly anything. Evidently the young guard had struck when they became sufficiently superior in fighting ability to the

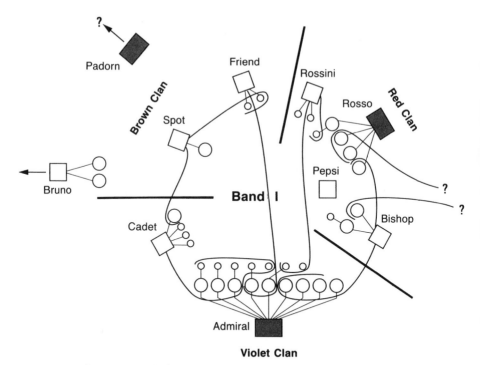

Violet Clan

Fig. 40. Revolutions in Band I from August 1972 to January 1973. Symbols as in figure 39. Old Padorn of the Brown Clan emigrated or died after losing his females. Three females of Rosso and Bishop are also missing. They were presumably taken by males of other bands. Bruno and his females have left the band or died.

family leaders, who were slowing down with age and wearing out their canine teeth. In support of this interpretation, all three old males were wounded in the uprising, whereas all but one of the five winners were unscathed.

That rival inhibition breaks down when the rival is not just slightly but far superior to the possessor follows an evolutionary cost-benefit logic that we can work through as follows:

· The female is worth more to the possessor than to the rival. She follows the former reliably and not uncommonly carries his child.
· Therefore the possessor fights harder than the rival.
· When one opponent fights harder, the fight becomes more dangerous and costly for both.
· It follows that for a particular degree of escalation, the risk of injury exceeds the value of the female for the rival, but not for the possessor.
· If the rival can assess this, he will let the possessor win in this cost/benefit range. Or he will not even attack, but rather will remain inhibited even when he is somewhat superior to the possessor.

- Unequal fighting force implies that the weaker is more likely to be injured than the stronger. As the rival grows stronger, his risk of injury decreases. The risk to the possessor rises, because his fighting strength declines with age.
- At a certain level of superiority, the balance becomes as favorable for the rival as for the possessor; although the female is still less valuable to him, the fight will also cost him less. Once this point has been passed, assuming that it has been correctly judged by the opponents, the rival attacks. The possessor must pay his higher costs for the fight or surrender.

Another aspect of the rearrangement, less clearly ordered than the influence of the males' ages, was the distribution of the females among clans and bands (28). Adult females were taken over by males of other clans just as often as by those of their own. In five and a half years, twenty-seven adult females of Band I changed possessors. Of these, six stayed in their clan, eight were taken into another clan of the same band, and eighteen actually moved into another band or troop. In contrast, almost all the little daughters, twenty out of twenty-six, were taken over by younger males of their own clan. This difference between the adult and the juvenile females could not appear by chance; it was statistically significant.

It follows that a young male has no particular prospects of acquiring a mature female in his own clan. On the other hand, he can most easily acquire juvenile females from the males in his clan. This is the only privilege we are certain a male has as a clan member, and it could explain his bonding to the clan.

A finding entirely counter to my intuition was that one oldest follower, at least, had turned against not just any elder male but his *own* family leader—the male with whom he had for years shared dangers, protected the family, and coordinated the marching formation, the one who was closest to him and may have mothered him when he was a youngster. My surprise was the result of looking through morally tinted glasses; from the viewpoint of an opportune strategy for the follower, his own clan boss was a good choice. Because the follower is a close associate of his family leader, he is in the best position to detect that the latter's powers are beginning to wane.

Does the family leader sense what is in store for him? Remember that in the inhibition experiments the possessors notified to their inhibited rivals remarkably often, but the rivals did not reciprocate. The only interpretation we can find of this friendly gesture from the vocabulary of sexual behavior is that it is intended to pacify the rival and get back on good terms with him. From September 1971 to July 1972, just before Padorn's harem was stolen from him, the Abegglens recorded every instance of notifying they observed among the males of Band I at the sleeping cliff (29).

Here are their results: as long as all three harem leaders still possessed their females, they notified to the initial-unit leaders ten times as often as to one another. The events in the uprising showed that the most dangerous rivals of the old males were indeed among the initial-unit leaders. Rosso and Admiral did not lose their harems until after July 1972; that is, months before the event, they were already trying to appease the group that included the eventual usurpers.

After Padorn had lost his harem, he no longer notified to the initial-unit leaders. Rosso and Admiral, who still had their females at this point, did it as often as before. That is, the old males do not simply notify to the younger ones—they do it only when they still have females to lose to these juniors.

As soon as the oldest followers Spot and Cadet had taken over their first adult females from Padorn, they in turn notified to the remaining initial-unit leaders considerably more often than they had previously done, but the latter by no means returned the compliment. The usurpers appeared to "know" that now the next-younger males were a menace to them.

Attentive readers may object that notifying does not seem very effective as a conciliatory signal, since the "conciliated" ones eventually stole the females anyway. But do we know how long the older males at least postponed their downfall by notifying? The fact that the consumption of quinine is highest in countries with malaria does not imply that quinine is ineffective against it.

What is certain is that the possessors addressed their notifying to the most dangerous of the haremless males long in advance. Does this mean that the harem leaders actually "knew" what the prospective usurpers had in store for them? As so often with animals, it is relatively easy to establish *that* they know something, but without sophisticated experiments we have no idea *how* the information is stored in their brains. In the simplest case, each male could sense his own physical condition and the ease with which he can guard his harem, as a particular degree of subjective security, which he gives away by a posture that the competitor need merely observe in order to compare the possessors' sense of security with his own. However, it could also be that a male looks for specific details about the others—that the possessor sees how long the canine teeth of his follower have become, or that the follower can discern how much effort his family leader has to make in climbing, how soon he gives way to another male, how skillful he is at herding, or how willingly his females follow him.

For the time being, all we know for sure about the notifying possessors is *that* they somehow sense or know the danger presented by their oldest follower. How emotional or conceptual this information is, we cannot tell. If we knew that, we would begin to understand how they see the world. Certain aspects of this immensely interesting area of research, which has gained new impetus under the term "cognitive ethology," are known. For instance, experiments by Verena Dasser (1988) have shown that long-tailed macaques, of their own accord, distinguish the relationship between mother and child from all other relationships. Once they have learned that they are supposed to put together color photos of one particular mother in their group and her baby, without further training they will correctly combine the pictures of all mothers with those of their children, but not the pictures of, say, two sisters. It follows that these macaques have a spontaneous perception of the mother-child relationship, which they apply correctly to the members of their group. Therefore it doesn't seem too far-fetched to surmise that a hamadryas male knows about the relationships in his band. Dorothy Cheney and Robert Seyfarth (1990) have obtained fascinating first evidence of the social and ecological knowledge of a group of vervet monkeys by ingenious experiments in the wild. In most cases of animal knowledge, however, we still have no idea how the image they have of the outside world is represented internally.

Hamadryas baboons are entirely capable of leading an orderly social life in the long term, even without laws and law enforcers, by a system of checks and balances—by acknowledgment of rank and possession. Only a *change* of power and possession can lead to bloodshed. Some human nations are not much different.

The Hidden Net of the Females

Among the hamadryas, the old net of female kinship has come into conflict with the new net of related males. Because one sex must leave the fold, both nets cannot remain intact. For the baboons at Cone Rock, the male net has the upper hand. While the males remain together, the females must release their ties several times in their lives, compelled by abduction and revolution. But on closer inspection it looks as though the broken female net can mend itself here and there under the surface of male domination, although only in parts. During the study of Band I, eighteen adult females changed their possessors. Fifteen of these eighteen, after one or two changes of spouse, again found themselves together with members of their first harem; the corresponding figure for juvenile females was thirteen out of sixteen (28). Even so, this cannot necessarily be counted as a success for the female kinship net, for two reasons. First, we did not know enough about the kinship relations among the females. And second, if the females successfully retied their net again and again, so that the females in a harem were often kin to one another, this should have been evident in their social interactions: they ought to groom one another frequently, as related females of other species do. However, they do not. Out of forty-eight female dyads of the same harem at White Rock, there were only two in which the females spent more than 10 percent of their resting time in mutual grooming. In contrast, females on average groom their males during 19 percent of their resting time.

It appears that the kinship net of hamadryas females has come to an end. Not because the females cannot find the way to one another—I believe they do that. But the fact that there is *so* little intense interaction among them, even less than would be expected if related females were taken into the same harem merely by chance, indicates that their kinship is no longer of any use to them. It has probably become unimportant for related females to stand by one another in conflicts. A male is a much more powerful defense against outsiders, and he will tolerate no disputes among females in his harem. If a conflict does arise in a harem, the females do not try to recruit one another as allies; instead, they turn to the male (fig. 41), as the zoo group had shown us. Alliances of mothers, daughters, and sisters were apparently useful only as long as there were no husbands—that is, among the ancestors that lived as the savanna baboons do now.

In the hybrid group at the Madrid Zoo, the net of female relatives still operates. Related females live in the same harem more often than would be expected statistically, and this is particularly true of mothers and daughters. Two female kinship groups in the same harem can fight one another and threaten its cohesion. When mothers and daughters are separated by male intervention, they nevertheless visit one another for grooming sessions across the harem boundaries. In doing so, the visitor enters the field of influence of the other male and can entangle him in a dispute with her spouse. When families fall out with one another, a female can actually take the side of her relative in the opposing harem, fighting against her own fellow harem members (Colmenares 1992 and personal communication). Such disorder can hardly suit the harem leaders, and it will come as no surprise that the males in Madrid try to suppress the alliances between related females, though not with such sweeping success as is enjoyed by the pure-blooded hamadryas males at Erer.

The reaction norm of a species contains far more potential forms of behavior than are manifest in any given group. A reaction norm is like a floating ball, only a small part of which shows above the surface. Often even a slight change in the composition of a population suffices to rotate the ball a little bit, bringing another part of its surface with other forms of behavior into view. For example, an otherwise concealed behavioral trait of the savanna ancestors might appear in a pure-blooded hamadryas

Fig. 41. Not a pretty picture. The male delivers a neck bite, but that does not make his females join forces against him. Instead, the other members of the harem also threaten the victim. (Photo: Walter Götz)

troop. In 1980, thanks to Willi Büttiker's efforts as intermediary and to the generous help provided by Abdulelah Banaja of the University of Jeddah, I was able to study the wild hamadryas baboons in Arabia for the first time (26, 31). In appearance and gestures they can hardly be distinguished from the hamadryas on the other side of the Red Sea. The Saudi Arabian hamadryas also live in one-male groups (fig. 42), which are accompanied by followers leading initial units. However, for reasons that can only be guessed, here there were only thirteen adult males per hundred animals rather than twenty-three as in Erer. Accordingly, the harems were larger (plate 2, top) and the herding behavior of the males, with so many females to control, was less radical than in Ethiopia.

The Arabian females were correspondingly more active and independent. Whereas the females in Ethiopia merely threatened one another and then sought the assistance of their male, in Arabia they actually fought one another, fencing with gaping jaws, hitting, seizing one another, and biting. In six weeks of observing the Saudi troops I saw more fierce fights between females than in twenty months in Ethiopia. There was one initial unit, with two juvenile females, in which one blocked all attempts of the other to approach the male, by pulling her companion away from him and imprisoning her with an almost masculine possession grip. This female claimed the other for herself, often groomed her and did not leave her side. On the other hand, certain females appeared to be close friends,

Fig. 42. At dawn, a hamadryas family in Saudi Arabia cautiously approaches the rubbish dump of the town Al Hada. At some places in the Saudi desert region, the baboons have become dependent on discarded human food and are beginning to invade the cities.

each holding the other's infants. It was much more common than in Erer for juvenile females to transfer unimpeded from one young adult male to another, grooming the first and then presenting to the second without incurring threats from either. This is the way hamadryas females who had been transplanted into anubis troops in Ethiopia conducted themselves as soon as they noticed that they were not herded there (p. 122). The Arabian males herded their females gently. As though they had more freedom in their mutual relations in the milder competitive climate of a society more determined by females, they fought one another less often, sat closer together, and interacted on a more intimate level than in Erer. Instead of notifying, a quick gesture in which contact is avoided, they presented to one another at length and even routinely mounted one another (26). In the Arabian population, with its excess of females, the females take much more control of affairs themselves and are not merely a prize to be won by belligerent males. It might be that this population has even preserved the female kinship net.

In Saudi Arabia, hamadryas baboons have recently discovered that the rubbish dumps on the outskirts of the cities are a rich source of food (fig. 42). They visit them in increasing numbers and are already entering the cities. For some years the French primatologists Sylvain and Véronique Biquand and the Saudi biologist Ahmed Boug have been exploring ways to control this potentially dangerous invasion. They, too, observed one-male families. Whether the Saudi hamadryas also form clans and bands, however, is still unknown (Biquand et al. 1991).

Pictures from Arabia

The souk, the old market in Jeddah. Sandy alleys between tall buildings. On the steps, men are sitting in conversation. The lights of the little shops shine up against the old, light-ochre stone facades. Far up in the darkness, the upper stories, delicately carved wooden structures with filigreed jalousies through which one can see without being seen, are cantilevered out over the alleys. Abdulelah, my colleague, is talking with a humble old man, the son of his childhood nursemaid. Abdulelah holds his hands, listens to him affectionately for a long time, finally seems to be offering advice.

A pause for rest when we reach the mountain city of At Taif. Under the eaves overhanging the courtyard of the inn we eat at metal tables with our bare hands: roast liver, flat bread, tomatoes, and peppers. For drink, there is water. Opposite us simply dressed men in red-and-white head-cloths are resting, sitting with legs folded like tailors on high benches with seats of woven string. The shiny brass hookahs gurgle as they smoke. Our Bedouin drivers ask me the purpose of this trip into the interior. Ahmed Randur translates. Their clever, interested, unprudish questions lead to a long conversation about the social organization of the hamadryas. It doesn't surprise them that someone would come such a long way to study the social life of an animal. We fall silent. Then the driver Muhammad declares that he knows where we should go. A few years ago, he says, he was in the Wadi Ranyah with a geologist and saw hamadryas baboons. With him in the lead, we drive into the night. He finds the way between the mountains with no road to follow. Only he knows where we finally put up our tents, at one o'clock in the morning (plate 6, top).

The unquestioning, classless equality of these men. They are self-assured without being unfriendly. When they help it is to help, not to serve. Our way of politely smiling with the lips is unknown to them, but sometimes—when our eyes meet after a long silence—a radiant smile transfigures their whole face. "Never command them," Abdulelah had told me. "Make a request!"

Wadi Ranyah. We are seated in a circle in a tent belonging to the geologists' camp. Only Arabs are present, only men. The dignified host, with his pointed beard, hands out the tiny coffee cups and pours the thin "gafua." Then he stands in the middle, holding the thin-spouted brass pot, ready to refill our cups. Whoever does not want any more swivels the cup from side to side. Muhammad sings while plucking the strings of a ruhaba, the body of which is made from a Shell Rotella canister. Then he asks about my daughter. "I'll give you 30,000 rials or my sister. She is eighteen and as beautiful as the moon." "That's too young for me," I reply. They laugh uproariously—eighteen is already too old for them.

Saleh recites pre-Islamic poems, and Ahmed translates. A song in honor of the poet's horse: it runs like a rock carried downstream in a torrent. To his beloved: her stride to the tent is like the floating of a cloud.

On a distant dune, two robed figures sit close together, facing each other. We would sit side by side.

The ten-year-old Bedouin boy Nasr visits us at suppertime and keeps us company with an earnest expression. Then he seats himself on a high cushion in the driver's seat of his father's Toyota pickup and drives off into the night.

Our trips take a long time, because it is not polite to pass a tent without entering and drinking coffee. You sit on the rug in the doorway and look into the golden evening. The host sits down next to you and pushes the gnarled branch deeper into the white ashes. While he serenely sets about making coffee, he talks to your traveling companion in a quiet voice. You need not say anything. Behind the reddish sand, the horizons flow over and under one another like voices in a chorus. On the right a single green shrub has rooted in black rock, forming a transparent lattice. In front of it, standing alone under an acacia, is the woman of the family, robed entirely in pink. She is holding a distaff and spinning.

Osayis, the driver, scans the distance through my field glasses, looking for a "Madame Bedou." Then he smiles broadly at me and points to the sacklike cloak he has just given me to use as a coat—maybe because he borrows mine every night to sleep in. He reminds me of my sons; they also like to wear my old jackets.

The Bedouin woman sits with me by the fire. This is an exception, Osayis assures me afterward. The woman is about forty, which means ancient. She grinds spices in a mortar, talks to me and about me, and by no means guards her eyes. She wants to exchange her necklace for my binoculars. The jewelry is beautiful, made of large engraved silver rings lodged between cubes of stone veined in black and white. I write the value of the binoculars onto Oseyis's palm in Arabic numerals:) . . . (1000). Unfortunately, I explain, I need them for my work. But the woman enjoys bargaining. She now lowers her black veil, showing me the golden star with the small turquoise in her nostril and the woven red and white band over her brow. At least I can give her my felt-tipped pen; she sticks it coquettishly into her coiffure. Between the rolls of material and the tin boxes in the back of the tent, a black baby goat rises unsteadily to its feet.

She takes it and lays it in my arms. But as it begins sucking on my thumb, she grabs it herself and kisses it on the mouth, through her veil.

I climb into the steep mountains, following the baboons. High above me a dark Asir goatherd bounds from one block of stone to the next. Bareheaded. His long locks swing around his shoulders; under his headband he has placed a bundle of fresh herbs. He sings with a hard, high voice, always repeating the same notes that sound like a bird's call. In the depths of the valley, the bellowing of the feral donkeys resounds.

A rocky desert ridge. A serrated line stretching into infinity. No one knows where you are. You keep going on in the silvery brightness through all times past and future, with increasing lightness. No animal would do this. Only this human searching for some freedom. On and on you wander in the clear light, borne by this maternal ridge above the glistening plain, among the hunched boulders and the poor, barren shrubs which hold their filigreed branches into the light. All of them silent, without pain, waiting. You walk as they wait. This is how life after death should be.

Going on and searching, instead of standing still and hacking the ground. Ovid's Golden Age was the age of the wandering gatherer whom we call the Paleolithic. "Spared the hoe, wounded by no plowshare, the earth gave everything of its own accord; satisfied with what grew for them unforced, they gathered from the arbutus branches and picked the mountain strawberries."

By wandering with animals, one can go this way again.

The Old Ones

The sudden loss of their females caused a change in the three clan elders at Cone Rock. Until then they had been the most imposing males in the band, robed in their massive mantles. Within a few weeks after they had been deposed, their faces turned dark and their mantles became sparse; they lost weight and looked old. Admiral's shoulders were soon almost bald, and the skin of his lower abdomen hung in folds (29). This was not the result of any wounds, as none had been serious and they had already healed. Similar battle wounds sustained by other males that had not lost their harems did not have such an effect. It must have been the profound experience of defeat and loss that changed the males in this way. While high-ranking males may respond to mild stress with an increase of their testosterone level (Sapolski 1990), severe stress uniformly lowers it. Testosterone causes the male sexual characteristics. It was precisely these sexual features of the adult male that the three oldsters had lost: the reddish face and the light-colored, dense mantle.

During the weeks after Padorn lost his females, his most frequent companion was his little son Hajo, who had stayed with him instead of going with his mother. The two of them groomed and defended each other, something that had never happened before the overthrow. Then the old male disappeared. Perhaps he died, or he may simply have left the troop into which he was born. On four occasions the Abegglens observed single adult males in the Cone Rock bands, males that were either wounded or had strikingly scanty mantles and that turned up alone, like itinerant visitors, and then went away again. One of them proved unable to follow the band; the family with which he was traveling, at the tail end of the band, left him alone. Presumably some deposed family leaders leave the clan where they had spent their whole life and wander alone, at an advanced age, from band to band. Why they do that is a mystery. Padorn never came back.

The other two defeated leaders remained in their clan and were still living there in 1977. Rosso kept his single female, and Admiral recovered some of his masculine glory. His face remained blackish and the hole in the roof of his nose, left by the fight for his harem, never fully closed. But his body hair grew dense again, though now it was dark and short. Neither of the two males tried to acquire new females—for example, by becoming followers again. Neither would look at his former spouses, even when they were resting only a few steps away. Like Padorn, Rosso and Admiral now spent time with their children as never before—mainly with their small sons, and not as protectors but in a leisurely way that involved much mutual grooming. We already observed this belated conversion in the zoo (see chapter 1), when after years of rule Pasha actually played with juveniles. I saw this last behavior only once in Ethiopia. A scrawny male with pale, sparse hair was walking behind a family. A young female came back to him several times, bit him playfully in the legs, and he pushed her away good-naturedly with one hand.

The new harem leaders distanced themselves somewhat from Rosso and Admiral. Three years later, however, Ruedi Wey observed just the opposite in another case. Rossini, whom the reader may remember from his arduous courtship of little Rosa (p. 224), had lost all his adult females and a little daughter to Band IV. Although he was still relatively young, within three weeks he too visibly lost weight and hair, grew darker in the face, and walked rather stiffly. His former female Rosa was now the single wife of a younger clan member, Bub. Bub displayed a benevolent tolerance toward his defeated colleague. The very day after his loss had occurred, Rosa was frequently allowed to groom her former spouse. Bub merely turned away and behaved as though he didn't notice. Four days later the brothers Bub and Rossini groomed each other for a long time, and this relationship continued. After two months, during which Rossini had literally been hanging his head, he had recovered somewhat. Bub gradually restricted the grooming sessions of Rossini and Rosa. But even then Rossini still sat motionless for long periods, and sometimes he could not be found with his clan.

Not every deposed family leader becomes a true exile, a miserable drifter from band to band. Until his downfall, Admiral had led nine adult females and thirteen children, and he again became powerful, calm, and influential after he had lost them all. On occasion he and a couple of other old males fought even more boldly than their younger clan mates. One evening in 1974 Stolba, Sigg, and I captured Rossini, who at that time still possessed two adult females. We wanted to test the feasibility of an experiment. The idea was that in the evening *one* male would be shown a place away from the sleeping cliff where corn had been newly scattered. The next morning we would try to see whether and how the male who had this information would convince the other ones to march by way of the cornfield. This would have been a major advance in our understanding of the collective decision process. The outcome of the test made us give up this plan, but it still taught us something.

We had just taken Rossini to the cornfield when battle cries sounded from the cliff. Fearing trouble for Rossini's harem, we immediately set him free and he galloped straight back. At the cliff a fight was going on between Rossini's Band I and another band, and it continued into the moonlit night. Next morning all the families were intact, including Rossini's. The defensive line of Band I had held. The only wounded were its three oldest males: Admiral, the ordinarily timid Rosso, and Spot—but the worst was Admiral, the one with no wives. What had *he* been fighting for? Because the battle had been against another band, the two oldest males would hardly have been trying to take over Rossini's females; such a thing would have been in stark contradiction to their extremely reserved behavior toward all females since they had been overthrown. Perhaps they only took direct action because they were infected by the fighting spirit of the others. In any case, the end effect was that they defended their own former females for those males who owned them now. The victims fought for the perpetrators.

Once again, we see something that confounds human empathy. The deposed leaders exacted no moralistic revenge for the suffering, so obviously severe, that the young males had inflicted on them—just as the latter had had no moral compunction about inflicting it in the first place. Biologically, for the old males to fight in aid of the younger made more sense than to stand aside spitefully, as many a man would have done in the old males' position, because some of the younger males were their relatives. Animals not uncommonly behave more "rationally" than we humans with our social standards, although they hardly ever know they are doing so.

Similarly, in the Madrid Zoo colony deposed leaders continued to defend their former families, including the young usurpers. In the Zurich Zoo the first time Pasha attacked his keeper Rehm was when he had already lost all his females and become a skinny oldster. The old ones risk nothing by fighting, as they no longer have any females to lose. They have realized their reproductive potential, for better or worse, and nothing can change that. All they can do for their genes now is to protect the clan, their relatives, and thereby help their brothers to have children. In this respect the old baboons resemble the sterile worker ants, which also have no reproductive potential of their own. Probably for this reason, the workers fling themselves into deadly battle against other ant colonies with very little concern for their own safety, to the advantage of their fertile winged sisters.

In 1974, when I visited my doctoral students Sigg and Stolba in Erer, I got to know the deposed Admiral. I wondered whether I could still manage the forced marches, which had tested me even as a young man. My young men recommended that I follow Admiral, and so we two elders traveled together. Admiral relieved my worries. He never ran. At a steady pace, he walked for hours on end a few steps ahead of me; at every erosion gully, he knew an easy way to cross, so I never again had to pull myself up vertical walls by clinging to roots. As an influential member of the band, he also seemed to know the day's route in advance, which meant that he and I did not need to make any detours. When my traveling companion dug for roots, his shoulder muscles played in a quiet rhythm, and every few strokes he brought something to his mouth. Nearby, youngsters were jumping from place to place, fumbling aimlessly in the ground and finding little.

Admiral seemed to know a lot. One early afternoon his clan, the Violets, had still not had anything to drink. We were moving northward in the sand of a dry wadi. Then Admiral veered off and, ahead of the others, climbed up to a bare hill with a single, dense patch of shrubbery growing at its top. A female and a juvenile overtook him and went a few steps past the bushes, paying no attention to them. When Admiral reached the shrubs, he did not hesitate and entered a gap between them. The baboons ahead of him hurried back, and those following rushed up. Singly and in pairs, the clan members disappeared into the shady bower. Afterward we looked into the bushes and found a hole in the granite, over three feet deep, with perhaps five quarts of water remaining at its shady bottom from previous rains. From outside, the hole was invisible. The female who had gone on ahead evidently had not known about it.

In that same month, we once trudged back to Erer in the midday heat, on the gravel of the single-track Djibouti railway line. On the ridge of a hill above us I noticed a baboon sitting alone in the glaring sun. Through the field glasses we recognized Admiral. He looked down at us, perfectly still, his dark face gleaming with sweat. From where he sat he had a good view of the railway line and the rolling plain extending to the Ahmar Mountains, but there was no shade at his observation post. Not until we had ascended a neighboring hill did we see that behind the ridge the members of his clan were gathered in the thin shade of two umbrella acacias, where the railway was out of sight. We could find no other explanation for Admiral's behavior than that he was keeping watch.

Admiral often occupied such observation points. That he was not doing this on some random whim was demonstrated most convincingly when it meant forfeiting some advantage, such as the shade in the previous scene. For instance, he might be the only one who was not digging for beetle grubs in the soil of an abandoned nomad kraal. Or, as in the following incident observed by Alex Stolba, he might place himself in danger. At 10:30 one morning before the baboons had drunk their fill, the Violets, Admiral's clan, had been driven away from a water hole by a nomad boy with a herd of cattle. Cadet, who now had more females than anyone else in the clan, retreated with his family into a little valley about a hundred yards away. Admiral, however, ascended alone to the rocky ridge above the water hole, sat down there on a dead tree in the full sun, and observed the water hole. Cadet and Bishop, a harem leader of the Red Clan, waited in the shade. At 11:10 more nomads approached. The baboon families withdrew a further 400 feet or so. Now Admiral was cut off from them, but he remained at his post.

Old females will also live more dangerously. From Hans Sigg's study we learned that the peripheral females, usually older, are just as willing to explore and take risks as the old males (p. 130). Old Narba was particularly prone to wander dangerously far away.

In time a baboon will become aged and decrepit. If it is a female, her male will wait for her a day or two, but no one will wait for a weak and lingering male. The crucial test, the decisive factor for survival, is the ability to follow the family for the many hours of the daily march. Sick and old adults are not carried, nor is food or water brought to them at the cliff. There have also been some human nomad tribes, according to John Koty (1934), that left their elderly members behind alone when they were no longer up to the demands of migration. Among the Manchu, sixty years was said to be the upper limit of life.

Among the hamadryas, those that can no longer keep up are left to their fate. But if they do manage to rejoin the others, they are given a friendly reception. One evening when the bands of Ravine Rock had settled down at their cliff, a thin male with a sparse, bleached-out mantle appeared just as night fell. He came up the ravine as the troop had done two hours before. At the foot of the cliff he filled the ravine with a resonant baahu call. When he appeared over the edge twenty yards away from the troop, two subadult males and, strangely, seven juvenile females went to meet him in a closed column. Without responding, he proceeded slowly through them to his sleeping place. The two subadults followed him, and half a dozen juvenile males sat down next to him. Years previously, a fragile old male had been received similarly at the same cliff. Two evenings in a row he arrived late and alone; on the third evening he did not come. He was not seen again (6).

Old Narba had begun to arrive late at the rock. One evening she was missing again long after the band had returned. It was already getting dark. Suddenly her male, Friend, got up, stared northward, and immediately set off in that direction. After ten minutes he came back with Narba. The family assembled with lively contact-rumbling. Narba then stayed away for a week, probably spending the night with a neighboring band in the north. After another short visit with her family, she finally disappeared forever. The infirm, going their lonely way, are very likely to fall prey to a hyena or leopard; severe weakness due to age or illness thus lasts only a few days. It is rare to see a sick animal whose forces hold out any longer than that. Several times at Awash I encountered a loner with a swollen tongue, which probably prevented him from chewing and swallowing. He was terribly thin.

Evolution has invented a thousand variations on ways to care for the young. Care for the old is unknown. What we think of as almost equally deserving poles of want do not even compete with one another in the process of evolution; old age has essentially no claim at all, because it is practically meaningless for the flow of genes to future generations. The fact that care for the old is unheard of, however repugnant it may be, is one of the many arguments in favor of the theory of selection. While a family member such as Narba's Friend may demonstrate his old affection once in a while, evolution has not produced any kind of behavioral *system* that serves exclusively to help the old. Friend's walk into the night does not contradict the theory; evolution does not generate individual scenes, but predispositions.

The old animal at the end of its reproductive phase is released to some extent from the guidance of its genes and so is relatively free. Genes have contributed to its behavior as a child and to its reproductive strategies; now, in old age, many of these are unemployed, and there are hardly any specific genes for behavior in the final stage of life. The lonely wanderings of old hamadryas males from band to band or their playing with youngsters cannot be explained in terms of adaptiveness. Maybe these restless males have been seized by an urge to travel inherited from the savanna ancestors, which they could never satisfy before; or maybe they are simply leaving the scene of their great loss. Who knows?

Of course, no biologist will maintain that human aging and caring for the old is pointless or wrong. The fact that something is natural does not make it right for those animals with a culture, that is, human beings. Wherever higher organisms are relieved of some of their struggle for survival, they use their free energy to realize individual and social aims that do not serve reproduction. In these free spaces, they emancipate themselves from the dictates of their genes and use the skills, motivations, and knowledge to which the genes have contributed, to pursue goals for which the genes have made no provision. Zoo animals play and become inventive. Humans create space for joy in their cultures. The old human, in particular, engages in a deeper search for spiritual meaning.

We know nothing of an equivalent of meaning in animals. Nevertheless, the behavior of the aging baboons can give us something to think about. Some of them never overcome their loss and release; they become miserable wanderers. But others remain, are more courageous than their younger companions, go further into the face of danger, and take on greater discomfort. This is just the opposite of retirement in a literal sense, as a withdrawal into a rather feeble self-indulgence. They have retired only from the compulsion to succeed.

The Function of the Male Clan

The time has now come to find out what the clan of related males really achieves. To prevent inbreeding among primates that live in groups, the members of at least one sex must leave the group in which they were born and join another. In the case of savanna baboons and macaques, their kindred species, the males leave voluntarily; in the hamadryas, the females are compelled to do so. Whoever remains at home, male or female, can form a net of alliances with relatives of the same sex. Female savanna baboons and macaques do just that. The daughters inherit their mothers' rank, and when one of their members is threatened, the net of the female clan holds together. It is not clear, however, whether females of these species really sacrifice more for one another's sake because they are related (Moore 1984).

It is also uncertain whether the males in the phylogenetically new hamadryas clans turn their kinship net to advantage by mutual assistance. All the prerequisites are there: paternity is guaranteed because female sexual "fidelity" is enforced, fathers and sons can recognize one another as such, and the sons stay with their fathers and older brothers all their lives. The males of a clan also interact more often and more intimately with one another than with those of the neighboring clan. Ninety-five percent of the time that males spend grooming males is reserved for fellow clan members. Family leaders tolerate their male relatives as followers, and little sons will actually leave their mothers in order to return to their fathers' clan. The cohesion of the clan is obvious, but what is it good for? One advantage could be that the males of the clan stand by one another in defending their females. However, we have observed such cooperation only at the level of the bands (pp. 147ff), and we could not tell whether the fighting males exposed themselves particularly in favor of males of their own clan. The mere synchronization of many defenders may be more effective than kin altruism among a few.

In the hamadryas colony at the Madrid Zoo, however, younger males joined their older brothers when the latter founded a harem. As followers, they turned out to be effective allies of their brothers when quarrels arose with other males; while the family leader went forth against the rival, his younger brother guarded the females from other males and also took this opportunity to have some sex. (Wild stallions in the Camargue have a similar buddy system to defend their common harem, but in this case it is the lower-ranking stallion that engages the rival, while his friend drives the mares away.)

A second possible advantage of membership in a male clan would accrue to the young male, in that he more or less inherits the females of the older clan males. In the Madrid Zoo this possibility was also confirmed. There the family leaders allowed their younger brothers and followers a degree of intimacy with the peripheral females. At first they drove the brother away when the female was in estrus, but later on he was permitted to copulate and even to take over females to establish his own marriage. Harem leaders were more tolerant in this regard, the more females they had (Colmenares, personal communication). This is reminiscent of the large harems of the Saudi Arabian hamadryas and the tolerance shown by the males there. Things were different in our Band I, with its small harems; it was only with respect to juvenile females that the young males had an advantage within the clan, and even then they had to spend months in courtship. But clan members were not favored as inheritors of adult females. And no solidarity prevented young Spot from taking his own clan chief's females by force. For the present, there is nothing to convince us of the nice theory that kin selection turned the clan of hamadryas males into a community of altruists. It is only the remarkable return of the two little boys to their fathers' clan and the events in Madrid that keep nagging at me. In some life situation that is important to them but unknown to us, the male clan may be of some use to its members. From their work at the Awash Falls, Phillips-Conroy and her coworkers (1992) suggest another explanation. Hamadryas males might not at all times and in all populations stay at home for life. They would sometimes migrate into other hamadryas bands just as they migrated into anubis groups at Awash. The Cone Rock males of the generations we saw would have remained in their clans as an exception because more females might have been available to them in their own troop than in neighboring ones. Unfortunately, the sex ratios of the latter at the time of the Cone Rock study have not been recorded; yet the suggestion is worth pursuing, since demographic changes are known to introduce significant variation into the social structure of a species. One should, however, consider that an immigrant hamadryas male trying to obtain females might meet more resistance from the hamadryas at Cone Rock than from anubis residents at Awash. Also, a bonanza of females at Cone Rock should have attracted more male immigrants from outside than the two that did arrive but were unable to obtain females. Even so, it is possible that hamadryas males have evolved no kin altruism because male migration is more frequent in the species at large than at Cone Rock in the seventies.

Social and Ecological Success

A social individual has to assert itself on two fronts—on the social front, vis-à-vis the members of its group, and on the ecological front, against the hardships of climate, refractory food sources, and the danger of predators.

The life history of hamadryas baboons makes clear the extent to which their reproductive success, and hence the direction of their behavioral evolution, depends on their *social* skills. Even a powerful fighter can make mistakes that will affect his whole career; the worst, as we can imagine, might be to commit himself as follower to a family in the wrong clan, or one with no daughter, or one in which older followers have priority over himself. He can court a juvenile female too vigorously and thus provoke her father. When he has finally established himself as harem leader, a lot depends on striking the right balance with the females, because dissatisfied spouses are more easily stolen. Escalating fights must be avoided, because in the turmoil he can easily lose the females he already has. At the same time, he has to stay on good terms with his own followers, to hold them off as long as possible. Dominance in terms of fighting force, however well known it may be, is only *one* factor in success; without subtle social skill it is not much use. Robin Dunbar, in his book *Primate Social Systems* (1988), estimated the likelihood of success of two strategies employed by gelada males: taking over a harem by force, and sneaking in from the position of follower. According to his model, both strategies ought to be equally successful, or else the inferior one would disappear. In the population he observed, in fact, they were used equally often. The implication is that the geladas commit few career errors, because they have the social knowledge they need.

The *ecological* knowledge and abilities of the hamadryas had just taken precedence in our research program when the conflict in Ethiopia brought the project to an end in 1977. From what little is known, we can conclude that they are well informed about topography and are experienced about the varying water levels at distant drinking sites. Presumably they also know about the blooming and fruiting seasons of their food plants, about what is good to eat and what is poisonous, about the places where the hidden dwarf carrots grow, and about the hyenas' dens, the leopards' hunting habits, and so on.

The relative importance of social and ecological abilities varies according to the animal species and its environment. When the individuals of a species live alone except for reproduction, ecological skill may well be the most important factor for success. Hamadryas baboons, however, are a social species. Even in the wild, their success depends to a great extent on how they treat their companions. But for all species there is an environment in which their ecological competence becomes quite meaningless—the zoo. Here all that matters is social success. Unfortunately, no one has investigated whether a different type of individual achieves high rank and success in the zoo than in the wild: the social artist, the forger of alliances, the courter, and intriguer, rather than the knowledgeable selector of food, the botanist, finder of water, and topographer.

Many modern city folk base their success on social skills almost as exclusively as a zoo baboon. In the primary and secondary sectors of the economy, people still need to be experts on plants and animals or on industrial materials and procedures, but in the growing tertiary sector it is almost entirely a matter of evaluating the customer's needs, advertising, and winning out over the competitor's strategies—all social skills. People in these professions know nothing from their own experience about the ecological conditions necessary for their survival. They have never worked in a mine, have never been on a leaking oil tanker or an overgrazed Sahel steppe, and they often don't know what the spices look like that flavor their food. But this type of human rules. Often it is only his subordinates who are experts in the world of objects. His political behavior is frequently like that of a captain who devotes endless consideration and debate to how the ship's crew should be commanded, to the market value of the freight, and to the trading strategy of the other shippers, but who dismisses the weather prediction as unproven or even as a hysterical rumor—as though his social and economic prognoses were better justified. This type knows a great deal about overcoming conflict, about commercial practice, laws, and markets, but nothing about seafaring. Probably one reason the ship of humanity has not yet run aground is that, on the scale of the history of the species, it has been drifting this way for a few minutes only.

A Complete Father, Once in My Life

Far off in the thornbush of Awash National Park there is a howl of terror. It is our five-year-old son Ruedi. I rush through the bush. After two hundred yards I come to a tiny clearing. Here Ruedi and his sister Kathrin, three years his senior, are standing in front of two black lava rocks, shaped vaguely like seated baboons. The children have collected these as toys, to paint when at home in the tukul. Ruedi looks at me with wide-open eyes, as though I were the Archangel Gabriel. Kathrin announces that she no longer knew in which direction the river and our tukul were, and woefully told Ruedi, "Now we'll never get back." (She has a sense for the dramatic.) And this fear was why Ruedi had trumpeted so loudly. But all of us are relieved. We experienced firsthand why children's screaming evolved, and for what purpose fathers were originally made.

It is evening twilight by the tukul on the Awash. The three children, in a tight group, have just gone off toward the little privy, a ditch covered by a shed of mud and branches, where they are going to do their last business of the day. Verena calls this "the outhouse march." The smallest one has his grubby little woollen blanket clamped under his elbows and is sucking his thumb. Then there is a crash in the bush, downstream, toward the falls. The two boys come running back, but Kathrin has fled to the outhouse and has to be fetched. The noise was made by our hippo, the young bull that had smashed the storage tent at night and mown down Götz's seedlings. I'm itching for a little mischief. "Ruedi, come along in the car," I say. My frightened son and the impudent hippo will both learn a lesson here. I start the Land Rover, search for the shiny, reddish humped back of the hippo with the headlights, and then push its heavy body away from the camp site with the bumper bar, gently but relentlessly forcing him into the bush. This does not diminish his attraction to our apparatus any more than Walter's scarecrow had done before, but Ruedi is delighted by our prank.

Ruedi knows the hippo from his first night in the tukul. The three children were lying in the low cots along the round, white-washed earthen wall of the tukul, Ruedi in the middle under the very low window that was covered only with a screen to keep the flies out. Suddenly our door creaked and the little fellow was standing in his pajamas next to us, in the light of the oil lamp. An animal had looked into his bed, he explained, and its eyes were "sooo far" apart. He stretched his arms out to the side, half laughing and half scared. I took the flashlight in one hand and led Ruedi out with the other. Outside the house I showed him the hippo outlined in the beam of light. He believed me when I said that the short-legged monster did not want to climb through his window. The hippo gradually became a jolly but often bothersome friend, whom we nevertheless encountered with all due respect. On long family drives in the Land Rover, the five of us composed a hippo ballad with a verse dedicated to each of his countless deeds (plate 8, bottom).

The children had few ready-made toys, so they turned crooked roots and branches into animals and took them for walks. The wooden animals had names denoting their species. For instance, there were the "Upernies," so called because they held their heads upright. The children told us about the habits and evolution of the various species in great detail. Our professional conversations around the dinner table had colored their imaginations. When my wife threatened to throw a "Downerny" into the Awash because it had once too often waited just outside the door to trip her, they were outraged. She mustn't do that, because there were only two "Downernies" left in the world.

The children watched us: observing the baboons and capturing them, doing experiments in the camp, and soldering the car radiators. They were especially enthusiastic about our forceful expressions when we had to take a radiator out again after the fourth failed attempt to mend it. What they saw, they turned into games. Next to the tukul miniature sleeping cliffs were constructed, with baboons made of modeling clay. Seated in front of them were little dolls with field glasses from which came, in Kathrin's voice, the most amusing versions of our note-taking talk: "E gives a neck bite to F, interval change, still the same"—as if a neck bite lasted forever. Above all, they wanted me to watch their own rough-and-tumble play through the glasses and describe it into the dictaphone in ethogram language. We would laugh so hard that we had to sit down. I understood then how wonderful it is for children, and for the father, when they can see him at work and, at least superficially, understand what he is doing.

At the campsite, under the trees along the river, lay chains, gasoline drums, baboon cages, ropes, and pieces of wood. The children included all of this material in their games. They would catch one another in traps, and the prisoner would then threaten the trapper as a baboon would. In the rainy season they lay down naked in the puddles and imitated the crocodiles on the other bank of the Awash, using small pieces of wood to show how fish were propelled from mouth into throat by snapping movements of the jaws.

Only two things were forbidden: the bank of the river and the high, dry grass. The morning after they arrived I took each child by the hand, led it to the river, and showed it the crocodiles and the swiftly flowing brown water. I explained to each of them, very seriously, that I would probably not be able to pull them out if they fell in because they would immediately be lost from view in the turbid stream. Six hundred feet downstream roared the Awash Falls. We went to look at them. I even let two-year-old Urs, the one we were most concerned about, slide down the steep bank near the tukul, holding him by one hand, so that he could feel how slippery it was. The high grass had to be avoided because of the poisonous snakes. This, too, I explained seriously and objectively, without creating a panic. The practical lesson was provided by a small spitting cobra that I had to fish out of Walter Angst's tent. The "Two Commandments" were not transgressed—maybe because everything else was allowed, and because the prohibited things were understandably and obviously lethal dangers.

When we were back in Switzerland, there were beds in the garden that should not be walked on, and I planted fruit trees with delicate branches that should not be struck by footballs. To look nice, the garden had to be cleaned up occasionally. Prohibitions and commands piled up, until one day it dawned on me how ridiculous they all were in comparison to the Two Commandments at Awash. I had just gathered into a basket all the odds and ends the children had scattered around the garden, when suddenly the disheveled Awash campsite came to my mind, and I wholeheartedly scattered everything around again.

Two months or so after our return, I came home from the university in the evening, carrying my briefcase. "Daddy, what do you actually do all day long?" asked Kathrin.

"I sit in my office and write and read and talk with students."

"What a pity. Why don't you become a zoologist again?"

I know that fathers are also important in the "civilized" world—as companions, role models, listeners. But they are not altogether necessary for the family's survival; there is such a thing as life insurance, after all. It was good to be a primitive father for a year—an ecological father, so to speak—whom wife and children needed when things got scary. What a father was once supposed to be.

CHAPTER SIX

Experts in
a Thorny Land

Baboons versus Predators and Nomads

The ecological abilities of a wild animal revolve around two main jobs: finding food, and not becoming someone else's food. This chapter is concerned with the second. How do hamadryas baboons keep away from their enemies? In the hills and gorges of Erer, there were jackals, spotted and striped hyenas, and, rarely, leopards, cheetahs, and lions. The nomads were also not favorably disposed toward the baboons; they dug water holes in the river sand for their cattle and themselves, and when the baboons drank there, the walls sometimes collapsed.

Full-grown males often position themselves between danger and the weaker members of the group. Old Narba liked to go her own way, and once she fell so far behind that a nomad boy cut her off from her family. Her male raised himself up on two legs to keep an eye on her and waited, even though the boy was only ten yards away from him. Hunched down, Narba hurried around the boy; her male let her run past him, and then fled after her, bringing up the rear. When threatened by hyenas or the nomads' dogs, adult males form a shield. Once a dog ran toward Band I, barking. The clan in the lead, the Reds, hurried on while Hacky, Coci, and old Admiral of the Violet Clan stayed at the side, forming a barricade against the dog. Then the rest of the Violets fled past. As a rear guard, Bub from the Reds and Minimus and Admiral from the Violets made up the shield against the dog while it yapped at the band from behind.

Eagles have a preference for the black infants, and there is no male shield against attack from above. But on one such occasion I saw a male jump high into the air, reaching for a diving Verreaux's eagle. The eagle veered off.

Crocodiles cannot be driven off and are almost invisible in the yellowish brown river water. An anubis group at the Awash River did not drink at the foot of their sleeping trees, where the bank descended steeply into the deep water. They went to a more distant part of the bank where the water was shallower and where three large stones were lodged in the river, three feet away from the bank, forming a drinking place protected from the open water.

On their sleeping cliff, the baboons are fairly safe from terrestrial predators. In one case, however, the cliff's protection was not enough. One gray morning I could hear the baahu calls of the males of the Issa cliff when I was still far away. I found them observing a leopard that was moving with lowered head through the bushes on the other side of the river. When the baboons started out for the day, the females of the hindmost family marched on with the troop, but their male stayed seated on the cliff edge and intently watched the spot where the cat had disappeared. Then he looked down at the foot of the cliff. His females came back and joined in his calling. Not until the troop had vanished behind the southern heights did the family run after their companions.

From the lowest levels of the cliff, a trail of fresh blood ran down to the brook. In the water lay a dead hamadryas female, barely adult, with bite marks on her neck and face but otherwise unharmed. Had the males driven the enemy away? Ninety feet farther downstream, the sandy bank was soaked with blood. Leopard tracks and the trail of something being dragged led through the stream and into the bush on the other side. There I found an arm, a leg, and the viscera of a second baboon—another female, judging by their size. One large and one smaller leopard were seen slinking away through the bushes. Presumably mother and offspring had attacked almost simultaneously and, being good climbers, had pulled their prey down from the lowest ledge of the cliff. Later Walter Angst and Walter Götz found remnants of the first female, including the head, up in a tree. The leopard had put its prey there, where it was safe from hyenas.

A subadult hamadryas male living at White Rock lacked one forearm. This may also have been the mark of a meeting with a leopard. Not only had the male survived the bleeding, he was even able to climb vertical rock walls one-handed. Using his single arm, he pulled himself up with such momentum that his hand could release the rock briefly and take hold again higher up.

Regions where humans have exterminated natural predators are sad experiments with nature. In such areas one can tell which of the hamadryas' strategies are used against their predators; for when predators are no longer there, these strategies die out. My observations in Saudi Arabia (26) indicated that the hamadryas baboons sleep on cliffs due to danger from predators. Saudi Arabia was once the home of leopards, cheetahs, wolves, and hyenas, but all are almost gone now. In Wadi Hesswa, on the western slope of the Asir Mountains, the cadaver of a donkey lay untouched for days. One evening a nomad set up his tent there, next to a sleeping cliff on which the baboons had already installed themselves. The baboons left the cliff casually and at nightfall settled down unprotected on the flat, exposed, scree-covered ground. I could not believe they would spend the night in such a place, and at two in the morning I left my tent to have a look. They were still sitting there; I was able to sneak up to within ninety feet and back again without being noticed. This may have been an exception because Biquand et al. (1992) never observed Arabian hamadryas sleeping anywhere except on cliffs, in caves, or within piles of large boulders.

Primatologists have discussed four possible reasons for primates to live in groups: defense against predators, protecting food sources from conspecifics, the exchange of information on places where food is concentrated, and, finally, collaboration in caring for the young (Dunbar 1988). The following observation in the Wadi Hesswa is consistent with the first explanation. When the Hesswa baboons left their cliff in the morning there was no decision process to determine the direction of the march. The males in the party that set out first looked back if the rest of the troop did not follow them, but they did not wait long, nor did they notify as the baboons in Erer did; each went his own way with his family. The families were far apart from one another as they moved along the slopes, and they did not even assemble at the water holes, where the hamadryas of Erer come together in bands. The little groups were connected only by their frequent baahu calls. Free of predators here, the hamadryas had given up the higher organizational units of the daily march.

That larger groups detect enemies sooner than small ones has been documented for a number of animal species. The best defense for baboons that live on the ground is most probably to stay in sufficiently large groups. So why do the hamadryas troops break up at all—and do so precisely when it is daylight and they are far from their safe cliff?

To explain this, we must look into the other main job of wild animals: finding food.

Separating and Rejoining: Response to an Extreme Resource Distribution

During the dry season, a few baboons often sit at the foot of the sleeping cliff early in the morning, consuming what to us was a puzzling breakfast. They put some tiny thing into their mouths and crack it between their molars. Hans Sigg solved the puzzle: at close range, he saw a male baboon poking with two fingers at one of the sun-dried balls of baboon feces that lay near the cliff in great numbers. He crushed the fecal ball and extracted a small spherical object, which he cleaned carefully with fingers and incisors and then chewed up. It was the pit of a fruit of the Jerusalem thorn (*Paliurus spinachristi*, a shrubby tree related to the euphorbias). In the rainy season the baboons had picked the fruits for the sake of their scanty flesh and swallowed them without breaking the pits. Now, when food was scarce, they utilized the harvest a second time by eating the seeds.

Anyone who is this economical with food must really be hard up. There are objective measures for such economy. One is population density, which reflects the productivity of the land. In the savannas, where the anubis and yellow baboons live, there are on average 9.7 individuals per square kilometer (Whiten, Byrne, and Henzi 1987); the figure for the hamadryas at Erer is only 1.8 (6). The second measure is the length of the daily march in search of food. The fifty-six primate species for which data are available travel an average of one kilometer (just under two-thirds of a mile) per day. In the Bole Valley in Ethiopia, the savanna baboons march 1,200 meters daily and the geladas only 630 meters (Dunbar 1988). The hamadryas are an isolated extreme, traveling far above all other species, 8.5 kilometers routinely and 20 kilometers at peak performance. Clutton-Brock and Harvey (1977) found that the smaller the proportion of leaves in a species' diet, the longer its daily marches. Leaves are more abundant than fruits, so that fruit eaters have to travel farther. Hamadryas baboons are among the species that rely heavily on roots, flowers, and fruits; in the dry season acacia pods are their most important food, and in the rainy season it is the acacia flowers and grass seeds. All these are sparsely scattered through the semidesert, which explains the long daily marches of the hamadryas.

Anubis baboons travel a longer distance per day when annual rainfall is low, when resources are scarce, and when the group is large (Barton et al. 1992). But a march cannot be prolonged indefinitely; the limit comes when the animals are expending more energy than they obtain from their food. Extreme marches in the heat of the dry season, when most trees and shrubs have lost their leaves and give little shade, can be beyond the powers of mothers and children especially. Hamadryas baboons need another solution: the foraging groups must become smaller. In their comparison of species, Clutton-Brock and Harvey also found that primate groups march longer each day, the greater the total body weight of the group as a whole (and hence the more food they need). From their graph one can make a very rough estimate for the hamadryas: a troop of one hundred hamadryas, weighing a total of 2200 pounds, would have to travel more than twenty-five miles to find enough food for all of them in the semidesert. They can manage with the actual five-mile daily march only if the troop splits up (fig. 21), for fewer baboons have to go less far, to visit fewer groves and root patches, in order to find enough to eat.

The family is the smallest group in the hamadryas society; it never splits up. In the region of Erer, which receives about twenty-three inches of rainfall annually, even isolated families are seldom seen. The typical foraging group here is the half-clan or the clan, with about ten or twenty members, respectively. In Wadi Hesswa in Saudi Arabia, there is only about two-thirds as much annual rainfall, and here even one-male units travel alone. The reason, in addition to the absence of predators, may be that the food supply is even more widely scattered there. The chacma baboons in the Drakensberg Mountains of South Africa, where there are no predators at all, show that food density in itself can determine the size of the baboon groups. In one study the food supply was found to decline from the low-land to the high plateaus, in parallel with the population density of the baboons. At an altitude of about 4,800 feet the chacmas formed groups with an average of forty members; at higher altitudes the groups gradually became smaller, until at 9,000 feet there were groups of only ten animals, with a single adult male (Whiten et al. 1987; Henzi et al. 1990).

A primate group is a compromise between the large group for protection against danger and the small one for protection against hunger and too-long marches. Most species choose to have one intermediate size group, like that of the savanna baboons. In the semidesert, though, the range of optimal group sizes is extreme. The hamadryas have solved this problem with a building-block society, a system of groups and subgroups that separate and rejoin along preformed seams, depending on the concentration and distribution of resources. At the rare but large sleeping cliffs, they spend the night in troops of hundreds of individuals. The troop is much larger than the groups of other baboon species and, in fact, represents a fusion of these. The largest troop we knew lived near the town of Dire Dawa and comprised 750 members, all of whom found room on the same cliff.

The permanent water holes in the wadis are the next-smaller resources. Here the hamadryas baboons gather in bands, which correspond to groups in the savanna baboons.

To search for food, the band must usually be subdivided. An acacia forest in the loop of a wadi, where there is groundwater, can supply a whole band with flowers and pods during the growing season. On the high plains, however, where the tiny, tasty root vegetable *Boerhavia repens* grows in the stony ground in stands covering about five hundred square feet, isolated clans can be found digging. At the bottom of the scale are the berry bushes and dobera trees standing on the barren ground of the hillsides, a hundred yards or more apart. These offer just enough room for one family.

The divergent requirements imposed by the resource distribution have both combined the old savanna baboon groups and torn them apart, producing the fusion-fission system.

This ecological explanation is plausible, but it has not been established with hard data. One would have to show that the nutrition obtained, in calories per minute, is actually less for foraging groups that are too large. The animals at the rear would have to find less food than those in front, as Prins (1987) showed for the buffalo of Manyara. Small groups would have to lose more of their members to predators than larger groups, and so on.

When food is scarce and baboons are reduced to eating even the horribly bitter white bases of the hard *Sanseveria* leaves, the females and young would seem to be at risk. Don't the males drive them away from

everything edible? Where small tidbits are concerned, respect for possession comes into play, and finders are keepers. Since the hamadryas baboons' food consists almost entirely of little pods, berries, grass seeds,
storage roots, grasshoppers, and beetles, the weak also get their share.
However, they are displaced from the areas where the little things are
growing most densely. Here it helps them to be lighter; in the trees, females and young can climb onto the thin, fruit-bearing branches that
would bend down vertically under the weight of the males—and hamadryas are not very good at brachiating. This food source, then, is reserved
for the smaller ones. Often family leaders do not even climb into the
weaker trees; instead, they gather from the ground what their family has
knocked down while climbing. On thin branches, a female in estrus can
also find a refuge from her importunate male.

It is astonishing that hamadryas baboons do not systematically hunt
small mammals; they are capable of doing so, and the nutritional value of
such prey ought to be highly desirable, considering the tiny servings of
vegetables that make up their normal diet. But just look at this excerpt
from the notebooks of Sigg and Stolba:

> The slim subadult male Hacky catches a hare. Rossini, Rosso, and
> Bishop instantly dash up to him, and it is the full-grown Bishop who
> finally eats the hare.
>
> When foraging in the bush, the Reds scare up a miniature ante-
> lope, a dikdik. Bishop catches and eats it. His female Bethli watches
> for twenty minutes, but is not given a single bite to eat. The same
> thing happened to Rosinante, when her male Rossini caught a rabbit.
>
> In two of the nine hunting scenes in our files, females were the
> hunters. Rabiata immediately had to give her hare up to the male
> Cadet, who consumed it all by himself. The only female to get any-
> thing from the nine animals that were caught was Labile. She had
> stronger nerves than her name would suggest:
>
> Labile catches a hare. Her whole family surrounds her, but she
> covers the prey with her body. Her male, Cadet, threatens her, but in
> vain. Even the herding glance he throws back at her as he walks
> away doesn't work; she makes the standard kecking response and
> follows him, with the hare under her arm, but then she turns her
> back and goes on eating. The family has to wait for her several times,
> until eventually she has finished. Like the others, she did not share
> her prey with anyone.

We saw in a laboratory experiment that a female's possession of large
portions of food is not respected (p. 186). Add to this the fact that in the
wild most prey animals are caught by adult males, none of whom shares
the meat with females and young, and it becomes clear that hunting cannot become established as a way for the species to obtain food. The

spouses and children of the hunters would have to waste time waiting, and go hungry. Although the baboons are physically quite capable of hunting, they are let down by their social inability to give, or at least to allow others to take. Ants, birds, wild dogs, and lions share their prey with adults and juveniles, being motivated by their hereditary predispositions. Most primates lack a genetic program for giving. Welker (personal communication) had a captive howler monkey that regularly fed marmosets in the neighboring cage from hand to mouth—a remarkable blossoming in the socially fertile conditions of captivity. In the wild, food sharing has been regularly seen only among chimps. The male chimpanzees in the Tai rainforest on the Ivory Coast hunt successfully in cooperative groups (Boesch and Boesch 1989), and here the possessor of a piece of meat will sometimes let another take a bite. But in only 6 percent of the observed cases does a possessor actively hand a piece to another chimp.

Of all the primates, only humans have made hunting a way of sustaining their lives. The precondition for this breakthrough was a new willingness to donate something to a companion. This may have become possible only when people developed the ability to empathize with one another. Although the role played by the invention of weapons is usually given priority in the development of hunting, in my opinion this was initially less important. It became crucial only later on in the hunting of large animals that were able to defend themselves.

I have compared my daily marches in the tracks of old Admiral to a survival course. By watching him I could have learned what edible things can be found in the semidesert; but even if I had been his brother, he would never have given me any of them.

Do They Plan the Day's March?

The flexible system of fission and fusion, like so many solutions, raises new problems. The hamadryas baboons separate from one another so smoothly because each of them is more strongly bound to the smaller unit than to the next-larger one, at each level of organization. But how do they rejoin one another? Are these haphazard encounters, anytime and anyplace? Sleeping cliffs are no doubt meeting points, but some bands use various cliffs, several miles apart. The Cone Rock troop alone spends its nights on at least seven different cliffs. To arrange a rendezvous, the baboons would have to employ a communication system that can refer to what is far away and into the future, just as the waggle dances of the bees convey information about where distant food can be found. Nothing of the sort had been observed in primates. Yet the members of a band do manage to meet at the same water hole at midday.

Getting together again is not the only problem involved in choosing a route for the day. To save time or energy, planning is necessary. A commercial traveler who has to cover a number of cities on the same day cannot simply start off at random. To calculate the one route that is absolutely the best, that includes the most cities with the minimal mileage, would keep even a computer busy for some time. The "traveling salesman problem" is a standard example in courses on optimization in information systems, with good reason. Hamadryas baboons that start their march face a similar problem. In fact, on closer examination it is more difficult. Let's think about it a little.

Choosing among visible objects is easy, as the choice can be guided by perception. The traveling salesman cannot see his customers while he is eating breakfast, and so must imagine them. A hamadryas baboon sitting on top of his dome of rock also sees only a small portion of the twelve square miles or so that constitute the home range of his band. The acacia forests are hidden behind the ridges, in the curves of the wadis, and in any case they are too far away for the animal to see whether the pods are ripe yet. No water hole is visible from here, and certainly not the beetle larvae in the thick goat dung of abandoned nomad camps, the little roots in the soil, and the groundwater under the sand. To plan, he would have to imagine these things. He would need an internal map, plotted with what he knows. In this sense his problem is like the salesman's.

But now it gets harder. The salesman travels alone. He does not need to consult anyone when he spreads out his map on the breakfast table and sketches the possible routes. His fellow-salesmen are elsewhere, planning their own routes on their own terms, and his family does not have to travel with him. Of all the animals, only the highly social insects are organized as well as a commercial company. Among bees and ants, only the oldest workers do the foraging; in certain cases, each one actually covers a specific territory, while the company—that is, the queen, brood, and nurses—stays home in the hive. Among the African wild dogs and mongooses that live in groups, at least the young stay home in a safe den with someone to watch over them, and their food is brought to them. But primates are unable to share food, so everyone must go along: the old, the pregnant females, and the infants holding on tightly to their mothers. Who should do the planning here, and for whom?

Given that the whole group has to travel, it would be best if an experienced member went ahead as an uncontested leader. Some animal species do function in this way. For example, when the dwarf mongooses of the Taru Desert in eastern Africa go in search of food, the group mother—the alpha female—leads her male and the young (Rasa 1986). But when they are confronted with snakes or hostile neighbor groups, the father takes the lead. The male alpha wolf leads his pack in the hunt. When a mother shrew is disturbed in her nest, she guides her children in convoy to a new one, making sure that each one takes firm hold of the hind end of the one in front with its mouth, so no one gets lost.

This original guiding system, in which an expert leads the way for those not so well informed, is common among mammals, but practically the only instance surviving among the social insects is found in the relatively primitive ponerine ants. The species *Paltothyreus tarsatus* uses it when the colony's nest has been destroyed by a downpour. Then the colony moves house immediately, even though many of the workers are away looking for food and hence will not know where the new nest is. When a forager that does know meets one that has not been informed, it presents the scent glands on its abdomen to the stray ant and leads it to the new nest (Hölldobler 1984). In the normal case, however, bees and ants no longer need direct guidance. When a lone collector discovers a rewarding food source or an enemy, it marks the way with scent so that the other group members can follow. There are species with five different scent signals that have evolved to detect the various things that can be expected at the end of the trail.

Hamadryas baboons do not set up such signposts, nor does anyone go up ahead as a guide. Old, experienced males such as Admiral, remarkably, usually stay toward the back of the marching group and are overtaken by ignorant juveniles. Furthermore, sometimes the band travels as a closed column, and at other times the clans and half-clans go off by themselves. One finds that a particular pool has dried up, and another discovers that a clump of acacias is already in bloom. When they all come together again, can one clan somehow tell what another has learned?

If the hamadryas really made good plans for the long march through the semidesert, they would have to have some way of combining the knowledge acquired by many. Even without a recognized leader, they would have to reach an agreement, despite their varying needs. For instance, the leader of a family with nursing mothers who need extra water must visit more water holes than a bachelor. We ourselves would not find this easy. I can imagine that my human neighbors, including the children and the old people, would not obtain their meals under such circumstances. Mrs. Z. walks with a stick and doesn't like cabbage. The B's are vegetarians and have let the hedge grow head-high on the side of their garden adjoining the property of Mr. F., who is an enthusiastic hunter. We would probably need a committee to draw up a list for an extensive joint shopping trip. However, the comparison with us sedentary individualists is unfair. Let's see how a genuine human nomad group handles the problem.

As reported by Barth (1965), the Basseri nomads in southern Iran decide by mutual consent when it is time to strike their tents and move on with their herds. Having come to this decision, they have to agree on which way to go and where the next campsite would be. There is no command from a leader. In fact, the Basseri do not even assemble for debate. Instead, the evening before, people visit each other's tents, back and forth. Individuals and groups, mainly relatives, discuss the pros and cons, but hardly anyone offers a straightforward opinion. Even the important members cautiously blend in with what seems to be the majority. The group often goes to sleep before a decision is reached. The shepherds, however, must leave before daybreak. They make a preliminary decision, one that leaves room for the strongest tendencies the group has shown the night before. In the morning, finally, those most eager to go take down their tents without more ado. In minutes, the others follow suit. The caravan starts out, its destination still undetermined. Individual men at the head of the caravan turn aside here or there and unobtrusively check whether the others are following. If not, they swerve back again and announce that the place they have in mind is unsuitable just now. Eventually the caravan does follow one of the proposers, and the new campsite is finally selected. This is a lengthy procedure, protracted by the fear of being alone in one's opinion. We shall now examine how the procedures of the departing hamadryas baboons compare to those of the Basseri.

A Two-Male Team in Conflict

We were just starting our first field study. The troop at the ravine cliff in the Ahmar Mountains had become smaller day by day. One group after another had moved away into the plain and were now sleeping in the north, at Stink Rock. Only two families were still spending the night at the favorite place in the ravine, under the huge cube of rock overhanging the smooth wall: old Pater with one female and a little son, and Circum, a male in his prime, with four females and their children. They granted me an extraordinary day by demonstrating, with rare clarity, how hamadrys males confer about which route to take (6). In the following description taken from my notes, be aware of the direction in which each of the two males is striving to direct the party (fig. 43).

7:05 A.M. The two families are sitting near the cubic rock.

7:09. Now the younger male, Circum, gets up and walks over to old Pater. They look into each other's faces. Then Circum leaves the sleeping place, going *north*. His females follow. Pater's female and the young ones join them, and after half a minute the old male goes along behind. The column climbs down to the brook and settles there for another social session.

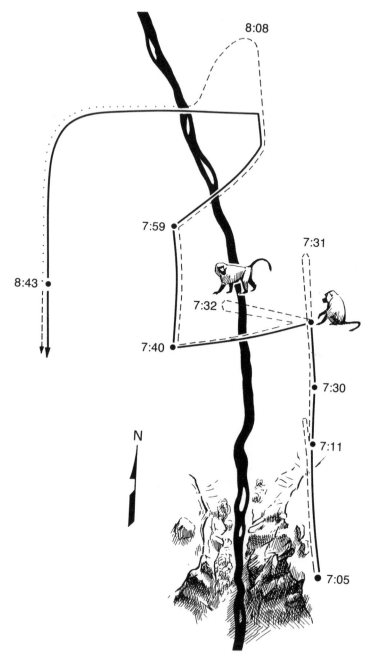

8:08

7:59

7:31

8:43

7:32

7:30

7:40

7:11

N

7:05

Fig. 43. Two males disagreeing about direction. The younger family leader Circum repeatedly tries to lead northward. The older one, Pater, refuses to follow until Circum yields to him and leads toward the west and southwest. The large dots indicate stopping points, and the bold lines show Pater's route. Circum's route is shown by dashed lines when he was leading, and by dots when he brought up the rear.

7:30. Circum rumbles a contact sound and starts off down the brook, toward the *north*. Again the rest follow. Having gone about 20 yards, they all sit down again in the same order as above.

7:31. Again Circum gets up, casts a glance back at the others, and proceeds another 20 yards *north*ward, but this time no one follows. He stops, comes partway back, and sits down. All the time, Pater has been watching him. (Circum's suggestion that they go north has not prevailed.)

7:32. Circum rises but now, observed by Pater, goes *west* over the brook. Only his youngest female dutifully follows. Pater does not move an inch. Circum notices, comes halfway back, and sits.

7:33. Again Circum makes a move to go, this time toward the *southwest*. Now, finally, Pater gets up; all of them follow Circum, in the same order as at the beginning, with Pater bringing up the rear.

7:40. On the other side of the brook, however, Circum again turns *north*ward. Everyone follows him to an umbrella acacia in bloom; they climb it and begin to eat the flowers.

7:58. Pater climbs down and sits facing *north*. He extends his arm toward the north and scratches it. (For a moment I think he is pointing there, but I later found out that baboons and other monkeys never point.) At once Circum hurries down to him, stands still next to him for a moment, and they look each other in the face. Then Circum again leads the way *north*ward. Pater lets all the females and juveniles go past him and follows as the last one. After 20 yards they all sit down, in the established formation.

8:07. Circum gets up, looks back, and leads off. But after a few steps he turns right, crosses the brook again, now going *east*, and on the other bank again leads the group toward the *north*. (This is where the two families would have been if Circum's first attempt to depart had been accepted by Pater.)

Now, however, for the first time Pater leaves his position at the rear and gradually moves forward along the column, passes Circum, and, now in the lead, swerves back to the *west*. This takes him across the brook for the third time. Circum goes a few yards on toward the north, and the single file of females stretches out between the two males. Then Circum gives up and follows the others westward. Pater is leading for the first time, followed by his family, then Circum's, while Circum himself acts as rear guard. Pater is leading the group toward the *southwest*. (This was the direction of Circum's third "proposal" at 7:33, which Pater finally "accepted.")

8:43. The group rests on a hill.

8:52. Circum gets up and goes along the row of resting baboons, passing close by Pater, and with his family behind him positions himself at the head of the column—toward the *south*. (He seems to submit to what Pater wants.) . . .

10:35. A sudden thunderstorm. The air is so full of water that I can hardly see the group from my distance of 50 yards. Fortunately, they are all sitting still, heads lowered and backs to the wind, the little ones sheltering at their mothers' breasts.

11:00. The storm is subsiding; Pater lifts his head, looks over at Circum, and starts out toward the *south*. Circum goes along for a few yards, far behind, but then turns away to the *northeast*. (He has evidently still not given up his original intention.) His four females and all the juveniles in the group follow close behind him. Pater and his female are left alone, looking after them. Finally they also follow, Pater last.

1:15 p.m. The group has paused to feed. Now Circum gets up very slowly and goes *north*, but looks around toward the others several times. Only his family goes along, and even overtakes him. Pater stays put.

1:19. Pater gets up and goes in the opposite direction, toward the *south*. Within three seconds all the females and juveniles are coming after him, even the Circum family. Trailing well behind, Circum also follows. . . .

This process continued all afternoon. It was almost two o'clock when Circum finally gave up for good, moving to the head of the line and leading the group back to the ravine cliff, where we arrived at 4:20. What he had probably intended was to travel northeast to Rotten Rock and rejoin the rest of the troop. For me, this stormy day in April 1961 is unforgettable. It taught me the general principles of leadership among the hamadryas; having been demonstrated so clearly, they were detectable later on in the intricate movements of the whole troop. They are as follows.

The females and juveniles rarely initiate travel in a particular direction, though they can tip the balance by following a male immediately and closely.

The males, on the other hand, have certain directions in mind (plate 6, bottom) and stubbornly insist on them. The younger, more dynamic male goes ahead and seizes the initiative. However, even though he could defeat the older male in a fight, in this case he does not necessarily get his way. The decision is almost always made by the older male who, from his position at the rear, watches which way the younger one starts out and follows—or stays where he is. By trial and error the young male learns what his senior's intentions are. During these tugs-of-war we never saw a male direct even the slightest threat to the one disagreeing with him. In moments of decision, they merely move close together, look at each other, or notify.

While observing the White Rock troop I accompanied such two-male teams at various age levels. In a young team the junior member is still subadult, a follower of an older male in his prime to whose wishes he conforms like a female, without suggesting a direction himself. Having reached adulthood, the younger male gradually leads the way more often, checking the older male's reaction to see whether he is right. As the years go by, he acquires females and the senior member loses his, but the pattern of their travels together does not change. The younger male, now a family leader, still pays attention to the scrawny oldster with no females at the rear of the column, consulting him about the direction of march and waiting for him until he can no longer keep up.

Why is the younger, stronger male content to go ahead as initiator and leave the decision to the older male following behind? That the young one goes ahead could simply result from his youthful energy. But that he acquiesces to the older male must have some other reason. Has he found out that his older companion knows more? In that case, he ought not to make proposals of his own. Or is it that old age in this case enjoys a degree of respect quite unrelated to physical strength? Once more we are on the brink of ignorance.

If the old male really is better at planning the route, the younger one's attempts to lead the way give him the chance of an education. The young male probably learns more by making his own suggestions and having them rejected than if he merely followed the older one. As initiator he can learn how profitable his companion's ideas turn out to be in comparison with his own. However, all this can hardly mean that the older male intentionally teaches the younger by "correcting" the latter's "errors" in the disciple's best interest. There are very few examples of such pedagogy in the animal kingdom (Premack 1991). Finally, if the two males are equally competent, the tug-of-war about direction can inform each of them about the intended destination of the other. They might plan more successfully if they can mark on their own internal map the place to which the other male is thinking of going.

But do the hamadryas baboons think about destinations at all? Or do they travel like trains on the rails of traditional, standard routes, disagreeing merely about whether Route 13 or 28 would be best today?

Baboon Geography

There are no constant, standard routes but only standard sections a few hundred yards long, which Sigg and Stolba called "street segments" (27). Each street segment is traveled time and again, with the advantage that the condition of its resources is known. Each route, however, is made up of a different set of street segments; this offers the advantage that no leopard that has discovered the baboons can know in advance where it will be able to ambush them later in the day. We could not tell, either. Two flies with one blow, then, but how much more difficult does this arrangement make it to agree on the day's route before departure?

If the baboons do not travel on fixed routes, they must be able to think of particular places as destinations. Sleeping cliffs are certainly such destinations, because the baboons can find their way back to them from anywhere. Hans Sigg and Alex Stolba collected data showing that the hamadryas also plot feeding regions on their internal map. If they want to stay in one place longer than fifteen minutes, the baboons walk faster before reaching the stopping place, even if it is not yet in sight. That is, they know that it is going to be good up ahead.

The following observation points in the same direction. In general, groups of baboons spend most of their time in the large wadis with abundant vegetation. Here water and food are more plentiful and more visible than in the dry side valleys and on the barren plateaus where the hidden roots grow. The less frequently the baboons visit a region, because it is at the edge of their home range or even in the range of another band—that is, the less well they know a region—the stronger is their tendency to keep to the large wadis there. In the barren areas it is probably necessary to know exactly where the food sources are. But in the wadis even a stranger can find food. Similarly, the hamadryas visit unfamiliar regions more often when it has just rained, so that they can expect to find fresh, easily spotted greenery and puddles everywhere.

The broad wadis are also the most reliable zones for drinking water. Even here, though, in a dry spell the water level soon sinks below the surface of the sand. The hamadryas know where a bar of rock holds the groundwater back, and there they dig holes and wait until the water fills them. When an exposed pool is covered with slimy green algae, they dig a hole next to it, allow some time for seepage, and drink the filtered water.

The first prerequisite for planning a day's march is that the hamadryas have some knowledge of the terrain, a brain map to which they can refer. What Sigg and Stolba reported suggests that they do. It would be especially impressive if a few strong animals, perhaps groups of subadult males, occasionally went exploring, and instead of eating what they found right away, led the whole clan there the next day. We have never observed such a thing, but the young Dutch researcher van Roosmalen (1980 and personal communication) saw females of the South American spider monkey (*Ateles paniscus paniscus*) doing almost that. This species lives in a fusion-fission system, the subgroups being led by dominant females. In the evening, when a subgroup climbs through the forest crowns to its sleeping tree, the dominant female often branches off to the side and goes alone to some fruit trees. Even if she finds ripe fruit there, she doesn't eat any of it, nor does she summon the members of her group. She simply returns to the group. What is missing is the observation that if she does discover fruit while reconnoitering, she would lead the group there the next morning. However, van Roosmalen is convinced that the dominant females "investigate feeding sites and plan economical collecting routes."

Now we must try to deal with the more difficult second prerequisite: can the hamadryas on their cliff communicate with one another about their knowledge of the terrain, so as to decide on the day's march? The problems could keep a planning expert busy. The clans and half-clans should go separate ways, along new combinations of the old, familiar street segments, then come together as a band at a water site at noon. In the process, predators or herders at the water sites might force them to make detours. On top of all this, their foraging should be productive and the route as short as possible. The Traveling Salesman Problem is comparatively innocuous. We can be sure that pedantically to plan every aspect would be pointless, even for humans. The only thing to do is make a general plan that is flexible in its details.

Let us take a look at what actually happens in a troop before departure. Again, as you read pay attention to the compass directions of the various movements.

Voting for Direction at the Cliff

During the night, a stormy rain had fallen. Wet and bedraggled, the baboons of the White Rock troop sat on the scree-covered slope above the cliff. Not until sunbeams broke through the dark cloud banks was there any activity among the huddled clusters. Then a family got up here and there, to settle a few yards higher on the slope. Barely an hour later, the band that occupied the right part of the cliff sent out a sort of offshoot to the upper right, toward the north. But this venture got nowhere. Some families, remaining under the acacias above the scree slope, hesitantly moved a little to the left, in the western direction. The baboons in the offshoot at the upper right did not respond. The males in this group looked away from the rest, toward Table Mountain in the north, on the other side of White Rock River. In recent days most of the band's marches had gone that way, through the dry riverbed.

Time passed. The rock walls had long since dried, and the youngsters played there tirelessly. A few males in the northern offshoot had turned around and were looking back at the stationary part of the band, which was still sitting under the umbrella acacias above the slope.

Finally a haggard old male by the trees lifted his long muzzle out of his chest hair, scratched himself at length, and stood up. In long, leisurely strides, without looking around, he moved off toward the southeast and vanished in the acacia woods. No one else had so far moved in this direction. But now within ten seconds baboons were getting up everywhere. The little western group overtook the old male. The baboons in the northern offshoot came back and brought up the rear. Their evident intention to depart toward the northeast, as they had done the day before, would today have been thwarted after a few hundred yards by the brown water flooding the wadi. Did only the old male know that?

The formation of offshoots before departure is typical (6). It evidently corresponds to the proposal of a direction by the younger male in a two-male team. A band changes shape while staying in place, like an indecisive amoeba; it extends a pseudopod in one direction and then in another, sometimes pulls it back in, and waits until finally one of them elongates faster and faster (plate 2, bottom left), absorbs the whole band, and flows away (fig. 44).

An offshoot is created when one male and his family shift beyond the periphery of the band. He does this hesitantly, scratching himself more frequently than usual before making his move, and he rarely advances more than five yards at a time. If his foray meets with approval, other males follow with their families at intervals of several minutes, pass the first male by a few yards, and sit down. The direction in which a male faces while seated is usually the direction in which he will move next. When several males sit facing the center of the band, the offshoot is about to pull back. During and between their changes of position, the males go up to one another and present each other with face or hindquarters. This notifying behavior is much more frequent now than at other times of the day.

As among the Basseri nomads, the individual tries not to be too obvious with his proposal—hence the long conflict scratching and the small, cautious shifting of position. Only the haggard old male dared simply to start out, without looking left and right. In the first field study I saw only old males making such decisive starting marches that were immediately accepted by all the others. It was not until Alex Stolba completed his dissertation (22) that we were given a detailed analysis of the decision process. Here is what he found.

Although several bands may be sitting close together on the cliff in the morning, each is a distinct amoeba, gravitating toward a different sector. At Cone Rock, the home range of Band I lay mainly to the north, and that of Band II to the south. By the time they are a hundred yards from the cliff, each band is marching separately. But earlier, at the cliff, the departure of the other bands has a magnetic effect. When one leaves, another tends to be carried along. A little later, though, it sits down again, makes its own decision, and turns off into its sector when the other bands have

Fig. 44. A band from White Rock, shortly after departure in a wadi bed.

disappeared over the horizon. The Cone Rock bands even let themselves be dragged along when a band departed from the opposite cliff, 600 feet away on the other side of the riverbed, or from Wart Rock, over half a mile away. This dragging is an anonymous mass effect, not an independent decision by a band. The bands communicate with one another as little before departure as at any other time.

Even before departing, the males of a given band spin a tight-meshed web of mutual attentiveness. When one male moves a few feet, his male clan mates watch him particularly closely. The way they watch one another also shows that the decision about departure is largely a matter for the males. If a female *and* a male walk past seated males, the gazes of the latter follow the male almost five times as often as the female.

The most common interaction of the males is notifying; we have come across this before, as a friendly gesture of conciliation that the possessors of females direct toward their rivals (p. 180 and p. 229f) Near departure time it has another function: it invites the recipients to come along. Initially, when the band is resting on the cliff, the males notify rarely—2.3 times per male per hour—and mainly within the clan. Then comes the descent from the cliff, in fits and starts. During this phase the rate of notifying jumps up to 6.1 times per male-hour. The clan members are now mostly in agreement. When a male advances a few yards, his clan mates more often reply by moving in the *same* direction, whereas the neighbors belonging to other clans often propose another direction. That is, during the descent the clans in their turn must be coordinated. And indeed, the males now direct their notifying toward other clans distinctly more often than they did while the band was at rest.

When they begin marching away, the notifying score again increases significantly, to 7.8. Afterward, on the route, it drops to a minimum of 1.4. Notifying is thus concentrated in the phases in which the clans are coming to an agreement with one another about their common marching direction.

In addition to shifting and notifying, Alex Stolba's analysis revealed other forms of voting. When a seated male lowers his head abruptly to his chest in response to the vote of another male, so that he no longer sees what is happening, then he himself will not budge from the spot for at least two minutes (fig. 45); for a while, his neighbors also change position less, as though his refusing to see were a No vote. In contrast, when a male stands on outstretched arms and legs, as stiff as a sawhorse, it is fairly certain that he will soon advance in the direction of his body axis, even though someone has just voted for another direction.

The amoeboid changes in the outline of the band in the morning are the external signs of a decision process in which each male can vote. Offshoots form when several males make the same proposal. Do the votes of the old males have greater weight, as was the case in the two-male teams, and as was suggested by the episode at White Rock when the wadi was flooded? Alex Stolba counted how many times a male first moved in a new direction, and how often such an initiative was adopted by other males, in that they moved in the same direction. The initiatives of the younger males in each clan clearly prevailed less often than those of the older family leaders. The aging Admiral, however, did not enlist more males to follow his short moves than did the family leaders in their prime. Nevertheless, when the old ones really intervene, they have an electrifying effect. In four out of twenty-six departures from White Rock, an old male managed to get the entire band underway in ten seconds by striding directly out of the center with conspicuously long steps. These elders did not even stop to look around, as the younger males always do. They seemed to reserve their influence for special cases, which are buried in the overall statistics. Occasionally the old ones also exert a veto by simply not following the proposals of the family leaders.

So the second prerequisite for a planned route has been met. The males in a band communicate with one another and arrive at a joint decision, which determines the direction in which everyone will depart. An agreement was reached in 98 percent of all the observed departures.

Fig. 45. A vote against the direction proposed by another member of the band. The male on the right abruptly lowers his head as another notifies to him in passing.

Why is it that the males make this decision and not the females? A first guess might be that it is due to herding by the patriarchal males. The females are indeed secluded within their families, and only the males have access to a network of relationships that crosses clan boundaries. However, this difference between the sexes exists before the age at which the females are guarded by a male. We recorded the age and sex of the three nearest neighbors of an individual while the hamadryas were resting (6). It turned out that even three-year-old males were most often found resting with three other males of about their own age. The neighbors of the three-year-old females were a random mixture in terms of age and sex. Only when such a female was in estrus was her nearest neighbor often a three-year-old male, a little sex buddy, whom the family leader evidently tolerates. He would surely also allow the young female to be associated by other females, but she does not seek them out. Of their own accord, then, the juvenile males live in the company of their own kind, but the females do not. The lack of a female net, which would be needed for group decisions, may also suit female inclinations. The old hamadryas females, in particular, are probably as much connoisseurs of the thorny land as the males and no doubt know as well as they do the best marching direction, but they do not communicate with one another about it.

To be a leader, one must dare to advance alone, before everyone else. Among the male baboons only the elders are sufficiently confident to do this. They would be influential enough to lead the bands permanently, but they are not interested in that role. Power over all others does not seem an end in itself, to them.

No one has yet studied the way savanna baboons make group decisions. I suspect that there the females take the lead, because there it is they who stay in the groups where they were born and know the resource geography of the home range from childhood on.

Where to Drink? A Long-Distance Decision

Something in all this is puzzling. What is the point of the daily voting and tugging in different directions, from the descent until the march begins, if the clans soon afterward separate from one another in any case? Alex Stolba had an idea: that the important thing is not the communal departure as such, but only its direction, which identifies a distant meeting point. Only one station on the route is important enough to justify such a laborious decision process—the drinking place where the band reassembles at midday (plate 8, top).

In the home range of Band I there were only eight pools that rarely dried up. Here rock barriers in the dry riverbeds retain the groundwater, so that the water level stays above the sand for weeks. At these water holes, which are often surrounded by dense vegetation and may harbor predators, all the clans of a band reassemble around noon in 72 percent of the observed daily marches. Alex Stolba wondered whether the direction of the communal departure might designate which of the distant, still invisible water holes would be the meeting point for the clans that day. Close observation revealed that the movements of the bands during the departure process were aimed progressively more accurately toward the day's midday water (22). Stolba divided the compass directions into eight

45-degree sectors, centered on the sleeping cliff. The first movements, as the baboons began to leave the cliff, pointed into the 45-degree sector that included the water hole on only 24 percent of the days. As the departure proceeded, they aimed toward this sector more often, and when marching away they did so 86 percent of the time. After the clans had separated from one another, the sector was again less likely to be targeted, only 68 percent of the time halfway along the route.

This result fits Alex Stolba's hypothesis. But the following test is crucial: when something unpredictable disrupts the plan, so that clans go to a water hole other than the one they had earlier agreed on, the expected result is that they will not all choose the same one. Here no march should be counted in which the clans saw one another again during the morning, so that they might have "discussed" the matter again. There were only sixteen marches for which such a later agreement could reliably be ruled out. In ten of these the noon water lay in the direction of the joint departure; in all ten cases, all three clans met there. In the other six departures, the direction of the water hole that was actually visited by the majority deviated by more than half a sector from the direction of the departure. On these days, some of the clans must have been disturbed in their original intentions. In none of these six marches did all three clans go to the same water hole. This difference is highly significant. Stolba's hypothesis can be cautiously accepted: the decision at the cliff applies to the meeting point "noon water," and the direction of the departure stands symbolically for this choice. The hamadryas cannot point out this direction to one another, so at the beginning of their march they must "walk it" together for a while, even though immediately afterward they may branch off toward closer destinations in other directions. Apparently all that is decided at the cliff is this most important, distant destination.

The band's plan for the day is thus limited to what the band actually does together: visit the water hole. The details of the foraging routes are left to the clans and can be flexible. Occasionally the clans are actually observed to stop, form offshoots, and make a new decision.

Alex Stolba told me a nice anecdote about the flexibility of the foraging groups. When the nomads move camp, they often set fire to what they are leaving behind. Stolba saw a resting group of hamadryas get up immediately when a column of smoke ascended out on the plain, and all the baboons disappeared in that direction. The smoke promised an abandoned goat kraal and a thick layer of dung with beetle larvae.

The hamadryas' long-distance decision about their noon water is by no means as elegant and precise as the bees' means of designating to others in the hive a source of pollen and nectar. In the famous waggle dance, a successful collector indicates the direction of her find with an accuracy of a few degrees by the way she moves on the vertical comb. The bee runs in alternating semicircles and straight lines, during which she waggles her abdomen. The direction straight up on the comb corresponds to the direction of the sun. When the straight run of the bee's dance points 15 degrees to the right of upward, that means, "You will find a food source 15 degrees to the right of the sun." Furthermore, the speed with which the dance is performed lets the others know the exact distance to the food— the slower, the farther away. Over the geologically brief duration of their evolution, the mammals have produced nothing similar, as far as we know. Their way is not to depend on precise, genetically based programs, but to evaluate special situations with the aid of a great capacity for learning. They know their conspecifics as individuals and make use of their individual characteristics. Bees cannot do that. The hamadryas baboons, deciding where to go when they leave the cliff in the morning, are on the way to knowing what their companions are thinking. Among the nonhuman primates, the ability is beginning to dawn that in humans produces such odd people as behavioral researchers, who even want to know what an animal is thinking.

The Diviner

The baboons' search for resources in the hills of Erer reminds me of a little story about another search for resources in the same region. I had returned to my tent, liberated my feet from the thick woollen socks and the prickling grass husks they had picked up, and strolled over to the Erer Hotel to sit on the veranda with Fred Kurt and rinse the dust out of my throat. On the round rim of the well in the inner courtyard sat a monk in a brown cowl. He was watching a little silver ball at the end of a thin chain he was holding in his hand circle slowly over the well water.

I am not so superstitious as to conclude without evidence that divining with a pendulum is a superstition, and I was curious about such undertakings, so I approached and greeted him. He turned out to be a Frenchman and responded cordially to my questions. He was not divining but somehow measuring with the ball the mineral content of the hot-spring water that feeds the well. The blue eyes behind the steel glasses followed the path of the ball, and his lips whispered numbers. Then he gathered up the ball and penciled some neat entries into a table. He went down his list, one mineral salt after another; each circle made by the ball represented one milligram of mineral per liter.

The mineral composition of the Erer spring was already posted under glass in a frame on the wall by the dining tables, so my curiosity was not satisfied. I asked the friar for another test.

"Would it be possible for you to distinguish between a glass of water from the Erer River and one with water from this mineral spring?" "Why, certainly, with pleasure," he replied amiably.

Meanwhile, a traveling companion of my new acquaintance had joined us, and so had Fred. All of us sat down at a table in the dining room. The old monk carefully spread a black felt cloth over the tablecloth and opened a large red box containing crystals, colored papers, and other mysterious utensils. The box bore the label of a Parisian company. I had asked Fred to go into the kitchen and put six drinking glasses on a tray, two with mineral water and four with river water, to cover each with a piece of paper, to number them, and to make a note for himself of the contents of each glass. The kitchen doors opened a crack and Fred's arm emerged, handing me the tray. He himself stayed out there. This way, even I did not know what result would be right; this is called a blind experiment. The monk swung his pendulum, and I took notes. To the disappointment of all of us, he got only three glasses right and was wrong on three. His companion encouraged him to try it again. The result of the second test was still worse: five of the six glasses were wrongly identified. Our guest was certainly acting in good faith, and for just that reason I regretted putting him to our smart-alecky test.

There was one good aspect, however. An Ethiopian official, a Blatta, had been observing us from the next table. Now he came over, took my sheet of notes, and signed it with a flourish. Then he sat with us. In the ensuing conversation it turned out that the monk had offered to find deposits of metal ores in the Erer Hills for him, by swinging his pendulum over the map. Now, of course, nothing came of that, and it was a good thing. Better disappointed than deluded.

Fred and I later visited the friar in his mission school and were impressed. He knew the local problems to the core from living so long among the poor, and despite his naiveté he had probably done more good here than the well-paid foreign development consultants who wanted to teach the Ethiopians all about Ethiopian agriculture in three years, without knowledge of either their language or their circumstances.

Before leaving for home we presented the monk with our thermometer and hygrometer. He was glad to have them, and I will assume that they served his nature studies better than the magic box from Paris.

CHAPTER SEVEN

Anatomy
of the Social
Relationship

The Hidden Substructure

Let us return from the high plane of band decisions to the basis of social life: the relationship between two individuals, the building block and the primary puzzle of any social system.

What exactly is a relationship, this invisible web that is woven between two visible individuals? What combinations of individual characteristics determine whether a relationship becomes intimate or remains distant? And what are the rules by which individuals arrange themselves in the constellation of the group, as atoms with certain affinities come together to form a molecule? Can there be a chemistry of social constellations, allowing a prediction such as the following: individuals of type H and type O form an especially stable group consisting of two H and one O, H_2O?

Perhaps the greatest wish of a scientist is to penetrate the world of phenomena he or she studies sufficiently to begin to understand the greater order behind it. One night, when I had been thinking for a long time about a scientific problem, I finally fell asleep and dreamed of an endless line of deer crossing a forest meadow in the dark. In the foreground, superimposed on the waves of dim gray backs and antlers, a constellation of stars gradually took shape; its shining geometry hung immovably in front of the restless procession, and in its figures I thought I could discern the order at work in the gray column.

The idea of looking for the blueprint of a global design behind the colorful garlands of phenomena is not as naive as it may at first appear. In solving fundamental problems of life, evolution has often first done some experiments and then settled on a basic principle that was only modified from then on. In all the higher plants and animals, genes are stored in chromosomes and sorted by spindle fibers. Large organisms are all composed of cells. To conduct and process signals, evolution has equipped ants, octopuses, and humans with nervous systems made of the same kinds of cells, the neurons. The problem of getting energy from the sun has been solved with photosynthetic pigments; although there are several types in the algae, in the higher plants chlorophyll has won out.

At the level of social life, evolution has achieved a masterpiece in producing cooperation among conspecifics, each of which is by nature a competitor of the others. This is the basic social problem. Its solution must lie in the internal structure of the two-partner relationship, which exists among primates and all other vertebrates with an individualized social life. From the anonymous mass of competitors, an individual selects one other, one that it recognizes and knows personally, and develops the ability to collaborate with—even behave altruistically toward—this partner in spite of all types of conflicts of interest. How did evolution ever manage such a thing?

Sociobiology is no help here. Researchers in this field are concerned only with where in the life of a species cooperation or altruism might have been useful and, in terms of population genetics, possible; then they try to find out whether evolution has in fact produced such behavior where predicted. They do not deal with the practical problem of *how* animals or humans accomplish these things at the level of motivation. It is this *how* that is the subject of this chapter. Given the conservative tendency of evolution discussed above, it would be surprising if every species had invented a new method to achieve the same end.

It is not easy to discern the substructure of social relations by examining the superficial activities of the society's members. Observing in itself is often not enough. Since Babylonian times astronomers scrutinized the stars without recognizing the principle of gravitation. It took the genius of Newton to comprehend the underlying order. Biologists had to become anatomists, microscopists, experimental electrophysiologists, and chemists in order to discover the neuronal structure of the brain and begin to understand it. We hear a lot lately about the need for holistic consideration of intact systems. That goes without saying, in my opinion. However, large ecosystems and social systems are usually so complex that they cannot be understood just by observing the whole. Even a genius might not succeed. To perceive order underlying the whole, it is necessary to begin by shielding a subsystem from the bewildering impacts of the overall system, so that the pure, undisturbed function of the subsystem can be analyzed. Both methods are needed—observation of the whole and experimenting with the part. "Observation sets the problem; experiment solves it, always presuming it can be solved," wrote Jean-Henri Fabre in 1919.

The study of the inhibition of fighting in hamadryas baboons (pp. 170ff) was an experiment on a crucial subsystem of hamadryas society: the triangle comprising a pair and a rival. It excluded the influence of the troop and the familiar place; it also ensured that none of the three relationships had an unknown history. What remained was the essence of the triangle, and it was only then that a simple principle came to light: the triangle situation drew two individuals still closer together and shut the third one out.

Moreover, the inhibition experiment achieved something else that is common to all behavioral experiments with animals that are initially strangers to one another. That is, the baboons played their roles in an especially explicit manner. They communicated with a clarity hardly ever seen in everyday life, when they are among familiar members of their band. The experiment not only concentrated on the essential elements, it exaggerated them.

This is easily explained. The reason lies in the nature of the social relationship itself. A relationship is the result of a history—it has developed through times past. The partners have learned from previous interactions what is possible between them and what is not. Relationship is the matured potential of two individuals for doing certain things together. Once both partners know their potential, they no longer demonstrate it constantly on the surface. Humans are also familiar with this; and here I come back to a comparison made earlier. The relationship of an old married couple or a team of mechanics that has worked together for years functions largely without detailed discussions and explicit decisions. The questions, "Do you love me?" and "Will you do the bookkeeping?" are superfluous. The partners know how their roles are assigned, who can do what better, and how each responds in particular situations. Even the simple rank order is the result of such an interactive learning process.

It is the same with animals in established relationships. Many everyday signals merely hint at a part of the known potential in a kind of shorthand. A tiny threat calls to mind a crucial fight in the past; a greeting gives reassurance that nonaggression still holds. The full potential is no longer visible on the surface.

When we, as behavioral scientists, encounter an established group of animals, we have none of this prior knowledge; for us, the history of their relationships is a blank. We start out like unprepared newcomers to the conversational circle in an exclusive club, ignorant of the insiders' references and allusions. But when we assemble animals that have never met before in an experiment, we circumvent this handicap. If these animals are experienced adults of a social species, their first concern is to work out a new structure of relationships, and to do so they send one another plain signals at full intensity. They are ahead of us in only one kind of knowledge: they know the rules by which their species builds up a group. These they show us in the experiment. Animals know nothing of the polite ways in which humans in similar circumstances feel one another out. They act openly and often dramatically. The exclusion of historic factors brings out the immediacy and urgency that we cannot see in the animals' ordinary lives. Otherwise animals behave so informatively only during social upheavals, and those are rare.

In 1967, between two field studies of the hamadryas, I had an opportunity to study gelada baboons (*Theropithecus gelada*) at the Delta Primate Research Center near New Orleans. We have already met these primates in the high mountains of Ethiopia (pp. 11, 65ff). Like the hamadryas baboons, they organize themselves into one-male families, but the male hardly herds his many females. Although he defends them against rivals, he is not the central figure in the family as the hamadryas male is. Gelada females have closer relationships with one another than is ordinarily the case among the hamadryas. I wanted to find out from the geladas what could be learned about the nature of a relationship *newly* formed by individuals that had been strangers to one another. I planned to begin with two-individual relationships, then investigate the reciprocal influences in groups of three, and finally study the "chemistry" of one-male groups (Kummer 1975).

This study showed that individuals unknown to one another can produce an especially well-defined social order. In one experiment, to anticipate somewhat, we put two adult males and five adult females together in a field enclosure measuring about 90 by 300 feet, where grass and pines were growing. We observed the baboons from the window of a booth built into one long wall of the enclosure. The geladas were socially experienced, having been captured from the wild in Ethiopia. So that we would not miss any phase of their group formation, we put them together for only four hours a day and watched them constantly during this time. They began to organize themselves at once. By the third day, two one-male families had already taken shape. The females of each family had fought out a rank order among themselves. The unusual thing, never so clearly seen in the field, was the way the geladas represented their new order precisely in their spatial arrangements (fig. 46). The two males, like two-male teams of hamadryas, formed the end points of a straight line, and between them each of the females had her particular place. The two alpha females occupied the places next to their males. The next toward the middle, on each side, was the corresponding beta female, and further inward came the place of the gamma female of the larger group. The reason for this linear formation became clear from the interactions: in this arrangement, each female was capable of keeping all females of the other family, as well as the lower-ranking ones of her own, away from her own male. During disputes she did this with a sharp attack, and while they

Fig. 46. Linear formation of two newly founded gelada families. The two males occupy the end positions, and their females are distributed toward the middle in order of their rank.

were grazing quietly in the meadow she simply corrected slight bends in the line by taking a few steps. She would sacrifice a better feeding place for the tactically better blockading site.

During the next three weeks, however, the linear formation visibly deteriorated, although there was no change in the composition of the families or in the rank order. Disputes about position became rare; as the relationships became part of everyday life, a certain negligence developed. It was easy to guess why: the females had maintained the linear formation only as long as they were not secure in the positions they had won.

To test this hypothesis, every morning for eight days we kept a different female waiting for half an hour in a cage at the entrance to the enclosure; only then did we allow her to go through the sliding door and join the others. Even this brief absence put the female's position in jeopardy. Her spouse often had to defend her from the rival again. Uncertainty and strife among the females reappeared—and with them, the linear formation in which place was dictated by rank. The experiment confirmed that the social order is fully revealed at the surface, demonstrated and defended by positions and interactions *only* if the group members are uncertain of it. Once a credible social order has been accepted by everyone, it sinks out of sight. Internal and external order are reciprocal, in the sense that the clearer the one, the less clear the other. Therefore the confrontation of strangers generates not disorder but rather an especially obvious order, the expression of an underlying substructure that is ordinarily known to all but not exhibited.

Our research program did not actually begin with this group experiment, though; we started at the bottom, with the two-partner relationship. Every morning two adult geladas that did not know each other were brought together in the large enclosure for four hours. We hoped that by watching them, we could discern the anatomy of the social relationship.

Steps in the Pair Relationship

Two strangers might be expected to build up mutual trust in a gradual, tentative process. They could first observe one another from a distance, then slowly move closer together and finally try out the first reassuring session of grooming.

The actual sequence of events was quite different. In every experiment the two unacquainted baboons engaged each other immediately, often in battle. Their relationship developed not smoothly but in a sequence of clear steps or stages. Each step was marked by the first appearance of a new kind of behavior. The first fight, the first presenting, the first mounting, and the first grooming occurred in just this order.

It was as if two singers began a joint song including four tunes, and these tunes had to be introduced in a given order. It was irrelevant who of the two was the first to begin the tune, but sequence of tunes was important. Also, the two partners had to advance more or less together; if one persisted in the fighting tune, the other could at best introduce the presenting tune. Once a tune was introduced, it could appear later on. But if it had not been introduced in its proper place in the beginning, it was banned from the rest of the song.

This sequence of first occurrence was maintained with uncommon consistency (fig. 47). Twenty-eight pairs together made only three errors, by changing the order of two consecutive steps—for instance, the first presenting before the first fight or the first grooming before the first mounting.

To my astonishment, the sex of the partners, normally so important, does not affect the *order* in which the behaviors are first performed. Although presenting and mounting are actually sexual behaviors, pairs composed of two males or two females included them in their program as a matter of course, in the same way as a mixed pair. With respect to the *speed* of the whole sequence, however, sex was a crucial factor. A male and a female took the shortest time. They always skipped the fighting step, began presenting at once, and after six minutes, on average, were engaged in the first grooming. Male pairs always started with fighting. They needed many repetitions at each level, and by the time they had reached the step of grooming they had taken an average of four whole hours. Two of the nine male pairs never got that far; they stayed at the sexual steps. This was not because they had no interest in each other. They, too, tried to advance their relationship, but they were visibly reluctant to touch each other. Male pairs evidently have special problems.

This difference in the abilities of the baboons to get along, depending on their sexes, is also reflected in the distances separating the individuals. The average distance between a female and a male was 3 feet and 3 inches; two females, 4 feet and 1 inch; two males, 24 feet. Such a thing is not entirely unfamiliar to us humans.

In 1972 we carried out the same experiments with pairs of unacquainted hamadryas baboons; we found the same four kinds of behavior, in the same order of first occurrence. The times required for the three combinations of the sexes to reach the grooming stage were almost the same as those of the geladas. Later on, Hans Sigg (1981) found the same sequence of steps among male rhesus monkeys.

All three species, then, developed their two-partner relationships according to the same basic plan, even though their social systems are different. We had evidently touched upon a core structure of the partner relationship in these primate species.

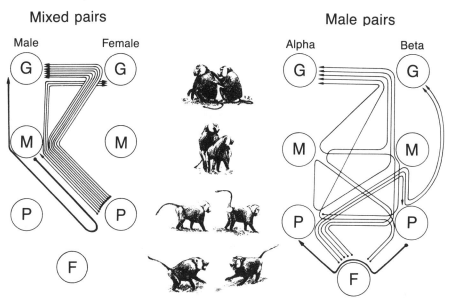

Fig. 47. The development of two-partner relationships in twelve male-female pairs (left) and nine pairs of males (right) of gelada baboons. The behavioral steps or stages in this development are illustrated from bottom to top: the first fight (F), the first presenting (P), the first mounting (M), and the first grooming (G) directed to the partner. Each curving arrow shows the route of one pair through the steps, shown as circles. The routes showing rule infractions are indicated by bolder lines. Only one of the twelve male-female pairs broke the step rule: the male mounted before the female presented to him. One of the nine male pairs also advanced irregularly, in that the lower-ranking male (beta) presented to the higher (alpha) prematurely, before they had engaged at the fight level; the fighting had to be done later. Mixed pairs reached the grooming step after an average of 6 minutes, whereas male pairs took 245 minutes.

The Landscape of Relationships in the Hamadryas Troop

If the sequence of steps is the expression of a true substructure of the pair relationship, we ought to see glimmerings of it, in some form, in the wild troops as well. We never studied geladas in the field, but Jean-Jacques Abegglen pursued this question with the hamadryas baboons at Cone Rock. The step sequence existed here too, in the distribution of the four forms of behavior at the different levels within the troop. The lower steps of behavior are used in the interactions of a hamadryas with many other conspecifics, while the higher ones are directed toward only a few selected individuals. Roughly speaking, the situation is as follows.

In the *whole hamadryas population*, the troops get out of each other's way if they should ever meet. They do not even fight. That is step zero, the normal step for the population as a whole.

Within a given *troop*, the bands relate to one another mainly on the fighting step. The battles between bands described on pages 147–153. are their typical form of interaction.

Within a *band*, presenting in the form of male notifying is the typical relationship. Ninety-three percent of all notifying is directed to other males in a male's own band. Mounting was not recorded numerically, but that too seems to occur between males almost exclusively within the band.

Within the *clan* the step of social grooming is reached. Ninety-one percent of the time that males spend on grooming other males is devoted to members of their own clan. The interactions of females outside their families are impeded by their males' intolerance, but even females occasionally groom followers or females of another family in the clan.

In the *family*, again, grooming is characteristic. Family members spend 98 percent of their grooming time on one another.

There is also a fifth step, which has not been mentioned before: embracing. It is rare between adults, but when it occurs the adults are very close friends. In the field, married couples embrace one another when faced with the threat of forceful separation by a rival. The true domain of embracing, however, is the relationship between *mother* and *infant*, the smallest and most intimate group in the social system of the hamadryas and of primates in general.

This social structure could be represented as an abstract landscape in which the steps correspond to altitude curves. The lowlands join large parts of the population with low-level interactions. At higher altitudes, the number of partners rapidly decreases as the step level rises. Bands and clans are mountains, families are the peaks. The highest, sharpest points in the landscape are the mother-infant pairs.

The step sequence is the route to ever closer relationships with ever fewer partners.

A relationship gains the highest steps only through the lower ones. The great exception is the relationship of a child to its mother. It alone *begins* with the highest step, the embrace. The child is born into it. This highest level, which adults reach hardly ever and only with effort, is a gift to the newborn from its first partner in life. Like mother's milk and warmth, it provides a resource the newborn is unable to obtain by itself: a secure and advanced relationship.

A Chain of Symbols?

What does the step sequence mean? Why does it involve precisely these four or five forms of behavior, and why do they appear in just this order in the pair relation?

First we must note that in our experiments none of these types of behavior had any material effect. The fights were neither for food nor for a
partner, because these were not present in the two-individual experiment.
Presenting and mounting of course could not result in impregnation when
both individuals were of the same sex; furthermore, in the experiments
the females were usually not in estrus. Even grooming had no tangible
benefit, because our baboons were kept in clean surroundings and had
neither ticks nor plant debris in their hair. In the absence of any material
function, we can only conclude that the actions were meant to communicate something. I think the two partners were communicating about their
relationship: they were testing whether the next-higher step was already
within their potential, and if the test succeeded, they had shown to themselves and to one another that the new step was possible.

But why do the geladas, hamadryas, and rhesus monkeys mark the
progress of their relationships with precisely *these* forms of behavior?
When I consider the content and the order of appearance of the four behaviors, I am overcome with a quite unscientific admiration for the way
each symbolizes a higher degree of social dependence. Let me speculate a
little.

Fighting is the essence and the most intense form of *competition*, the
inevitable undertone of any partner relationship. In our experiments it
occurred most frequently between two strong, dangerous individuals—
that is, full-grown males. Dominance is decided at this stage and, as a
result, the fear of at least one partner—the dominant one—is diminished.
For the sake of this outcome it is necessary to risk injury.

Sexual behavior—presenting and mounting—is the most visible form
of *cooperation*. Indeed, it is the prime example of cooperation, because in
sexual reproduction there is no other way for an individual to achieve its
highest biological goal than to cooperate closely with another. In general,
cooperation means dealing with the same task simultaneously in such a
coordinated manner that each partner gains more than he could have by
acting alone. In sexual reproduction, acting alone gets you absolutely nowhere. In the wild troop, presenting in the form of notifying is the level at
which males in the same band interact. Presenting goes together with
their ability to coexist and cooperate despite the ever-present competition
for females.

Grooming of one adult by another, finally, is the most visible form of
altruism, the rarest and highest degree of sociality. That it may be only a
medium of exchange, offered for a service in return, is unimportant here.
At the least, care for a weak individual is altruistic. And in its origins,
grooming is care for the weak, because it is derived from the unilateral
cleaning of a child by its mother.

Embracing is clearly limited to relationships in which the embracer is
prepared to stand up for the partner, even if it means a fight. I suspect that

for the animals themselves their behavior is determined not by altruism as sociobiologically defined above, in which the altruist has to accept that his reproductive success may be impaired, but rather by an independent, direct motivation to care for and defend another that is linked to claiming a relationship from which third parties are excluded. Males in a relationship involving merely presenting and notifying do not reserve their partner for themselves alone. But as soon as the relationship reaches the level of grooming, exclusivity can be claimed; even two males in a given clan will compete for a third male if the latter is desired by both males as a grooming partner. And finally, relationships at the level of embracing always include a claim of exclusivity. Perhaps it is exclusivity, more than altruism, that is communicated at the highest levels of interaction.

To me the sequence of steps looks as though two new partners were employing exemplary forms of behavior to explore the potential of their relationship in the realms of competition, cooperation, and exclusive care. But as I said, this is speculation.

In the field of communication theory a distinction is sometimes drawn between the aspect of content and the aspect of relationship of a communication (Watzlawick et al. 1967). The content aspect is concerned with what one partner tells another about objective details of the outside world; an example is the communication among hamadryas baboons about a distant water hole. However, almost every communication also has a relational aspect, which conveys information about how the transmitter sees his relationship to the receiver. The statement "I am strong" not only has an objective content, it also signifies something about the dominance or protective aspects of the relationship. The head-lowering vote during the decision about where to drink at noon described earlier does not only mean "the green pool is now too overgrown with algae"; it can also signify "I am ignoring your suggestion, go away." If my interpretation of the step interactions is correct, then as communications they include *only* the relational aspect.

A monkey in the free-living group rarely needs to develop a new relationship with a strange adult, because the groups outlast seasons and years, and the young animal gradually grows into most relationships. There are animal species, however, in which new relationships are constructed at the beginning of every reproductive season: those between mates. Here we find a parallel to our pair experiments. Among the monogamous fishes and birds, too, aggression and fear are the great obstacles to cooperation, and the means for overcoming them are the same as among the primates—conciliatory submission, sex, and caring behavior. The weak partner, usually the female, is first chased away, but soon, instead of fleeing, it uses gestures to signal its subordinate rank. For example, when choosing her spouse a female herring gull approaches the threateningly upright male with her head pulled down between her shoulders and walks around him while jerking her bill upward in a conspicuous movement. After that, the male no longer attacks her. As the days pass, she gradually comes closer until finally her bill jerks are clearly aimed at his bill. And then, after many repetitions he begins to regurgitate; a piece of fish appears in his throat, and she swallows it. The bill jerk is a begging gesture, later used by the chicks in eliciting feeding from their parents. In many bird species courtship includes feeding of the female by the male, a caring action borrowed from the inventory of the parent-child relationship.

In the crisis of confronting a stranger, geladas, hamadryas, and rhesus monkeys fall back on the ancient aids to vertebrate courtship. The only new thing is that they use them not only to form heterosexual pairs but also to develop relationships with adults of their own sex. To achieve this they borrow sex and grooming behavior, just as the herring gulls borrow chick-feeding to cement the marriage bond.

We may well ask why monkeys still unacquainted with one another do not jump to the fourth step at the outset, and win one another over with conciliatory grooming. But consider that the higher the level of a relationship, the more intimate and prolonged is the physical contact required. Initially the animals are deterred by fear. Even a social animal will not immediately put itself at risk to the extent demanded by grooming and embracing. The redoubtable Pasha in the zoo, for example, so intimidated the young females that they could groom him only with one index finger, and the young males dared regard his mantle only from a distance.

This fear is most obvious in the case of male pairs. Armed with sharp canine teeth, they understandably take a long time to rise to the level of grooming or never make it at all. The effect of fear can be observed at each step. After several rounds of a fight, with long pauses during which they stay far apart, the victor eventually approaches his subordinate opponent but then hesitates; the subordinate tries to present his unprotected rear end; the victor, still at a distance, extends his hand an inch at a time as though intending to mount, but suddenly this approach becomes too ominous for the weaker male; in a flash, he turns around and attacks. The relationship has plunged back to the fighting step.

It seems as though the only way a relationship affected by fear *can* advance to prolonged contact is by slowly feeling its way. This can be illustrated by comparison with the gears of a car. Although the car goes fastest in the highest gear, you cannot shift into it without starting in first gear, especially when going uphill. For two male baboons the road is so steep—that is, their incompatibility is so great—that some of them never get past second gear; their relationship stays at the level of presenting. A male and a female have a relatively easy ride downhill, so they can start out in second gear with no danger and then shift rapidly into third and fourth.

Triangle Dynamics

Hamadryas baboons and geladas do not limit themselves to one relationship with a marriage partner; they maintain several simultaneous relationships, with partners of both sexes. This has its problems. As everyone knows, pair relationships readily enter into competition. Of all groups, the triangle is under the greatest tension because it is fairly certain that one member will be crowded out. Just recall the difficulties the young baboons in the zoo had when they grew out of the reliable alliance with the mother and did not know whether, in case of conflict, the strong subadults would protect them or their opponents. Protected threatening was the triangle tactic that resulted from such a situation. After participating in a three-individual experiment, our adult hamadryas not uncommonly lay down in their home cages and went to sleep in the middle of the day.

With the geladas as well as the hamadryas, we extended our experiments to three-individual groups. Even in this situation each pair relationship ascended the four-step ladder, and it could fall down and climb back up again. But here a new instrument was added: intervention, used by an animal to obstruct the relationship between two others. For instance, a male gelada approaches a low-ranking female and smacks his lips in a friendly way. She presents to him. But the higher-ranking female is already coming between them; she stares at the subordinate female with raised brows. Or the high-ranking female has been grooming the male for a long time and finally lowers her hands, whereupon he goes to his lower-ranking female and grooms her. The high-ranking one, who a moment before had had enough of grooming, rushes up and begins busily working on the male again. He is satisfied and abandons the lower-ranking female.

The triangle experiments with the geladas proceeded as follows. In the first series of five experiments, on each trial we put *two males* together and let them ascend to the level of grooming; then, an hour later, we put a female into the enclosure with them. In every case, the same phases then followed in almost stereotyped order. The alpha male instantly left his companion and joined the female, and the two of them hurried up the steps to grooming. Making no challenge, the beta male withdrew into a distant corner. No fight was needed now, because the rank of the two males had already been determined in the two-individual relationship. In a second phase, the alpha male occasionally left his female, repeatedly visiting the beta male and presenting to him; that is, he was beginning to repair the disrupted relationship. One of the beta males rejected these approaches and chased the alpha back to his female. Another eventually replied to the alpha's presenting but stayed away from the pair. The remaining three beta males, all not quite full-grown, came closer and seated themselves at a respectful distance from the pair, like followers. Of these three pairs of males, one restored their relationship to the level of mounting and another even ascended to grooming.

The alpha males did not have to protect their marriages by intervention, because all the beta males acted as though they did not see the females, as the inhibited hamadryas rivals had done in the earlier experiments.

One of the females, however, knew the beta male from a pair experiment and had not forgotten him. It was only after some vacillation that she opted for the alpha male, and when he approached her previous companion she screamed at him. Later on, when Beta was lying apart in the grass, the female went to him several times, but he did not stir even when she mounted and then groomed him. That was too much for Alpha. He put an end to the whole thing with a brief threat.

In these three-way experiments the relatively uneasy male relationship, the friendship between two strong individuals, succumbed utterly to the more compatible male-female relationship.

Relationships between *two females* are more resilient. They were not so easily destroyed in the reverse three-way experiment, and were broken up only by intervention. We left two females in the enclosure until they had reached the stage of first grooming and an hour later we introduced a male. At the arrival of the other sex, the female relationships at first also tumbled to the bottom of the ladder or to the fighting step. Then the higher-ranking female turned to the male and presented, he mounted, and she groomed him. But the male soon became interested in the beta female. He would surely have ascended to the highest step with her as well, but the higher-ranking female did not permit it. She intervened whenever the male approached the secondary female and drove her away with threats. Then came the most surprising thing. When the secondary female presented to the male, the primary female behaved as though she were the intended recipient and mounted the other female. Step by step, she renewed *her* relationship with the secondary female; she would not permit sex in the secondary marriage until she herself had again reached the still higher-level relationship of grooming the other female. She insisted on the precedence of her own relationship with the secondary female, and the males acquiesced. The alpha females always sat between male and beta female.

The rules for the step sequence in pair relationships are thus accompanied and superseded by rules for groups of three. They determine which pair relation has precedence. The rules are:

1. Relationships among two incompatible individuals succumb when they have to compete with compatible relationships and fall to a low step, usually irretrievably. (Think of the hamadryas males, which give up their grooming friendships when they form marriages and from then on relate to one another only at step 2, by notifying.)

2. Compatible relationships compete with one another by way of intervention. The success of the intervention determines which relationship survives on the fourth step and which is tolerated only at lower levels from then on. The relationship between male and secondary female, compatible in itself, is repressed by the primary female's intervention and even yields to the relationship between the two females, which in itself is less compatible: the females groom one another, but in the secondary marriage, only sex is allowed.

According to these rules, females, compatible from the outset, were able to share a male, but males, whose relationship with one another is basically incompatible, could not share females. The substructure of the polygynous family of free-living geladas had already been clear in the three-individual groups, but now we wanted to go further and observe the process in the organization of whole families.

Tactics in the Battle for a Place in the Group

In a group of three there are three pair relationships; in a group of seven, there are twenty-one. Can a baboon with so many companions be expected to know at every moment where it stands with each of them, and never get confused? My assistants Dagmar Werner and Fernando Alvarez doubted it as we began the next series of tests. Twice we put together gelada groups consisting of two males and four or five females. These were the same animals we had observed in the experiments with two and three individuals, but we combined them in such a way that as many group members as possible were unknown to one another.

Each group was assembled in the large enclosure and observed daily, from 8:00 A.M. until noon, for several weeks. After 12:00 each day we separated the baboons into the subgroups they had formed previously and kept each subgroup in one of the adjacent cages until the next day. When we drove the powerful animals into the cages at noon, both sides carefully weighed up their courage—a human front standing against a phalanx of geladas. There were no actual assaults on either side, though once Fernando Alvarez had to save himself from a male gelada by making a toreador's leap onto a high platform.

Each group took about a week to build up the families natural to the species. Never have I learned so much about substructure in so short a time. The geladas never let chaos develop. At every moment the group was "working" only on a triangle basis; that is, two animals would try to climb to the next-higher step with one another, while one or more other animals attempted to prevent them. And even though the triangles kept shifting, each animal went through the step program with each other one and never mixed up its relationships, although it was still on the fighting step with some partners and already at the level of grooming with others. There were more departures from the basic step sequence than were observed in the pair experiments, but so few that the sequence itself was never in doubt. This was all the more remarkable because the whole process was seriously retarded by the barrage of interventions. Now pairs of females took an average of ten hours to reach the first grooming, if they ever got there at all, whereas a pair alone had taken only sixteen minutes.

The geladas obviously knew at all times where they stood with whom in this simultaneous interplay. When we put them together in the morning after a twenty-hour break in the experiment, the partners usually quickly recapitulated the step they had gone through the previous day, as though they wanted to confirm what had been achieved, in analogy with our custom of reading the minutes at the beginning of a meeting.

In these experiments it became clear that some of the baboons themselves perceived the steps as symbols for the different states of a relationship. They intervened against high interaction steps but tolerated the next-lower step for the same pair. For instance, an alpha female permitted all sexual behavior between her male and the secondary female, but she attacked the secondary female whenever the latter tried to groom the male. Evidently sex was not the highest step in her view of marriage.

The notes spoken by the assistants into their Dictaphones sounded like hectic football reports. I tried to concentrate on the larger picture and noted only the major lines of events. They were the same in both groups. As in the three-individual experiments the alpha female instantly attached herself to the alpha male of the whole group, and the two established their bond. But now there were other strong females. Soon one of them attacked the alpha female and tried to occupy a position between the married partners. It was amusing to someone familiar with the hamadryas when the male gelada fled from the two females while they hurried after him, fighting one another.

The attacking female was defeated. She seated herself off to the side, as beta female. Still more isolated was the beta male, who had not attempted anything so far. Like the hamadryas rivals, he was so inhibited that he did not even respond to the advances of lower-ranking females. Everything revolved about the alpha family. As in the triangle situation, the alpha male tried to approach the other females. The alpha female intervened, then accepted one or two lower-ranking females as peripheral, secondary members of her family; finally she allowed herself to be groomed by them and only then granted them the freedom of limited access to her male.

Nothing happened for days among the baboons on the outskirts. Even the defeated beta female seemed inhibited, though she recovered sooner than her fellow-sufferer, the beta male. In both groups it was the beta female who finally took the initiative in forming a beta marriage. This happened on the third day of the experiment, and I shall describe it in detail for the first group. To follow the action, as in any drama, you have to keep track of the cast of characters.

The alpha male Killer had been claimed by the alpha female, Juliet. Mooge, the beta male, had withdrawn and was oblivious to the others. Vicki, the beta female defeated by Juliet, sat apart. Juliet had begun to invite Vicki to join the alpha family after all, as her subordinate: she made friendly overtures and no longer intervened when Killer mounted Vicki.

Vicki, however, would not accept subordinate status. She avoided the alphas and spent more time near the inhibited Mooge, the beta male. He gazed rigidly off into the distance. Only the small, delicate Lolita, who had joined Mooge, responded to Vicki's approaches. She had no chance of prevailing against the more massive Vicki by direct intervention, so she ran to Killer, positioned herself in front of him, and staged a classical protected threat against Vicki. And it worked: not only Killer but also his alpha female Juliet ganged up with Lolita and drove Vicki away from Mooge. (It was not uncommon for lower-ranking females to seek help in the other family when they could not get their way in their own family.)

Killer and Juliet were well-chosen allies, because a little later they took it upon themselves to thwart the Mooge-Vicki marriage. Vicki fled and sat down close behind the passive Mooge. That was a good move. Killer, who would have liked to have Vicki for himself, hurled himself after her, followed by his mate Juliet. This almost direct attack finally roused Mooge—himself a powerful baboon—from his inertia. He attacked not the superior Killer, but the less dangerous opponent Juliet. (This was repeated several times; indeed, it was the frequent repetition of the same ploy that enabled us to be sure we had identified their tactics.) When Killer again harassed Vicki, she gave a piercing scream. Now Mooge regained his full courage. He left Juliet alone, rushed to Vicki's side, and with her chased away the mighty Killer.

That settled the matter. An hour later, Vicki presented to Mooge and he mounted her for the first time. Although Killer and Juliet immediately ran toward them, the new pair held them off. Vicki stayed with Mooge and, for the first time, groomed his disheveled mantle. The two of them were no longer intimidated by the alpha family's subsequent interventions. After this episode Mooge's bare breast area, previously pale, turned glowing red.

Vicki easily prevailed over Lolita to become Mooge's primary female. The two families were now established. The next day Killer and Juliet made one more unsuccessful attempt to break up the Mooge family. Then the interventions ceased.

The two one-male groups now grazed in the linear formation described

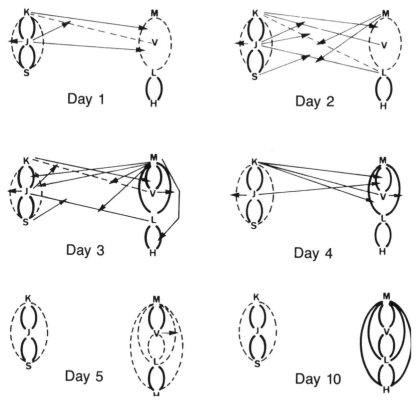

Fig. 48. Emergence of two gelada families. The interactions within and between the families of Killer (K) and Mooge (M) on the first to fifth and the tenth day, after we had put the individuals together. Killer's females are Juliet (J) and Susi (S); Mooge has got together with Vicki (V), Lolita (L), and little Harriet (H). Solid arcs indicate grooming between the individuals they connect, and dashed arcs indicate mounting. Arrows point from an individual to the interaction against which it intervened.

above, with the males at the two ends. The triangular interplay sank to the everyday level of mere traces, and two weeks later the tactical arrangement of the straight line also disintegrated. Figure 48 illustrates the whole course of events schematically.

The gelada study revealed fifteen rules for substructure, the most important of which I summarized in the preceding section on the triangle. In a triangle, the most compatible relationship survives intact on the highest step, the least compatible ones fall spontaneously to lower steps, and relationships with intermediate compatibility are shifted to lower steps by the intervention of others. These rules were confirmed in the larger groups. We have not yet discovered any rules that apply specifically to groups of more than three animals. Even large social networks operate in triangles, although one of the three roles may be played by several individuals at once.

In the life of an established gelada family, the rank of its members is of considerable importance. Each of them tries to groom partners of the highest possible rank who would probably make the most useful allies. But each member also prevents those below her from grooming those above, as though it were necessary to go through official channels. The end result was that each family member mainly groomed the member next higher in rank. The linear formations in the first days of the group experiments made this blockade chain obvious. Among the lower ranks, grooming became visibly less frequent; for the female at the bottom, the one second from bottom is not much use as an ally. This principle was put in the form of a model and confirmed in several primate species by Robert Seyfarth (1977).

The lowest-ranking female, at the bottom of the family chain, hardly ever manages to groom the male. Recall that the hamadryas males in the Munich Zoo got around this problem by making a particular point of grooming the lowest-ranking female themselves. The gelada males in our groups did no such thing. In one case the consequences were enlightening: the strong female Fea was the lowest ranking in her own family. So she deserted and set out to achieve the highest rank in the other family. She would have succeeded easily if the other females in her own harem had not intervened in concert, frustrating her efforts and eventually bringing her back.

Fea's desertion suggested to us that the low-ranking females do not value the marriage with their male very highly, impeded as it is. At the end of the group experiments we checked this with an experiment we called the "fidelity test." We gave every female the opportunity to be entirely alone for an hour in the enclosure with the male of the *other* family. During this time we kept her own male in an outside cage behind a little wall, where he could hear the pair but not see them. Our suspicions were confirmed: alpha females presented to the "wrong" male less often than beta females, and they resisted the attempts of the interloper to approach them twice as long as the beta females, often for the full hour. "Fidelity" depended at least in part on how much a female had to lose in her own marriage.

The males in the "false" pairs did not restrain themselves in the fidelity test except for one small detail. Normally when a female begins grooming a male, he yawns with a loud sound of pleasure. These males opened their mouths widely, but silently; they knew that the female's spouse was behind the wall.

Geladas confronted with strangers developed and combined their new relationships according to rules so clear as to be reminiscent of a simple chemical reaction. The general rule is: each individual, male or female, tries to build as many relationships as possible and take them to the highest possible level, simultaneously trying to keep the others from doing the same thing.

Our geladas formed their groups on the basis of only two characteristics of the members: rank and sex; in so doing, they demonstrated that these alone suffice to produce the one-male families typical of the species. To the best of our knowledge, the members of these groups had no prior history in common to complicate their social organization. In the natural gelada troops of the Semien Mountains, the third, historical factor that had been excluded in our experiments comes into play: the kinship of individuals and the gradually developing individual friendships. Since our experiments were published, the British primatologist Robin Dunbar observed wild gelada families and analyzed the elaborate, delicate marks this factor engraves on the family structure. The females are most obviously affected; among the geladas their kinship net remains intact, in spite of the one-male families.

Free-living gelada families comprise considerably more than the two females that make up the average hamadryas harem. Certain sets of females that groom one another preferentially are particularly noticeable: a mother and her adult daughter. These pairs are genuine cooperatives. Basically, the females in a gelada family are vigorous competitors with one another, as our experiments had shown. Low-ranking females are threatened and kept apart; they suffer from stress and, probably for that reason, bear fewer offspring than females of higher rank. The alliance between mother and daughter in these confrontations is so persistent that it affects their reproductive success: a female with an ally bears more children than one that must fend for herself in the family. The females prefer other females as allies, rather than their male. He has to compete with the intense grooming among females; it is thus impossible for him to make contact with all members of "his" harem, and in very large one-male groups he tends to lead a peripheral existence.

Robin Dunbar inferred that the hamadryas males are able to disrupt their females' kinship net because their harems are too small for the females to form a sufficiently numerous alliance against the male. This seems plausible, in view of the relative independence of the hamadryas females in the larger families that live in Saudi Arabia. Extreme polygyny could have its advantages for female baboons. However, in Erer even harems of seven or ten females never joined forces against their male. In chapter 8 I shall suggest another explanation.

There is an interesting side issue here. Although several females in the same family compete for the male, they can also cooperate, sometimes against him. Doesn't something similar happen when there are several *children* in the same family? The first child may be jealous when the mother turns her attention away to the newborn second child, but the new sibling also serves as a companion with whom to face the adult world. It is curious how differently our culture's norms evaluate the two kinds of jealousy.

A Germ of Politeness

To be a good fighter is a two-edged sword. It makes a male attractive in compatible relationships with weaker individuals, and in conflicts between competitors it ensures access to resources. But where friendship with other strong individuals is concerned, fighting ability gets in the way.

Close observation of male relationships makes it clear that fear is the great obstacle. This may at first seem astonishing; after all, we would expect it to be mainly the *weak* who are deterred by fear from forming a relationship with the strong. But that is not so. Infants let themselves be cuddled by nearly adult hamadryas males. Marriages are quickly established despite the tremendous physical inferiority of the females. The trouble arises when the partners are both males, each of whom has reason to fear the canine teeth of the other one.

In the Zurich colony, when we put unacquainted hamadryas males together in pairs for the first time, the degree to which they got along with one another was inversely proportional to the sum of their body weight— and hence to their strength, since fat contributes very little to the weight of a healthy hamadryas. That is, two strong males had the most difficulty in making friends. In contrast, a *difference* in strength increases compatibility; relationships are promoted by a clear decision about rank. When the difference is large, at least the stronger individual has nothing to fear. I suppose that one partner's fear communicates itself to the other and enhances his own fear. It would be worthwhile to study just how this process of escalation actually operates.

Occasionally an external enemy can unite even strong males. The window of the observation booth at the geladas' enclosure was angled so that from a certain direction the baboons could see a pale mirror image of themselves. Once two males found themselves on this line at the same time. They began to threaten the "strangers" in the glass, casting quick glances at each other between threats. Soon they would let slip a friendly lip-smack along with these glances. As the hours passed, they returned to the mirror several times, and each time they came closer together. Their relationship, which had been arrested at a low level, was again underway; they began to present to one another and eventually reached the stage of grooming. Triangular differentiation can work for males, too, but it can never prevail over the competition for relationships with females.

For friendships between two strong males, the borrowed behaviors of sex and grooming are often insufficient motors. The unifying effect of a mutual opponent whitewashes this problem but does not solve it. However, something new is appearing on the horizon of evolution, though it is still indistinct and barely effective. Judge the following scenarios for yourself.

First example. Two hamadryas males were sitting in their transport cages, having been brought to the observation room for an experiment. Warto, the largest and highest-ranking in the colony, eagerly peered through the cracks at Turk, a subadult whom he did not yet know. The Dictaphones and timers clicked on, the cage doors slid up, and the two males were free to enter the room. Warto and Turk hurried out of their cubicles, looked at one another and smacked their lips in an eager, friendly way. For two minutes nothing happened. They cautiously kept five paces apart, looking pointedly past one another but lip-smacking immediately whenever their eyes did meet. Then Warto, the higher-ranking one, rose slowly and approached his companion. Turk lip-smacked briefly back and cautiously gave way, but the larger baboon followed him. When Turk saw that, he stopped and presented his hindquarters with tail raised, looking back at Warto. Very slowly, Warto advanced; the closer he came, the more anxiously Turk strained forward, away from him. At the very moment when Warto's fingertips touched his hips for mounting, Turk's self-control collapsed. He jerked around and attacked. The two fought for three seconds with manes flying, then broke apart. Turk ran away, through the whole room, and Warto fled into a transport cage. For a while they stayed five yards apart.

As usual Turk, being lower ranking, had tried to take over the first presenting, but despite Warto's careful response this attempt came to nothing because of Turk's fear of being touched. After a while Warto acted as though he could feel the other's dilemma. Smacking his lips, he came a little closer to Turk and then *he in turn presented* from a considerable distance. Instead of punishing the lower-ranking male for his recent attack, he himself took on the role of lower-ranking partner, along with the risk of attack from behind.

But even this renunciation got nowhere with Turk. Every few minutes Warto—and only he—repeated the presenting visits, but Turk recoiled. Only during the moments in which Warto's hindquarters were turned toward him did Turk sometimes smack his lips briefly. He refused to mount. Finally, Warto gave up. The relationship was stuck at the level of presenting.

Second example. Warto first presented at a distance to another fearful lower-ranking male, then sat down and, still seated, slid gradually toward him *back first*, a position in which he was harmless. The smaller male was about to flee but then restrained himself and stayed sitting behind Warto.

The relationship between them progressed very slowly. In both scenes Warto acted as though the development of the relationship were more important to him than insisting on maintaining his alpha role.

That alpha males, both hamadryas and gelada, would behave in this way was also reflected in the numerical data. In female pairs and mixed pairs, the lower-ranking partner regularly began the first presenting, and it was up to the higher-ranking to do the first mounting; however, the male pairs of both species departed significantly from this rule. The alpha males were almost always the first to present, and in half of the cases they allowed themselves to be mounted by the beta male. Presenting by the alphas might just possibly be interpreted as an expression of *their* fear. However, Warto's novel method of coming closer by sliding backward, exactly what the situation required, is not the behavior of a fearful male, nor is it a phylogenetically old strategy. It may be the dawning ability of a primate to imagine itself in the place of another.

"Nothing new," you may say. We humans do the same thing every day. Consciously to relinquish a momentary advantage for the sake of a cooperative relationship in the future is the very essence of politeness: give precedence to another, offer the preferable place, hand over the better tool.

Among the aggressive mountain and desert baboons, sexually tinged subordinacy—if necessary, that of the stronger one—is the narrow gateway to cooperation, allowing animals dangerous to one another to join in defense against predators and hostile conspecifics. For us Western humans, the small gesture of polite renunciation seems to have been reduced to a formula, one often scorned by the young. At best, it is a drop of oil into the gears of commerce. So I thought. Until my wife Verena explained to me that when local politicians and board members praise one another's merits so lavishly in after-dinner speeches, that is just as necessary as notifying at the baboon cliffs. These people often had clashing opinions but nevertheless had to find a way to proceed together, she said, and the way was smoothed by this special affability.

Since then, I have had respect for after-dinner speeches.

The Town of Dire Dawa

The hottest part of the day has passed. The old Arab with the henna-red beard examines the steps of the Bank of Ethiopia through his wire-framed glasses, then places his stick on the bottom one and ascends, past the guard and into the large room. He is followed by an Ethiopian servant with a jute sack on his back (plate 7, top right). At one of the counters the servant carefully empties the sack while the old trader watches, supported by his stick. Piles of unbundled, crumpled banknotes, hundreds of Ethiopian dollars. The two walked through the streets completely unprotected. At that time a servant here earned about two Ethiopian dollars a day.

On the way through the streets of the town, bordered by gardens on both sides, I meet our Amharic friend Ghirma. Laughing, I admire his perfectly ironed white shirt. "You are too elegant to be seen with me, Ghirma."

"Washed and ironed it myself," he smiles. His job with an import company doesn't compel him to go to these unusual lengths. "How should our people learn that work is good, if everyone avoids it whenever he can? Have you seen how long the men in our offices let the nails on their little fingers grow? They do that to show that they don't have to work with their hands. That's bad."

Camp Danayu in the Ogaden. Fred Kurt and I have been invited by the Elwerath Oil Company of Germany, which is doing seismic investigations here for the Ethiopian government. Day after day the equipment installed on four huge Magirus-Deutz trucks is used to drill holes over thirty feet deep for explosives; when they are detonated, the echoes are picked up by geophones and analyzed in search of the tectonic structures associated with oil. The German technicians do not instruct their African helpers with words. They merely take the tools from their hands and do the job themselves, whenever it should be done differently or faster. And that works. Where necessary, the boss himself sets surveyor's rods in place, and when a Land Rover has to be pushed out of the mud, he pitches in. Speed and precision. And good-natured banter.

We fly back to Dire Dawa with the Elwerath people who are going on leave; they work every day for six weeks at a time, and then they have a week to relax and swim. At the takeoff, a visitor from the capital causes some cheerful laughter among the other Ethiopians. He buckles the safety belt around his hips and sits down, without securing the belt to the lug on the bench. They show him how, but when we land, he again puts the belt on without attaching it.

On the way home to Erer, I stop at the Agip gas station. The young attendant pulls his kerchief over his mouth to protect him against the dust, and sets his book aside. It is an English biology textbook, open at the chapter on circulation of the blood. My professional curiosity is aroused.

"Do you now know how the blood flows through the body?"

"I think so. From the left ventricle through the aorta into the systemic circulation. Then into the right atrium, then into the right ventricle, which pumps the blood into the lung. From the lung into the left atrium, and then it starts over from the beginning."

"Perfect! And did you teach yourself English, too?"

"I couldn't go to school." Together we put my 44-gallon gas drum into the middle of the Land Rover's cargo space, set the nozzle in place, and open the hose valve. We have known each other for a while now, and because I always give him a decent tip, I let him take care of the rest.

"Would you tie the drum down with that rope, please, so it doesn't slide around? I'm going over for an espresso." He sets to work.

Ten minutes later, the end of the rope is tied firmly to one corner of the cargo space. From there it runs once around the drum and back to the same corner, and then crisscrosses the cabin, from lug to brace, without ever touching the drum again.

I think of Ghirma, and no longer feel like laughing.

How can this intelligent young man with his book learning ever become a doctor if he doesn't even know how to use a string?

At Camp Awash I replace the broken upper leaf of one of the Land Rover's springs. The Ethiopian park mechanic helps me. We have to use tire irons to press the back eye onto the bolt, using just the right amount of force to counteract the spring tension. But the mechanic has no intuitive feeling for the law of the lever. He usually applies force in the wrong direction. Seven years earlier, when I was on the way to Dire Dawa, two Ethiopian workers had replaced a similar upper spring leaf for me with a gnarled acacia branch. Using wire cable and tire irons, they lashed it in place so cleverly that the spring action was nearly the same as before. At what age does that have to be learned?

Fred Kurt and I have brought along a couple of Dinky-Toy cars for the children in Garbellucu. All day they carry the colorful little lumps of metal around, clutching them to their round stomachs, and they can hardly be persuaded to give them up long enough for us to demonstrate how the cars can roll down the tin cover of the well. The children themselves never play with them.

Jean de Stoutz, the Swiss chargé d'affaires in Addis Ababa, once told us about a little boy who stopped him on the street and showed him a letter from a woman who had just left the country. In it she asked that someone pay the boy's school fees, as she had previously done. De Stoutz did as she asked. He went on to explain that the emperor had built a school big enough for a thousand children. Every day fifteen hundred crowded around the door, hoping to be allowed in. Some of them slipped past the person who checked the students in and hid under the benches until they were discovered.

The old walled Arab city of Harar, once the capital of the Sultanate of Adal, crowns a hill in the mountains behind Dire Dawa. The poet Rimbaud had lived and worked here. The old couple from England have invited us to spend the weekend in the modern new city, where the Teachers' Training School is located. Our hosts are German Jews who emigrated to England in 1933. After the husband retired, they decided to devote their last working years to Ethiopia. He is a geographer and trains the future teachers here.

We visit the practice-teaching school on Parents' Day; the pupils come from an elevated stratum of Ethiopian society. The teaching methods are modern. By the plots in the school garden, each child explains how to cultivate particular plants, usually European varieties of vegetables. The nine-year-old son of a general talks about the art of composting, showing us the heap itself. The pupils speak freely, fluently, and with a good knowledge of the subject. Languages and the law are preeminent talents of highland Ethiopians. But will these children of the upper classes ever cultivate a garden when they grow up? There is also an agricultural school near Harar, and the problem is the same there. The sons of the rich are most likely to be accepted, and their goal is a desk in a ministry.

In the wooden shower room at the Omedla Hotel, someone is singing "Ave Maria." It is Francesco, the rotund young Ethiopian who sits at a little table in the courtyard every day, hammering on his portable typewriter while listening to European music with his radio turned up too loud. This does not prevent him from shouting greetings and jokes to his many acquaintances, using expansive gestures. He prefers speaking in very rapid Italian.

In 1936 his parents were killed during the Italian invasion. He was brought up in Italy, attended university there, and became a lawyer. Then he moved to Mogadishu, where he worked as a tax inspector for the Somali government and as a tax attorney. Three months ago, he had returned to his country for the first time and applied to the government here. They gave him a position in the Propaganda Ministry. But no work, just the salary. "Cas, cas," they told him when he asked about his duties: slowly, slowly. Fine, he said, I'll have a look around my country in the meantime. That's why he is here. Francesco has talked with farmers, nomads, and ministers. He tells me about the results of his analyses, which he does not keep secret from anyone: about the officials' fear of responsibility, with which we are already familiar: "Io sono niente. Bisogna domandare il ministro" ("I am nothing. You have to ask the Minister"); about illegal, ruinous taxation of new businesses—even of international aid efforts. We exchange our impressions of the education of young Ethiopians abroad. The few Ethiopian physicians all practice in Addis Ababa. In the provinces we found only white doctors. A few years later that situation improved; sufficiently well-trained barefoot doctors appeared. What the country needs is not academics so much as competent craftsmen. Here these are the Greeks and the Italians. However, the tax burden is so great that they want to emigrate as soon as they can find an indigenous buyer for their businesses, and there are none.

To counteract the basic evil of addiction to prestige, development funds are of no use. Francesco had shrewd plans. On my next visit to Ethiopia, he was no longer to be found.

For the last time, I take the train from Addis Ababa to Erer. Soon after we pass Miesso, someone hesitantly opens the compartment door. A young nomad in a gray loincloth, with a large curved knife in his belt, comes in and slowly lowers himself into the available seat, next to a corpulent highlander in a dark suit who is evidently an official from the capital. The official gives the nomad a brief side glance and then pushes him roughly from the seat. I become rigid. But the herdsman does not touch his knife. He gathers himself up and slinks out onto the platform.

Ten years before, no highlander would have dared enter nomad territory without an armed guard.

The Net and
the Sword

The gelada study made me aware of a difference in the fighting behavior of the sexes. Eight of the nine combinations of two gelada males fought even in the pair experiments, when there was no third baboon to compete for. Out of seven pairs of females, only one fought under these conditions. The females tended not to fight until they were in *groups*, and then fighting occurred in no fewer than eleven out of sixteen relationships. They fought only when they could form alliances. Why?

Among the baboons, the macaques, and some other species, the male fights with the sword, and the female with the net of her allies. The male uses his canine teeth in the struggle for a higher individual rank, then changes to a new group and starts over again. The female is endowed in her youth with her mother's rank, and in most species she stays with the group where she was born and from then on fights within a permanent alliance of females.

The principle of the male sword and the female net is practically the norm in the higher primates, except for the monogamous species, and it has a profound effect on the life-styles of the sexes. It originated long ago.

The males in polygynous mammalian species evolved their strength in the battle for females; since they made only a slight contribution to the costs of bearing and raising the young, they could afford to develop massive bodies and expend effort on fighting. Burdened by their children, the females could not become great warriors as well, so they had to choose another weapon, a beta strategy: the alliance. This is not a sexual characteristic but simply the only form of fighting available to the weaker.

The females' net is not at all inferior to the males' sword. For example, consider what happens in troops of free-living geladas. Here a male acquiring new females often takes over the whole female net of a one-male group, intact. First he has to defeat the previous leader. But when he does, his victory is useless if the females reject him. Then they join forces to chase him away and stay with the loser.

Patas monkeys (*Erythrocebus patas*) are terrestrial African relatives of the vervets. These females can also form an alliance to drive away their harem leader. In the enclosure at the Delta Primate Center, two slender females chased a powerful male, who would have been far superior to them in an open fight, until he screamed and I had to rescue him.

Among the long-tailed macaques in our Zurich colony, it was not sufficient for one male to vanquish all the other males in battle. The winner
became alpha male of the group only if he could then hold his own
against the females' net. At the first opportunity, the females formed a
semicircle around him and threatened him with deafening screeches. If he
stood firm until the females left him alone, he was the new alpha male; if
he fled, the other males would immediately renew their attacks. In that
case he was usually beaten, and a new victor had to confront the females'
net. The superiority of the swordsman was not of much use against the
female front. What was needed here was the courage of an individual to
stand up against the crowd. A predator is sometimes confused by a
swarm of his weaker prey and may even run away when the mob charges
at him, screaming, although they never even brush his body. Similarly,
within a species the sword can be defeated by the net without one blow
being struck. In the fable, the mouse releases the lion from a net. Certain
Roman gladiators, the retiarii, specialized in net fighting and were greatly
feared; without armor, carrying only a trident and a net, they faced warriors bearing shield and sword.

Canine teeth are permanently attached, but allies can be chosen and
exchanged. Female primates take advantage of this. For example, in Amboseli National Park in Tanzania, when female and juvenile vervets have
a choice between two potential allies, unrelated to themselves, they
choose the higher-ranking one—the one superior to their opponent (Cheney 1983). Female rhesus monkeys offer support preferentially to their
close relatives. The lower-ranking they themselves are, however, the more
likely they are to desert their relatives and turn against them in collaboration with a less closely related but higher-ranking female. The literature
of the field contains many examples of such opportunistic alliances.

The net is such an effective weapon that in some cases males, too, form
alliances. Among wild turkeys and lions, brothers successfully ally themselves to fight for females. Low-ranking anubis males threaten a higher-
ranking one in pairs, and so manage to get his estrous female away from
him (Noë and Sluijter 1990). Among the geladas, the young follower
helps his family leader defend the females, and a deposed male will even
help his successor (Dunbar 1988, p. 241). Male chimpanzees enlist the
help of a lower-ranking male to attain the highest rank in the community
(Goodall 1986).

However, the incompatibility of males is so great that their alliances
are fragile. Male entellus langurs who have allied in conquering a group
of females come into conflict as soon as they have obtained it (Vogel and
Loch 1984). Among patas monkeys, pure male groups maintain their cohesion only if no females are present (Gartlan 1975). Perhaps the fragility

of male alliances is one reason for the finding that in rhesus monkeys and chimpanzees, conciliatory behavior is more common between males than between females (Dunbar 1988, p. 240).

In fact, the geladas, the hamadryas baboons, and we humans are the only primates whose males live in permanent marriages and nevertheless can simultaneously cooperate with one another. In the two-male alliances of the geladas, at least one of the two is a bachelor. A hamadryas band does comprise several married males, but each keeps his females close to him. Humans are different in that men can usually leave their wives to their own endeavors, while they themselves go hunting or herding, without losing them to rivals: this is a unique achievement.

In all three species, the married males form alliances; but only the hamadryas males have in addition cut the females' net of alliances. They now have both sword *and* net, while the females have neither. The males' superiority is total. How could that have happened?

Researchers were so impressed by the alliance nets of female families in the macaques that for a long time blood kinship was regarded as a crucial cornerstone of stable nets of allies, which were thought to be formed primarily by kin selection (p. 160)—that is, to involve only the sex that stayed with mother and siblings in the group of birth.

This interpretation has now been called into question. In the first place, a female helps even her relatives only if she is superior to the opponent. Second, in some primate species the *females* leave the group of their birth, and hence are separated from most of their relatives, but nevertheless proceed to form alliances in their new group (Moore 1984). The females in our gelada study had no relatives in the groups of strangers, but they adhered to the principle of the net. In the group experiments, after only a few days the females intervened together as an allied front. Hence female alliances can also be formed by unrelated individuals. That the females in a hamadryas harem do not support one another against their male may not have anything to do with the fact that they have no mothers and sisters in the harem.

I can imagine that it goes back to their childhood experiences. Even as infants they are taken away by young males, who embrace them and carry them around. A juvenile female is deprived of her mother by her first male, who imposes himself on her as a substitute mother; although he keeps her warm, defends her, and carries her through dangers, he also restricts her freedom forever, as no mother would. Once married, the female still seems to be like a child of her male, inwardly incapable of defending herself or allying herself with someone else against him. She even takes his part against her fellow females (p. 232). This is how a patriarchal system could develop.

The behavior of the hamadryas males also gives no evidence of a tendency to form a net of alliances only with relatives, although all the prerequisites are available: husbands make sure of the sexual "fidelity" of their females and hence know who their sons are, and all the related males stay together in the home clan until they grow old. Therefore kin selection could operate here. But we found no higher degree of cooperation among clan members than among the much more distantly related males in the same band.

Perhaps we did not look closely enough. On the other hand, perhaps we need to rethink our assumptions. Kin selection is necessary when help is provided one-sidedly. When help is reciprocal, however, so that both stand to gain, alliances can in theory be formed by unrelated individuals.

So what is the basis of the hamadryas alliances? According to our observations, they are formed by males that *grew up together*. A shared childhood is automatic for relatives; anyone who does not leave his group, but stays with mother, father, and siblings, necessarily grows up in close association with them. It may be this *familiarity* from youth onward, and not kinship at all, that forges alliances.

Certain findings indicate that animal primates threaten and attack their closest relatives not less, but more often than nonrelatives (Bernstein and Ehardt 1986). In our colony of long-tailed macaques, the mothers take food by force only from their *own* children (Kummer and Cords 1991). Kin are not necessarily paradigms of unselfish love.

It may be, therefore, that hamadryas males stay with their fellow clan members not because they are their fathers, brothers, and sons, but because the males of this species have evolved a strong inclination to stay with others of the same sex who have been well known to them since their early youth, and progressively to strengthen these relationships. Hence the male net formed in youth by grooming and embracing can later survive the strain of the marriage bond to the females, when the strings of the net are stretched out to the thin threads of mutual presenting, barely keeping the net alive. There would be a way to test this idea: hamadryas males would be expected not to ally themselves with males they had first met as adults.

Both net and sword have a price. The sword can wound; fear of it keeps the sword bearers at a distance and can drive them into isolation. The price of the net is the constriction and lack of freedom in a bond that lasts for life. In Gombe, Jane Goodall showed me how adult female chimpanzees with children of their own still followed the authoritarian lead of their old mothers, who alone determined where and for how long food would be gathered. An adult, highly skilled termite catcher had just fashioned some probes out of bark and was going to use them to fish in a termite hill. But when her mother imperatively reached out her hand for the tools, the younger female anxiously showed her teeth, pressed the probes to her body, and then, quite suddenly, threw them into her mother's lap. A net like this is not only a weapon, but also a prison. The female cannot free herself as long as her mother lives.

The danger of the sword is the loss of bonds due to fear; the danger of the net is entanglement in a few tight bonds.

It was my fascination with these two means of fighting and their history that made me decide to write this book.

Chapter Nine

The Eye of
the Beholder

Humans see the world through different glasses, depending on their culture and profession. The Egyptian scribe in Akhenaten's time wrote down the wisdom with which he was inspired by the hamadryas of Thoth. To the people of the Middle Ages, the monkey was a symbol of vanity and obscenity. We, too, read into the animals something of what we are ourselves, each through his or her own glasses.

A German engineer who was mapping the locations of water in the Danakil flatlands in 1960 told me how he had noticed a troop of hamadryas baboons from his helicopter and, just for fun, flew in a circle to herd them together. "Then the old males lifted up large flat stones and held them over their heads, and the little ones fled to shelter under them." These were a technician's glasses.

The fiery-eyed Armenian bar owner on the outskirts of Dire Dawa was relating his hunting adventures. "One evening my wife cried out in the garden. The baboons were in my orange trees. I ran for my gun, crept up to them and shot at the chief baboon. But in the confusion I lost sight of him. Stealthily I pursued them. When I got to the ridge of that hill over there, I saw the troop sitting close together. From a large tree four old males were walking toward them; they lifted the corpse of a gigantic male and carried it back to the acacia. They had evidently prepared a grave there. I could not see what they did, but after a while the four old ones came back without the dead baboon. When they reached the others, all of them howled and cried. I saw it all with these very eyes," he swore, placing his index finger against the bag under his eye. He also assured us that some Issa nomads turn into hyenas at night. He himself, he claimed, had found a silver Issa earring in the ear of a hyena he had shot. An Italian sculptor, a local resident for many years whom Haile Selassie had appointed to direct a sculpture school, asserted that while hunting he had noticed that the black-and-white colobus monkeys never descended from the trees on Fridays. "Sono forse superstiziosi?" he asked. "Maybe they are superstitious?" These two men wore magical glasses.

While preparing for the first Ethiopian trip I read a recently published book by a man described on the cover flap as "a successful writer and journalist." It was a narrative of his adventures with hyenas and hamadryas baboons in Ethiopia. According to his eyewitness report, hamadryas mothers correct their offspring by boxing their ears and slapping their hindquarters. At night, he said, the lowest-ranking baboons were sent out to act as guards. Before leaving the country, this author caught ninety hamadryas baboons for European zoos. When he and his helpers approached an occupied sleeping cliff, the baboons hurriedly climbed down. They were probably beginning to retreat from the humans, but the writer interpreted it differently: "We were lost if we did not manage to escape in time." They managed. With their captive baboons, the trappers reached the harbor of Massawa. By bad luck, the drinking water had run out there and all they could get was mineral water. He had no recourse but to press a bottle into the hands of each of the dangerous monkeys. "And while the animals wandered over the harbor quai to the steamer— in a nice, orderly column—they poured the sparkling water into their dry throats." Are those the glasses of a sensationalist or a joker? I found the book in the children's department of a well-known educational library.

On my visit to consult with the Siggs and the Stolbas in Erer, one evening for fun we donned our human glasses; each of the two students, independently of the other, wrote a completely unscientific profile of the male hamadryas Spot of the Cone Rock troop.

According to Hans Sigg, Spot was "elderly, steady, calm. Takes a long time before he explodes, but then he really does; allows his females much freedom, does not herd them, protects them well from conspecifics and enemies; has little relationship to young animals."

Alex Stolba characterized him as: "Strict, deliberate, does not take the initiative, in the group is quiet, attentive, sexually devoted to Mother Brown. Does not concern himself with the young, except when external danger threatens. When he becomes aggressive, then massively and with a clear target. He is stubborn, introverted. Doesn't mind the rain. Able to cut himself out of the males' net. Even in a friendly mood, he can be brusque. An evening type."

Jane Goodall, Barbara Smuts, and Shirley Strum have shown us how much color and character can be revealed if one's interest is focused on individuals. The glasses of us male primatologists tend to focus on the impersonal and general. We try to discern the evolved strategies that most members of an age or sex class use in a particular context of life. We start to describe the behavior of the Adult Male, or of the Female in Estrus. But the large category of Adult Males turned out, in the course of our projects, to consist of the smaller classes of Followers, Initial-Group Leaders, Family Leaders, and The Aged. Our Aged Males class comprised just three baboons. Eventually the individual will have to become a subject of research. It makes no sense to process Alexander, Caesar, and Napoleon

statistically as members of the class of Great Field Commanders. Is primatology approaching a phase of biography and the description of individual histories, in which quantitative documentation is no longer possible?
My natural-scientist glasses prevent me from finding that an entirely desirable prospect.

In any case, the crucial aspect of the scientific approach is not the quantitative analysis of large samples but rather the attempt to cast aside the
distorting glasses we usually wear, which give us a rough, inconsistent
picture laden with emotions and cultural prejudices—to strive for a differentiated view, free of contradictions, one that does justice to the object
observed and corrects our prejudices. I knew someone with this kind of
vision who grew up outside our own cultural circle, with no formal education. It was the Bedouin boy Mahdi, at the Wadi Ranyah in Saudi Arabia. He deserves a chapter of his own.

Mahdi

"The ink of scholars is more precious than the blood of martyrs"—a saying of the Prophet, according to Ahmed and Saleh, my companions from the University of Jeddah. I thought I must have misheard. Such a thing could not have been written in the West in any century. But later I found in the literature that Ahmed and Saleh had been quoting accurately. Furthermore, the Prophet had not meant only the ink of Muslim religious scholars, because he is said to have continued, "Seek knowledge even as far as China" (Mansfield 1978). As the three of us talked, Ahmed, the parasitologist, gradually opened up. He said that he often read the Koran late at night, and that he found what it said "scientifically pleasing."

We were sitting at the Wadi Ranyah in the evening twilight, around a blanket striped blue and red that was spread out on the sand, serving as both prayer rug and tablecloth. In the southwest the sky glowed orangered behind the black silhouette of the granite tower Djebel al Ossobrae, which looks like an upward-pointing finger and is so named. We fell silent. What I had just been hearing made me think of our experience with Mahdi, the twelve-year-old Bedouin boy who lived in his father's tent, within shouting distance of our own (fig. 49). A week before, we had arrived after midnight in two vehicles from the University of Jeddah and had gone to sleep under the open sky. The Bedouin driver Muhammad, who had led the convoy at breathtaking speed and mysteriously managed to find his way between the moonless desert mountains, had a few years ago seen hamadryas baboons almost daily here at Djebel Ablah.

By sunrise we were already seated on a round granite outcrop, peering into the mouths of the valleys. At 10 o'clock there was a distant baahu call, but otherwise nothing. At 1:00 in the afternoon Mahdi climbed up the rock and released us from our waiting. He wore a long, brown cloth coat and a white skullcap, and he smiled shyly. After a while he asked, according to Saleh's translation, whether we would give him money if he touched a baboon. Laughter. But then he showed us that all this time we had been sitting above the cliff where the baboons slept. Mahdi pointed out their dried dung. Then he led us to the places where the baboons eat, drink, or rest. The tracks in the sand and his reports of what the monkeys did here and there at each site proved to me that Mahdi knew what he was talking about. Saleh and Ahmed, who were translating, could hardly have filled this in, as they knew nothing about such details.

Fig. 49. Mahdi, visiting me, sits outside my tent.

"The monkeys sleep over there when people have disturbed them here." Yes indeed, there was another cliff. "Here they dig between the goat droppings and eat something." I know, dung beetles. The hamadryas in the Danakil dig for them at abandoned nomad camps, and we were now standing at an abandoned Bedouin kraal. Next to a donkey's wooden pack-saddle lay an automobile tire, witness to the new civilization.

I have the translators ask: "Where do the baboons drink?"

"There is no water here, except for one place. There they dig for it." And he demonstrates, correctly.

We do not find the baboons, but on the way home to the camp Mahdi tells us what he knows about the hamadryas, bit by bit, mostly without our asking. Some things he imitates.

"The male baboons are much bigger than the females. In this group there are about five males and five females. And many young. The females and young always walk in the middle. There are two kinds of young: smaller than the mother, with light face and no hair on their cheeks; and large ones, larger than the mother, with hair on their cheeks." He calls the large ones "brothers." They are obviously the followers, with the cheek beards of subadult males. "If someone wants to take the mother, the brother attacks him."

Then he tells us something that he probably observed only once. "When a male from another group comes and sees that a female is open [evidently: has a swelling] and that her own male is away, he does with her what the man does with the woman. At first she does not want to, but he makes very strong eyes at her [brow-raising?]. And at last she also speaks, with her mouth [lip-smacking?]. Her own male sees it and runs up and chases and bites the other one until he is gone."

"What does the male do then with the female?" I ask.

"He grabs her by the shoulders and shakes her." He demonstrates movements like those I saw in Ethiopia during a neck bite. "And at the end he hits her with his hand. As though a person were saying, 'Why did you do that?'"

"After she is punished, does the female run away?"

"She does nothing. She pulls her elbows against her body." That is probably what we call pressing.

"What does a male do when he wants to get married for the first time?"

"The male can take any of the young females, and later she becomes his wife." The initial unit!

I was moved by my little colleague. What he said bore the stamp of accurate personal observation. Still more convincing were his imitations, because there could be no mistake in translation. What the male "says" to his fallible female was preceded by the cautious formulation "as though," a turn of phrase that elegantly separates interpretation from observation—the primary virtue of the scientist.

As it happens, Mahdi was also clever in practical matters. When one of our drivers had to drive the other to the hospital, we ran out of gas and water. I was already planning a night march to the geologists' camp when, before sundown, a Toyota truck turned into our own. I stared at it in disbelief—there was no driver. Mahdi was so small that his skullcap could hardly be seen above the edge of the side window. He drove to our canisters, got out, and matter-of-factly, without speaking, filled them from the water hose on his truck. I asked about it. No one had brought our problem to his attention; he had simply observed and decided what should be done next.

There are, of course, tensions between science and religion in Islam. Evolution is a difficult topic. It is discussed, but also rejected. A Saudi colleague at the university, a biochemist, took a statement in the Koran as the subject of his research project, which he carried out with the most modern techniques.

Imaginative storytellers are found here as elsewhere. A traveling emir, whom we met in the geologists' camp, told us that baboons had kidnapped and raised a human infant whose mother had let it briefly out of her sight. When he was six years old, people rescued him from the troop by force of arms. Asked where the boy was now, he did not answer.

At the same time, though, there was a nomad boy who had never been to school and, purely for his own interest, had observed a wild animal and understood it just as I try to do. Compare this with the improbable stories we had been told about the hamadryas by the German engineer, the Italian hunter, and the Armenian bar owner in Dire Dawa. They may very well have seen something special, but they instantly distorted it by their projections. Mahdi was a born scientist, more than I am.

I was not in Saudi Arabia long enough to judge the extent to which science is accepted by religious teaching in Islam. Maybe Mahdi's culture had nothing to do with his personal openness. But the evening conversations with my colleagues at the Wadi Ranyah made me think how unfortunate the relationship between religion and science has been in the West, for long periods. At first the church threatened scientists with burning at the stake, and later science treated the church with contempt. The two have found one another in individual humans, but hardly at all in the culture as a whole.

CHAPTER ELEVEN

The Likely Evolution
of Hamadryas
Society:
A Reconstruction
and a Summary

The main perspective from which today's behavioral scientists view animals is that of evolution. We see an animal species as the result of a gripping history during which characteristics emerged in the stream of external conditions, later occasionally assumed new functions, receded again, and were overgrown by other solutions. It has been a history in which solutions bring fresh problems, and these in turn call for solutions of their own. To us today, a species appears as an idea of survival—one way of coping with the world. In this chapter I want to show how I think the evolution of hamadryas society came about. The history of a species' adaptation can never be reconstructed with certainty, for it has been partly determined by the small events with great consequences that we generally refer to as "chance."

The hamadryas baboons in the Red Sea region are phylogenetically related to the four species of savanna baboons: the yellow baboons in eastern Africa, the Guinea baboons in the west, the anubis baboons in the center, and the chacmas in the south (see the Introduction). Savanna baboon society is very similarly organized in the various species—they have no marriage and live in groups that neither separate nor reassemble. The Guinea baboons and some highland populations of chacmas show signs of organization in one-male groups. Only the hamadryas, however, has developed it fully. It is likely that its social system originally, about 340,000 years ago, arose from that of the savanna baboons.

At that time, the hamadryas presumably lived like the present-day savanna baboons, in large closed groups that included many adult males. The females were allied in a kinship net; mothers, daughters, sisters, and grandmothers groomed one another preferentially and stood by one another. The females were lifelong members of their group, whereas the males transferred to another group after reaching sexual maturity. Individual males probably copulated with some females more than with others and protected their children; nevertheless, in the days of her swelling a female was still an object of dispute, and she would enter into brief sexual bonds with various males in succession during the same estrus.

Somewhere—maybe in Arabia, maybe in eastern Africa—the hamadryas baboons must have struck out in a new direction, on the way to their present society of fission and fusion. The groups that were to become the bands of the modern hamadryas began to assemble in troops at night, and in the daytime they split up into the subgroups we now know as clans and families.

The selection pressures, the external conditions that made these changes advantageous, were probably the extreme distributions of the most important resources (p. 254). Places suitable for refuge at night were few but large, so it was useful to assemble there in troops; feeding sites were poor and widely scattered, so that foraging was better done in small groups like those formed by chacma baboons on high, barren mountain slopes. Even in their small foraging groups, present-day hamadryas baboons have to travel much farther every day than any other primate species.

According to current understanding, a society does not evolve as a whole, like an organism. The organs of our bodies are genetically the same, 100 percent related, so to speak; they are not in competition with one another. The members of a group, however, have different genes and different strategies and are predisposed to try to outdo one another in procreation. Therefore, when thinking about how the hamadryas society developed, we must consider for each evolutionary step which alternatives were open to the males and which to the females, and what was likely to be the best choice for each of them.

The selection pressure toward the small foraging group probably acted mainly on the females (Wrangham 1980). When they are pregnant or nursing, they need to have a high nutrient income without expending great effort on traveling in search of food. Dietmar Zinner (1993) of the German Primate Center found that hamadryas females in an experimental group study had a better energy balance (energy consumed minus energy expended) than males. Let's assume that females would also be the first to favor small foraging groups when food was scarce in the wild. They would hardly have done this by leaving the group without male protectors—their centripetal tendency in two-male teams contradicts such a notion—but by joining males that struck out on their own. As such fissions became more common, the males were pressed to evolve their strategies for gaining access to the dispersed estrous females. A male could oscillate between the foraging groups, trying to win females with swellings wherever he found them. However, this strategy would have been costly, requiring a lot of traveling and frequent fights against other interested males. Furthermore, with this kind of sex tourism a male would have left his female before his child was born and could not have protected it. A second strategy seems preferable, one that can be seen in the incipient one-male groups of the mountain chacmas: to attach himself permanently to a group of females and defend it, as its sole possessor (33).

This solution seems more beneficial to the female, too. Instead of being harassed, pursued, and tugged back and forth in frequent male contests, she has the permanent company of one male, who protects her children. The long-term one-male unit is evidently the hamadryas' response to a widely scattered food supply.

The reproductive success of the family leader, and hence the propagation of the male tendency toward married life, now depended largely on his ability to prevent his females from having sex with other males. Protection of child by father, too, could have evolved only if the children of his females were really his own. As far as the interests of the individual mother are concerned, it would suffice for the male to *think* her children are also his, so it is not surprising that hamadryas females occasionally go astray in secret. However, the male is under selection pressure to make sure that they do not.

The male could achieve this by going his own way with his family, keeping them away from other males at all times; this is what happens now in the Wadi Hesswa in Saudi Arabia, where there are no predators to fear, and what the male mountain chacmas evidently are trying to achieve when they drive their females away from a neighbor that appears in the distance. In relatively dense forest habitats, many primate species live in isolated one-male groups. But in the perilous savanna or semidesert, ground-dwelling one-male families have to become secretive and inconspicuous, like the present-day patas monkeys. Such a development was incompatible with the predator strategy already adopted by savanna baboons, which depends on the combined efforts of many large males to drive a predator away. By maintaining this strategy, the hamadryas males exposed their now permanent females to rivals, but that is a problem that a hamadryas male must solve in any case while he is in the dense crowd at the sleeping cliff. It is probably for this reason that he has retained the strategy of defense against predators by a cooperative alliance of males, at least at the dangerous water holes.

However, he did not simply accept the associated chance of female "infidelity" but counteracted it, by evolving a more effective guarding method. He elaborated the simple behavior of driving the female away from a rival, as the savanna baboons do, into an aggressive herding behavior in which his threats bring the female from the rival to himself (p. 101). If he nevertheless has to fight, after each round he runs to the female and, with his opponent watching, encloses her in his arms. In this way he exploits the probably much older convention that where something valuable is at stake, the possessor actually holding on to it has precedence (p. 179). The events observed in the "Rape of the Sabine" (p. 107) show that this hamadryas herding strategy can sometimes prevail even against a stronger anubis male. To sum up, the hamadryas male gained the benefit of cooperation with other males against predators at the cost of another danger, that his females would take advantage of being near so many other males and deprive him of his paternity. The herding technique was his evolutionary countermove.

However, he also faced a different problem: that one of the nearby male rivals might rob him of his females by force and forever. This difficulty may be one reason that apart from humans, the geladas, and the hamadryas, no primate species has evolved closed families within a larger social unit. This danger was counteracted by the evolved convention that a rival respects the possession of females, as long as the possessor is not too far inferior (p. 228). This convention has been documented only for the hamadryas, but it could ensure the long-term safety of a marriage in geladas and humans as well. It is not a matter of morality but can be explained by evolutionary cost-benefit logic. Once she is established as the companion of a male and the mother of his children, a female is of more value to him than to a rival. Therefore even a weaker husband can benefit from a fight, if fighting costs the rival more than he would gain by winning the female. This balance can be tilted the other way only if the rival is much stronger than the husband (p. 229). Probably at this stage the dominance displays and dominance orders that are so conspicuous among savanna baboon males amazingly vanished from sight in hamadryas society. The vulnerable possession of harems could not have survived frequent aggressive unrest, and even a strong owner did best if he led his females away from a fight (p. 149).

In this phase, the special morphological features of the male hamadryas had probably been fully developed: the mantle, which attracts grooming by the female, and the red hindquarter with which to appease rivals.

New solutions created new problems. The maturing young male was faced by an establishment in which the females belonged to marriages that demanded respect. Here, again, evolution found ways around the difficulty. As a follower, the young male acquires immature females that are barely defended by their fathers, and he keeps them in reserve in a provisional marriage until they reach sexual maturity (p. 219). Later, when the family leaders he knows well grow weaker, he takes their adult females away by force. The property convention can protect marriage for years without morality or sanction, but eventually fighting power does prevail and the old order is overthrown (p. 225).

Kidnapping and abduction severed the old kinship net of the females. Young males separated daughters from their mothers. When a male is overthrown and his females are redistributed, it is still possible for previously separated females to get together again. Among the hamadryas, however, females no longer groom one another frequently, and they now seek to form an alliance not with their relatives but with their male. A female prefers some males over others, and in experimental tests males even respected these preferences: a female is less likely to be stolen when she "belongs" to the male of her choice (p. 191). In Arabian troops, where there are fewer males, there are indications that females choose males (p. 234).

Newly secure in his paternity, a father was able for the first time to know his sons, and the sons their father. This was the basis of a male kinship net. And in fact, sons now stayed with their fathers rather than emigrating as the savanna baboons do. Mobility was still necessary to prevent incest, but it was exchanged between the sexes: males kept to their groups, and the females left them. Within the band clans of males were formed, and from their appearance and their lifelong adherence to the clan we must conclude that these males are related to one another. As yet it seems that the clan offers no great advantages to its members. Only one benefit is clear: from his clan a young male acquires a juvenile female to hold in reserve for marriage. Clans are also often marching units in the search for food. But they do not oppose one another as cooperatives for the defense of females; only whole bands do that.

The male net thus seems to make little use of kinship. Nothing compels us to conclude that kin selection operates among the males. To be more effective, the meshwork of known kinship would have to extend beyond the clan to include the whole band—and that it does not.

In experiments, pairs of males proved not to be very compatible (pp. 279ff). By resorting to the phylogenetically old vertebrate courtship rituals of sex and grooming, males in the presence of females just barely manage to keep their relationship with one another on the lowest nonaggressive step. Here, at the level of notifying, males are capable of cooperation. They fight in concert (p. 149)—though without unilateral sacrifice for one another, with the possible exception of the old males—and their efforts to decide on a mutual marching direction do not involve aggression. But the hamadryas have apparently gotten no closer than the savanna baboons to the highest level, where one gives altruistic help to another.

In summary, this viewpoint holds that the hamadryas baboons evolved in a region where food grew in such *small* and widely scattered areas that small foraging groups were necessary, and in these small groups marriage came into being. Sleeping cliffs and water holes were even more widely scattered, but they were so *large* that the families had to assemble there, and in these assemblies herding behavior, the property convention, and male alliances developed.

Some social peculiarities of the hamadryas can be found, in embryonic form, in certain populations of savanna baboons. In the Amboseli Park groups of these now and then gather into troops for the night. The mountain chacma baboons in South Africa occasionally form one-male groups at the highest altitudes, although three thousand feet lower down the same population lives in the normal savanna baboon groups (Henzi et al. 1990). In some of these one-male groups the females interact more with the male than with one another, as the hamadryas do, and the male "herds" them to the extent of driving them away from rivals, but he does not prevent his females from grooming and mating with the old second male of the group in addition to himself: the chacma marriage is not yet exclusive and impermeable to rivals. The hamadryas has combined these extreme variants from the reaction norm of his savanna ancestors, then consolidated and perfected them.

There are two evolutionary fronts, profitable in themselves, at which the hamadryas seem to have reached their limits. The first is *hunting*. Primates other than humans and chimpanzees are incapable of giving away any of their prey, and for that reason this ecological niche is closed to them (p. 256).

A second place where they run aground is in group planning of the day's activities. Hamadryas baboons can, with great effort, agree on a meeting point, as we saw in their decision about a distant water hole (p. 270). However, their inability to share food blocks their way to a *division of labor* that would profit at a much larger scale from splitting and meeting, such as the social insects, predatory mammals, and early humans developed, in which the weak are left at the home base with guardians while the strong and experienced, in separate groups, forage and bring back food for all.

Primates are social, but not in the sense of highly developed altruism. The horizon toward which they seem to be steering is knowledge about what another feels and thinks. This knowledge is an achievement that cuts several ways; it enables one to outwit the other, to make plans together, and to give genuine, sympathetic help.

CONCLUSION

The hamadryas field projects came to an end in February 1977. The Swiss ambassador in Addis Ababa had advised us to leave the Erer region, because the war in the Ogaden at the boundary with Somalia made it impossible to continue working in this turbulent, tormented region. Haile Selassie had been assassinated. The depredations of Mengistu's red terror were no longer limited to the capital. Gasoline and groceries were practically unobtainable, and people we knew in the village disappeared overnight. We were planning to come back in two years. After this intermission we would still have been able to recognize at least the adult members of the Cone Rock troop, and we could have partially reconstructed their biographies. But when the time came and everything was ready, the ambassador informed us that the region was again closed to foreigners. A few years later the newspapers reported the compulsory resettlement of poverty-stricken highland farmers into the eastern lowland. In a news magazine we saw a map on which the region around Erer was shaded as a prospective settlement area (*Spiegel*, March 1986). Unless he has help with irrigation, however, a highland farmer in the land of the nomads can only cut the few trees for fodder and fuel, and then starve. It was said that hundreds of those resettled in the south merely looked at the land and then set out on foot for the long trip home.

Since then, the Project Hamadryas has existed only in articles, in textbooks, and in our memories. I have often thought about what this research meant to me, and to remain true to my decision not to conceal the personal, I shall touch on these lasting imprints as well. Pure research has its origin in the subjective, in a human being's almost unconscious but powerful longing to feel at home in a greater order of things. Religion is the oldest path for this search. Since the Pythagoreans, half a millennium before our chronology began, developed the orphic mystery cult into a religion in which mathematics and astronomy guided perception of the world order, science has been a second path. As L. L. Whyte saw it: the mystic believes in an unknown god, the thinker and scientist believe in an unknown order, and it is hard to say which surpasses the others in his irrational devotion. Something of this search has survived through the Renaissance into our time, although modern scientists rarely admit it; for them, the emphasis is on objectivity.

A research project can be compared with a missile. It comes out of the depth of a person and in the end strikes this ground again. It is "objective" only on its visible trajectory. To this middle phase belong the strict methodology and self-discipline with which we try to wrench a more differentiated, consistent, and true picture of the world out of our prejudices and tinted glasses. But the ultimate effect of our science—the impact of the results—once again involves the whole person. That is why the end of the hamadryas project impelled me to begin this book. The "skeleton" of our research papers was not enough; I wanted to give some idea of the effects our discoveries had on the way I experience the world. They went deeper than my somewhat sloppy metaphors of meaty broth and colorful paths in the Introduction to this book might suggest. Here I should like to outline one example.

In his work on gnosis and existentialism, the philosopher Hans Jonas (1987) quotes Pascal: "Swallowed up in the infinite expanse of spaces of which I know nothing, and which know nothing of me, I am seized with horror," and Jonas adds; "Even more than the oppressive infinity of cosmic spaces and times, more than the quantitative disproportion, the ultimate diminution of man as a quantity within such dimensions, it is the 'silence,' the indifference of the universe to humans . . . that accounts for the loneliness of man in the sum total of reality." The effect of a materialistic theory of evolution can be similar. When I first encountered it at the age of sixteen, I visualized the lonesome human appearing from the black, primeval mud on a small planet in the darkness of space, opening his eyes and realizing that only he in all the universe can understand. The lower animals, twisting unconsciously around him in the mud, merely increase his dread. Now that I have experienced an animal's way of life at close hand, with the white baboons of the semidesert, and tried to decipher it as the result of evolution, this picture of extreme loneliness has receded. It has always been a consolation to the individual human to look beyond his personal end to a future for the larger circle of life with which he identifies himself.

This circle has long since expanded beyond family and tribe. It reaches as far as one can know and love, into different regions for each individual. As a biologist, I feel at home in the realm of nonhuman life. The history of life on this planet has built a living bridge between Pascal's indifferent cosmic spaces and me. However merciless the evolutionary process may be, it has lifted us above the material, even though at the price of countless fates of failure. Many a problem that we had considered our own is older than we are and has already been solved by other organisms. We have not been dismissed from the rest of the living world as completely as it might appear. I am comforted by the thought that other species will probably survive the possible failure of the evolutionary attempt toward humanity. The trial run of a large brain has just begun, on the geological timescale; it could be resumed along another branch, if ours should break off. What ultimately matters is whether a person feels at one with the twig alone or with the whole tree, to borrow a metaphor by Durkheim.

That the idea of evolution could seem merely terrifying has its basis in a misunderstanding of the objective scientific approach. We know something about the fundamental processes of evolution: mutation and selection. These are indeed merely cold processes of macromolecular material. These elementary mechanisms, however, are not all of evolution. The special organizations of life—the organs, individuals, behavioral systems, strategies, and finally communities—are built up layer by layer above them, in ever more incredible syntheses and transformations. And these, the creations of the history of life, demand an understanding of dimensions we have hardly begun to comprehend; they cannot be dismissed in terms of mutation and selection. For example, I see no compelling argument derivable from the efficiency criteria of selection that can explain why life should ever have arisen at all. Dead matter is considerably more stable and solid. So why life? I also know at present of no selection-based reason for the "invention" of affects and emotions. A machine can destroy perfectly well without rage, and it is entirely conceivable that an act of fertilization and the associated feedback mechanisms could be devoid of feelings of pleasure. Even the function of conscious experience is still a subject of speculation. It is seen, for example, as a means to imagine the mental states of others by inferring them from one's own states (Humphrey 1986). Most convincingly, it is a "means of freeing animal behavior from the tyranny of ongoing events" (Edelman 1989). Consciousness can create an imagined world of stimuli that can direct thinking and planning regardless of the stimuli that happen to surround us. This is an elegant solution. Behavioral systems are evolved to respond to sensory stimuli. Conscious experience capitalizes on this ancient kind of input by producing powerful *imagined* stimuli of things we may encounter tomorrow and that often are far more relevant to our present actions than the tablecloth now before our eyes. This amazing ability, too, is the working of evolution.

The English sociobiologist Richard Dawkins wrote that plants, animals, and humans are machines that the genes have built to propagate themselves more effectively. From the genes' point of view, that is right. The genes of a migratory bird can fly through the air and live in two parts of the earth only with the help of the machine "bird." However, it is just as obvious that the machines can emancipate themselves from their blind originators, can trick them now and then. Machines can do more than those who built them, or they would not have been built. Some can even think faster. The builder has reason to be wary of his machines, as we have found out by now. The genes are no better off. For instance, we have elaborated sex into an erotic culture, and at the same time we are able to deny it its procreative function. One of the most puzzling and dangerous characteristics that human genes gave their "machines," or at least allowed them to have, is the tendency to create myths—unproved and often apparently delusional ideas of how something is or should be. Myths of boundless growth, for example, or of the absolute uniqueness of humans that allows educated people to count only *human* deeds and thoughts as worthy elements of education. Myths are certainly not always in the interests of gene propagation. Thanks to myths, we are not only the most rational but also the most irrational organisms. Animals know no myths. Their behavior is comparatively matter-of-fact; the genes keep it aimed more accurately at survival. But even among the animals there are some that play with their behavioral systems.

Creation will experiment with itself whenever it is given the chance, as was shown in the section, "The Hothouse of Social Behavior," in chapter 3, and this is not always in the best interests of the genes. Inside the "machine" is a brain that looks for rewards and devises tactics. The genes have no such thing; they are chemistry. The machine is infinitely superior to its "builder" and takes advantage of its room for maneuver. Evolution is far more than the sorting of genes. When evolving species yield to the pressures of selection, they produce phenomena that leave the genes far behind in their kaleidoscopic richness and playfulness.

We are ungrateful when we dismiss the evolution of life as merely a cold game of chance with the macromolecules as dice. It has been nothing less than a road to ever-higher levels of freedom. Freedom in the right sense, of course: not merely an opportunity to make idle choices or not to be locked up in an external cage, however indispensable such liberty may be to the free organism. Freedom is primarily emancipation from the rigid rules governing primitive forms of existence, with their single tracks, fixations, and blindnesses. Freedom permits the organism to decide, but it also demands decision. And because decisions can be wrong, freedom is dangerous and exacts its price.

The first step toward freedom led from dead matter to life. What is alive generates its own shape by its metabolism and thus gains a new, higher independence. Its costs are high. At every moment living beings are in danger of sinking back into the dead substance, due to an external menace or their own mistakes.

The second great step toward freedom occurred when organisms developed the capacity for locomotion (Jonas 1973). That opened new ways of making a living. An organism that can walk, swim, or fly is able to live even where the resources needed for metabolism are widely scattered. A plant lives its whole life in one place and therefore must constantly be immersed in everything that it needs. If only one thing is missing, the plant dies. A hamadryas obtains safety here, roots there, and water under the sand of a far-away wadi. This kind of mobility is impossible without sense organs that can locate what is needed; it also requires motivation that recognizes an impending internal shortage soon enough and makes the animal persevere through time and space until the resource is found. The danger of making wrong decisions becomes many times greater when an animal can travel. And above all: this freedom, once won, *must* be used. An animal that sits still and makes no decisions will die. Freedom is uncomfortable as well as expensive.

The third step leads to an internal map of one's own home range and thus to an initial picture of the world. The organism can now exist where refuges, water, and various kinds of food are so far apart or so well concealed that it would not have the endurance to find them by random wandering; simple planning is required. With this ability it protects itself from becoming fatally lost, but now it *must* plan. When for its own safety it travels in a group of conspecifics, it must resolve not only its own indecision but also the conflict between its desires and those of its companions. Here an additional internal map is needed, on which are plotted the companions themselves and their knowledge and desires.

The ability to think out plans, to test actions internally before carrying them out, opens a new area of experience: organized knowledge, a general view and a life of the imagination—things that seem almost the essence of freedom and bring their own hidden dangers.

This simplified survey has now brought us to the threshold of becoming human. An animal's world-image map still lacks the dimension of time and an ego figure. As far as we know, both of these are almost exclusively human. The time dimension allows us to view the history of our personal life, our species, and the evolution of life. Thanks to the ego figure, in which we can see ourselves from outside, we can promote our own interests on a longer-term basis, refer the standards and values of society to ourselves and conform to or reject them, and finally put ourselves in another's place, knowing that the other is ultimately like ourselves. However, time dimension and ego figure have also loaded us with perhaps the most heavy burdens an organism can bear: fear of the future and doubt of one's own value. One person will respond by adopting a comfortable mythology. Another might dream of being a fish or a bird, but one with imagination and self-consciousness, of course. And no one would want to go all the way back to dead matter—which reveals the fundamental inconsistency of the dream of returning. The last freedom, which alleviates this dilemma, is the renunciation of some goals of the ego, the identification with something greater than oneself.

A biologist may do this by accepting all life on our planet as his wider home, but then he also takes upon himself a new kind of grief. This century has transformed many of the large wild animals into characters only in books: the animals themselves have vanished, and in their place we only have information about them. At the very moment in the earth's history when humanity is extinguishing the planet's organisms at an ever greater rate, it lets some of its researchers see what it destroys. Their knowledge resides in the journals of institutions and associations. On these pages, I have wanted to pass on a glimpse of what these biologists see.

Other researchers have followed us to Ethiopia and done excellent and thorough studies in the hybrid zone at the Awash National Park, but none have entered the eastern semidesert where the pure hamadryas live, away from any national park.

There is no return to Red Rock, not for me. The Project Hamadryas slowly faded from my life. The subconscious seeker in my brain, who sometimes made my head snap around when the merest fragment of a hamadryas silhouette appeared at the edge of my field of view, seeks no longer. At times the sight of a cliff arouses something in me that sees a row of figures climbing along a ledge high up there, gray shapes and between them smaller, earth-brown ones with tiny black riders on their backs. This something hears the rattle of pebbles and sees a mantle waving. For years after the end of the project, I would sometimes dream at night that I was reading or hearing forgotten reports of hamadryas troops that lived in hiding close to my Zurich home: in Balkan mountain forests, in the region southeast of Lyon, and finally in the woodlands above Zurich itself. In each of these dreams I was seized by an unbelievable feeling of happiness, tore my bicycle from the shed, and rode off. At last I found them. They sat with great gravity at the upper edge of a steep-walled gravel pit under the pines of the Loorenkopf, one of the haunts of Zurich schoolboys, and they gazed at me in the falling twilight.

BIBLIOGRAPHY

Publications by Authors Outside the Hamadryas Project

Altmann, J. 1980. *Baboon Mothers and Infants*. Harvard University Press, Cambridge, Mass.

Altmann, J., Altmann, S.A., and Hausfater, G. 1986. Determinants of reproductive success in savannah baboons (*Papio cynocephalus*). In T. H. Clutton-Brock, ed., *Reproductive Success*. University of Chicago Press, Chicago.

Andersson, M. 1982. Female choice selects for extreme tail length in a widowbird. *Nature* 299:818–820.

Barth, F. 1965. *Nomads of South Persia. The Basseri Tribe of the Khamseh Confederacy*. Universitetsforlaget, Oslo.

Barton, R. A., White, A., Strum, S. C., Byrne, R. W., and Simpson, A. J. 1992. Habitat use and resource availability in baboons. *Animal Behaviour* 43(5):831–844.

Bernstein, Irwin S., and Ehardt, C. L., 1986. The influence of kinship and socialization on aggressive behavior in rhesus monkeys (*Macaca mulatta*). *Animal Behaviour* 34:739–747.

Biquand, S., Biquand-Guyot, V., and Boug, A. 1991. Distribution and population structure of *Papio hamadryas* in Saudi Arabia. In A. Ehara, ed., *Primatology Today*. Elsevier Science Publishers B.V.

Biquand, S., Biquand-Guyot, V., Boug, A., and Gautier, J. P. 1992. The distribution of *Papio hamadryas* in Saudi Arabia: Ecological correlates and human influence. *Int. J. Primatol.* 13(3):223–243.

Biquand, S., Boug, A., Biquand-Guyot, V., Gautier, J. P. 1994. Management of commensal baboons in Saudi Arabia. In S. Biquand and J. P. Gautier, eds., Proceedings of the symposium "Commensal Primates." *Revue Ecologique* 49(3):213–222.

Boesch, Ch., and Boesch, H. 1989. Hunting behavior of wild chimpanzees in the Taï National Park. *Amer. J. Phys. Anthrop.* 78: 547–573.

Boese, Gilbert K. 1975. Social behavior and ecological considerations of West African baboons (*Papio papio*). In R. H. Tuttle, ed., *Socioecology and Psychology of Primates*. Mouton, The Hague.

Bunnell, B. N., Gore, W. T., and Perkins, M. N. 1980. Performance correlates of social behaviour and organization: Social rank and reversal learning in crab-eating macaques (*M. fascicularis*). *Primates* 21(3):376–388.

Byrne, R. W., Whiten, A., and Henzi, S. P. 1987. One-male groups and intergroup interactions of mountain baboons. *Int. J. Primatol.* 8:615–633.

Calhoun, J. B. 1973. Death squared: The explosive growth and demise of a mouse population. *Proc. Roy. Soc. Med.* 66:80–88.

Chatwin, Bruce. 1987. *The Songlines*. Pan Books, London.

Cheney, D. L. 1983. Extrafamilial alliances among vervet monkeys. In R. A. Hinde, ed., *Primate Social Relationships*. Blackwell Scientific, Oxford.

Cheney, D., and Seyfarth, R. 1990. *How Monkeys See the World: Inside the Mind of Another Species*. University of Chicago Press, Chicago.

Clutton-Brock, T. H., and Harvey, P. 1977. Species differences in feeding and ranging behaviour in primates. In T. H. Clutton-Brock, ed., *Primate Ecology: Studies of Feeding and Ranging Behaviour in Lemurs, Monkeys and Apes*. Academic Press, London.

Colmenares, Fernando. 1992. Clans and harems of hamadryas and hybrid baboons: Male kinship and the formation of brother-teams. *Behaviour* 121(1–2):61–94.

Colmenares, F., and Gomendio, M. 1988. Changes in female reproductive condition following male take-overs in a colony of hamadryas and hybrid baboons. *Folia primatol.* 50:157–174.

Dasser, V. 1988. A social concept in Java monkeys. *Animal Behaviour* 36:225–230.

de Waal, F. 1982. *Chimpanzee Politics*. Allen and Unwin, London.

———. 1989. *Peacemaking among Primates*. Harvard University Press, Cambridge, Mass.

Dunbar, Robin I. M. 1988. *Primate Social Systems: Studies in Behavioral Adaptation*. Croom Helm, London.

Edelman, G. M. 1989. *The Remembered Present: A Biological Theory of Consciousness*. Basic Books, New York.

Elliot, D. G. 1913. A review of the primates. *Amer. Mus. Nat. History*, vol. 2.

Fabre, J. H. 1919. *The Mason Wasp*. Trans. A. T. de Mattos. Hodder and Stoughton, London.

Gardiner, Alan. 1973. *Egyptian Grammar*. 3d ed. Oxford University Press, Oxford.

Gartlan, J. S. 1975. Adaptive aspects of social structure in *Erythrocebus patas*. In S. Kondo et al., eds., *Sympos. 5th Congr. Int. Primatol. Society*. Japan Science Press, Tokyo.

Gessner, Conrad. 1551–1587. *Historia Animalium*. 5 vols.

Goodall, J. 1986. *The Chimpanzees of Gombe: Patterns of Behavior*. Belknap Press of Harvard University Press, Cambridge, Mass.

Goy, R.W. 1966. Role of androgens in the establishment and regulation of behavioral sex differences in mammals. *J. Animal Science* 25 (supp.): 21–35.

Hall, K.R.L. 1963. Variations in the ecology of the chacma baboon, *Papio ursinus*. *Symp. Zool. Soc. London* 10:1–28.

Hamilton, W. D. 1964. The genetical evolution of social behavior, I and II. *J. theor. Biol.*. 7:1–16, 17–32.

Hammerstein, Peter. 1981. The role of asymmetries in animal contests. *Animal Behaviour* 29:193–205.

Harcourt, A. H., Harvey, P. H., Larson, S. G., and Short, R. V. 1981. Testis weight, body weight and breeding system in primates. *Nature* 293 (5827):55–57.

Henzi, S. P., Dyson, M. L., and Deenik, A. 1990. The relationship between altitude and group size in mountain baboons (*Papio cynocephalus*). *Int. J. Primatol.* 11(4):319–325.

Hölldobler, B. 1984. Communication during foraging and nest-relocation in the African Stink Ant, *Paltothyreus tarsatus* Fabr. (Hymenoptera, Formicidae, Ponerinae). *Z. f. Tierpsychol.* 65:40–52.

Huard, Paul. 1962. Archéologie et zoologie: Contribution à l'étude des singes au Sahara oriental et central. *Bulletin de l'I.F.A.N* 14(1–2):86–104.

Humphrey, N. K. 1986. *The Inner Eye*. Faber and Faber, London.

Jonas, Hans. 1973. *Organismus und Freiheit. Ansätze zu einer philosophischen Biologie*. Vandenhoeck & Ruprecht, Göttingen.

Jonas, Hans. 1987. *Zwischen Nichts und Ewigkeit. Zur Lehre vom Menschen*. 2d ed. Vandenhoeck & Ruprecht, Göttingen.

Kaumanns, Werner. 1983. Soziale Strukturen bei einer Zookolonie von Mantelpavianen (*Papio hamadryas*). Dissertation, University of Constance.

Koty, John. 1934. *Die Behandlung der Alten und Kranken bei den Naturvölkern*. Hirschfeld, Stuttgart.

Kummer, Hans. 1975. Rules of dyad and group formation among captive gelada baboons (*Theropithecus gelada*). *Proc. Symp. 5th Int. Congr. Primatol.*, Nagoya, 1974, pp. 129–159. Japan Science Press, Tokyo.

Kummer, Hans. 1978. Analogs of morality among nonhuman primates. In G. S. Stent, ed., *Morality as a Biological Phenomenon*. Life Sciences Research Report 9, Dahlem Conferences, Berlin.

Kummer, Hans, and Cords, M. 1991. Cues of ownership in long-tailed macaques, *Macaca fascicularis*. *Animal Behaviour* 42:529–549.

Macdonald, Julie. 1965. *Almost Human: The Baboon, Wild and Tame, in Fact and in Legend*. Chilton, Philadelphia.

Manning, J. T. 1980. Sex ratio and optimal male time investment strategies in *Asellus aquaticus* (L.) and *A. meridianus* Racovitza. *Behaviour* 74(3–4):264–273.

Mansfield, Peter. 1990. *The Arabs*. Rev. ed. Pelican Books, New York.

Martin, Robert D. 1990. *Primate Origins and Evolution: A Phylogenetic Reconstruction*. Chapman Hall, London.

Mirreh, A. G. 1976. Die wirtschaftlichen und gesellschaftlichen Verhältnisse der nomadischen Bevölkerung im Norden der Demokratischen Republik Somalia. Dissertation, University of Leipzig.

Moore, Jim. 1984. Female transfer in primates. *Int. J. Primatol.* 5(6):537–589.

Morrison, J. A., and Menzel, E. W. 1972. Adaptation of a free-ranging rhesus monkey group to division and transplantation. *Wildlife Monographs* 31:6–78.

Nagel, Thomas. 1981. What is it like to be a bat? In D. R. Hofstadter and D. C. Dennett, eds., *The Mind's I*. Penguin Books, Harmondsworth.

Noë, R., and Sluijter, A. A. 1990. Reproductive tactics of male savanna baboons. *Behaviour* 113:117–170.

Phillips-Conroy, J. E., Jolly, C. J., Nystrom, P., and Hemmalin, H. A. 1992. Migration of male hamadryas baboons into anubis groups in the Awash National Park, Ethiopia. *Int. J. Primatol.* 13(4):455–476.

Premack, D. 1991. The aesthetic basis of pedagogy. In R. R. Huffman and D. S. Palermo, eds., *Cognition and the Symbolic Processes.* Erlbaum, Hillside, N.J.

Prins, H.H.T. 1987. The Buffalo of Manyara. The individual in the context of herd life in a seasonal environment in East Africa. Dissertation, University of Groningen.

Rasa, A. 1986. *Mongoose Watch: A Family Observed.* Doubleday, Garden City, N.Y.

Reiners, Ludwig. 1967. *Stilkunst.* C. H. Beck, Munich.

Roeder, Günther. 1959. *Die aegyptische Religion in Texten und Bildern.* Vol. I. Artemis, Zurich.

Rowell, T. E. 1988. Beyond the one-male group. *Behaviour* 104 (3–4):189–201.

Saleh Mohammed, A. K. 1984. *Die Afar-Saho Nomaden in Nordostafrika.* Lit, Münster.

Sapolski, Robert M. 1990. Stress in the wild. *Scientific American,* January.

Schönholzer, Lili. 1958. Beobachtungen über das Trinkverhalten von Zootieren. Dissertation, University of Zurich.

Seyfarth, Robert M. 1983. Grooming and social competition in primates. In R. A. Hinde, ed., *Primate Social Relationships.* Blackwell Scientific, Oxford.

Seyfarth, R. M. 1977. A model of social grooming among adult female monkeys. *J. theor. Biol.* 65:671–698.

Shotake, T. 1981. Population genetical study of natural hybridization between *Papio anubis* and *P. hamadryas. Primates* 22(3):285–308.

Sigg, Hans. 1981. Entwicklung von Zweierbeziehungen bei jungadulten Rhesusaffenmännchen und ihre Beeinflussung durch Psychopharmaka. In M. Blösch, ed., *Die Beeinflussung angeborener Verhaltensweisen durch neurotrope Substanzen.* Erlanger Forschungen, series B, vol. 11. Universitätsbund Erlangen-Nürnberg.

Smuts, Barbara B. 1985. *Sex and Friendship in Baboons.* Aldine, New York.

Strum, S. C. 1987. *Almost Human: A Journey into the World of Baboons.* Random House, New York.

Sugawara, K. 1988. Ethological study of the social behavior of hybrid baboons between *Papio anubis* and *P. hamadryas* in free-ranging groups. *Primates* 29 (4):429–448.

Thesiger, W. 1988. *The Life of My Choice.* Fontana Paperbacks, Glasgow.

Topsell, Edward. 1607/1973. The historie of foure-footed beastes, with narrations out of scriptures [&c.] collected out of all the volumes of Conradus Gesner, and all other writers to this present day. 1607. Facs., The English Experience, no. 561, 1973. Theatrum Orbis Terrarum Ltd., Amsterdam.

van Lawick-Goodall, Jane. 1971. *In the Shadow of Man.* W. Collins, Glasgow.

van Roosmalen, M.G.M. 1980. Habitat preferences, diet, feeding strategy and social organization of the black spider monkey (*Ateles paniscus paniscus* L.) in Surinam. Dissertation, Agricultural University, Wageningen, Holland.

Visalberghi, E., and Welker, Ch. 1986. Sexual behavior in *Cebus apella. Antropologia Contemporanea* 9(2):164–165.

Vogel, Ch., and Loch, H. 1984. Reproductive parameters, adult male replacements, and infanticide among free-ranging langurs (*Presbytis entellus*) at

Jodhpur (Rajasthan), India. In G. Hausfater and S. Blaffer Hrdy, eds., *Infanticide: Comparative and Evolutionary Perspectives*. Aldine, New York.

Washburn, S. L., and DeVore, I. 1962. Ecologie et comportement des babouins. *La Terre et la Vie* 2:133–149.

Watzlawick, P., Beavin, J. H., and Jackson, D. D.: *Pragmatics of Human Communication: A Study of Interactional Patterns, Pathologies, and Paradoxes*. W. W. Norton, New York.

Whiten, A., and Byrne, R. W. 1986. *The St. Andrews Catalogue of Tactical Deception in Primates*. St. Andrews Psychological Reports, no. 10.

Whiten, A., Byrne, R. W., and Henzi, S. P. 1987. The behavioral ecology of mountain baboons. *Int. J. Primatol.* 8(4):367–388.

Wrangham, Richard. 1980. An ecological model of female-bonded primate groups. *Behaviour* 75:262–299.

Zinner, D. 1993. Nahrungskonkurrenz bei Mantelpavianen. Eine experimentelle Studie. Doctoral dissertation, University of Göttingen. Shaker, Aachen.

Zinner, D., Schwibbe, M. H., and Kaumanns, W. 1994. Cycle synchrony and probability of conception in female hamadryas baboons, *Papio hamadryas*. *Behavioral Ecology and Sociobiology* 35(3):175–183.

Zuckerman, S. 1981. *The Social Life of Monkeys and Apes*. Reissue of 1932 ed., together with a postscript. Routledge & Kegan Paul, London.

Publications on the Hamadryas by the Zurich Group
(in order of publication)

(1) Kummer, Hans. 1956. Rang-Kriterien bei Mantelpavianen. Der Rang adulter Weibchen im Sozialverhalten, den Individual-Distanzen und im Schlaf. *Rev. Suisse Zool.* 63:288–297.

(2) Kummer, Hans. 1957. Soziales Verhalten einer Mantelpavian-Gruppe. *Beih. Schweiz. Z. Psychol.* 33:1–91.

(3) Kummer, Hans, and Kurt, Fred. 1963. Social units of a free-living population of hamadryas baboons. *Folia primatol.* 1:4–19.

(4) Kummer, Hans, and Kurt, Fred. 1965. A comparison of social behavior in captive and wild hamadryas baboons. In H. Vagtborg, ed., *The Baboon in Medical Research*, pp. 1–16. University of Texas Press, Austin.

(5) Kummer, Hans. 1967. Tripartite relations in hamadryas baboons. In S. Altmann, ed. *Social Communication among Primates*, pp. 63–71. University of Chicago Press, Chicago.

(6) Kummer, Hans. 1968a. Social organization of hamadryas baboons: A field study. *Bibliotheca Primatologica* 6:1–189. S. Karger, Basel, and University of Chicago Press, Chicago.

(7) Kummer, Hans, 1968b. Two variations in the social organization of baboons. In P. Jay, ed., *Primates: Studies in Adaptation and Variability*, pp. 293–312. Holt, Rinehart and Winston, New York.

(8) Kummer, H., Götz, W., and Angst, W. 1970. Cross-species modifications of social behavior in baboons. In J. R. Napier and P. H. Napier, eds., *Old World Monkeys*, pp. 351–363. Academic Press, London and New York.

(9) Nagel, Ueli. 1971. Social organization in a baboon hybrid zone. *Proc. 3rd Int. Congr. Primatol. Soc.* (Zurich, 1970), vol. 3, pp. 48–57. Karger, Basel.

(10) Kummer, H., Götz, W., and Angst, W. 1972. Anpassung eines Anubis-Weibchens an das Haremssystem der Mantelpaviane (Freilandexperimente). Begleittext zum Film D 1095. *Publ. Wiss. Film, Sekt. Biol.* 6(1):1–9. Institut für den Wissenschaftlichen Film, Göttingen.

(11) Kummer, Hans. 1973. Dominance versus Possession: An Experiment on Hamadryas Baboons. *Proc. 4th Int. Congr. Primatol. Soc.*, vol. 1, pp. 226–231, *Precultural Primate Behavior*. Karger, Basel.

(12) Nagel, Ueli, 1973. A Comparison of anubis baboons, hamadryas baboons and their hybrids at a species border in Ethiopia. *Folia primatol.* 19:104–165.

(13) Kummer, H., Götz, W., and Angst, W. 1974. Triadic differentiation: An inhibitory process protecting pair bonds in baboons. *Behaviour* 49:62–87.

(14) Kummer, Hans. 1975. Dreiecks-Verhältnisse bei Pavianen. In H. Kranz and K. Heinrich, eds., *Psychiatrische und ethologische Aspekte abnormen Verhaltens*. 1. Düsseldorfer Symposium, 1974. Georg Thieme, Stuttgart.

(15) Angst, Walter, and Kummer, Hans. 1975. Soziale Organisation von Pavian-Gruppen. In G. Kurth and I. Eibel-Eibesfeldt, eds., *Hominisation und Verhalten*, pp. 56–73. Gustav Fischer Verlag, Stuttgart.

(16) Abegglen, H., and Abegglen, J.-J. 1976. Field observation of a birth in hamadryas baboons. *Folia primatol.* 26:54–56.

(17) Kummer, H., and Abegglen, J.-J. 1978. Gesellschaftsordnung bei Mantelpavianen. In R. A. Stamm and H. Zeier, eds., *Die Psychologie des 20. Jahrhunderts*, vol. 6, *Lorenz und die Folgen*, pp. 163–176. Kindler, Zurich.

(18) Kummer, H., Abegglen, J.-J. Bachmann, Ch., Falett, J., and Sigg, H. 1978. Grooming relationship and object competition among hamadryas baboons. In D. J. Chivers and H. Herbert, eds., *Recent Advances in Primatology*, vol. 1, *Behaviour*, pp. 31–38. Academic Press, London.

(19) Götz, W., Kummer, H., and Angst, W. 1978. Schutz der Paarbindung durch Rivalenhemmung bei Mantelpavianen (Gehege- und Freilandexperimente). Begleittext zum Film D 1168. *Publ. Wiss. Film, Sekt. Biol.* 11(8):1–22. Institut für den Wissenschaftlichen Film, Göttingen.

(20) Stammbach, Eduard. 1978. On social differentiation in groups of captive female hamadryas baboons. *Behaviour* 67:322–338.

(21) Fritz, Marietta, 1979. Beziehungsstufen als Struktur- und Rangkriterien beim Mantelpavian (*Papio hamadryas*). Diplomarbeit, University of Zurich.

(22) Stolba, Alexander. 1979. Entscheidungsfindung in Verbänden von *Papio hamadryas*. Dissertation, University of Zurich.

(23) Bachmann, C., and Kummer, H. 1980. Male assessment of female choice in hamadryas baboons. *Behav. Ecol. Sociobiol.* 6(4):315–321.

(24) Sigg, Hans. 1980. Differentiation of female positions in hamadryas one-male-units. *Z. f. Tierpsychol.* 53:265–302.

(25) Müller, H. U. 1980. Variations of social behaviour in a baboon hybrid zone (*Papio anubis x Papio hamadryas*) in Ethiopia. Dissertation, University of Zurich.

(26) Kummer, H., Banaja, A. A., Abo-Khatwa, A. N., and Ghandour, A. M. 1981. A survey of hamadryas baboons in Saudi Arabia. In W. Wittmer and W. Büttiker, eds., *Fauna of Saudi Arabia*, vol. 3, pp. 441–471. Pro Entomologia, c/o Natural History Museum, Basel.

(27) Sigg, Hans, and Stolba, Alexander. 1981. Home range and daily march in a hamadryas baboon troop. *Folia primatol.* 36:40–75.

(28) Sigg, H., Stolba, A., Abegglen, J.-J., and Dasser, V. 1982. Life history of hamadryas baboons: Physical development, infant mortality, reproductive parameters and family relationships. *Primates* 23(4):473–487.

(29) Abegglen, J.-J. 1984. *On Socialization in Hamadryas Baboons: A Field Study*. Associated University Presses, London and Toronto.

(30) Kummer, Hans. 1984. From laboratory to desert and back: A social system of hamadryas baboons. The Niko Tinbergen Lecture, 1982. *Animal Behaviour* 32:965–971.

(31) Kummer, Hans, Banaja, A. A., Abo-Khatwa, A. N., and Ghandour, A. M. 1985. Differences in social behavior between Ethiopian and Arabian hamadryas baboons. *Folia primatol.* 45:1–8.

(32) Sigg, Hans, and Falett, Jost. 1985. Experiments on respect of possession and property in hamadryas baboons (*Papio hamadryas*). *Animal Behaviour* 33(3):978–984.

(33) Kummer, Hans. 1990. The social system of hamadryas baboons and its presumable evolution. In Thiago de Mello, White, and Byrne, eds., *Baboons* (selected Proceedings of the 12th Congress of the International Primatological Society, Brasilia, 24–29 July 1988), pp. 43–60. Brasilia.

Films (16 mm)

Kummer, H., Götz, W., Angst, W. 1972. Adaptation of a female anubis baboon to the social system of hamadryas baboons (field experiments). 22 min. Film D1095. Institut für den wissenschaftlichen Film, Göttingen. Video cassette through BUIVC-British Universities Film and Video Council, 55 Greek Street, London W1V 5LR, England.

Götz, W., Kummer, H., Angst, W. 1978. Preservation of pair bonds through rival inhibition in hamadryas baboons (cage and field experiments). 27 min. Institut für den wissenschaftlichen Film, Göttingen. Also available from Pennsylvania State University, Audio-Visual Services, University Libraries, Special Services Building, 1127 Fox Hill Road, University Park, PA 16803-1824.

INDEX